# WHAT IS IN A RIM?

**Pacific Formations**
Arif Dirlik, Series Editor

# WHAT IS IN A RIM?

## Critical Perspectives on the Pacific Region Idea

### Second Edition

*Edited by*
## ARIF DIRLIK

ROWMAN & LITTLEFIELD PUBLISHERS, INC.
*Lanham • Boulder • New York • Oxford*

ROWMAN & LITTLEFIELD PUBLISHERS, INC.

Published in the United States of America
by Rowman & Littlefield Publishers, Inc.
4720 Boston Way, Lanham, Maryland 20706

12 Hid's Copse Road
Cumnor Hill, Oxford OX2 9JJ, England

Copyright © 1998 by Rowman & Littlefield Publishers, Inc.

British Library Cataloguing in Publication Information Available

**Library of Congress Cataloging-in-Publication Data**

Dirlik, Arif
    What is in a rim? : critical perspectives on the Pacific Region idea / Arif
Dirlik.—2nd ed.
        p.  cm.
    Includes bibliographical references and index.
    ISBN 0-8476-8468-7 (cloth).—ISBN 0-8476-8469-5 (pbk.)
    1. Pacific Area—Economic conditions. 2. Pacific Area—Foreign economic
relations. 3. Pacific Area—Politics and government. 4. Pacific Area—Social
conditions. I. Title
    HC681.W48  1998                                                              97-28861

ISBN 0-8476-8468-7 (cloth : alk. paper)
ISBN 0-8476-8469-5 (pbk.: alk. paper)

Printed in the United States of America

♾™ The paper used in this publication meets the minimum requirements of American
National Standard for Information Sciences—Permanence of Paper for Printed Library
Materials, ANSI Z39.48–1984.

# Contents

PART THREE
PACIFIC SOCIAL AND CULTURAL FORMATIONS

*Part One*

# Pacific as Concept and Fantasy

# 1

# Introduction: Pacific Contradictions

## ARIF DIRLIK

"Pacific Rim" and a variety of terms cognate to it, such as "Pacific Basin" and "Asian-Pacific," have become commonplace in geopolitical vocabulary over the last decade. And yet, what these terms mean remains unclear. The immediate reference is obviously physically geographic: Pacific Rim (or Pacific Basin) refers to societies situated on the boundaries of the Pacific Ocean and within it. Discussions of the Pacific Rim, however, rarely account for all the societies thus situated, more often than not referring primarily to societies of the northern hemisphere and sometimes using the term euphemistically as a contemporary substitute for what used to be called East Asia.

The terms sometimes include societies technically outside the physical boundaries of the Pacific Ocean even as some of the societies situated on the Rim or within in it are left out. These usages problematize the geographic reference of the term(s). Indeed, it is arguable that the terms represent ideational constructs that, although they refer to a physical location on the globe, are themselves informed by conceptualizations that owe little to geography understood physically or positivistically—in other words, that they define the physical space they pretend to describe.

We must resist the reductionism of the very concept of the Pacific: the Pacific is as much a realm of fragmentation as of unity, which therefore deprives any effort to describe it with the narrative unity that might lend a guise of comprehensiveness to an otherwise diffuse subject. Definitions of the Pacific are part of the very struggle over the Pacific they seek to describe. Nevertheless we should try to bring to the surface some of the significant problems that present themselves to any discussion of the Pacific that seeks not an ideological constitution of the region but a recognition of the complex and contradictory relationships that shape the Pacific discourse.

We can begin with several premises: The Pacific Rim (or Pacific Basin, Asia-Pacific) is an invented concept. But being an invented concept does not mean the Pacific has no material basis. This material basis is defined best not by physical geography, but by relationships (economic, social, political, milita and cultural) that are concretely historical. These relationships that give meaning to the notion of the Pacific are also relationships of contradiction that disrupt the very unity that they imply.

Such contradictions are not to be understood without reference to global forces that transcend the Pacific, as well as relationships of hegemony and exploitation that are internal to the region. The idea of the Pacific is intended as much to express the aspirations of the people who inhabit the region as it is to contain intraregional contradictions and the relationship of the Pacific to other regions of the world. Finally, the idea of the Pacific, therefore, is not so much a well-defined idea as it is a discourse that seeks to construct what is pretended to be its point of departure, a discourse that is problematized by the very relationships that legitimize it.

That the Pacific is an invented concept does not mean it does not exist except as an idea, but that what exists does so by virtue of human interactions and the conceptualizations that endow those interactions with meaning. There is indeed a Pacific region in a different (and more meaningful) sense than the physically geographic. Motions of people, commodities, and capital over the last few centuries have created relationships that traverse the Pacific in different directions and have given rise to regional formations with shifting boundaries. These formations have varied in the area they encompass, in accordance with the nature of the relationships restricted sometimes to portions of the area designated today as the Pacific, sometimes extending far beyond that area. Such motions continue to this day and account for the gap between the Pacific area (conceived physically) and a Pacific region conceived in terms of human activity. Emphasis on human activity shifts attention from physical area to the construction of geography through human interaction; it also underlines the historicity of the region's formation(s).

The Pacific and the areas situated on the rim were initially filled out by peoples moving out of Asia, and there had been all along movements of commodities and people in the area, at least locally. But the filling out of the Pacific from the sixteenth century on had a more compelling logic to it, whether we speak of geographical discovery or the pursuit of commodities: the logic was the logic of the capitalist world economy spreading out of Europe to conquer the world. The modern formation of the Pacific was dynamic in its transformative powers, persistent in its logic, and total in the sense that it affected all areas of life, from economic relations to culture (from missionaries to contemporary consumer culture). The important point is that the Pacific in the end would be a EuroAmerican invention (first of Europeans and then of the transplanted Europeans of the Americas), that what we today regard as the Pacific region was formed by forces that originated outside of the region. This does not mean that the inhabitants of the region had nothing to contribute to the region's formation, which they did, but only in resistance to the EuroAmerican conquest. Dynamic forces emanating from EuroAmerica, from the secular growth of capitalism to contingent political rivalries, were projected onto the Pacific and played the central part in its formation as a region as well as in its conceptualization.

The Pacific was invented by EuroAmericans in another sense: as a concept. From the very beginning, it was the Europeans who gave meaning to the area in terms of European (later EuroAmerican) concepts, visions, and fantasies. Just as they reconstructed the area in accordance with the logic of European capitalism and politics, Europeans and EuroAmericans projected on the area their myths, fantasies, and visions. To be sure, this process was not without its own internal contradictions and conflicts. The Pacific served as much to deconstruct inherited European myths (such as the existence of a southern continent) as to create new visions. But at a certain level, Eurocentrism and capitalism are indistinguishable. The Pacific in this regard has served an ambiguous purpose, reflecting the contradictions of capitalism itself—at once a "paradise" that offered relief from the harshness of life under capitalism and a frontier of capitalism that awaited the transfer of native powers of European dynamism. The beachcomber and the entrepreneur are two sides of the same coin.

In the end, it was the Pacific that was incorporated into the narrative of capitalism (by definition a Eurocentric narrative, even to this day when capitalism is deterritorialized), rather than the other way around. Hence the resistance to the discourse of the Pacific, described in some of the chapters that follow, in the name of localized regionalisms. To define, as to name, is to conquer: EuroAmericans were responsible not only for mapping the Pacific, but also for attaching names to the maps. Today, even Pacific peoples, in order to locate themselves in the area, have to go by EuroAmerican maps and the new names; which is why, in recent struggles for cultural autonomy, Pacific peoples have given some priority to the renaming of Pacific places. To use a distinction suggested by Joseph Levenson, a historian of China, the confrontation of the EuroAmerican and the Asian Pacifics entailed a vocabulary change for one and a language change for the other. From mai-tais to taboo and tattoo, a whole range of vocabulary has entered EuroAmerican languages. But for the people of the Pacific the confrontation has entailed the rephrasing of metaphysical and historical experience in a new language.

This transformation, however, does not negate the strong Asian presence in the Pacific, which justifies the use of the term "Asia-Pacific" throughout this volume. If the "Pacific" was a EuroAmerican invention, the invented region had an Asian content, which presents us with the central contradiction of the Pacific region. Asian peoples through their motions have played a highly significant part in the filling out of the region (including the initial peopling of the Americas). The China trade and visions of China were not only responsible for luring Europeans to the discovery of the Pacific, but provided the nodal point for much of the early economic activity in the area, from the Manila galleons to the pursuit of sea slugs, through which the Pacific was to enlarge as a region. The Asian presence in the region is presently more prominent than ever with the post–World War II economic emergence of societies in East Asia that for the first time have begun to challenge the nearly five century long EuroAmerican domination of the region. It may be arguable that this challenge has only brought to the surface contradictions that have been implicit in the region's formation from the beginning.

The emergence of East Asian powers has turned the former "American Lake" into a site of contestation between the United States and various East Asian competitors for power. Lost in the process are the peoples of the Pacific themselves, who do not find their way into much of the hegemonic literature on the Pacific. The struggles of island peoples first for survival and subsequently to acquire a voice of their own must be part of any critical account of the Pacific. Erased from history either through fantasy or narratives of progress, the many peoples of the Pacific are currently involved in their own struggles for self-assertion. The eloquent voice of a Haunani-Kay Trask sets indigenism against the global narratives of capital in efforts to capture Hawai'ian economic and cultural sovereignty. Equally eloquent, the Tongan writer Epeli Hau'ofa lays claims to the ocean spaces of the Pacific against the EuroAmerican imprisonment of island peoples in barely visible specks in the ocean. There is in these efforts not a negation of the history of colonialism and conquest, but its remembrance in rewriting history in keeping with Pacific peoples' historical experiences. Most eloquent of all these voices may be that of the unidentified Australian indigene who came up with the idea that the gods created EuroAmerican anthropologists so as to preserve the people's beliefs and practices.

The Pacific is a EuroAmerican success: an area of the world that did not even exist as an entity in human consciousness until only about two hundred years ago has been created in the image of EuroAmericans. The capitalist world system of which the Pacific as we know it today is a product presently draws sustenance from the creation of the Pacific; it has produced some of the most successful examples of capitalist development that now in their turn inject new energy into the system. Asian-

Pacific capitalism has produced new models of development that may be held before the struggling societies of the non-EuroAmerican world as proof of the success of capitalism; much the same as Asian Americans are held up before other less successful minorities within the United States as a "model minority."

The Pacific is also a failure, however, because these Asian-Pacific offsprings of capitalism in their success challenge the dominion of their progenitors, introducing a new conflict into the capitalist world system. The model of capitalism they represent, so-called communitarian capitalism, as it is held up before the Third World as a new model of development, also asserts with confidence its superiority to the "individualistic capitalism" of EuroAmerican societies.[1] Likewise, the premodern ideological legacies of successful East Asian capitalist societies, once viewed by one and all as cultural obstacles to development, are now re-presented as sources of East Asian dynamism, challenging the ideological hegemony of EuroAmerican culture. The competition has once again brought to the surface the Europe/Asia (or West/East) cultural confrontation that has played a part all along in the Pacific's cultural formation; the concern with the economic threat from Asia-Pacific to the European and U. S. economies finds explicit expression in a resurgent "yellow peril" vocabulary.[2]

The success/failure of EuroAmerican capitalism in reconstituting the Pacific is also visible in the intraregional division of the Pacific into First and Third Worlds. The Pacific contains within its boundaries some of the most successful examples of capitalist development in the world. It also contains some of the sorriest products of the capitalist world system; the Philippines and Indonesia, as well as many of the island societies of the Pacific once responsible for the image of the Pacific as an earthly paradise, now survive as nuclear and chemical dumps for the First World, inhabited by people who have been disoriented completely by their economic and cultural incorporation into the world system.

The discourse on the Pacific as part of a global discourse is a discourse of the powerful who seek to reconstitute the Pacific once again in their image; this time around not just a EuroAmerican image, but a homegrown image that is nevertheless no less the product of a discourse of capitalism. In its most recent manifestation, which is the manifestation in which it entered global consciousness, this discourse began to emerge sometime in the 1960s, accompanied by the first tentative efforts to institutionalize a Pacific region. Writers on the subject agree that the issue of a Pacific community originated in Japan, was picked up in the United States in the 1970s, and has been kept alive over the years by Australian efforts. One Filipina scholar describes the Pacific community idea as "a baby whose putative parents are Japanese and American and whose midwife is Australian."[3] Starting with semiofficial efforts on the part of scholars and business and government officials in the 1960s, efforts to institutionalize a Pacific community gathered momentum in the 1970s and 1980s with the closer involvement of governments. The first concrete steps toward cooperation were taken in the Asia-Pacific Economic Cooperation (APEC) meeting in Seoul, Korea, in Fall 1991.

What gave rise to a Pacific discourse in the 1960s is more problematic. It is possible that the Vietnam War and U.S. efforts to sustain power in the Pacific played a key role in the new attention to institutionalizing the Pacific region. Even if that were the case, however, the effort was given a new meaning with the emergence of Japan in the 1960s as a world economic power, to be followed closely by the other "miracles" of Asia in Taiwan, Singapore, and South Korea. Japanese initiatives toward the formation of a Pacific economic community also suggest a concern for an Asia-Pacific economic organization that would parallel initiatives in Europe toward a European economic community. The initiatives of the 1960s, in other words, would seem to have coincided with what would appear to be in hindsight a regionalization of the capitalist world economy into competitive blocs.[4]

What has made these efforts at institutionalization difficult in the Pacific has been the diversity of Pacific societies and the mutual suspicions that are the legacies of a past of imperialism and colonialism. Intraregional groups (or subregional groupings) continue to this day to interfere with and undermine an all-encompassing Asia-Pacific idea. Among a variety of such subregions, themselves tentative and diffuse, are: a North American free trade area, a South Pacific area, an East Asian free trade zone, a Northeast Asian free trade zone, a "Greater China" area, and the most successful subregion so far, the Association of Southeast Asian Nations (ASEAN). Intraregional groupings such as ASEAN are suspicious of the Pacific community idea because they see in it an effort to limit the less powerful Asian societies' autonomy in dealing with the outside world. Under conditions of unequal development, the efforts of societies such as the United States and Japan, themselves transregional world economies, to establish a Pacific community appear easily and justifiably as efforts to reserve for themselves a Pacific domain and restrict the autonomy of other (weaker) societies in the region while preserving their own autonomy as world powers.

The Pacific discourse, then, appears from these alternative perspectives as a discourse intended to suppress contradictions fundamental to the Pacific as a regional construct. The more prominent of these contradictions include the following:

First, there are contradictions between area and region: These are the contradictions between the Pacific as physical geography and the Pacific as a product of human activity that I have discussed above. It is the latter that gives meaning to the concept of the Pacific—but also problematizes it. In the Pacific's formation, and to this day, not all areas of the Pacific are included within the region. At the same time, areas outside of the Pacific's boundaries have played a significant part in its formation. Bostonians were active in the Pacific before there was a U.S. West Coast; and such a key player in the Pacific today as Australia was a product of the region's formation initially.

Second, there is the contradiction between the Pacific as EuroAmerican invention and its Asian content, both in terms of people's movements and in terms of Asia (East Asia) as a node in the movement of commodities. These motions, which in a concrete sense helped in the formation of the Pacific as a region, also continue to be a source of opposition and division economically, politically, and culturally.

Third, there is the contradiction between fantasy and actuality: There is a Pacific of actuality. But there is also a Pacific of fantasy. The one has nourished the other. European fantasies of immense wealth in the Pacific were responsible for luring Europeans to the Pacific. The same Pacific, however, has served to extend the frontiers of capitalist development. This fantasy presently drives capitalist utopianisms. The irony here (or is it tragedy?) is that EuroAmerican expansion into the Pacific has led to the destruction of the very "paradise" that EuroAmericans fantasized about from the destruction of entire peoples physically and culturally (especially in the Southern Pacific) to ecological destruction.

The fourth Pacific Rim contradiction exists between Asia-Pacific and the world system of which Asia-Pacific is a region: This is a contradiction within capitalism. The contradiction has become especially conspicuous as capitalism has become deterritorialized with the emergence of what has been called "global capitalism" or "flexible production"; that capitalism, in other words, that is based on a "new international division of labor" in production and is no longer nationally based but located in the narratives of transnational corporations. The Asia-Pacific idea as a conceptual construct that emerged in the 1960s may well be a product of efforts to "reterritorialize" capital, by establishing realms of control for transnational capital in constant competition internally. The effort has also brought to the surface different modes of production and organization within the capitalist mode of production (products of the development of capitalism itself from individualistic to managerial capitalism) that are presented nevertheless in terms of an older cultural vocabulary, especially the vocabulary of Eastern-Western cultures (themselves, ironically, products of a European cultural expansionism fueled by capitalist development).

Fifth, there is a contradiction that exists between region, subregion, and nation: Vis-à-vis the capitalist world system, Asia-Pacific might represent an effort to define and control one area of the world as a preserve of economic powers of world scope (such as the United States and Japan). Viewed from within the region, efforts to define or institutionalize a Pacific region appear also as attacks on subregional groupings (and divisions of labor), as well as attacks on the autonomy of nations to determine their fate. In a situation of inequality, a regional "community" serves only to disguise the subjection of individual nations and ethnic groups to the imperatives of a regional economy dominated by the powerful. The Filipina writer quoted above observes that an earlier term for the Pacific community was "co-prosperity sphere." That the initiatives for a Pacific community have come from the OECD (Organization for Economic Cooperation and Development) nations within the Pacific underlines the plausibility of this fear. Again, the global capitalism of the present reveals how real this fear is. The Pacific First World supplies the capital—the Pacific Third World supplies the labor. The situation has been complicated by the entry into the scene of the Pacific Second World, the so-called socialist society of China, which uses socialism to control labor costs so as to make China competitive with other Pacific societies.

Sixth, the contradiction, therefore, is not just between region, subregions, and nations, but between capital and classes/genders. The terminology of First, Second, and Third Worlds becomes irrelevant as parts of Los Angeles become a Third World, and Manila and Hong Kong turn into centers of capital. As the transitional corporations become genuinely transnational, the terminology of imperialism (and of Leninist Marxism) becomes largely irrelevant, because the managers of capital become authentically international. So does the working class, in actuality if not in consciousness. The "new international division of labor" recruits its laborers where it can and moves around laborers as it moves around capital. Most conspicuous in Asia-Pacific production are women from this or that Pacific Third World who, faced with the choice between starvation and exploitation, move around the area, selling everything from their labor to their bodies. On a Sunday afternoon, downtown Victoria island in "miracle" Hong Kong is a veritable sea of Filipinas, who also fuel the sex industries of Japan. Sexual fantasy has been a component of the Pacific fantasy ever since the first European set foot in Tahiti; sex tourism is today one of the booming industries of Asia-Pacific.

Finally, there are cultural contradictions at various levels: between the EuroAmerican Pacific and the Asian Pacific, between different cultural formations within the Asia-Pacific, and between regional forces of cultural homogenization and local resistances to it, all articulated within the context of a consumer culture that has spread throughout the area from the capitalist nodes in Los Angeles, Tokyo, and Hong Kong. We have already referred to the first contradiction between EuroAmerican and Asian-Pacific cultures. Examples of the second type of contradiction are dissonances between the "Confucian" cultures of East Asia, the Islamic and Buddhist cultures of Southeast Asia, and the Hispanic cultures of the Philippines and Latin America. In the midst of these broader cultural dissonances are efforts, such as those among the many ethnic groups in the area and on the Pacific islands, to assert some measure of local cultural identity.

In the four years since this collection was first published, there have been significant changes in Pacific configurations, as well as in the thinking of the editor and the contributors. Among the former may be included the reorganization of United States corporations in the late eighties and early nineties to gain supremacy over "Asian Models" of one kind or another, especially Japanese, the emergence as an economic power of the People's Republic of China, and the parallel diminution in Japanese influence, exacerbated by economic depression and political scandal in Japan. Regional formations already visible earlier have been formalized, as in the case of the North American Free Trade Agreement (NAFTA), or acquired greater visibility, as in the so-called "Greater China." Diasporic Chinese societies now seem to be on their way to constituting a new center of economic gravity, while Chinese states have become more expansive; as with the efforts of the PRC to create a China-centered East- and Southeast-Asia region, or the "Look South" policy of Taiwan which, mobilizing the mainland hinterland behind it, seeks to become a new "hub" of economic activity in the region. These self-assertions of Chinese societies, especially of the PRC, have triggered the reemergence of Cold War rhetoric between the United States and China, and even some Cold War strategies; recent United States political and military activity in the region is seen by the leaders of the PRC as efforts to encircle China. But the contradictions are not only those between the United States and the PRC. Controversy has reemerged over the Diaoyutai (or Senkaku) islands between Japan and Chinese societies. Elections in Taiwan earlier this year triggered military threats on the part of the PRC which, exaggerated or not, point to continued tensions among Chinese societies, which the political and corporate leaderships seek to defuse by stressing the importance of economic interactions over political conflicts. Finally, East and Southeast Asian societies have become exporters of antidemocratic ideologies, as their economic success has enhanced the prestige of what they choose to portray as their cultural legacies. The antidemocratic ideas of the former prime minister of Singapore Lee Kuan

Yew have been promoted to the status of "Lee Kuan Yew'ism," while the president of the United States is forced to refrain from referring to human rights for fear that he may offend his Indonesian friends (not just Chinese), who now seem to have a role to play in U.S. presidential elections. While the United States is still willing to promote human rights in "hostile" states such as China, it is instructive that on his visit last year to the PRC, former Secretary of State Warren Christopher met not just with the derision of the PRC government but also with the wrath of U.S. businesses in China for making an issue of human rights.

These changes are all very significant, but not unanticipated. Each of them requires extensive study, needless to say, which is not to be contained within a single volume. This volume was intended originally not to deal with events but with general configurations and patterns. In some ways, it is possible to suggest that events as they have unfolded over the past four years have demonstrated the validity of the conceptualizations that initially informed the contributions in this volume. Recent events, and the contradictions they reveal, are in keeping with the contradictions in Pacific formations that were identified in the first edition.

Changes in this revised edition, therefore, weigh toward the strengthening of the conceptual components of the earlier volume. Several essays have been added that stress interrelationships and formations, while limitations of space have forced the elimination of other essays that were country-based, or focused narrowly on specific issues. We have retained in this edition only those country studies with significant conceptual consequences. Unfortunately, we have had to drop the only essay on NAFTA and the maquiladoras because, with NAFTA becoming reality, the essay was seriously outdated. The changes do not reflect on the quality of the original contributions for which I, as editor, remain grateful. Two of the essays, on Chinese in Latin America and changes in the Chinese economy, have been revised slightly to account for recent changes. We have also added an essay that addresses more directly than any essay in the previous volume the Pacific peoples' perceptions of the Pacific. This is still too little, but it has been addressed more extensively in a volume that the author has coauthored.[5] I also regret that the collection does not contain any discussion of issues of labor in the Pacific. There are limits to what can be included in any single volume, and what is absent from this volume will hopefully find its way to other similar volumes. This volume was intended originally as an attempt to conceptualize and theorize an undertheorized field, and to introduce critical issues to discussions of the Pacific which seemed to be dominated by hegemonic discourses of states and capital. It is because it seemed to make a contribution in that regard that it seems worthwhile to reissue it, while acknowledging its deficiencies.

# Notes

1. See the discussion in *New Perspectives Quarterly* (NPQ) 9, no. 1 (Winter 1992), especially the interview with Lee Kuan Yew, the foremost proponent of a "Confucian capitalism" as the former prime minister of Singapore. There is more than irony in the representation as a model of "communitarian capitalism" of the fascist state Lee Kuan Yew brought into existence in Singapore.

2. For an example, see Ian Buruma's review of Michael Crichton's *Rising Sun,* "It Can't Happen Here," *New York Review of Books* 39, no. 8 (April 23, 1992): 3. According to Buruma, *Kirkus Reviews* found in *Rising Sun,* "the return of the 'Yellow Menace' "—in a "three-piece suit."

3. Valera Quisumbing in Jose P. Leviste, Jr., ed., *The Pacific Lake: Philippine Perspectives on a Pacific Community* (Manila: Philippine Council for Foreign Relations, 1986), 81.

4. For a history of the discourse on the Pacific and efforts to institutionalize a Pacific community, see the appendix in Leviste, *The Pacific Lake.* Hadi Soesastro and Han Sung-joo, eds., *Pacific Economic Cooperation: The Next Phase* (Jakarta: Centre for Strategic and International Studies, 1982) also contains a summary history of these efforts, as well as contributions by those who have played key roles in the process. For the U.S. perspective, see W. W. Rostow, *The United States and the Regional Organization of Asia and the Pacific, 1965–1985* (Austin: University of Texas Press, 1986).

5. Rob Wilson and Arif Dirlik, ed., *Asia/Pacific as Space of Cultural Production* (Durham, NC: Duke University Press, 1995).

# 2

# The Asia-Pacific Idea:
# Reality and Representation in
# the Invention of a Regional Structure

ARIF DIRLIK

Many efforts have been made to define the region that has been described variously as "Asian-Pacific," "Pacific Rim," and "Pacific Basin." But a basic question remains: How do we comprehend a region that appears in most discussions of it as something, in the words of one commentator, "akin to Pascal's horrible sphere, with periphery indeterminable and a center that may be anywhere?"[1]

I argue here that even to begin to confront the question, What is the Pacific?, it is necessary to define our terms by specifying *whose* Pacific— and when. This is not to suggest that there is no "objective" reality to the concept of the Pacific; it would be meaningless even to raise the question of defining the Pacific were it not for those human activities that provide links across the area, ranging from movements of people, to transfers of commodities and capital, to cultural interchanges. But these apparently "objective" forces integrating the area bear the mark of the historical relationships that produced them, and they are also open to manipulation and interpretation in accordance with configurations of interest and power that have informed those relationships. What the term *Pacific* means depends largely on location within these networks of relationships—or even outside them, for those inhabiting the area who have been marginalized by these very same relationships, or excluded from them altogether. The relationships that give rise to the question of the Pacific are neither coextensive with the totality of the area implied by such terms as *Pacific Rim* or *Pacific Basin,* nor necessarily confined within an area thus delineated in physical terms.[2] In a fundamental sense, there is no Pacific region that is an "objective" given, but only a competing set of ideational constructs that project upon a certain location on the globe the imperatives of interest, power, or vision of these historically produced relationships.

These constructs, which we may describe as alternative forms of a Pacific ideology, serve two major functions, neither of which is comprehensible without reference to a larger world system—a condition of any conceptualization of the Pacific. The first is to set up a domain of economic activity and power for those who play a hegemonic role in this area (at present, the United States and Japan), to contain within it the relationships that in and of themselves are not confined to it, and thereby to assert a regional identity (and power bloc) against other similar regions in the world system, of which the European Economic Community is the immediate instance. The contradiction here is, of course, that these hegemonic powers are themselves global powers, and they have little wish to be contained by the region they envision. This implies, second, that the Pacific ideology takes as its object—and may even express in the short term the interests of—the lesser competitors in the world system that inhabit the area, such as the newly industrialized countries (NICS) of East and Southeast Asia, the Association of Southeast Asian Nations (ASEAN), Australia and New Zealand, Canada, and Latin America. (The Pacific islanders, with whom the Pacific was initially identified, have been largely marginalized in this ideology.) In this perspective, the goal of a Pacific ideology is to bring into alignment economic and political forces that in and of themselves do not point to a common regional structure. The Pacific ideology in this guise necessitates a relinquishing of national sovereignty for the lesser powers that link their fates to the region, an act that may or may not benefit their societies as a whole but is desirable to those among their elites who are already engaged in transnational activities. It also serves to disguise as manifestations of regional cooperation and coordination relationships that are also instruments of domination and subordination; of development and marginalization; of class, gender, and ethnic exploitation. In a broad perspective, such relationships bear not just signs of regional vitality but also the scars of cultural and ecological destruction that are the legacies of four centuries of Pacific emergence. Any conceptualization of the Pacific that does not account for these contradictions in Pacific realities must of necessity remain incomplete and ideological.

My concern here is not to add another definition of the region to those already existing, a task that I take to be neither possible nor desirable; definitions exclude as much as they include, and where the problem at hand remains to be formulated, may hinder rather than help analysis. Rather, I focus on the procedures of conceptualization that underlie such definitions (and the terminology that we employ in describing the region). The problem with most definitions of the region, whether or not they pretend to precision, is a geographical bias—in other words, a tendency to view the region as a geographical given, a physically delineated stage, as it were, upon which human beings play out their various activities. The task of definition appears then as one of delineating the boundaries of the region, determining its center(s), and deciding which of all the peoples who inhabit the region to include within it as serious participants in its activities. This unmistakably positivistic bias is related in subtle and sometimes not so subtle ways to the motivation for understanding the region. It is important to elucidate the question of the Pacific Rim, Peter Gourevitch writes, "for two communities who have a need to know: the community of social scientists, interested in making sense out of general social activity and the location of a particular goegraphical region within a theoretical context; and the community of policymakers who, faced with the compelling need to make decisions, seek information pertinent to those decisions."[3]

What Gourevitch ignores is that these reasons—the location of the region in a theoretical context (a euphemism in the particular context of his discussion for modernization studies), and policymakers' need to know (whether the policymakers be government, business, or military)—to move inquiry in directions consistent with the satisfaction of the interests of "the two communities who have a need to know," inform the construction of the region in accordance with those interests.

It is this aspect of the problem that I pursue here. I suggest that while geography is an indispensable component in the definition of the region, if only to locate it on the globe and distinguish it from other regions, any definition is at best an abstract representation that seeks to contain within physical categories the spatial and temporal motions of the human activity—including the activity of conceptualization—that constitutes its reality. If it is impossible to delineate the boundaries of the region with precision, or to identify its centers, it may be because both are subject to change, as the activity changes that constitutes the region as a region. To complicate matters, such activity is often contradictory (as it expresses contradictory interests in the constitution of the region) and, in its refusal to reproduce the structures that produced it, generates contradictions that disrupt the self-contained coherence of its geographical premises. Efforts to define the region, under the circumstances, reveal their underlying motivations in their search for a regional construct that is most consistent with the particular interest and perceptions of their purveyors. Gourevitch, for example, recognizes this implicitly when he states that "the definition of the Pacific Rim is itself an object of controversy and struggle. Many writers see it as a shorthand for Asian Pacific, the arc of countries resting on Japan and extending southward toward the newly industrializing countries (NICs). Often the term is extended to include the whole relationship of the Asian Pacific region to the United States."[4] Gourevitch himself is interested, we might add, in bringing Latin America into the definition of the Pacific Rim because of the "reality" of growing Latin American participation "in the dynamics of East Asian North American relations."[5] His statement has the additional virtue of revealing that inhabiting the region does not serve as qualification for inclusion in its definition, and also that those who are so included are not included equally.

Recognition of the fluidity of both the extent and the structure of the region reveals the difficulty of definition viewed as a historical problem: that is, in order to comprehend the region concretely, it is necessary to account for changes in its scope and structure (as well as its conceptualization) in terms of the human activity and the economic, political, and cultural relationships that in all their contradictoriness have dynamized its transformations. I do not propose to trace these developments in their historicity; rather, I will analyze briefly a basic contradiction in the region's construction that appears when it is viewed in historical perspective: a contradiction between its Asian and Pacific content—the people who inhabit it, in other words—and a regional formation that was very much a EuroAmerican invention. This is not to suggest either that this is the only contradiction in the region or that there are no contradictions internal to the region, but it seems to me to be the fundamental contradiction when the region is viewed in global perspective. We may see it as something like Mao Zedong's primary contradiction in the part it has played in shaping those contradictions internal to the region, perhaps even in producing those "secondary" contradictions.

The alternative terms that are available in descriptions of the region suggest the difficulties involved in its definition, and they therefore provide an appropriate point of departure in discussing problems of conceptualization. I will say a few words here on the most physically geographic of those terms, *Pacific Rim* and *Pacific Basin,* to illustrate the problems they present in the definition of the region; I will then illustrate the structural contradiction that is essential to comprehending the region by analzying, in historical perspective, two other terms, the commonly employed term *Asia-Pacific,* and a term that I have coined (and I will seek to justify), *EuroAmerican Pacific.*

Viewed as it appears on contemporary maps, the Pacific region covers an area that stretches from the Bering Strait to Antarctica, from California to Korea and China, from Alaska to Tasmania, from Tasmania to Southeast Asia, and from Kamchatka to Chile. The terms *Pacific Region* or *Pacific Basin,* in their suggestion that they refer to this whole region, seemingly have the advantage of comprehensiveness and an egalitarian inclusiveness (in suggesting the copresence of all those who are physically located in the region), but they are misleading for precisely these reasons. Taken literally, in their strongly physical associations, they are not as comprehensive as they sound at first hearing: *Pacific Rim,* the more commonly used of the two, is unsatisfactory because it focuses too exclusively on the edges of the region, leaving out the picture that is inside, which historically played an important part in the formation of the region. One recent discussion of the Pacific goes so far as to deliberately exclude the islands![6] *Pacific Basin,* with its suggestion of a center to the region somewhere in the ocean, is unsatisfactory for the opposite reason—at least in our day. In their inertly physical associations, moreover, achieved by identifying the boundaries of the region with a certain conception of those boundaries at one moment in time, both terms exclude the possibility of the expansion and contraction of those boundaries in accordance with activities initiated or played out somewhere in that physical area. We need only recall that the physical delineation of the region in contemporary maps was not available to human consciousness until after Captain James Cook completed the exploration of the area in the late eighteenth century—long after the beginning of the activities that would structure the region as such. Even after the physical boundaries of the region have been delineated, moreover, where to place the "rim" remains a problem. We all know, for instance, that California, Oregon, and Washington are U.S. locations on the Pacific Rim. But how significant was that fact in the early nineteenth century, when these states did not yet exist as they do at present, but when Pacific whaling played an important part in the New England economy? And what do we miss when today we place California on the Pacific Rim, yet ignore an Asian-American population in North Carolina that has economic ties to the Pacific or, equally if not more significant, that has strong cultural associations with its point of origin somewhere in that physical area? The terminology that appears concrete with reference to the region's physical delineation on maps is revealed as an abstraction when viewed in terms of human activity. And geography, conceived in terms of human activity rather than inert physical features, appears not as a point of departure for, but as a product of, human activity, reverting to its original etymological sense of "earth inscription."

More serious may be the misleading suggestion of the copresence of all participants in the region of a crudely physial geographic terminology. Historically, the formation of the region entails more than the gradual recognition, integration, and structuring of a physical area of which there was no knowledge at all among Europeans until the early sixteenth century, and only a local knowledge among its various inhabitants. It also involves a series of suppressions, maringalizations, and, in the case of one human group, total extinction (I am referring to the Tasmanians who did not survive the modern transformation of the area, and live on now in Saturday-morning cartoons in the United States).[7] In our day, a term such as *Pacific Rim* is but a euphemism for the powers that dominate the region: the United States and Japan, as Gourevitch suggests, and to a lesser extent societies of Chinese extension, as well as nations created by British imperialism, such as Canada, Australia, and New Zealand. But this was not always the case. Indeed, when these societies did not yet exist or were at best of marginal importance, the Pacific owed its formation to societies that appear marginal to it today: the Spanish colonies of Latin America that spearheaded the exploration of the area and created the first regional structure through the galleon trade with what is now the Philippines; the Russians whose Russian-American Company integrated another local region in the northern Pacific; the Pacific islands that served as the bases of EuroAmerican trade activity and provided the commodities whose flows integrated the whole of the Pacific into one superregion; and, of course, China, which served as the focal point of this intensifying activity. Only in the nineteenth century did the forces emerge that would ultimately give the Pacific the shape that it has at present.

While the exact list of those who have played a part in the region's formation (and continue to do so) may be debatable because of the historically dynamic nature of the region—what is not so problematic is that those who are located either on its physical boundaries or within them do not play equally important parts in its constitution or structuring. Physical terminology offers little clue to the dialectic of the region's formations, above all to the contradictions that have played a significant part in its formation as inevitable consequences of the very process of its constitution as a region. Having said this, let me note that remaining aware of the area as it appears on maps does serve an important purpose, for it is a reminder of the gap between region and area, of what is included within the region's structure and what is excluded from it. This gap, more than anything else, is indicative of the construction of a region out of an area in accordance with changing economic and political relationships.

In the procedures of its conceptualization, the problems that the Pacific region presents may be no different than for any other region on the globe. In his book, *The Western Hemisphere Idea*, Arthur Whitaker observes that while the term *Western Hemisphere* has as "an essential ingredient of it . . . a geographical concept," from its origins in the late eighteenth century, "a large cluster of related ideas, social and cultural as well as politico-geographical, and mystical as well as rational, began to grow up about it."[8] Much the same may be said of the "Pacific region" idea which if anything has been richly nourished by fantasies ranging from dreams of oriental markets to longings for earthly paradise, and is even more blurred in its boundaries than the "Western Hemisphere," which is at least identifiable with the boundaries of a continent. The Pacific region *is* an idea, if not *just* an idea, and terminology that pretends to a physical concreteness in its delineation is misleading to the extent that it conceals its origins in the human activity that produced the ideas.

In a richly suggestive study published some thirty years ago, *The Invention of America*, Edmundo O'Gorman wrote of the region that was his concern: "America, as such, literally does not exist, even though a mass of land exists which, in due course, will be endowed with that meaning, with that being."[9]

What O'Gorman was saying is that the term *America*, which we have come to use to describe that landmass, does not refer directly to the landmass but rather to a conception of it. To the extent that the term is meaningful, it is so not because it is descriptive of some inert reality, but because it is representative of some conception of that reality. Indeed, the reality itself is an "invention" of the concept: "Only that which has been conceived can be seen," O'Gorman quotes from Heidegger, "but that which has been conceived is that which has been invented."[10] The focus on "invention" directs O'Gorman's exploration of the term *America* away from the relationship between the term and the physical landmass it describes and toward the historically grounded activity of conceptualization that produced the relationship in the first place. While the descriptive content of the term as we have it is by no means irrelevant (for it refers to a specific landmass at a specific location), what is more crucial in grasping its significance (its *historical* meaning) is its conceptualization, with all the ideological and experiential presumptions and consequences attendant upon it.

O'Gorman's analysis hinges upon the distinction he draws between discovery and invention:

"Discovery" implies that the nature of the thing found was previously known to the finder, i.e., that he knows that objects such as the one he has found can and do exist although the existence of that particular one was wholly unknown. Thus an astronomer who is already aware that some heavenly bodies are classed as planets may be said to have "discovered" a planet when he detects for the first time one of those bodies. But the astronomer who first has the conception of such bodies as "planets" may be said to have "invented" that class of heavenly bodies, since it was he who formulated for the first time the concept itself.[11]

We need not restrict the definition of *discovery* as O'Gorman does (consciously) or take *invention* to be an initial formulation after which the only possibility is discovery, in order to recognize validity in the distinction that he draws. The distinction remains valid I think, even if we include in the definition of *discovery* its everyday sense of finding, or stumbling upon, something previously unknown, and even if we view invention as a historical process of conceptualization (in contrast to a single discrete historical act) or as a series of conceptualizations, or reinventions, that take place as that which is invented is endowed with new meanings (like the term *Western Hemisphere* referred to above). O'Gorman, moreover, moves too much in the abstract realm of ideas to concern himself with human activity as a process of invention. What is crucial, however, is the question of meaning that he raises, which itself is a historical question, because central to it is the part human agency plays in the production of meaning.

With reference to the Pacific region, in the consideration of available terminology the question is not (or should not be) which term best describes it, but rather precisely what alternative terms mean or, as I prefer it, represent. The search for descriptive accuracy may satisfy a positivist longing (or a policymaker's need) to establish a one-to-one correspondence between concept and reality, but what such a search yields is not very significant or interesting, and is generally misleading as well, as I have argued about with regard to terms such as *Pacific Rim* and *Pacific Basin*. The terminology is meaningful not because it is descriptive of some inert reality, but because it is representative of some conception of that reality, which itself points to the human activity that intermediates the description and what is being described.

In this perspective, two terms best capture the realities of the Pacific region, terms that are quite different (almost antagonistic) but equally indispensable to comprehending the region as a region: *Asian Pacific* and *EuroAmerican Pacific*. The former refers not just to the region's location but, more important, to its human constitution; the latter refers to another human component of the region (at least at present) and also to its invention as a regional structure.

To start with the latter term, I suggest it not in spite of but *because* of its Eurocentric or, more accurately, EuroAmerican centered implications. The Pacific region, *as* a region, is a EuroAmerican invention. In his editorial preface to a study of the region by Ernest Dodge, Boyd Shafer notes that the use of the term *discovery* with regard to the region is embarrassing because it suggests that the people who inhabited the region before the European arrival did not know that they were there.[12] The sentiment is one we may share, but the important question lies elsewhere. The people in the region obviously did not require a place in EuroAmerican consciousness to know that they existed, but regardless of their autonomous consciousness or history (more accurately, histories), the production of the region as a region, that is to say its modern history, was very much a consequence of EuroAmerican activity. What Whitaker says of the Americas may be said with equal validity of the Pacific: "The idea that America possessed a unity of any kind . . . was one—which, before the arrival of the Europeans, had never occurred to anyone in all the agglomeration of atomistic societies that inhabited America from Alaska to the Tierra del Fuego."[13] This is not to say that people in the Pacific did not interact with one another, but from the perspective of the region that had emerged by the late eighteenth century, these interactions were local, and so was the inhabitants' consciousness of them.

The production of a Pacific region begins with the global expansion of Europe, which is the premise of the region as a region. While Europeans entered the area from both its western and eastern ends, it was the entry from the east, around the Horn, that gave it the name *Pacific;* this initial entry, we might add, was consequent upon European efforts to come to terms with problems created by the new and unexpected landmass that Columbus had stumbled on just decades earlier on his way to Asia. On the one hand, Columbus's original intention linked Asia and the newly discovered Pacific; on the other hand, the Pacific emerged in historical consciousness as an extension of the conquest and consciousness of the Americas.

More significantly, over the next two centuries, it was the activity of Europeans, and of the transmuted Europeans of the Americas, that constituted the region as a Pacific region and gave it its form, which also transformed the localized consciousness of the area's original inhabitants (including, the highly developed societies of China and Japan) into a broader regional consciousness. The movement of EuroAmericans—not just in explorations but also in search of gold and silver, silks, spices, whales, seals, and sandalwood—over the length and breadth of the area eventually integrated localities into a region that extended over the area in all directions.[14] EuroAmericans invented the Pacific region because they created a structure out of the area that had not been there earlier; that this invention was not by design but was the result of often haphazard human motions does not mean that it had no logic to it. As the foremost historian of the Pacific, O. H. K. Spate, writes in a brilliant piece tracing the transformation of the "South Sea" (the original name given to the ocean by Balboa, who was the first European to sight it in 1513) into the "Pacific":

El Mar del Sur was in origin a merely local reference to little more than the Bay of Panama. One factor in its extension to the vast ocean was simply that the entry was always southabout; to Mariners, there was no other way in until the opening of the Suez and Panama Canals. Of the factors in the change from "South Sea" to "Pacific" the progress of geographical discovery was important, especially as the northern bounds of the Ocean were traced out; and except for rather vague knowledge in western Europe of the earlier Russian probes to Alaska, this had to wait until Cook. But probably more important were changes not just in the delineation of the Ocean, but in its patterns of trade.[15]

The logic rested with an expanding European world economy and in the competition it fueled among the European powers that in succession, through conquest and trade, extended it over the face of the globe. Entering the Pacific from the west or the east, the Portuguese, the Spaniards, the Dutch, the Russians, and the English, as well as their colonists in the Americas, all contributed in turn to the creation of a regional structure, in which Asian and Pacific societies provided the building blocks and the globalized interests of EuroAmerican powers furnished the principles of organization. The Pacific was "invented" as it was conceptualized in terms of a EuroAmerican global vision that incorporated the region's peoples into a new inventory of the world and established relationships that bound them together in a regional structure. This structure expressed the demands of the nascent capitalist order that informed the new vision, rather than expressing needs intrinsic to the region.

The EuroAmerican Pacific also gave birth to the Asian Pacific. The Pacific as it assumed conceptual form, did so as a periphery to an expanding EuroAmerican world economy, which structured the incipient region in accordance with its own economic and political logic. But from the beginning there was a strong Asian component present in the Pacific economy that complicated this logic and introduced into it a contradiction that disrupted the region's status as a periphery to a European core. This was the Chinese economy, a world economy in its own right, as Braudel has observed,[16] which stimulated a Pacific trade with its hub concentrated in Guangzhou (Canton). China had always played a major part in shaping the Southeast Asian trade. As Europeans arrived in the Pacific, the Manila galleon trade, which initially shaped the Pacific region, was based on trade between China (through the Philippines) and, first, the Americas and then, indirectly, the Iberian peninsula. At a later phase, Guangzhou served as the hub through which British opium was exchanged for Chinese tea. Less obvious, but from a Pacific perspective highly significant, was the fact that European economic activity over the Pacific Ocean and the American coast was oriented to the satisfaction of Chinese demand for commodities, ranging from sea otter furs to edible sea cucumbers.

The Pacific economy, in other words, had a strong Asian orientation even as EuroAmerican activity built it into a regional structure. The regional structure derived its logic from the requirements of two world economies; for that very reason, it appears problematic as a regional structure or, phrased somewhat differently, as a world economy in its own right with a coherent structure. Braudel has observed that a world economy, to be a world economy, presupposes a center (a core).[17] The Pacific economy as it took shape was decentered, or rather took shape through the interaction of alternative centers with their contradictory demands. It is nevertheless highly significant that EuroAmerican intermediation between the two world economies was responsible for its construction, which would gradually render the region peripheral to a EuroAmerican core, with East Asia never completely eliminated from the competition, but increasingly reduced to the status of a regional core. The Pacific economy was in this sense no different from other regional economies, which were rendered peripheral to a EuroAmerican economy that, as it invented a global economy (the world economy, in Braudel's distinction), subjected earlier world economies to its own demands.

The Asian component of the Pacific region had another aspect, relevant to understanding its future dynamics: the people who inhabited the area. It is arguable that the early conception of the region, very much bound up with EuroAmerican activity (and, therefore, economic and political interests), also served as the medium through which the original inhabitants of the area became aware of it as a region and, we may venture, of their place within it.[18] The EuroAmerican invention of the region, however, had to be produced out of the societies that inhabited the region. Their characteristics—and their resistance—are also indispensable to understanding the constitution of the region. In other words the original inhabitants of the area were not just passive objects of EuroAmerican activity but also shaped the course of such activity by their resistance, which included, in extreme (and rare) cases, eating the intruders. As Spate has written: "The outsiders named the Ocean, gave it bounds, and in a not trivial sense 'the Pacific' as a concept is a Euroamerican artifact. But it was not just 'made in Europe'; the local materials were not inert."[19]

We may recall here that long before the beginning of the activities that were to constitute it as a region, the Pacific area was peopled by human beings who had their origins in Asia. I am referring here to the peopling not just of East or Southeast Asia and the Pacific islands, but of the Americas as well. In spite of continuing debate over details, there is little serious doubt among paleontologists that the original inhabitants of the Americas, North and South, shared origins with the inhabitants of East Asia and the Pacific. The formation of the region in the modern world itself facilitated the movements of Asian and Pacific peoples; as a byproduct of the EuroAmerican integration of the Pacific area, the Asian and Pacific diaspora would play a part in the structuring of the region. While in the early modern period Chinese diffusion over Southeast Asia may have been the most readily visible (and significant) instance of this diaspora, since the mid-nineteenth century human flows have become a regionwide phenomenon, moving primarily in an easterly direction from Asia and the Pacific to the Americas. The Asian presence in North America is no longer just a local demographic detail of Los Angeles, San Francisco, or Vancouver, and citizens of Asian descent play a dynamic role in North American societies out of proportion to their numbers. One country in the Americas even has a president of Asian descent, President Alberto Fujimori of Peru. There is also, however, a south-north movement of peoples within the region, the most visible among which may be the Filipino migrations to Japan and Hong Kong. There are diverse reasons for these human movements, ranging from war and poverty to the transfer of capital, but the result of the Asian and Pacific diaspora is to enhance the structural integration of the region (albeit bringing with it, dialectically, previously unknown structural tensions). It may also have transformative consequences for the region's structure that are at present barely visible. Suffice it to say here that the region is linked not just by the flow of commodities or capital but also by human ties. EuroAmerican intermediation produced the regional structure; Asian and Pacific intermediation now plays the most significant role within it.

A historical perspective suggests, then, that the Pacific region as it assumed a regional structure was at once EuroAmerican and Asian. EuroAmerican activity, in giving the region its form, also shaped consciousness of it and resulted in an ideological hegemony that paralleled the invention of the region in actuality. Historical literature recognizes this in the depiction of the successive phases of Pacific history as a "Spanish lake" (during the sixteenth century and into the seventeenth, when Spain, largely through the intermediation of its colonies in the Americas, dominated the Pacific); an "English lake" (during the eighteenth and nineteenth centuries); and, finally, an "American lake" (from the late nineteenth into the twentieth century). EuroAmerican domination of the region assumed a political form from the mid-nineteenth century, when the economic competition between EuroAmerican powers was resolved by political arrangements that reduced societies in the region to the status of colonies or semicolonies.[20]

The Asian contribution to the region's formation, while no less real, was not as readily evident until the late nineteenth century, because up until that point it took the form of resistance to EuroAmerican activity rather than active participation in the region's structuring. Japan's emergence as an economic and political power in the late nineteenth century, which paralleled the ascendancy of the United States among EuroAmerican powers, was to bring to the fore a contradiction between the region's form and its content that had been there from the beginning.

Japan had been economically involved in the region's formation from its origins, through the intermediacy first of the Portuguese and then of the Dutch. Its emergence as an active participant in the region, however, begins in the late nineteenth century when EuroAmerican colonialism was turning the region into a periphery of a core that lay outside it. Japanese modernization from the beginning drew upon the lessons of Euro-American colonialism. As Bruce Cumings has argued, from the late nineteenth century on, Japan sought successfully to establish itself as a regional core with a periphery of its own, which would stretch ultimately beyond the colonization of its immediate neighbors to the Pacific islands.[21] Japan's rise would perpetuate the "decenteredness" of the region and sharpen the contradictions between its Asian and, by this time, American aspects. There is no need to belabor the point here that World War II in the Pacific, although a fundamental moment in this contradiction, did not resolve the problem. On the contrary, Japan's emergence as an economic world power has extended the periphery of Japanese economic dominance to the Americas and, with the opening of the People's Republic of China and the Soviet Union, may well establish Japan as the economically dominant power on the East Asian mainland as well.

Given the significance of the role Japan plays in the dynamics of the Pacific, it is important to spell out the context and consequences of this role. The immediate, and obvious, context is U.S. domination of the Pacific and the construction in Northeast Asia of a Japan-centered order under U.S. hegemony.[22] Less obvious but no less important is the historical context I have suggested: a Pacific that was a EuroAmerican construct, a product not of an Asian core but of the organization of the Pacific as an extension of a capitalist world economy emanating from Europe. It is arguable that Japan and the United States rose to power within this context almost simultaneously in the late nineteenth century, but it was the United States rather than Japan that dominated the regional construct, if only because the United States played a part in creating it from the eighteenth century onwards. World War II did not initiate but rather consolidated U.S. dominance. Japan, on the other hand, sought to carve out an Asian space within this construct; it was able to do so to the extent that it was willing to play according to the rules of the game (including colonialism)—rules that had been devised by others. It is necessary to emphasize here that the competition between Japan and the United States lies within the same capitalist social formation; the question is who is to dominate it.

This helps explain, I think, the ambiguity in the role Japan plays in the region, in spite of its unquestionable economic ascendancy at the present.

Japanese ascendancy has not brought about an alternative structure for the region, or even an alternative vision of it, if only because Japan itself is a product of the very forces that produced the region—the forces of the EuroAmerican-rooted capitalist order. To be sure, Japan from the beginning has called for Asian control of the region, and voices are to be heard in Japan even today that would represent Japanese ascendancy as a "liberation" of Asian peoples from EuroAmerican hegemony.[23] Rather than pointing to a new vision of the Pacific, this adds up to little more than the capture of the inherited regional structure for Asian (read Japanese) domination; in and of itself, it does not promise a restructuring of the region in a way significantly different from that created by the Euro-American capitalist order. Hence, rather than encourage unity or cohesiveness around a Japan-centered Pacific economy, the claims to a Japanese "liberation" of the Asian-Pacific region from EuroAmerican hegemony arouse immediate suspicion and divisiveness among Japan's Asian neighbors who suffered from Japanese colonialism, as well as among the less powerful societies in the region. The latter justifiably feel that within the Asian-Pacific world economy, their relationship to Japan is that of a Third World periphery to a dominant capitalist core, or of South to North. Writing of the Japanese promotion of a Pacific community, a Filipina scholar, Purificacion Valera-Quisumbing notes that "for a time, another term for community-building was colonization."[24] Moreover, given the importance of ties to the United States, as well as of extra-regional ties, other societies in the region do not see themselves merely as participants in a world economy with Japan at its core, but rather, on the strength of those ties, as competitors to Japan. Indeed, the economic emergence of South Korea and the Chinese-based states of Taiwan, Hong Kong, and Singapore introduces uncertainties into the structure of the Asian-Pacific economy and might alter the situation radically were Chinese and Korean unification to be realized. Reinforced by memories of colonialism, these ties undermine Japanese efforts to make Japan the core of an Asian-Pacific world economy. Under the circumstances, geographical proximity and intensity of economic ties distance these societies from one another rather than serving as the basis for unity, as evidenced by a perceived need among Japan's neighbors to include the United States within any regional organization as an antidote to Japanese power. This perpetuates U.S. domination of the region not only economically but politically and militarily as well.

Japan's emergence as an economic power in the Pacific region disrupts the Euro-American hegemony established during the region's formation, which had made the Pacific region as a whole a Third World vis-à-vis Europe and the United States, without offering a substitute structure or an alternative vision. This lack may be responsible for continued uncertainty over the meaning of a Pacific region—as well as mutual fears and antagonisms. The persistent dominance of the EuroAmerican legacy in the region's structure is most readily visible in the Japanese sentiment, quite justifiable, that for all its status as a world economic power, Japan is not a hegemonic but a hegemonized society, a merely regional power that differs little from other Third World societies in its political and ideological relationship to Europe and the United States. The dominance is also evident in the seeming inability of the Japanese to come up with an alternative vision of the region, except to call for a Japanese self-assertiveness within it, in which a justifiable resentment of being the object of EuroAmerican domination and disdain finds outlet in atavistic claims to national and racial superiority. Rather than challenge the principles and language of domination, such claims seek Japan's admission into the ranks of the dominant. A core power in the capitalist world system, but one that perceives itself to be peripheral culturally and politically, while lacking any genuine identification with the Third World: such seems to be the contradiction of an Asian power ascending to dominance within a structure not of its making.[25] It disrupts the structure and evokes suspicion, fear, and resentment both in the United States, whose hegemony it challenges, and in its Third World neighbors, who are not easily beguiled by Japan's claims to be one of them.

My insistence here that the regional structure invented by EuroAmerican activity persists despite the emerging power of the Asian-Pacific societies within the region is not intended to imply that such change is therefore of little consequence; rather, I seek to point to a fundamental contradiction in the region's constitution. It is important to emphasize here that the relationships that shaped the Pacific region in its origins have now been reversed. The Pacific region took shape originally through EuroAmerican activity that was oriented to an Asian world economy (China); it is now shaped increasingly by an orientation to a North American market through the activity of Asian peoples. The unmistakable transfer of initiative in the structuring of the region (its reinventions so to speak) to its Asian peoples justifies more than ever its description as an Asian rather than a EuroAmerican Pacific.

This may be in the ideological and cultural reassertion of the region's Asian identity. As one scholar from the Philippines writes:

> Geography does not change, but the way of looking at it definitely does. It was not too long ago when many Pacific countries—due to their shared fate of Western colonialism—looked towards Europe and North America. Hardly were they conscious about the need to look inwards to the region and among themselves. Owing largely to the demise of the colonial era, the momentum of nationalism, the imperatives of economic survival and secur-

ity, to studies underlining the importance of the region and other factors, many states in the region are now asserting their Pacific orientation.[26]

"The Pacific way of development," as it has been called, not surprisingly is subject to different interpretations, depending on status within the region. Among the dominant and rising economic powers of East Asia, it is asserted through a revival of Confucianism, so-called, as the characteristic feature of Asian development. The Confucian revival, which stretches all the way from Japan to Singapore on the East and Southeast Asian rim, may be viewed as an antihegemonic cultural movement that seeks to stamp upon the Pacific region the ideology of its East Asian protagonists. This "Confucianism," however, is different from any Confucianism that had been available earlier, for its protagonists seek to articulate it to a managerial capitalism at which East Asian societies have been remarkably successful; inasmuch as it is antihegemonic, it seeks not to question the capitalist structure of the Pacific region but rather to assert an East Asian identity within it.[27] That may be the reason that it has had more appeal among managers of capitalism in North America than among the peripheral societies of the Pacific region (whether of Latin America, the Pacific islands or Southeast Asia) whose cultural characteristics it marginalizes. Some of the region's peripheral societies have turned their attention to other alternatives within a Pacific framework. One Filipino scholar, Jesus Estanislao, welcomes the idea of a "Pacific community" because

> by its implementation we would be given another opportunity to be in closer contact with our ASEAN counterparts and also with Mexico, and along with it the major Latin American countries bordering on the Pacific. We have a sentimental reason for this because for centuries we maintained a thin but vital link with Mexico and through it with Europe and the world. We are certain that in the next decades, we will have more than sentimental reasons to try and work for mutual prosperity with Mexico and the Pacific countries of Latin America.[28]

Similarly, a Malaysian scholar, critical of tendencies to emulate Japan in development, calls upon another cultural tradition when he writes that Malaysia should base its "program of social reconstruction upon a philosophy that is culturally rooted. Islam and the other great religious traditions have the capacity to perform this role."[29]

The "Pacific way of development," in its assertion of Asian cultural identity in such a way as to articulate its traditions to the forces of capitalism that initially shaped the Pacific region, reveals the fundamental contradiction that is the region's legacy; the appropriation of "the Pacific way" for these different traditions is likewise indicative of the "controversy and struggle" (recalling Gourevitch's words) over the definition of "the Pacific rim." This is not just a debate among social theorists, but a real-life struggle over hegemony and counter-hegemony within the region—which is no less a region because it is the object of struggle.

What is the Pacific? We may paraphrase O'Gorman to state that "the Pacific does not exist; even though an area exists that has been endowed with that meaning, with that being." What the Pacific is seems to be inextricable from another question that is implicit in most discussions of the subject: whose Pacific? There is a discourse on the Pacific that originated in the European invention of the region, *produced* the region as we know it, and holds hegemonic sway over consciousness, including that of the people who inhabit the region. But the discourse is also subject to conflicting appropriations in accordance with different perceptions and interests. To define, or to name, is to conquer. The debate over definitions that Gourevitch refers to is also a struggle over domination of the region, over its constitution, as well as over whom to include within and exclude from it.

A historical perspective on the region helps us formulate its problematic, but the problems of the present are not necessarily those of the past. I will conclude this discussion with a few words on the problem as it appears in our day, in the efforts to organize the Pacific into a structured community, which are the most recent guise in which the discourse on the Pacific (and its appropriation) appears. These efforts, I suspect, are responsible for the prominent place the region has acquired in our consciousness over the last two decades. To be sure, the economic success of Pacific societies has drawn attention to the region, but these organizational efforts, and the problems they have brought to the surface concerning the region's constitution, give an urgency to the problem of definition. There is by now an ideology of the Pacific; the problem is how to give form to this inchoate ideology through organization.[30]

The problems the Pacific presents to organization are somewhat differents from those we find in other regions. Whitaker observes that the Western Hemisphere idea, as it took form, was primarily a political idea.[31] The Atlantic region, in addition to economic and political relationships, binds the two sides of the ocean with real or perceived cultural ties. The Pacific region emerged as primarily an economic region. Since the late nineteenth century, some semblance of political form has been imposed on the region, but the diversity of political forms in the area perpetuates a political fragmentation. Above all, however, is the problem of the diversity of cultures. It may be possible in our day to speak of the emergence of an Asian-Pacific culture through the medium of the movements of Asian peoples, as well as of the absorption by peoples in the region of EuroAmerican, especially U.S., cultural forms. But any common culture remains marginal against cultural differences.

Valera-Quisumbing has observed that "it would be useful to think of the Pacific Community concept on three distinct levels: as an ideal; as an institution and process; and a reflection of an underlying reality".[32] The underlying reality is that of transactions of commodities and capital, as well as movements of peoples and, to a lesser extent, of cultural forms. "Institution and process" appear in the efforts to give organizational form to the Pacific, which are yet to be realized. And the ideal, shared to a greater or lesser degree by societies in the region, and as yet indistinguishable from ideology, appears at the one extreme as fantasy, at the other as a disguise for the contradictions in the region.

The idea of Pacific unity implicit in the Pacific community idea appears to the less powerful within the region as a barely disguised effort on the part of the powerful to control it. Valera-Quisumbing has described the Pacific community idea as "a baby whose putative parents are Japanese and American and whose midwife is Australian."[33] Luz Del Mondo states even more bluntly that Japan, seeing the intensifying relations of ASEAN societies (Malaysia, Thailand, Singapore, Indonesia, Brunei, and the Philippines) with Europe, western Asia, and Latin America, seeks through the Pacific community idea "to preempt the ASEAN as its own preserve."[34] The wealthier societies of the region, united in the Organization for Economic Cooperation and Development (OECD), consisting of the United States, Japan, Canada, Australia, and New Zealand, have far fewer qualms about the Pacific community than do societies of the Pacific Third World. The latter seek to balance Japan with the United States, even as those two powers go on bashing one another over their status in the world and in the region. The question of where communist societies in the area belong in the region remains highly problematic. Latin America remains suspended between continued U.S. hegemony and increasing Japanese (and, to a lesser extent, Taiwanese and South Korean) economic incursion. And, of course, few bother any longer to speak of the islands, around which the idea of the Pacific first took shape.

The contradictions within the region are further complicated by a number of factors, some of them old, some products of the contemporary world. First are the extraregional commitments of powers that are not merely regional but global. Chief among these are the United States and Japan, but also included is China which, in spite of its poverty and economically dependent status, claims extraregional powers. The existence of other regional formations (or potential formations) on the periphery of the area is a second factor. The United States, crucial to any definition of the Pacific, nevertheless is anxious also to promote a North American region; how this region would relate to the Pacific region is highly problematic. So is the potential region in East and Southeast Asia centered on

Japan. In other words, the issue of an American Pacific versus an Asian Pacific remains to be settled.

Finally, the uncertainties of developments in the world economy also render uncertain the structure of the Pacific region. I am referring here to what has been called a "global factory," with its workshops and production processes scattered around the globe, which may consign to the past the organization of the world in nation-states. The societies of the region owe their impressive development to an export orientation (now emulated even by the likes of China) that shifts attention from the national to the international context; in the words of Gary Gereffi, "export networks thus are replacing the nation-state as the key units of analysis in the contemporary global manufacturing system."[35] A prominent market analyst such as Kenichi Ohmae can even argue that we should stop thinking in terms of nations, and pay greater attention to pockets of development within nations that tie together global development. According to Ohmae, it is no longer meaningful, for instance, to speak of the United States as a whole; rather, we should think about, in his words, "Orange County or North Carolina," where new dynamic forces are being forged.[36] If there is any significance to the "borderless world" for which Ohmae is an articulate spokesperson, it may also be meaningless to speak of divisions between the First and Third World, or North and South; for in the Third World as well, there is an economic elite that participates actively in the workings of the "global factory," just as in the First World, such as the United States, parts of society are being reduced to Third World status in the midst of economic growth. Border economics and special economic zones flourish while the national economy languishes.

It is possible that the Pacific region impresses the world today because societies of the Pacific have taken the lead in the development of these new economic forms, showing the rest of the world its future. If that is the case, we are once again in the midst of a reinvention of the Pacific, which heats up the struggle over definitions. As the future form of the region dimly appears through the haze of fantasy and ideology, of struggle and conflicting claims, however, that future is likely to be, more than ever before, an Asian-Pacific future.

## Notes

1. Tom Magnuson, "From Mist in the Pulpit to Fog in the Pews," *Naval War College Review* 42 (1990), sequence 332, p. 122.

2. For the sake of clarity, I use *area* in this discussion to refer to the Pacific as a physical geographic entity, and reserve *region* for the constructs of human activity, whether material or ideological.

3. Peter A. Gourevitch, "The Pacific Rim: Current Debates," *The Annals of the Academy of Political and Social Science* 505 (1989): 8–23.

4. Ibid., p. 9.

5. Ibid., p. 10.

6. Lau Taik Soon and Leo Suryadinata, *Moving into the Pacific Century: The Changing Regional Order in the Asia-Pacific* (Singapore: Heinemann Asia, 1988), p. 177.

7. This statement needs to be amended in light of individuals of Tasmanian origin who have come forward in recent years to reclaim their Tasmanian identity.

8. Arthur P. Whitaker, *The Western Hemisphere Idea: Its Rise and Decline* (Ithaca: Cornell University Press, 1954), pp. 1–2.

9. Edmundo O'Gorman, *The Invention of America: An Inquiry into the Historical Nature of the New World and the Meaning of Its History* (Bloomington: Indiana University Press, 1959), p. 73.

10. Ibid., p. 73.

11. Ibid., p. 9.

12. Ernest S. Dodge, *Islands and Empires: Western Impact on the Pacific and East Asia* (Minneapolis: University of Minnesota Press, 1976), pp. ix–x.

13. Whitaker, *The Western Hemisphere Idea,* p. 7.

14. The observations here are based on a number of works that proffer comprehensive accounts of the ways in which Euro-American economic and political activity integrated and structured in the region, ultimately rendering it peripheral to the Euro-American economies. Douglas L. Oliver's *The Pacific Islands,* 3d ed. (Honolulu: University of Hawaii Press, 1989), offers a detailed account of the consequences of these activities for the Pacific Islanders, with much empathy for the latter. Ernest Dodge's *Islands and Empires* and *New England and the South Seas* (Cambridge: Harvard University Press, 1965) offer clear accounts with emphasis on the role of U.S. traders and missionaries. O. H. K. Spate's magisterial three-volume study, *The Pacific Since Magellan,* is indispensable to understanding the formation of the region from the sixteenth to the early nineteenth centuries (vol. 1: *The Spanish Lake;* vol. 2: *Monopolists and Free Booters;* vol. 3: *Paradise Lost and Found* [Minneapolis: University of Minnesota Press, 1979, 1983, 1988]). Given the spatial problems presented by the idea of the Pacific, it may not be surprising that this most comprehensive account of the Pacific should have been the work of a geographer.

15. H. K. Spate, " 'South Sea' to 'Pacific Ocean,' " *The Journal of Pacific History* 12 (1977): 210.

16. Fernand Braudel, *The Perspective of the World,* vol. 3 of *Civilization and Capitalism* (New York: Harper and Row, 1986), pp. 484–533.

17. Ibid., pp. 29–31.

18. Thus Chao Ju-kua (Zhao Rugua), in *Records of Foreign Countries,* which dates back to the twelfth century, observes that east of Java, "you come to the (Ocean)-Sea and to where the waters flow downward; there is the kingdom of women. Still farther east is the wei-lu, the end of the habitable world" (Chau, *Records of Foreign Nations,* trans. Friedrich Hirth and W. W. Rockhill [St. Pe-

tersburg: Printing Office of the Imperial Academy of Sciences, 1911]). The work, quite detailed with regard to Southeast Asia, betrays little awareness of the Pacific of Borneo. Chinese awareness of the Pacific as an area of significant concern goes back to the post-Opium War (1839–42) period. See Fred W. Drake, *China Charts the World: Hsu Chi-yu (Xu jiyu) and His Geography of 1848* (Cambridge, Mass.: Harvard University Press, 1975). Similarly, Honda Toshiaki's *Tales of the West*, written in 1798, betrays little knowledge of the Pacific, although it is extremely interesting for the ways in which the Dutch presence in Japan provoked one Japanese at least to relocate Japan in what is clearly a Pacific perspective. See Donald Keene, *The Japanese Discovery of Europe, 1720–1830* (Stanford: Stanford University Press, 1969), pp. 205–26. Within the Pacific Ocean itself, the areas that have come to be known (following the arrival of the Europeans) as Polynesia, Melanesia, and Micronesia were areas of trade and other interaction, but it is doubtful that consciousness of the Pacific extended beyond this "local" consciousness. Much the same may be said of Native Americans of the Pacific Northwest.

19. Spate, *Paradise Lost and Found*, p. 211.

20. See Akira Iriye, *The Cold War in Asia* (New York: Prentice-Hall, 1974), chap. 2; Dodge, *Islands and Empires,* chaps. 12 and 13.

21. Bruce Cumings, *The Origins of the Korean War: Liberation and the Emergence of Separate Regimes, 1945–1947* (Princeton: Princeton University Press, 1989), pp. 6–7.

22. John Dower, "Occupied Japan and the American Lake, 1945–1950," in Mark Selden and Edward Friedman, eds., *America's Asia* (New York: Vintage Books, 1971), pp. 155–73. See also Bruce Cumings, "The Origins and Development of the Northeast Asian Political Economy: Industrial Sectors, Product Cycles, and Political Consequences," *International Organizations* 38 (1984) 3–40.

23. Arif Dirlik, " 'Past Experience, If Not Forgotten, Is a Guide to the Future': The Politics of History are Sino-Japanese Relations," *Boundary 2/19* (1991): 48.

24. Jose P. Leviste, Jr., ed., *The Pacific Lake: Philippine Perspectives on a Pacific Community* (Manila: The Philippine Council for Foreign Relations, 1986), p. 80.

25. This is one of the grievances that seem to have provoked Shintaro Ishihara's "America bashing" in *The Japan That Can Say No* (New York: Simon and Schuster, 1990). However, it is by no means restricted to Ishihara and the right wing in Japanese political circles with which he seems to be associated. Akio Morita of SONY Corporation obviously shared Ishihara's views (although his name does not appear in the English version of the book), and the view that Japan's cultural relationship to the United States resembles a Third-to-First-World relationship has been suggested also by writers with impeccable political credentials (in my view), such as Oe Kenzaburo and Masao Miyosli.

26. Leviste, *The Pacific Lake*, p. 2.

27. The "Confucian revival" is not new, but it has gathered force over the last decade, and has been tied during those years to the economic success of East Asian societies in the "Confucian cultural sphere." One discussion traces the recent revival to Michio Morishinia's *Who Has Japan Succeeded* (New York:

Cambridge University Press, 1988). See John Wong and Aline Wong, "Confucian Values as a Social Framework for Singapore's Economic Development," unpublished paper presented at the "Conference on Confucianism and Economic Development in East Asia," Taipei, 29–31 May 1989. This rather novel interpretation of Confucianism is one European and U.S. specialists have come to share. It has also piqued considerable interest in the People's Republic of China, in search of models of development to substitute for a waning socialist ideology. For a sampling of writers, see the contributions to the conference mentioned above.

28. Leviste, *The Pacific Lake*, pp. 112–13.

29. Lee Poh Ping, "Malaysian Perceptions of Japan Before and During the 'Look East' Period," *Asia Pacific Community* 13 (1985): 103.

30. A useful summary of efforts to establish a Pacific community, or a Pacific economic community, is to be found in Leviste, *The Pacific Lake*, app. A. See also Norman D. Palmer, *The New Regionalism in Asia and the Pacific* (Lexington, Mass.: Lexington Books, 1991); and W. W. Rostow, *The United States and the Regional Organization of Asia and the Pacific, 1965–1985* (Austin: University of Texas Press, 1986). A sampling of differences is to be found in *The Pacific Community Concept: Views from Eight Nations*, Proceedings of the Asian Dialogue at Oiso, Japan, 1980 (Tokyo: Japan Center for International Exchange, 1980).

31. Whitaker, *The Western Hemisphere Idea*, p. 1.

32. Leviste, *The Pacific Lake*, p. 88.

33. Ibid., p. 81.

34. Ibid., p. 116.

35. Gary Gereffi, "Development Strategies and the Global Factory," *The Annals of the American Academy of Political and Social Science* 505 (1989): 100.

36. Kenichi Ohmae, "Beyond Friction to Fact: The Borderless Economic," *New Perspectives Quarterly* 7 (1990): 21. Ohmae is an advocate of "triad power," which seems to be a Japanese version of trilateralism. For a recent explanation of his views, see *The Borderless World: Power and Strategy in the Interlinked Economy* (New York: Harper Business, 1991). His views would seem to have great appeal in the world of transnational corporations.

# 3

# The Asia-Pacific Idea as a Mobilization Myth

ALEXANDER WOODSIDE

The recent history of the Asia-Pacific region has been converted into a myth, or sacred narrative, which invites the fulfillment of a certain kind of future, rather than just explaining and justifying one version of an ideologically contested past. Political, economic, and academic elites on both sides of the Pacific use the myth to protect programs and policies in the present to which such elites have become attached, and to mobilize people for their future achievement. Relatively commonplace observations of contemporary reality become transmuted into visions of governments' (or universities') sense of the future meaning of reality in relation to themselves and to the peoples they govern or instruct.

Such visions have their fervidly utopian side, as expressed in books like the U.S. futurologist John Naisbitt's *Megatrends 2000,* published in 1990. In Chapter 6 of his book, entitled "The Rise of the Pacific Rim," Naisbitt and his coauthor make relatively modest predictions about the immediate future in Asia: Japan rather than France will lead the world in the 1990s in fashion, design, and the arts; Korea, "heir to the samuari's crown," may overtake Japan economically by the year 2010; "the whole world is moving toward greater democracy and China will follow," despite what happened in China in June 1989; in the world economy, "education is the Pacific Rim's competitive edge," and allegedly greater investment in education will allow Asian-Pacific countries to maintain their economic ascendancy.[1] But Naisbitt's ultimate conclusions storm the futurological heavens with their optimism: "On the threshold of the millennium, long the symbol of humanity's golden age, we possess the tools and the capacity to build utopia here and now. . . . The Pacific Rim has rewritten the history of economic development, jumping right over the industrial period and into the information economy, where the important resources do come not from the ground but from people."[2] Naisbitt, evidently, is widely read in the Asian countries he describes or invents. His earlier *Megatrends* book, for example, was quickly trans-

37

lated into Chinese and published in China by the prestigious Chinese Social Sciences Publishing House.[3]

Apart from its utopia builders, the Pacific Rim prophetic culture also has its less euphoric medicine men, obsessed with the need to find cures for stagnating economies on the Western side of the rim. A good recent example of a minimum version of such reformism may be found in S. B. Linder's book, *The Pacific Century: Economic and Political Consequences of Asian-Pacific Dynamism,* published in 1986. Asserting that the Pacific region is too "heterogeneous" to rely on "particularized growth theories," Linder rejects the claims that Asian-Pacific economic prosperity is due to Confucianism or to the Japanese national character or to East Asia's supposed traditional reverence for education (for which Linder's index does not even have a reference). Rather, Linder sees the secret of Asian-Pacific economic dynamism as being nothing more than the region's apotheosis of export-oriented market economies, relying upon historic policies that once gave the rich Western countries their own affluence. "It is exciting to see these policies succeeding again."[4] However valid it might be, the self-congratulatory argument that Japanese or South Korean economic success might come in effect from an adoption of the principles of the nineteenth-century British economy, is cearly meant to be confidence building for Westerners. Beleaguered nineteenth-century Chinese conservative intellectuals' rhetorical supposition that Western chemistry had all been invented by *Zhuangzi* was meant to comfort them in the same way.

We meet a more extreme version of the sort of reform proposals the Pacific Rim prophetic culture inspires in recent books like the veteran U.S. journalist Robert Elegant's *Pacific Destiny,* published in 1990. Elegant concludes this huge book:

> We must now take a profound lesson from the patient perseverance that is central to the Asian ethos: the tenacious accretion of power and virtue that lies beneath the dazzling surface of present-day Asians. . . . Asian societies do change, sometimes dramatically. But they change only after attaining an almost mystical consensus regarding their new course—and the old values endure. Individualistic Westerners living in laissez-faire societies are unaccustomed to arriving at fundamental decisions by such patient and profound processes.

To hold their own in the Asia-Pacific region, Elegant counsels, Western countries do not need "authoritarianism, which could cripple initiative, but a structured consensus such as normally prevails in wartime."[5]

Despite this apocalyptic language, Elegant, Linder, and Naisbitt are agreed that, in Naisbitt's words, "The rise of the East need not mean the decline of the West."[6] Writers like Elegant are really vulgar latter-day mercantile Leibnizes; they preach the need for a synthesis, or convergence, of Asian and Western economic planning behavior, just as Leibniz's far more sublime *Novissima Sinica* once pleaded for an East-West synthesis in natural theology, to be aided by the stationing of Confucian missionaries in Europe.

This particular renewal of the old dream of convergence implies that the West should conform at least in part to an "Asian" example. Technically, moreover, the idea of an Asia-Pacific economic community itself seems to have originated in Asia, in Japan in the middle of the 1960s. As the Beijing economist Luo Yuanzheng, himself the author of significant Chinese books and articles on the subject, has pointed out, Japanese politicians, and famous Japanese economists like Kojima Kiyoshi, proposed the notion of a Pacific Ocean free trade zone in the 1960s, only to meet with a rebuff from the United States and caution elsewhere; the U.S. attitude underwent a "major" change and became far more receptive only in the late 1970s.[7] Yet the paradox is that the Pacific Rim prophetic culture, like much of the rest of Pacific Rim thought, is as Arif Dirlik has rightly argued, a "EuroAmerican construct" whose imaginative hegemony is in Western hands.[8] It is surely significant that most of the roots of such thought may be traced back in the West to a time when no Japanese-made or Korean-made machines of any kind offered the slightest threat to Western countries' manufacturers.

If we merely confine ourselves to Britain's hegemonic "invention" of Japan before World War I, we could cite Alfred Stead's book *Great Japan: A Study of National Efficiency* (1905), in the preface of which a former British prime minister (Lord Rosebery) praised the Japanese for their patriotism and self-discipline; or *A Modern Utopia* (also 1905), by H. G. Wells, in which the members of Wells's ideal ruling elite were called "samurai"; or *Universities and National Life* (1911), by the British cabinet minister R. B. Haldane, who also urged British students to imitate the "disciplinarianism" of the Japanese.[9] Despite the Pacific Rim futurologists' exhilarating reminders of the inadequacy of our inherited conceptual schemes and paradigms for understanding the future, the main modes of their own thought are hardly new.

Three principal such modes are easily detected. The first one might be called Saint-Simonianism, in honor of the French thinker of the early nineteenth century who located the golden age in the future, not the past, and anticipated a future industrial civilization, ruled by an elite of scientists and engineers, undergoing repeated progressive transformations in which supposedly more primitive political struggles disappeared or were marginalized. The second mode of thought could obviously be said to be a genteel social Darwinism—the belief in a competitive struggle between civilizations in varying degrees of economic fitness—minus the original social Darwinism's tedious fascination with national physique sizes, and with the possiblity of peace and prosperity for all through convergence benignly substituted for the older, more brutal outcome of the wholesale elimination of unfit civilizations. (Linder, for example, says that there must be "adjustment without tears.") The third mode of thought, as Elegant's moonshine about the "almost mystical consensus" of the "Asian ethos" suggests, is Orientalism. A series of reductive analytical categories is applied to Asian societies, with the object of savoring the exotic profundity of their differences from the West and then making this a stimulus to mission-oriented action of some kind; although again a hope of redemption through convergence softens the process.

One could add to these three modes the chief U.S. extension of them, particularly of the Saint-Simonian mode: a cybernetics-flavored managerialism that stresses "communications" research and seeks to control the effects of technological change through the measurement of "feedback" information about the intended and unintended consequences of such change. If Asian societies enjoyed the "mystical" powers of consensus building that Robert Elegant and others attribute to them, they would presumably have only a weak interest in such forms of political management. In fact such techniques, dressed up as theory, have become a major U.S. export to Asia. In the 1960s, for example, the U.S. National Aeronautics and Space Administration mobilized U.S. "communications" researchers like Raymond Bauer to study such unintended and potentially damaging "second order consequences" of the terrestrial expansion of the NASA space exploration empire as the displacement of local businesses by NASA land acquisitions. "Social indicators" research was born. The Chinese National Statistics Bureau transferred it, giving full credit to NASA and to Raymond Bauer, to China in the early 1980s; by 1987 the Chinese Ministry of Public Security had its own "Public Security Statistical Indicators System," complete with 470 separate "indicators" of "social order," "public security," and "safeguard prerequisites."[10]

Of course not all these inspirations are fully shared by everyone who writes about the Pacific Rim. But the cardinal modes of Pacific Rim thought, whether they are found in the heads of Western economists or Chinese police officers, usually do serve the overall purposes of what Gao Fang—a politics professor at People's University in Beijing, and one of the few serious present-day Chinese critics of U.S. futurologists like Alvin Toffler—calls international capitalist utopianism.[11] The Pacific Rim prophetic culture in its current form could probably not survive an abrupt or cataclysmic termination of the extraordinary prolonged boom global capitalism has enjoyed since World War II.

In the meantime, however, the prophecies, which are essentially Western in origin, do not just respond to the possible realities in the Asia-Pacific region, they go far to shape and create them. One of the contemporary Pacific Rim's most noteworthy cultural transactions is the spread of their practical influence. Consider agriculture. Toffler is perhaps the Asia-Pacific region's most popular Saint-Simonian prophet. He suggested in his book *The Third Wave* in 1980 that economically lagging countries like China could bypass earlier strategies of modernization by means of previously unexampled "postindustrial" breakthroughs in education and in high technology. The "Third Wave leads us in unconventional directions. . . . Ultimately we may see the convergence of weather modification, computers, satellite monitoring, and genetics to revoluntionize the world's food supply."[12] In 1983 Toffler paid what could be called a state visit to China, as the guest of Premier Zhao Ziyang and the Chinese Academy of Social Sciences, lecturing to audiences in Beijing and Shanghai who "listened to him as if he were an oracle."[13] When a Chinese language version of *The Third Wave* appeared in 1984, purged of its anti-Marxist references, it became one of China's great modern best-sellers, selling more than 13,000 copies in the city of Changsha alone in the first six months of 1985. Young Chinese research scholars publicly informed their superiors that Toffler's thought was the truth and that Marxism was moribund.[14]

The chief traces of the Toffler cult's contribution to the construction of the technocratic side of Pacific Rim thought are probably to be found in the more than 5,000 national "research and development organs" or government think tanks that proliferated in China by the end of the 1980s. The Chinese State Council's Village Development Research Center, for instance, published a massive work (almost 700,000 words) in 1985, *Zhongguo nongcun fazhan zhanlue wenti* (Strategic problems of the development of Chinese villages), which called in a Tofflerian manner for the introduction into China of intellectualized farming, or "thinking agriculture" (*sikao nongye*). Such wonders as plant genetics could be used to transcend earlier "developmental models."[15] Numerous references to, or invocations of, Toffler could be found in the hundreds of economic development journals that flourished in China in the same decade. Thus one Chinese researcher, calling in 1987 for a transfer of "surplus labor" out of Chinese agriculture, said that this transfer could not occur without a rise in the peasants' cultural and technological levels. But Toffler's enthusiasm for educational sky satellites, he added, had shown how this could be made to happen.[16]

That the times are so propitious for the reception of such optimistic futurology on the Asian side of the Pacific Rim is probably to be explained by the buoyant expectations associated with East and Southeast Asia's recent economic success. At least fourteen Asian countries or units had annual economic growth rates of 6 percent or more in 1984, a benchmark year in the transfer of the newer Saint-Simonianism across the Pacific. Moreover, optimism about the miraculous powers of science and technology is perhaps more likely in countries for which the experience of industrialization is relatively recent. It is less seductive in more middle-aged industrial societies where familiarity with the costs of sicence and technology is greater, and which may thus suffer from what some analysts have jokingly called "development fatigue." The Asia-Pacific region may well be riddled not merely with trade imbalances, but with psychological imbalances related to national variations in the loss of industrial innocence. But why are there so few Chinese or Thai or Indonesian or Vietnamese Alvin Tofflers or John Naisbitts? Why is the futurological business the reverse of the car-making and shipbuilding businesses, with the intellectual trade deficits apparently all occurring in Asia?

One answer to this question would point to cultural differences. People with rich historical consciousnesses are rarely good futurologists. Left to their own devices, most East Asians and Southeast Asians might well continue to be tempted to think of the future on the basis of more thickly historical models than would (say) Americans. Although the term "Asia-Pacific region" is current on both sides of the Pacific, the very different formula "Pacific Rim" seems to be most fashionable in the English-speaking Pacific democracies, with some important echoes also in Japan. Whatever its practical usefulness to physical scientists like oceanographers or seismographers, the notion of a "rim" induces us to think of the Pacific community as a frontier. On the Western side of the Asia-Pacific region, it undoubtedly reflects the traditionally positive view of frontiers in North America as historically almost virgin realms where humankind could be remade. As always, John Naisbitt marks this triumphant return of the old frontier myth with the least subtlety and the most parochialism: "The Pacific Rim is emerging like a dynamic young America but on a much grander scale."[17]

On the Asian side, fewer people are capable of thinking of the Asia-Pacific region as an open-ended frontier, as a sort of giant inequality-transcending Homestead Act of the imagined future. A Chinese economist like Ma Bohuang of Shanghai stubbornly writes about the Pacific community in more prosaic terms, as being merely the modern world's fifth great epoch in the exploration of the development of export-directed economies, albeit a more culturally demanding one than the earlier four epochs, a series he sees as beginning in Europe in the sixteenth century.[18] On the rare occasions when Chinese do imagine the Pacific community as a frontier, they do so in much more dialectical terms of cultural collision and confrontation. Thus in the memorable last episode of Su Xiaokang's sensational Chinese television series "River Elegy" in 1988, the supposedly ugly, despotism-engendering Yellow River is urged to surrender to the beautiful great blue Pacific Ocean beyond it that allegedly bears democracy on its waters.

A second, more simple kind of answer to this question might suggest that although many Asian intellectuals and politicians are wishful consumers of the products of the region's prophetic culture, actual history so far has given far fewer of them the confidence to be extravagant creators of its more flamboyant visions. Ma Bohuang, the Shanghai social scientist just quoted, stated baldly in 1988 that China was too weak to do what Japan, Taiwan, or South Korea had done and convert other countries into being China's own commercial goods markets or suppliers of raw materials, and use its scientific and technological superiority to "control" the "labor services" of other countries' people.[19] Thus there could be no common Asia-Pacific region strategy based on such an ambition. Is China even properly one of the countries of the Asia-Pacific myth, with all of the advantages attributed sometimes to such countries by Western futurologists? Or is the Asia-Pacific region ideology a device for supplanting a very different earlier agenda more concerned with the tragedy of the world's "North-South divide" between haves and have-nots? The battle of agenda-defining metaphors here is hardly just academic. The older North-South divide runs right through the newer Pacific Rim, as a genuine fault line between its richer and poorer countries, if no longer the most fashionable apocalyptic symbol of the world's unperfected present. And there are still many Asian "Asia-Pacific" thinkers, like China's Ma Bohuang and others, who are driven to preserve both agenda-defining metaphors, rather like the late medieval scholars in Europe who tried to accommodate both the geocentric and heliocentric views of the universe.

The technological innovations the Pacific Rim prophetic culture celebrates are, of course, perfectly real. If ever there were a master institution of the emerging Pacific Rim community of which a Toffler or a Naisbitt might approve, with their interest in genetic engineering and the international diffusion of science, it would surely be the International Rice Research Institute in the Philippines. It is responsible for some of the Asia-Pacific region's most significant technological transfers so far. Since about 1970, for example, Vietnam, though the victim of an unrelenting U.S. trade embargo, has imported and widely planted more than fifty different fast-growing, high-yield IRRI rice strains, with the tangible result being an annual increase in Vietnam's rice productivity of about one million tons of paddy each year. The traditional Vietnamese farming world of inadequate fifth-month and tenth-month rice crops has vanished.

But the prophetic culture goes beyond the mere description of obvious economic and scientific transactions like this externally inspired agricultural revolution. Vietnamese elite thinkers now try to consolidate imaginatively this limited but real scientific internationalization of Vietnamese village life by redefining Vietnamese villages themselves in the "contemporary scientific language" of "management studies" as "open systems" (*he thong mo* in new-speak Vietnamese)—to quote from a recent study of a north Vietnamese village by two well-known Hanoi social psychologists.[20]

Within Vietnam's thousands of years of history, this is an extraordinary change in the elite conception of what a village is. A century ago, the Vietnamese elite hardly thought of villages as being "open systems." They thought of them as being religious communities, with their own tutelary deities, located inside a greater national hierarchy of religious communities. The new notion of villages as "open systems" is an elite image, borrowed from the largely U.S. storehouse of Asia-Pacific region managerial vocabulary, which still has only an imperfect capacity to summarize actual Vietnamese village life. In the 1980s, indeed, the Vietnamese army had to be used to naturalize the new definition of the village as an "open system," in the sense that most of the villagers who left their supposedly "open" villages were young men conscripted into the army: they learned scientific skills outside the village, while in the army, and then supposedly brought the skills back with them if they returned. That the minds of the villagers who must stay put and harvest the new IRRI rice crops—poorly educated, middle-aged Vietnamese females—remain quite remote from Pacific Rim "scientific language" is suggested by the fact that the Vietnamese government must recurrently round up the legions of soothsayers, fortune-tellers, and sorceresses who still exist in abundance in rural Vietnam and make them sign statements promising to give up their occupations. They must, in other words, give up their efforts to continue to define village life in the prescientific magical way. The old prophets do not mix well with the new ones.

Thus it might be useful to think of the intellectual construction of the emerging Asia-Pacific community in anthropological terms, as involving—in the long run—the imposition from above of an alien and complex new Great Tradition of thought—especially managerial and scientistic as well as scientific thought—upon villages all over China and Southeast Asia. In the short run, however, the belief in an Asia-Pacific community described above amounts to less than the regional internationalization of even a single ruling-class ideology that genuinely unites diverse political elites on both sides of the Pacific in the pursuit of common goals or shared interests. What the belief does is more modest. It helps to maintain separate national elites with an identical concern for its perpetuation in very uneasy coexistence with each other, while encouraging them to think that they must take greater account of each other than they need take of the vast populations they govern. In its early stages the acceptance of the belief is more the sum of provisional elite alliances within a large region than it is the reflection of even the beginning of the unification of an "Asia-Pacific" consciousness that might weaken the region's far-flung ethnic or racial divisions.

On the surface, political leaders on the Asian if not on the North American side of the Pacific Rim have taken full account of this. As the Chinese Foreign Minister Qian Qichen told a Chinese audience at the end of 1989, the national differences within the Asia-Pacific region—uneven economic development levels; differences in "social systems" and "ideology"; dissimilarities in language, religion, and culture—make the emergence of an integrated or "organic" security system there, comparable to that of the European Community, "impossible."[21] Few politicians in power apply the language of a Toffler or a Linder to the continuingly sin-riddled landscape of international relations, which—unlike armchair economics—stubbornly resists easy utopianization. The most fashionable and superficial way of exploring the region's disharmonies is to point to the fact that its states are less similar in size and in assets than the European states. A huge and provocative disproportion in power or potential power is said to exist between China, Japan, India, and the United States on the one hand, and all the other countries, not excluding Indonesia, on the other.

In this context, the one enormous problem of how to coexist with Japanese power necessarily haunts the government-sponsored research centers and think tanks that proliferated in China and in some Southeast Asia countries in the 1980s. Discussing the advent of the "new Pacific era" in 1985, one Shanghai political economist foresaw three possible outcomes, all centered upon Japan. The first was that the future industrial successes of the region's other countries would undermine the Japanese economy, forcing it into allegedly European-style conditions of "structural stagnation" and unemployment; the second was that Japan would adapt harmoniously to its new Asian competitors and would work out a new "horizontal" division of labor with them, involving genuinely cooperative regional industrial diversification; the third was that Japan would preserve the old, unequal "vertical" division of labor between itself and other Asian countries, constantly reinvesting its profits in improving its technologies and competitive edge. He concluded that the first possibility "underestimated" the vitality of the Japanese; the second possibility was "ideal" but unlikely, in part because of the limited capacities of the other Asian countries; the third posibility was thus the most reasonable prediction, though it falsely assumed that relations between states could be "frozen" in such unequal circumstances.[22] The barely disguised paternalism of some Japanese policymakers toward Southeast Asia, if not China, reflects their probable confidence in the third scenario. As a Japanese Ministry of International Trade and Industry official wrote in 1984, Japan's duty to Southeast Asia was similar to the European duty to Africa or the U.S. duty to Latin America.[23] There is a tension between the implicit state-transcending egalitarianism of the Asia-Pacific myth and much older reflexes for imagining regional relationships that continue in unreformedly hierarchical ways.

But this tension is merely the symptom of larger and more treacherous ones. The pretense in the Asia-Pacific myth that it portends some regionally specific "ethos" of economic success that can belong to or be imitated by everyone masks the absences of any common moral culture across the region. Back in 1944, a famous British analyst of the European colonial order in Southeast Asia, J. S. Furnivall, described Dutch-ruled Indonesia as a "plural society" in which various ethnic groups—the Dutch, the Eurasians, the Chinese, various kinds of Indonesians—lived side by side, interacting with each other economically, without having any discernible "common will" or common social conscience. The marketplace was their only common ground. As Furnivall put it: "The fundamental character of the organization of a plural society as a whole is indeed the structure of a factory, organized for production, rather than of a state, organized for the good life of its members." In such a "plural society," the moral apartness of the various ethnic groups, in outlook and in standards, meant that capitalism was freed of all restrictions other than those imposed by written laws, which were themselves underdeveloped. There was, therefore, a concentration on materialism, and on purely economic ends, that was far more complete and absolute in the colonized Indies than in the West European homeland of capitalism itself.[24] What Furnivall wrote about the islands of the Indonesian archipelago in the 1940s might well be pressed into service to cover the regional Asia-Pacific society of the 1990s. It is a factory-like "plural society" of the Furnivallian sort writ large. The highly technocratic nature of the Asia-Pacific myth does little to create even the rudiments of a moral "common will" that might cross ethnic barriers.

The result is that the myth mobilizes the poor of the region without representing them. Evangelical "Pacific Century" theorists such as S. B. Linder argue that the "basic commonality" of the region that explains its prosperity is that the Asia-Pacific economies are all "market economies"; interventionist government policies are supposedly not one of the region's talismanic "commonalities."[25] In Southeast Asia, at least, the facts qualify if they do not confound this generalization. As of 1990, the Indonesian government wholly owned at least 189 companies, ranging from Garuda Airlines to Krakatau Steel to fertilizer maker Pupuk Kujang. In the lucrative regional cigarette industry, government tobacco monopolies reigned supreme in such countries as Thailand and China, and high import duties, enforced licensing systems, or limits on the foreign ownership of cigarette making otherwise controlled the huge cigarette markets of Indonesia, the Philippines, and Malaysia.[26] Even in Singapore, such crucial assets as shipyards were owned by government-controlled companies. Monarchies with royal business monopolies, not free trade traditions, shaped the precolonial economic history of the region. Even today the Thai royal family is the largest shareholder in Southeast Asia's biggest cement producer, the Siam Cement Company.

The real key to much of the economic success on the Asian side of the Pacific Rim is the repression of the consumption rates of subaltern social groups and classes. Here is the authentic similarity the region has with industrializing nineteenth-century Britain, although most Asia-Pacific futurologists hardly emphasize it. The region's working people still possess what Walter Bagehot once memorably called, with reference to the nineteenth-century lower-class English, the "deferential" reflexes of incompletely defeudalized lives. For the average Western citizen, it is probably enterprises like the expanding Western cruise ship industry that make this situation most obvious: it would hardly be viable without Indonesian and Filipino sailors. The deference, of course, is a product of repression as well as of custom. Roy Hofheinz and Kent Calder, who do raise this issue of consumption control at least obliquely, are right to explain Singapore's triumphs by pointing to the Central Provident Fund. This was a compulsory savings scheme, initiated by the Singapore government in 1955, that allowed that government to impose the highest savings rate in the world upon its people, in the interests of obtaining capital for industrial expansion.[27]

It is not fashionable anywhere in the Pacific Rim these days to use the strength of labor unions as a touchstone of progress. But it is worth comparing the percentage of workers who were unionized, even in tame government-manipulated unions, on the Southeast Asian and Australasian sides of the Pacific, as of 1986: 4.8 percent of the Indonesian work force; 8.7 percent of the Malaysian work force; 1.1 percent of the Thai workforce; but 42 percent of the Australian work force and 52 percent of that of New Zealand.[28] Some Southeast Asian governments (for example, Malaysia) have guaranteed foreign investors that there will be no "union disturbances" in such countries' "free trade zones," where workers are not allowed to join unions.

The repressed popular consumption rates in Asia that Asia-Pacific rhetoricians take for granted without acknowledging as central to what reality their myth possesses will not vanish soon. These rates are linked to the continued cohesion of military governments such as the one in Indonesia that "virtually wiped out bodies which articulated the interests of less privileged groups" during the mass killings in Indonesian villages in 1965–1966.[29] But they are linked also to the region's high rate of population growth, which hardly favors lower-class bargaining positions. The "deference" of the lower classes in Southeast Asia, such as it is, is also partly cultural, just as it was in Walter Bagehot's Victorian England. The tropical neo-Victorianism of the Pacific Rim features the same situation of technological change occurring more rapidly than cultural or political defeudalization.

Nineteenth-century Thai society, for example, was organized like a hierarchical military regiment, in which there were nine or more different status pronouns just for the word "I," and noble patrons commanded commoner clients; contemporary analysts suggest that Thailand remains an "as you please, sir" political culture, with little consciousness of individual rights that could be exercised against politically superior people.[30] The eminent journalist Mochtar Lubis charges his fellow Indonesians with preserving a timeless "feudal mentality" in which underlings submissively serve their bosses or "fathers" (*bapak*).[31] In Vietnam, neotraditional forms of state exploitation of the peasants, such as labor conscription laws that compel each adult male between the ages of eighteen and forty-five to donate ten days a year of unpaid labor to the state (as in a law of 1988) reflect the survival of premodern village expectations about corvée labor, not merely a dictatorship with Stalinist characteristics that are weakening only slowly. One remembers Matthew Arnold's comment in nineteenth-century England that railways were dealing a death blow to feudalism; it is possible that labor transfers within the contemporary Pacific Rim (more than 600,000 Filipinos were registered to work outside their country in 1990; hundreds of thousands of Vietnamese workers were sent to the Soviet Union and eastern Europe in the 1980s) may eventually have a similar effect there. But the advanced technological achievements the Asia-Pacific myth celebrates, such as the genetic redesigning of Southeast Asian agriculture, occur in a far less advanced moral universe. About this fact the myth has little to say.

In its present form, the Asia-Pacific myth mobilizes the poor of the region for economic production without representing or encouraging their political and social claims. Yet it does provide one important palliative in the realm of ethnic or racial relations, which is not greatly discussed by the usual architects of the myth but cannot be ignored. The myth rationalizes and gives optimistic coloring to a formidable historical event: the de-Westernization or cultural diversification of capitalism, and the shift of its center of gravity. White EuroAmerican capitalism has been in relative decline, in much of Southeast Asia at least, since the 1940s and 1950s; the myth makes the gigantic contemporary capture by the Japanese and Asian offshore Chinese of that system seem like an inevitable stage in a common enterprise of human improvement. The moderation of the relations among the three hegemonic business cultures in the region—the Japanese one, the Chinese one, and the Western one—is not easy. Tensions exist between the two "Asian" capitalisms, as well as between Japanese or ethnic Chinese capitalism on the one hand and Western businesses on the other. One Japanese scholar recently even went so far as to accuse the ethnic Chinese business world in Southeast Asia of being "ersatz capitalism," because of its supposed cronyism and preference for licensed monopolies over competition.[32] The language of the Asia-Pacific myth, with its invocation of "Third Wave" civilizations and its focus upon the "basic commonalities" of economic prosperity, rhetorically reconciles the tensely coexisting multiple rival capitalisms and usefully blurs potential battle lines among them. Its votaries on both sides of the Pacific Rim become imaginative shareholders in a common utopianized marketplace.

But if the Asia-Pacific myth blurs the battle lines among competing ethnic capitalisms, it may sharpen the battle lines between regions within nation-states, and between ethnic majorities and minorities whose identities coincide with regional distinctions. Here the effect of the myth can be traced to places a long way away—geographically, that is—from the Pacific. Chinese administrators, for example, in the name of the doctrine that the twenty-first century will be the "century of the Pacific Ocean," inform the restless Turkic peoples in Xinjiang that the Chinese language is the "key" to entering that century and that such minorities should therefore graciously accept the bilingual schools they do not want.[33]

In Southeast Asia, the myth undermines the solidarity of whole nation-states that were the recent creations, in many instances, of poetic nationalists. Such nationalists were—in the words of one of them, Indonesia's Sukarno—"bound in spiritual longing by the Romanticism of Revolution," rather than by what a "Pacific century" writer like Linder calls "outward-oriented export strategy." They believed (Sukarno again) that revolutions could not "be measured by the standards of textbooks, even ones written by bald-headed professors from Oxford or Cornell University"; they saw their national future as being "like the melody of a distant *gamelan* on a moonlit night,"[34] rather than a series of sovereignty-surrendering transactions with multinational corporations and international monetary funds. The states they created were fragile, as the artificiality of their names suggests. (The term "Indonesia" was borrowed after World War I by anticolonial patriots in the Netherlands Indies from the writings of anthropologists like Adolf Bastian; Burma and Cambodia have both changed their names at least once in the past twenty years; the country between them changed its name from Siam to Thailand in 1939, after a debate over whether the new name should be spelled Tai or Thai; Malaysia, in political name and substance, came into existence only in the 1960s.) These states sometimes covered territory and people who had no overwhelming historical reasons for belonging to them.

Although a Canadian scholar in particular may have little business being surprised by such a phenomenon, it is nevertheless true that the new Pacific Rim economics stresses the maximization of regional advantages within nation-states, as part of the particularized pursuit of export earnings. This emphasis has political consequences that are yet to be measured in Asia-Pacific countries less psychologically self-contained or ethnically homogeneous as Japan or Korea or Taiwan or Singapore or Hong Kong. Painful regional differences within countries that an earlier generation of nationalists through faith and poetry (and war) had tried to overcome, threaten to reappear. One could cite many examples of regions within Asia-Pacific nation-states in which the relatively pure capitalist economic rationality of the Asia-Pacific mobilization myth could dissolve the solidarities developed by an earlier nationalism. Aceh, for example; or northeast Thailand; or Mindanao; or Sabah.

South Vietnam might well be the most poignant example. French colonialism in Indochina strengthened an imbalance in Vietnam between a densely populated but economically backward north and a commercial capitalist economy, based far more upon French laws, in the less densely populated south. South Vietnam, because of its more generous land-to-people ratios and its weaker adherence to precapitalist village social and economic norms, then came to dominate the Indochina export trade the French promoted. The port of Saigon exported more than three-quarters of the two million tons of rice French Indochina was shipping abroad by 1907. Vietnamese nationalists attacked such structural imbalances as the legacies of Western economic colonialism. Now they are abruptly transformed into the regional economic superiorities the Pacific Rim celebrates. As one Vietnamese economist recently put it, south Vietnam is better able than north Vietnam to make a "military breakthrough" in "infiltrating" the Asia-Pacific economy with its exports.[35] The policy-making corollaries of this rhetorical militarization of regional advantages are far from trivial. They lead to proposals that all state investment in agriculture in Vietnam be concentrated in the south's Mekong delta, rather than divided evenhandedly between the Mekong delta and the Red River delta up in the north—where more people live, and where malnutrition is pervasive.[36]

Like Siva, the Asia-Pacific myth both creates and destroys. Insofar as it remains a capitalist myth, it renews an old tendency of capitalism to rationalize all behavior in the name of economic production. Despite a pretense of satisfying more general millennial human cravings that transcend economics, in practice the myth works against noneconomic faiths and spiritual concerns. For better or for worse, it contributes to the imaginative dispossession of much postwar Asian revolutionary nationalism, especially with respect to internal stability and ethnic self-assertion. The economics of the myth have a partial kinship with the more classical colonial economic arrangements of the prewar period that several generations of Asian nationalists condemned. It remains to be seen how provocative this kinship will prove to be in any major future regional trade breakdowns.

## Notes

1. John Naisbitt and Patricia Aburdene, *Megatrends 2000: Ten New Directions for the 1990's* (New York: Avon Books, 1991), pp. 184–227.
2. Ibid., pp. 336–337.
3. For an interesting Chinese discussion of the Chinese interest in the writings of such U.S. futurologists as Naisbitt, Alvin Toffler, and Daniel Bell, see the article by Shao Wenjie in *Guangming ribao,* March 18, 1984, p. 3.
4. Staffan Burenstam Linder, *The Pacific Century: Economic and Political Consequences of Asian-Pacific Dynamism* (Stanford, CA: Stanford University Press, 1986), p. 4.
5. Robert Elegant, *Pacific Destiny: Inside Asia Today* (London: Hamish Hamilton, 1990), pp. 510–511.
6. Naisbitt and Aburdene, *Megatrends 2000,* p. 217.
7. Luo Yuanzheng, *Shijie jinji yu Zhongguo* (The world economy and China) (Changsha: Hunan renmin chubanshe, 1985), pp. 157ff.
8. Arif Dirlik, "The Asia-Pacific Idea: Reality and Representations in the Invention of a Regional Structure," *Journal of World History* 3, no. 1 (Spring 1992), pp. 19, 21.
9. G. R. Searle, *The Quest for National Efficiency: A Study in British Politics and Political Thought 1899–1914* (Oxford: Basil Blackwell, 1971), pp. 57–59.
10. See the discussion in Chinese Academy of Social Sciences, comp., *Zhongguo shehuixue nianjian 1979–1989* (Chinese sociology yearbook, 1979–1989) (Beijing: Zhongguo Dabaike quanshu chubanshe, 1989), pp. 182–188. See also Raymond Bauer, ed., *Social Indicators* (Cambridge, MA, and London: MIT Press, 1966).
11. See Gao Fang, *Ping disanci langchao* (Criticizing *The Third Wave*) (Beijing: Guangming ribao chubanshe, 1986).
12. Alvin Toffler, *The Third Wave* (London: Pan Books, 1981), pp. 350–351.
13. Andrew Mendelsohn, "Alvin Toffler in China: Deng's Big Bang," *New Republic,* April 4, 1988, pp. 15–17.
14. Gao Fang, *Ping disanchi langchao,* pp. 1–2 of Preface.
15. Tong Dalin, "Yige xinde 'nongye daguo' jiang chuxian zai shijie shang" (A new agricultural great power is about to appear in the world) in Guowuyuan nongcum fazhan yanjiu zhongxin, comp., *Zhongguo nongcum fazhan zhanlue wenti* (Strategic problems of the development of Chinese villages) (Beijing: Zhongguo nongye keji chubanshe, 1985), pp. 38–41.

16. Yu Mei, "Qianyi Woguo nongye laodongli yu shengyu laodonglide zhuanyi" (A simple comment on our country's agricultural labor force and the transfer of surplus labor), *Zhongguo nongcun jingji* (Chinese village economy journal) (Beijing) 12 (1987), pp. 23–28, especially pp. 27–28.

17. Naisbitt and Aburdene, *Megatrends 2000*, p. 184.

18. Ma Bohuang, "Waixiangxing jingji de jinxi guan" (Present and past conceptions of export-oriented type economies), *Shehui kexue* (Social sciences) (Shanghai) 8 (1988), pp. 32–35.

19. Ibid.

20. See the profile of An Binh village, Hai Hung province, by Nguyen Duc Uy and Bach Van Tho in *Nhan dan* (Hanoi), August 13, 1980, p. 3.

21. See Qian's interview in *Liaowang* (Outlook) (1989), p. 52; as reprinted in *Xinhua yuebao* (New China monthly report) (Beijing) 1 (1990), pp. 162–163.

22. Guo Zhaolie, "Taipingyang xin shiji de daolai he Ya-Tai diqu jidai jiejue de tike" (The advent of the new Pacific Ocean era and questions of the Asia-Pacific region that urgently wait for resolution), *Shehui kexue* (Social sciences) (Shanghai) 1 (1985), pp. 3–6.

23. See Kinju Atarashi, "Japan's Economic Cooperation Policy Towards the ASEAN Countries," *International Affairs* (London) 61, no. 1 (Winter 1984–1985), pp. 110–111.

24. J. S. Furnivall, *Netherlands India: A Study of Plural Economy* (New York: Cambridge University Press, 1944), pp. 350, 446–450.

25. Linder, *The Pacific Century*, pp. 27, 29.

26. See the special feature article by Carl Goldstein et al. in *Far Eastern Economic Review*, 29 March 1990, pp. 62–68.

27. Roy Hofheinz, Jr., and Kent Calder, *The Eastasia Edge* (New York: Basic Books, 1982), pp. 142–144.

28. See the articles by Elizabeth Cheng, Suhaini Aznam, Jose Galang, Paul Handley, Colin James, V. G. Kulkarni, Hamish McDonald, and Paisal Sricharatchanya in *Far Eastern Economic Review*, 3 April 1986, pp. 43–67.

29. Hamish McDonald, *Suharto's Indonesia* (Sydney: Fontana Books, 1981), pp. 171–172.

30. Tulyathep Suwanachinda, as quoted in J. L. S. Girling, *Thailand: Society and Politics* (Ithaca, NY: Cornell University Press, 1981), p. 148.

31. Mochtar Lubis, *The Indonesian Dilemma*, trans. Florence Lamoureux (Singapore: Graham Brash, 1983), pp. 21–23.

32. Yoshihara Kunio, *The Rise of Ersatz Capitalism in Southeast Asia* (Singapore: Oxford University Press, 1988).

33. Ding Wenlou, "Guanyu 'Shuangyu' jiaoxue de sikao" (Reflections on the pedagogy of 'bilingual' education), *Xinjiang shehui kexue* (Xinjiang journal of social sciences) (Urumqi) 6 (1990), pp. 72–75.

34. Herbert Feith and Lance Castles, eds., *Indonesian Political Thinking 1945–1965* (Ithaca, NY: Cornell University Press, 1970), pp. 32, 114, 119.

35. Le Hong Phuc, "Mien nam Viet-Nam trong phan cong lao dong quoc te" (South Vietnam in the international division of labor), *Nghien cuu kinh te* (Journal of economic research) (Hanoi) 8 (1989), pp. 9–15.

36. See the proposal by Nguyen Kien Phuoc in *Nhan dan* (Hanoi), August 22, 1989, p. 3.

# 4

# Rimspeak; or, The Discourse of the "Pacific Rim"

## BRUCE CUMINGS

Most of the literature on the Pacific Rim is prognostic, and most of it isn't very interesting once a year or two of history flits by, disproving predictions and revealing flawed assumptions. Murray Sayle must have agreed with me when he penned this forecast for "the Pacific Rim in the 21st century":

> Britain and Ireland could respectively be Japan's Hong Kong and Macao, well placed for the European entrepot trade, the U.S. will be Japan's fabulously wealthy India, *terre des merveilles*, while Australia can be Japan's Austrialia, land of rugged adventure and heavy drinking, the appropriate place of exile for Japanese dissidents and remittance men. This would leave only table scraps for the others: Holland, perhaps, for the Indonesians, France for the Vietnamese.[1]

I do not wish here to contribute to this sort of literature on the Pacific Rim, since I find explaining the past or figuring out the present hard enough without moving into a different century, that is, the dawning twenty-first. I would like instead to seek an explanation of the currency of the term, Pacific Rim: where does it come from? The first answer is, currency. In the late 1970s a hue and cry suddenly emerged about the unfolding era of the Pacific, especially up and down the West Coast and particularly among academics trying to find some way to interest donors in funding Asian or international studies. "Pacific Rim" was a discourse searching out its incipient material base, targeted upon exporters with Asian markets, or importers of Asian products.

One example is the Henry Jackson School of International Studies at the University of Washington (where I taught for several years), started in 1978 (although not named for Senator Jackson until 1983), and funded by Boeing, Weyerhauser, and other corporations, in a Seattle that was otherwise sleepwalking into the Pacific century. Another is the newer School of International Relations and Pacific Studies at UC-San Diego. By now we have many other academic centers of "Rim studies."

"Pacific Rim" is not an academic subject so much as a field for academics working in the present and looking toward the future, as well as for transnational technocrats and policymakers. According to the director of the San Diego school, Peter Gourevitch, Pacific Rim inquiry is important for the "two communities who have a need to know: the community of social scientists . . . and the community of policymakers."[2] That is an apt summary of one meaning of rim studies: our academic pundits and government policymakers need to know. (But to know *what?*)

Let's call this "Rimspeak," a discourse of recent origin, but one with considerable immanent power. "Pacific Rim" was a construct of the mid-1970s for revaluing East and Southeast Asia, as Westerners (mostly Americans) recognized and defined it, in ways that highlighted some parts and excluded (or occluded) others. The centerpiece of this construct was Japan, a newly risen sun among advanced industrial countries—indeed, "Number One" in Ezra Vogel's perfectly timed book,[3] published in 1979. Organized into the region were "miracle" economies in Japan, South Korea, Taiwan, Hong Kong, Malaysia, and Singapore, with honorable mention for Thailand, the Philippines, Indonesia, and post-Mao (but pre-Tiananmen) China. The miracles were "NICs" (newly industrialized countries) and their story spawned a prolific literature on Asian miracles.[4]

"Miracle" is one trope always found in the rimster's repertoire. Another is "dynamism," as in "dynamism of East Asian-North American relations" (Gourevitch again), or Linder's "Asian-Pacific dynamism."[5] The miracles of the rim, of course, do not truck with Joseph Schumpeter's notion that capitalism's dynamis is through waves of creation and destruction: it is all on the up-and-up, a whoosh of progress transforming the region.

Rimspeak is a curious discourse with a half-life of months or years, depending on the source. Situated in the dynamic present, casting one's eyes to the yet more dynamic future, all things seem possible—until something like the Tiananmen bloodletting demolishes the incorrigible optimism of this genre and sends a handful of recent books to the instant oblivion of secondhand stores. Rimspeak opens a window on the future, but it also clouds one's optic on the present. Consider this statement leading off a new book entitled *Pacific Rising* (admittedly one of the more interesting and thoughtful texts in the genre): "Rarely indeed is one fortunate in being able to live through times in which a major shift in the world's history can be seen to be taking place. . . . One such event . . . came about when the fifty-odd countries now grouped around the Pacific

Ocean seemed to take the torch of leadership from those hitherto grouped around the Atlantic. . . ."[6] A torch passes from Atlantic to Pacific; but into whose hands? Fifty countries including the sultanate of Brunei? The Four (or is it Five?) Tigers? A Japan that went catatonic at the mere hint that it do something significant about Iraq's invasion of Kuwait? And when exactly was that torch passed? (The answer is, of course, that the flame still burns brightly along the Atlantic Rim.)

In the subterranean text of all this palaver about "dynamism," Saint-Simon meets the theory of the Asiatic mode of production, as in, "I thought they were vegetating in the teeth of time over there in Asia. But suddenly they make better cars than we do." Behold, a miracle has occurred. Tropes of dynamism and miracles also convey this: capitalist universalism is the only thing I can see; thus I discover the Pacific Rim.

The latter point is not facetious, but precise: the people of the Pacific Rim did not know they inhabited a bustling new sector of the world system until they were told, just as our "Indians" didn't know they were in America (or "West India") until Columbus told them so. "Rim" is a EuroAmerican construct, an invention just like the steam engine, incorporating the region's peoples "into a new inventory of the world"; "Pacific" is a EuroAmerican name in itself, measuring, delineating, and recognizing living space for the people who live there.[7] That these are Western social constructions does not mean that the natives think them unimportant or have self-confident definitions themselves. For example, former Chinese Premier Zhao Ziyang invited certified twenty-first-century rimster Alvin Toffler to lecture at the Academy of Sciences in 1983, to audiences who "listened to him as if he were an oracle."[8]

After the NICs come the pretenders to this throne: pre-NICs, near-NICs, would-be NICs, miracles-in-the-making if they "do the right thing." Take the Philippines, for example: bit of a basket case, not clear if those people know their comparative advantages. Digging itself out of decades of "irrationality" in the mid-1970s, China under the "enlightened" leadership of Deng Xiaoping (after his resurrection and reforms in 1978) might bid fair to make it. By 1991 the newest of the NICs was Thailand, "doing the right thing" by exporting cheaply made goods (and since the mid-1980s, allowing an ocean of Japanese capital to slosh around). Defined out of the Pacific Rim in the 1970s were North Korea, Mao's China, and Indochina—especially Vietnam, which had just won its thirty-years' war, only to find itself in the pale of the rim. OINKs, they were sometimes called: old industrialized kountries. Sometimes Rimspeak ropes in Latin American countries, too. Candidates include post-Allende Chile, *maquiladora* Mexico, even Atlantic Rim Brazil (but also in its pre-debt-crisis phase of "miracle growth").

In other words "Pacific Rim" painted the entire region differently than it had been since 1945. Paint it Red, the pundits said until 1975. Paint it black, was the post-1975 artistry. (Hollywood followed suit, with a number of films in the late 1970s and 1980s seeking "to put Vietnam behind us." This was Francis Ford Coppola's stated goal for *Apocalypse Now.* Another film that parodied the U.S. "Vietnam syndrome," Stanley Kubrick's *Full Metal Jacket,* ends with the Rolling Stones singing, "Paint it Black.") "Pacific Rim" heralded a forgetting, a hoped-for amnesia in which the decades-long but ultimately failed U.S. effort to obliterate the Vietnam revolution would enter the realm of Korea, "the forgotten war."

When East Asia was "painted Red," it held an apparent outward-moving dynamic the core of which was Beijing: "400 million Chinese armed with nuclear weapons," in Dean Rusk's 1960s scenario, threatened nations along China's rim with oblivion: South Korea, South Vietnam, Taiwan, Indonesia, Thailand, and the big enchilada, Japan. Thus another secretary of state, Dean Acheson, drew a "defense perimeter" through island Asia in 1950. China and North Korea were among the most rapidly growing industrial economies in the world in the 1950s and early 1960s, "success stories" sadly to be contrasted with basket case South Korea (as AID people always named it up through the mid-1960s), running sore Indonesia (with a formidable internal Communist "threat" until 1965), incompetent South Vietnam, mendicant Philippines, and Lucian Pye's hopelessly obtuse and retarded Burma.

"Pacific Rim" revalued all that. Suddenly the rim was the locus of dynamism, bringing pressure on the mainland of Asia. The basket cases were any countries still foolish enough to remain committed to self-reliance or socialist development (from Burma to North Korea), the success stories were any countries that sought export-led capitalist development. The new discourse was deeply solicitous of the benighted and laggard socialist economies, however, and therefore sought a formal end of ideology: "Pacific Rim" invoked a newborn "community" that anyone, socialist or not, could join . . . as long as they were capitalist. Rimspeakers of course continued to look with curiousity if not disdain upon anyone who did not privilege the market. (But only *sotto voce.*)

With hindsight the decade 1961–1971 was the cirtical turning point toward Rimspeak. In 1961 Soviet Chairman Nikita Khrushchev fashioned a voluntarist programmatic ideological vision that anticipated the overcoming of capitalism on a world scale within a few decades. At about the same time Mao's "East is Red" theme placed socialist Asia in the van and the Great Leap Forward sought to overtake Great Britain in fifteen years. At Bucharest in 1961 the socialist camp openly split, however, and Mao's private writings laid the cause of the failure of world socialism at Khrushchev's feet: his revisionism consisted of replacing two world systems within a single planet with one world system, which the Soviets wished to join (symbolized by Camp David in 1959), and through which it would exploit other socialist bloc nations in an international division of labor. State capitalism in Moscow prefigured Russia in the capitalist world system, according to Mao.[9]

W. W. Rostow joined the Kennedy administration in 1961, with his "non-Communist manifesto" of capitalist growth by stages, a view deeply influenced by technological determinism. One of his first projects was to get South Korea and Taiwan moving toward export-led policies and to reintegrate them with the booming Japanese economy. Facing the first U.S. trade deficits, the Kennedy administration sought to move away from the expensive, draining security programs of the Eisenhower years toward regional pump priming that would bring an end to the bulk grant aid of the 1950s and make allies like Korea and Taiwan more self-sufficient. The economism of the Kennedy years inaugurated the phase of export-led development, but was short-circuited by Vietnam. Richard Nixon later revived these ideas through his Guam Doctrine and opened relations with Red China: policies that were in place by 1971 and that thereby completed the Kennedy agenda. "Pacific Rim" was now incipient, as Nixon hinted in an influential 1967 article: "The U.S. is a Pacific power. . . . Europe has been withdrawing the remnants of empire, but the U.S., with its coast reaching in an arc from Mexico to the Bering Straits, is one anchor of a vast Pacific community. Both our interests and our ideals propel us westward across the Pacific, not as conquerers but as partners. . . ."[10]

The many working-class and antisystemic movements of the region in the past decades suddenly became poxes, irrationalities that bespeak immature "political development" in the rim. Standing above all else was the nearly instantaneous revaluation of China. The very real slaughters of Mao's failed Cultural Revolution—many directed against the intellectual class—became for U.S. intellectuals the signifier to rename and parenthesize the entire history of the Chinese Revolution, not to mention occasioning a vast rewriting throughout the scholarly apparatus of the China field. But the same thing has happened throughout the rim: when South Korean students protested the pipe-beating murder of an activist by police in the spring of 1991, many U.S. editorials greeted this with exclamations of sheer amazement, that students or workers should be "radical" in a world in which—as all agreed—the role model was the democratic and market-driven United States, led by George Bush and Dan Quayle. The logic seems to be this: Stalinism has palpably failed, therefore why should we have day care centers?

"Pacific Rim" has a class-based definition of Asia. The "community" is a capitalist archipelago, based on indigenous labor power and purchasing power—although mainly labor power until recently. It has thus been the "workshop of the world," using cheap and efficient labor to manufacture exports for other regions with consumer buying power; the vast U.S. market has been and is its mainstay. The archipelago runs through, but also divides, the Pacific and Asian region.

Capitalist classes, obviously, are organized into the archipelago. Peasant Asia (Vietnam; Kampuchea; much of India, Indonesia, and China) is out. Dense, developed, highly differentiated urban nodes are in; the two most important are Tokyo and Los Angeles, but city-state nodes like Hong Kong and Singapore are also critical. China's old Treaty Ports and new Special Export Zones like Shenzhen are in; vast reaches of interior China are out. South Korea is in, North Korea is out (unless Kim Il Sung "does the right thing"). In other words the majority of the populations in Asia are either out or participate only as unskilled or semiskilled laborers.

The class-based archipelago is also a hierarchy—not just the core urban nodes, the peripheral peasantries and the intermediate zone of strivers (NICs and OINKs), but a virtual pyramid of power on C. Wright Mills's model (in *The Power Elite*)—at the top, a transnational power elite, intertwined in various networks and educated at top-rated U.S. or British universities; then an echelon of urban middle and working classes; and finally a vast mass below. The echelon connoted by terms like democracy and pluralism encompasses at best a decile or two of the stratification, but legitimates the whole. In *The German Ideology* Marx said that the bourgeoisie views the world as if in a *camera obscura,* that is, upside-down; a narrow echelon claims its particular view to be universal and thus paints the whole in its hue.

This hierarchy reproduces itself throughout the region. Los Angeles is the perfect example: first, in its contemporaneous polyglot Hispanic, black, and Asian masses, its putatively universal Yuppie life-style, and its world-class elite drawn from financial, industrial, and mass culture industries; second, in its sanitized history that paints black a homegrown Asiatic mode of production and paints white an elite liberalism.

That is, Los Angeles was created through hydraulic engineering that brought water to the arid coast, and the city to the water through vast suburbanization,[11] by Anglo-Saxon despots who corruptly utilized privileged public position to make vast private fortunes in real estate, a history collapsed but not violated in the film called *Chinatown*. The interior history of Los Angeles capitalism until the 1940s was of a "private sector" distant from the central state and taking upon itself innumerable works of irrigation, transportation, port building, and the like (infrastructure and "social overhead") that places it at opposite poles from the "state-dominant" capitalism of Japan, and that energizes a free market myth that deeply influenced (among other things) Ronald Reagan and his furious 1980s deregulation.

In the film *Chinatown,* John Huston plays Noah Cross, a man who owned the city water system and then gave it up to "public" control by nepotistically inserting his son-in-law as head of Water and Power; it is Oriental despotism in our own backyard. The film ends with the knowing detective being led away from a scene of incestuous murder by his friend: "Forget it, Jake, it's Chinatown." This might be the perfect metaphor for the history of Anglo-Saxons in the Pacific Rim.

## Manifest Density:
### "Pacific Rim" as Anglo-Saxon Lake

Roland Barthes used Japan as a system of difference[12] to develop a radical critique of the West and its assumptions, instead of a mirror to reflect back to the West what is good and true here, and sadly lacking there. Barthes developed an optic that offers a parallax view, or a salutary boomerang, to question ourselves. As he said, Japan afforded him "a situation of writing . . . in which a certain disturbance of the person occurs, a subversion of earlier readings, a shock of meaning." And later, "Someday we must write the history of our own obscurity [or provincialism]— manifest the density of our narcissism."[13]

Nietzsche used the term "emergence," *entstehung,* to mean "the principle and the singular law of an apparition." Emergence does not mean "the final term of a historical development"; "culminations" are "merely the current episodes in a series of subjugations," and so, "Emergence is thus the entry of forces; it is their eruption, *the leap from the wings to the center stage* . . . emergence designates a place of confrontation. [emphasis added]" An event (or an emergence) is not a decision, a treaty, a war, but "the reversal of a relationship of forces, the usurpation of power, the appropriation of a vocabulary turned against those who had once used it." And thus his conclusion: "The body [or history, or the descent, or the present] is molded by a great many distinct regimes."[14]

Barthes and Nietzsche help us to ask the question, Where do tropes come from? Whence come the dynamics and miracles of far-off Asia? They help us understand our own density and a history in which "Pacific Rim" and "Japan" seem to emerge suddenly and mysteriously not just in the 1970s, but at several points throughout the past 150 years. They also underline a central point in my argument: we have had "emergence," but we have not had "the reversal of a relationship of forces." The torch has not been passed. Throughout the Pacific industrial era, Japan has been junior to Anglo-American hegemony save for six years or so, from 1939–1945. But we know what happened then . . . and it doesn't go under the title "Pacific Rim Community."

"Pacific Rim" was there from the beginning, soon after Commodore Perry's "Black Ships" arrived in Tokugawa port. A famous secretary of state, William Seward, found in world history a movement of empire making its way "constantly westward, and . . . it must continue to move on westward, until the tides of the renewed and the decaying civilizations of the world meet on the shores of the Pacific Ocean."[15]

The high-tech conveyance of that era was the steamship, so much less expensive than the ongoing building of continental railroads that it rendered the Pacific as a vast plane traders could skate across, toward the putative China market. These longings brought U.S. ships to Hawaii, where more Noah Crosses subdued the natives and gave the islands over to pineapple and sugar production, and to Manila Bay in 1898, seen as the first important colonial waystation to the treasures of the rim itself.

Somehow, then as today, Japan was thought to be separate from the rest of the rim—honorary Westerner, pearl of the Orient, good pupil, or as Dean Acheson put it in the 1940s, "the West's obstreperous offspring"; earlier, in 1852, the *Edinburgh Review* reported: "They are Asiatics, it is true, and therefore deficient in that principle of development which is the leading characteristic of those ingenious and persevering European races . . . but amidst Asiatics the Japanese stand supreme."[16]

The steamships skated toward Asian markets, but also toward a presumed earthly paradise offering occult knowledge unavailable to the rational Westerner. That the second theme persists today is evident in the pages of the *Economist:* a recent article on the "Pacific Idea" is subtitled, "There Is a Better World." The Pacific idea, the article alerts us, "is important for the mental well-being of the world," because it stands for "belief in the survival of innocence." The accompanying map centers the globe on various tropical islands in the middle and south of the Pacific (described in the article as "a village pond for the Seventh Fleet"), unwittingly placing Bikini at the epicenter—an island the United States made uninhabitable with H-bomb tests in the 1950s. The British did better, destroying by the same means an island called Christmas. The French still test nuclear weapons in the region, and the United States uses Johnston Island for the destruction of chemical weapons. Meanwhile the *Economist* speaks wistfully of Gauguin's women, Melville's lory-lory, Marlon Brando's Tahiti and places the burden of rim exclusion on the natives: "The places that people call Eden and Paradise can really become so, if only the Pacific islanders will heave themselves to their feet [translation: get dynamic]."[17]

The Pacific Rim in the nineteenth century was a realm of formal empire for the European powers, and so the United States enunciated the "open door" in 1900 to deal with other empires and made its effective if informal alliance with Great Britain in search of Anglo-Saxon condominium. Japan was the junior partner, in formal alliance with Great Britain from 1902 onward, in informal alliance with Teddy Roosevelt's United States.

Japan was also a junior partner in a hierarchical, product cycle driven regime of technology (the productivist aspect of U.S.-British hegemony). Viewed temporally, Japan has been a "late" industrializer, just as South Korea and other NICs have been "late-late" (to use Albert Hirschman's term for mid-twentieth century industrialization), benefiting from the adaptation of core technologies. Japan maximized its economic power in the one region not claimed by other imperial powers (except for Tsarist Russia)—Taiwan, Korea, Manchuria—creating a closely linked regional political economy that has promoted and skewed the development of East Asia ever since.[18]

In Japan's first wave of industrialization in the 1880s, we find fish canneries in Hokkaido, the pioneer Kashima Cotton mill, the huge Kobe Paper Factory, the first cigarette company, tanning and leather firms, the Osaka Watch Company, the Tokyo Electric Company with its own brand of light bulbs, even tasty Kirin Beer: and every last one based on U.S. technological startups or U.S. expertise. And we would find that Japan's favorite economist in the 1880s was an American, Henry Carey. Marx thought Carey was the only original U.S. economist, inveighing against "English economics" (see his wonderful essay "Bastiat and Carey," in the *Grundrisse*); actually Carey was a protectionist who learned much from Friedrich List, whose theories were also favored in Japan.

General Electric was dominant in the delivery of electricity, and by the 1890s Standard Oil had placed both Japan and China well within the world oil regime, which was increasingly dominated by U.S. firms. Standard's comparative advantage was financial and technical, but also resided in innovative marketing schemes: monopoly on a world scale, combined with creative ways to sell "oil for the lamps of China."[19] The joint British-U.S. condominium is perhaps best symbolized by the British-American Tobacco Company, a subsidiary of the Duke tobacco interests in North Carolina, which got Japan and China hooked on something else, a cigarette habit so deep that "non-smoking sections" can hardly be found anywhere in either country today.[20]

Japanese textile firms, leading sector in Japan's first phase of industrialization, for decades bought their machines from the famous Pratt Brothers of Great Britain—until about 1930 when they came up with their own "high-tech" equipment and quickly became the most efficient textile producer in the world, becoming Great Britain's bête noire of industrial dumping, market stealing, and general villainy. A few years later Japan's obsolescent machines were stoking Korea's first textile conglomerate, courtesy of "technology transfer."

During the halcyon days of the British-Japanese alliance, however, Japan was a model of industrial efficiency for Great Britain in incipient decline. As Phillip Lyttleton Gell put it in 1904: "I shall turn Japanese for they at least can think, and be reticent! [Witness] their organization, their strategy, their virile qualities, their devotion and self-control. Above all, their national capacity for self-reliance, self-sacrifice, and their silence!"[22] Or as a Fabian put it in 1907: "Witness the magnificent spectacle of Japan today; the State above the individual; common good above personal good; sacrifice of self and devotion to the community. . . ."[23] By the 1930s matters had descended from that subline point, however, as British business publications vented their rage at "The wily Jap [who is] determined to stop at nothing in his efforts to bamboozle shoppers in this country [and is] STEALING OUR MARKETS! [*sic*]"[24]

## Japan as Number Two

What about today: Is Japan the core power of the Pacific Rim? I do not know what the future will hold, but today the answser is: not yet. However close Japan may be to hegemonic emergence, in "concrete reality" for this entire century it has been a subordinate part of either bilateral U.S. hegemony or trilateral U.S.-British hegemony. Here is our metaphor for 1900–1991: Japan as Number Two.

An archaeology of Japan in the twentieth century world system unearths the following time lines:

1. 1900–1922: Japan in British-U.S. hegemony
2. 1922–1939: Japan in U.S.-British hegemony
3. 1939–1945: Japan hegemonic in East Asia
4. 1945–1970: Japan in U.S. hegemony
5. 1970–1990: Japan in U.S.-European hegemony

Three of the periods (1, 2, and 5) are trilateral, and none are colonial or necessarily imperial. A bilateral regime is predictable in the temporary phase of comprehensive hegemony (1945–1970 for the United States), a trilateral regime in the rising and falling phases of transitional hegemonies.

Shortly after World War I ended, in 1922 to be exact, the United States came to be the major partner in the trilateral hegemony. This was the period when U.S. banks became dominant in the world economy;[25] in general, the British-Japanese alliance had become tattered, and the United States became more important than Great Britain in Japanese diplomacy. The Washington Conference was the occasion for this transfer of the baton, a "locking in" with the critical element of global military reach, the U.S. navy.[26]

Japan accommodated to these trends with a very low posture diplomacy throughout the 1920s. Meanwhile it girded its loins at home for trade competition, inaugurating tendencies in its political economy that remain prominent today. Here was an early version of NIC-style "export-led development." Both Johnson and Fletcher date Japan's national industrial strategy and "administrative guidance" from the 1920s, and both the Americans and the British were receptive to Japan's outward-turning political economy.[27] We can note that it has only been in 1931–1945 and the 1980s and 1990s that this strategy has been perceived as a problem for the United States.

The Export Association Law of 1925 was an important turning point, stimulating industrial reorganization, cartels, and various state subsidies to exporters; Japan was careful to direct these exports to the noncolonial semiperiphery and not to the core markets of the United States and Great Britain.[28] The 1920s also inaugurated a period of import-substitution industrialization[29] that went hand in hand with the exporting programs, although it was more pronounced in the 1930s, when Japan accomplished its heavy-industrial spurt and its virtuoso mastery of the industrial product cycle.

Japan's "old" empire in Northeast Asia was, from 1910 to 1931, the empire the United States and Great Britain *wanted it to have,* and even when Manchuria was colonized in 1931, the United States and Great Britain chose to do little about it, save for a lot of rhetoric about the "open door." The reason they did little was that Japan preserved a modified open door in Manchuria until 1941 and encouraged U.S. and British investment—of which there was much more than generally thought. And in the postwar period, from 1947 to the present, U.S. planners have urged a modified restoration of Japan's position in Northeast Asia.

Dean Acheson and George Kennan masterminded this repositioning of Japan in the world system, by deciding in 1947 to place Japan as an engine of the world economy, a U.S.-defined "economic animal," shorn of its prewar military and political clout. Meanwhile the United States kept Japan on a defense dependency and shaped the flow of essential resources to it, thus to accumulate a diffuse leverage over all its policies and to retain an outer limit veto on Japan's global orientation. This strategy was articulated precisely at the time of the formal onset of the cold war, in the spring of 1947. The post-war U.S. empire has not rested upon territorial exclusivity like the old European colonies. It has been an "open door" empire, policed by a far-flung naval and military basing system and penetration of allied defense organizations (e.g., the prohibition on the use of military force in the Japanese constitution; U.S. command of West German and Korean militaries).[30]

Japan would also need an economic region "to its south," in Kennan's words, and Acheson came up with an elegant rim metaphor to capture this restoration; a "great crescent" from Tokyo to Alexandria linked

Japan with island Asia, around Singapore and through the Indian Ocean
to the oil of the Persian Gulf. It was this crescent that lay behind Acheson's famed "defense perimeter" speech in January 1950.[31] This definition
was hammered out coterminous with the emergence of the cold war and
deepend as Japan benefited from U.S. wars to lock in an Asian hinterland, in Korea and Vietnam.

Here we intuit a truth that Rimspeak would rather forget: the "Pacific
Rim community" has been a region fashioned in warfare. The United
States was "at war with Asia" from 1941 to 1975, to use Noam Chomsky's term. If Pearl Harbor functions as original sin for Americans, Hiro-
shima and Nagasaki connote a cataclysmic rendering of "Japan as
Number Two." The Korean War drew the Northeast Asian boundaries
of Pacific capitalism until the 1980s, being also "Japan's Marshall Plan"
(Chalmers Johnson's term)—war procurements propelled Japan along its
world-beating industrial path. In Korea, too, original sin came on a Sunday morning, when Kim Il Sung's forces invaded, seeking to overturn a
Korean original sin: the U.S. decision to divide Korea, carried out by
Dean Rusk at John J. McCloy's request in August 1945. Original sin was
harder to determine in Vietnam; Ho Chi Minh resembled neither Tojo
nor Kim. For some Americans it was the Tonkin Gulf incident; for the
Vietnamese perhaps it was Acheson's decision to link Indochina to the
revival of Japanese industry, bringing the United States in on the side of
French imperialism.[32]

In this era, which ran from Truman through Johnson, Japan was a
dutiful U.S. partner and the partner was tickled pink at Japan's economic
success. As the U.S. capacity unilaterally to manage the global system
declined in the 1960s, however, a new duality afflicted the U.S.-Japan
relationship: Japan should do well, yes . . . but not so well that it hurt
U.S. interests. Richard Nixon was again the agent of change, with his
neomercantilist "New Economic Policy," announced on V-J Day in
1971. U.S. thinking about Japan remains firmly within that duality
today, symbolized by the inability of elites to do more than oscillate between free trade and protectionism, between admiration for Japan's success and alarm at its new prowess.

In short, Japan has been thriving within the hegemonic net for ninety
years, but nonetheless "emerges" in the Western mind—leaps from the
wings to the center stage—at three critical and incommensurable points:
at the turn of the century when it was a British wunderkind (but a "yellow peril" to the Germans); in the world depression of the 1930s, when
it was an industrial monster to the British (but a wunderkind to the Germans and the Italians); and in the 1980s, when it was a wunderkind to
U.S. internationalists and a monster to U.S. protectionists. The Four Tigers, Three or Four Tiger Cubs, and all the others tread the same path:

do well, please, but not so well that you threaten us (whereupon the tropes all reverse, and you move from miracle to menace, from market-driven dynamo to crypto-fascist upstart).[33] The main point is that there has been no fundamental reversal of relationships; no torches have been passed, nor are likely to be passed for "the near term."

## The Near Term: Trilateral Futures

As I said earlier, I am not good at prognosis: I find it hard enough to predict the past. In the near term of the next couple of decades, however, I would hazard the guess that the world system will have three nodal, central points, symbolized by New York, Tokyo, and Berlin, and a core point of hegemony, headquartered in Washington. New York will have a tendency to connect with Europe, Los Angeles with East Asia, and Washington will seek to manage a trilateral condominium. In other words, we are not in the eve of a regionalization of the world economy, but a period of prolonged North-North cooperation propelled by a historic "peace interest," to use Karl Polanyi's term, on the part of high finance and the modal capitalist organization of our era, the transnational corporation.[34]

The Pacific Rim is neither a self-contained region nor a community, but just that: a rim—peripheral and semiperipheral societies oriented toward Tokyo and the U.S. market. Consumer purchasing power is still lower than in Western Europe or the United States, and labor cost advantage still orients the region toward assembly and finishing work using Japanese or U.S. technology. It is still a region under dual economic hegemony, held by a unilateral U.S. security network. No common culture unites the region: Japanese do not interact culturally with Koreans, Koreans have little noneconomic intercourse with Filipinos, Indonesians do not interact with Thais.

Instead the lineaments of "culture" run through Los Angeles and New York: Hollywood and the global center of television, purveying U.S. mass culture throughout the region. South Korea has three networks, of which one is the Armed Forces Korea Network, broadcasting in English. The other two run dubbed versions of "Dallas" and "Miami Vice," and Korean shows on similar themes. Most Americans have never seen a single Korean movie. Japanese films play in U.S. art houses, if at all; U.S. films play throughout the region. The unrelenting seductions of Hollywood's vision of a universal bourgeois lifestyle are apparent ultimately in two scions of the antisystem being unable to resist it: Mao's wife, Jiang Qing, watched *Gone With the Wind* in the Forbidden City, and Kim Il Sung's heir-apparent son, Kim Jong Il, reportedly has a personal library of 20,000 films, most of them American. Travelers even to remote Nepal report street urchins tug at their sleeves yelling "Michael Jackson, Michael Jackson." Japanese investors' recognition of the epicenter of late-twentieth-century culture led, of course, to their purchase of Columbia Pictures and MCA.

Since the mid-1980s, it is true, Japan has deepened its regional influence in Asia, with much higher levels of direct investment in Northeast and Southeast Asia. Its direct investment in the region has grown sixfold since 1985, its trade with Taiwan tripled in the same period, and its manufactured imports from the Asian region as a whole more than doubled from 1985 to 1988 (contrary to pundits who argue that its economy is basically closed). Japanese investors have been especially active in Thailand: on the average one new Japanese factory opened every working day in 1989.[35] The Pacific region inclusive of Northeast Asia, the ASEAN countries, and Australia will have a GNP of $7.2 trillion by the year 2000, according to current projections, which will be bigger than that of the European Union (EU); the number of effective consumers will be about 330 million, as large as the EU, but not as affluent.[36]

Japan has also been assiduous in breaking barriers to trade with the Asian socialist countries: it is North Korea's biggest capitalist trading partner (which is not to say much), and may normalize relations with P'yongyang soon; it went back into China much more quickly than other investors in the wake of the Tiananmen bloodletting in June 1989. As the Asian "Berlin walls" crumble, Japan will be poised to pursue a "German" option, that is, to deepen its market position in socialist China, Korea, and Vietnam as Germany has been doing in the old semiperiphery of East Europe. Indeed, Japanese experts have been asked to come back and renovate industrial technology in Manchuria, and even to revive big gold mines in North Korea formerly owned by Japanese and U.S. firms.

All this regional activity is grist for the mill of those who find a developing tendency toward regional economic blocs. But this is unlikely short of a major world depression; a trilateral regime of cooperation and free trade linking Europe with East Asia and the Americas is much more likely, with the three great markets of each region underpinning and stabilizing intercapitalist rivalry in the world system, and encouraging interdependence rather than go-it-alone strategies that would be deleterious to all. Japan's regional investment hedges against exclusion from the European Community after 1992, but it has other hedges in the form of direct investment in manufacturing in Great Britain and East Europe. The United States is strongly pressuring its European allies not to exclude Japan from the post-1992 arrangements, in favor of trilateral cooperation.

Japan is also constrained regionally, in that "actually existing socialism" persists, above all in "the East." There is no break yet in Asian communism, with the predictable exception of Soviet-aligned Mongolia. China has thus announced that "the center of socialism has moved East." With the demise of the "people's democracies" in Europe, predictably, the *Wall Street Journal* ran an article under the title, "The Coming Collapse of North Korea."[37] Strange, therefore, that the most recalcitrant outpost of communism today is in North Korea, which seems almost a museum of 1950s–1960s revolutionary socialism. Today it is the most interesting Communist nation, because it is the last unadulterated redoubt of what all the others used to be—the last Communist. Furthermore, for forty years it has been a state organized as an anti-Japanese entity, an apotheosis of the resistance to Japanese penetration that exists throughout the Asian rim.

The simplest answer for the seeming anomaly of persisting Asian communism in "Pacific Rim community" is precisely the Chinese claim that "the center of socialism has moved East." It's just that they are off by a few decades: it moved there after World War II, or perhaps in the 1930s, when formidable revolutionary nationalist movements emerged in China, Korea, and Vietnam. Today octogenarians in China and septuagenarians in North Korea and Vietnam are guardians of that deep-running anti-imperialist tradition. In China, of course, "Marxism–Leninism–Mao Zedong Thought" remains today little more than a justification for one-party rule. The post-1978, rim-joining economic reforms hang in a balance, or along a spectrum, from a young urban and coastal crowd that is following the capitalist road blazed by the Four Tigers, an old crowd whose preferred Marxism is the Stalinist variety (central planning; heavy industry first), and the still-vast peasantry for whom nobody but Mao had a policy—other than that they should disappear as a class, by becoming workers, urbanites, or the latest slogan, "getting rich." (In forty years of industrialization perhaps half a billion of them have done none of the above.)

Centrist national security elites in the United States have frankly promoted a reviving trilateralism. Internationalists are sure they know which direction the U.S.-Japan relationship should take: deepened collaboration, pointing toward a joint condominium, in which Japan will continue to play second fiddle.[38] The trilateral logic also expressed itself at the dawn of German reunification in the fall of 1989. Henry Kissinger and David Rockefeller both journeyed to Berlin and Tokyo in September; Kissinger was second only to U.S. Ambassador Vernon Walters in announcing his support for German unity. By not opposing what soon became a fait accompli, U.S. leaders succeeded in keeping Germany within the postwar settlement, and "containment" continues apace: not of the old enemey, the USSR, but of the old ally, Germany, just as U.S. bases still dot Japan in spite of the end of the cold war.

How long this will last is anybody's guess, but it makes of the enormous U.S. commitment to the Persian Gulf in 1990–1991 something less than the "first post–cold war crisis." U.S. forces are there to shape the flow of resources to Japan, Germany, and the other industrial economies, thus to maintain "outer limit" hegemonic lines that were central parts of the post-war settlement. (Imagine the reverse: a German or Japanese airlift of 500,000 troops to Saudi Arabia!)

The ultimate logic of trilateralism for the near term resides in Japan being for the United States today what the United States was for Great Britain in the 1920s: the emergent financial and technological center, but a long way from assuming hegemonic responsibilities. As the recent Gulf War demonstrated, Japan (and Germany) will be content to "let George do it" for some time, there being no interest in taking on an expensive security role when the United States is willing to do so, and in the absence of major security threats from the USSR or anyplace else.

North-North cooperation, including the Soviet Union (or whatever Russia and its allied republics will come to call themselves), is thus the order of the day in what is perhaps the most bourgeois era in world history. It is the Third World in our midst, another archipelago running from Los Angeles through Seoul and Manila to the hinterland masses of China and Indonesia, that will find no exit in the "Pacific Rim community," save hard work at low pay. The Third World is dominated by the advanced countries in a way unprecedented since the colonial era, with no convincing antisystemic model to follow. It is outside the loop of the prosperity of recent years, and therefore is the prime source of war, instability, and class conflict.

## Conclusion: The Significance of the Rim

Is there a way of constructing "Pacific Rim" other than that which I have given you in this chapter? Is there an indigenous path toward reconstituting Western Rimspeak? The people of the rim have tried two ways before: the imperial pan-Asianism of Japan in the late 1930s and early 1940s, never very successful in gaining non-Japanese adherents; and the Communist pan-Asianism of the 1950s, when Mao's China deeply influenced Korea, Vietnam, and various socialist movements in Asia. It had a brief heyday after North Korea and China fought the United States and its allies to a standstill in Korea, with the high point at Bandung in 1954. It is as dead as dead can be today, when China courts the NICs, and like Russia, tries to wash its hands of North Korea and Vietnam.

Perhaps capitalism Chinese-style will provide an alternative model. Southeast Asia is not Northeast Asia, but both are part of the rim. It was a historic trading area for another world economy, the Chinese, and it was the centerpiece of Great Britain's "Pacific Rim" empire. It has been shaped recently by a number of anticolonial independence movements (Vietnamese socialism, Indonesian nationalism, Malayan and Philippine guerrillas, Burman autarky, etc.) that make it less open to U.S. and Japanese ministrations than Northeast Asia. Today Southeast Asia has an alternative organization of capitalism, the long-standing interstitial commerce of "island China," the Chinese diaspora. Some pundits think this might provide a different way of organizing rim capitalism, with Hong Kong and Vancouver being principal nodes, patrimonialism and family-based entrepreneurship the means, and Chinese the lingua franca. A reorganization of the region under Chinese auspices seems remote, however, until the mainland itself is so organized; otherwise Chinese commerce will continue to operate in the pores of the system.

So we are left, I think, with but one grand event symbolized by "Pacific Rim," and that is the rise to power of Japan. It is the only true entrant in the past century to the ranks of the advanced industrial core, with the possible exception of the (now-deindustrializing) Soviet Union. It is the only non-Western entrant. If it does not wish to be, and cannot today be, the lodestone for an autonomous non-Western reorganization of the region, one day it will be. When that happens, an old soldier and charter Pacific rimster, General Douglas MacArthur, Japan's benign U.S. emperor, will have been right: in an address in Seattle back in 1951, MacArthur opined that "Our economic frontier now embraces the trade potentialities of Asia itself; for which the gradual rotation of the epicenter of world trade back to the Far East whence it started many centuries ago, the next thousand years will find the main problem the raising of the subnormal standards of life of its more than a billion people."[39]

It is a classic piece of Rimspeak.

## Notes

This chapter is a revision of my keynote address to the 15th Annual Conference on the Political Economy of the World-System, Honolulu, Hawaii, March 28, 1991.

1. Murray Sayle, "Bowing to the Inevitable," *Times Literary Supplement,* April 28, 1989. I am grateful to Gavan McCormack for drawing my attention to this statement.

2. Peter Gourevitch, "The Pacific Rim: Current Debates," *Annals of the American Academy of Political and Social Science* 505 (September 1989), pp. 8–23.

3. Ezra F. Vogel, *Japan as Number One: Lessons for America* (Cambridge, MA: Harvard University Press, 1979).

4. Chalmers Johnson, *MITI and the Japanese Miracle* (Berkeley: University of California Press, 1982); see also Thomas Gold, "State and Society" in *The Taiwan Miracle* (Armonk, NY: M.E. Sharpe, 1986); Gary Gereffi, ed., *Manufacturing Miracles* (Princeton, NJ: Princeton University Press, 1991). According to Gereffi, he wanted to title his book *Manufactured Miracles,* but the publisher changed it (to go along with the trope).

5. Gourevitch, "The Pacific Rim," p. 19; Staffan Burenstam Linder, *The Pacific Century: Economic and Political Consequences of Asian-Pacific Dynamism* (Stanford, CA: Stanford University Press, 1986).

6. Simon Winchester, *Pacific Rising: The Emergence of a New World Culture* (New York: Prentice-Hall, 1991), p. xiii. Sociologists will be happy to know, even if East Asianists will drop to their knees in mortification to find out, that in Winchester's view, Max Weber offered "the most complete, if not the most readable, account of Confucius" (in his *Religion of China*—see p. 487). Weber famously sought the source of East Asia's failure to develop capitalism in the absence of the Protestant ethic, or its equivalent; generations of graduate students got this as an explanation for why the West was dynamic and the East was not. But at least it *was* readable, especially compared to the East Asianist texts.

7. See Arif Dirlik, "The Asia-Pacific Idea: Reality and Representation in the Invention of a Regional Structure," *Journal of World History* 3, no. 1 (Spring 1992).

8. Andrew Mendelsohn, "Alvin Toffler in China: Deng's Big Bang," *The New Republic,* April 4, 1988, quoted in Alexander Woodside, "The Asia-Pacific Idea as a Mobilization Myth" (Chapter 3, this volume). Woodside notes that there are no Chinese, or Indonesian, or Vietnamese Alvin Tofflers.

9. I have argued this point at length in "The Political Economy of Chinese Foreign Policy," *Modern China* (October 1979), pp. 411–461.

10. Richard M. Nixon, "Asia After Vietnam," *Foreign Affairs,* 46, no. 1 (1967), pp. 111–125.

11. See Mike Davis, *City of Quartz* (London: Verso, 1990).

12. Barthes, *Empire of Signs* (New York: Hill and Wang, 1982).

13. Ibid.

14. Friedrich Nietzsche, *On the Genealogy of Morals,* ed. and trans. by Walter Kaufmann (New York: Vintage Books, 1969), pp. 15–23, 77–78.

15. Quoted in Richard Drinnon, *Facing West: The Metaphysics of Indian-Hating and Empire-Building* (New York: New American Library, 1980), p. 271. This book is a wonderful antidote to Rimspeak.

16. Quoted in Jean-Pierre Lehmann, *The Image of Japan: From Feudal Isolation to World Power, 1850–1905* (London: George Allen & Unwin, 1978), p. 46.

17. "The Pacific Idea," *Economist,* March 16, 1991.

18. For more elaboration see Bruce Cumings, "The Origins and Development of the Northeast Asian Political Economy," *International Organization* (Winter 1984), pp. 1–40.

19. By 1894, U.S. kerosene exports to Japan had reached 887,000 barrels of

42 gallons each. Standard entered the production field in Japan with its International Oil Company, 1900–1906. See Harold F. Williamson and Arnold R. Daum, *The American Petroleum Industry, 1859–1899: The Age of Illumination* (Evanston: Northwestern University Press, 1959), p. 675; *Söritsu shichijù-shùnen kinen Nihon sekiyu shi* [seventieth anniversary history of Japanese petroleum] (Tokyo: Nihon Sekiyu K.K., 1958).

20. James B. Duke formed BAT in 1902, in league with a chief rival, the Imperial Tobacco Company; Duke held ²⁄₃ of the stock. By 1915, BAT had almost $17 million in investments in China and was one of its two largest employers. (Michael H. Hunt, *The Making of a Special Relationship: The United States and China to 1914* [New York: Columbia University Press, 1983], pp. 282–283.)

21. Carter Eckert, *The Origins of Korean Capitalism* (Seattle: University of Washington Press, 1991).

22. Quoted in Colin Holmes and A. H. Ion, "Bushido and the Samurai: Images in British Public Opinion, 1894–1914," *Modern Asian Studies*, 14, no. 2 (1980), pp. 304–329.

23. Sir Oliver Lodge, quoted in Holmes and Iron, "Bushio and the Samurai," p. 321.

24. Quoted in Isohi Asahi, *The Economic Strength of Japan* (Tokyo: Hokuseido Press, 1939), pp. 207–209.

25. See Harry N. Schreiber, "World War I as Entrepreneurial Opportunity: Willard Straight and the American International Corporation," *Political Science Quarterly*, 84 (September 1969), pp. 486–511; more generally see Carl P. Parrini, *Heir to Empire: The United States Economic Diplomacy, 1916–1923* (Pittsburgh, PA: University of Pittsburgh Press, 1969).

26. Akira Iriye, *After Imperialism* (Cambridge, MA: Harvard University Press, 1965). Although Iriye's analysis is different from mine, he demonstrates more the failure than the success of the "Washington system," and underlines the upper hand that the United States now had in East Asian diplomacy.

27. Johnson, *MITI*; William Miles Fletcher III, *The Japanese Business Community and National Trade Policy, 1920–1942* (Chapel Hill: University of North Carolina Press, 1989).

28. Gö Seinosuke, formerly head of the huge Oji Paper Company and director of the Tokyo Stock Exchange for 12 years, drafted a report in 1929 recommending, among other things, "a new national committee . . . to rationalize industrial production in order to 'aid industrial development' "; "Gö endorsed the principle of export planning—selecting products that might sell well abroad and fostering their growth." The plan led to the Export Compensation Act of May 1930, and other measures to aid export industries; the plan was to help exports to Central America, Africa, the Balkans, "central Asia Minor," and the USSR, and it later expanded to include "the whole world except for Europe, the U.S., India, and the Dutch East Indies" (Fletcher, *The Japanese Business Community*, pp. 59, 61–62).

29. Ibid., p. 28.

30. See Robin Luckham, "American Militarism and the Third World: The End of the Cold War?" (Working paper no. 94, Peace Research Center, Australian National University, October 1990), p. 2.

31. See Bruce Cumings, *Origins of the Korean War,* vol. 2 (Princeton, NJ: Princeton University Press, 1990), Chapter 2.

32. See Andrew Rotter, *The Path to Vietnam* (Ithaca, NY: Cornell University Press, 1986).

33. By the 1990s pundits have already begun to suggest that Japan and South Korea may represent a different, "third" kind of political economy—"what we used to call fascism," in Jude Wanniskie's words ("Some Lines on the Rest of the Millennium," *New York Times,* December 24, 1989). Karel von Wolferen, in an important book called *The Enigma of Japanese Power* (New York: Knopf, 1989), hints at a similar perspective with his discussion of the mysterious "system" at the core of Japan's political economy.

34. For an elaboration, see Bruce Cumings, "The Seventy Years' Crisis and the Logic of Trilateralism in the 'New World Order,' " *World Policy Journal* (Spring 1991). For Polanyi's explanation of *haute finance* and the 100 years' peace (1815–1914), see *The Great Transformation* (Boston: Beacon, 1944).

35. *Far Eastern Economic Review,* July 21, 1990, and August 30, 1990.

36. *Far Eastern Economic Review,* August 9, 1990.

37. *Wall Street Journal,* June 26, 1990.

38. See for example Zbigniew Brzezinski, who advocated a U.S.-Japan condominium called "Amerippon" in "America's New Geostrategy," *Foreign Affairs* 66, no. 4 (Spring 1988), pp. 680–699.

39. Speech in Seattle, 1951. Quoted in Michael W. Miles, *The Odyssey of the American Right* (Oxford: Oxford University Press, 1980), p. 170.

# 5

## On the Outs on the Rim: An Ethnographic Grounding of the "Asia-Pacific" Imaginary

### DONALD M. NONINI

The notion of "Asia-Pacific," or the "Pacific Rim," poses an analytical problem on one hand, but on the other, it is a concept that theoretically at least, is difficult to take seriously. A focus on the regions of the world central to strategic military and economic interests of the United States, its allies, and its ruling elites led to the emergence and codification of "area studies" in the social sciences in the 1950s and 1960s (see, e.g., Horowitz 1971; and Roberts 1971), with much definitional controversy about what constituted an "area."[1] There is presently a similar haphazard and hazy appearance on our disciplinary horizons of something called the "Asia-Pacific," or "Pacific Rim," quite clearly again tied to these interests, with its correlative forms of institutionalization and discursive inscription.[2] Can the whole thing be considered with a straight face, without irony? My skepticism is of particular relevance to the topic I intend to address here: labor, gender, and ethnicity—within the area, however we end up defining it, under discussion.

As an anthropologist, I have certain implacable disciplinary loyalties toward locale and place—toward the understanding of how people lead their lives, in all their specificities, in certain "small" spaces: in their households, neighborhoods, communities, towns, and villages. My emphasis is therefore on the everyday, the pedestrian, the local. From the perspective of those people I have studied and done research among, something so grand as the "Asia-Pacific" or "Pacific Rim" has no meaning; it does not even exist as illusion. Yet, as Henri Lefebvre reminds us, "The *unrecognized,* that is, the everyday, still has some surprises in store for us"—and this arises, above all, from the fact that the "everyday," *la quotidienne,* has a history as a "modality for extending the capitalist mode of production" (Lefebvre 1988: 78–80) with all the intrinsic dynamism this implies. This is as true for the societies of those countries referred to as being part of the "Asia-Pacific" as elsewhere in the capitalist

73

world order. All this must be conceded and, more than that, conceptualized.[3]

What I have observed from ethnography as part of the everyday has been persons and groups implicated in various ways with something that I recognize on other, theoretical grounds as being the "Asia-Pacific," or to be more precise, implicated in *processes of relation* with something identified closely with the "Asia-Pacific"/"Pacific Rim" neologisms. Thus, I have seen the factory buses circulating through the outlying neighborhoods of a Malaysian market town, picking up throngs of young Malay and Indian women who are employed in the foreign- and state-owned electronics and textile factories of the industrial estates and free trade zones of the Penang area; I have witnessed Chinese men, women, and children in Malaysia engaged frenetically in the piecework of home labor—sewing, shoemaking, packaging, and the like—to produce commodities for the international market; I have talked with Chinese men who aspire to work as illegal laborers in Japan or Taiwan, then return to Malaysia with money saved to open their own businesses.

I thus find it incumbent on me to make some sense of this "Asia-Pacific" that links these disparate experiences together. But not as such. Rather, I reject the notion of "Asia-Pacific" as unitary, as a thing. At worst, it is an intellectual construction that serves those who serve state and corporate power—as in the case of "area studies" in the immediate postwar period. At best, it refers to a set of economic, political, and cultural processes creating relationships within an area—perhaps one could call it a "supraregion"—that link up different regions each with their own social and cultural integrity: regions with households, neighborhoods, towns, centers, hinterlands, cores, and peripheries.

Because the "Asia-Pacific" imaginary appears to presuppose, even if it is not coextensive with, such linkages—flows of people, capital, commodities, ideas and information, microbes, sources of energy—there have been many groups, in the United States as elsewhere, who will be able to construct histories—*their* histories or autobiographies—from memories of experiences of earlier migrations traced across this supraregion. This is as it should be. Thus, for instance, there are the memories carried by an author such as Maxine Hong Kingston of her parents come from China to the American mainland (Kingston 1980); there are the life stories created by the Japanese sugar plantation laborers and studied by Ronald Takaki (1983) of early years in Japan and the ordeal of working in Hawaii; there are the accounts of Mexican-American migrants laboring in the food-crop plantations of California (Galarza 1971). But these histories, centrally important as they are to the identities of Asian Americans and Mexican Americans, do not as such validate or privilege the "Asia-Pacific" imaginary, for they like all experiences on a human scale, are lived through in small spaces step by step: in itineraries, paths, voyages, passages from one small space through others, arriving at yet others as sojourners, migrants, or pilgrims. Memory and experience cannot constitute either a past or present "Asia-Pacific": such a grand conception can only arise through the act of theoretical construction. In what follows, I first set out some theoretical propositions about the recent social and material history underlying the new "Asia-Pacific." I then turn to the theme of the place of labor, gender, and ethnicity within this history. My focus tends to be on those countries within the Southeast Asia "edge" of the "Pacific Rim," and especially on Malaysia, which I know best in terms of an ethnography of the everyday. I believe that the generalizations I advance will, however, have broader application to other regions bounded by the imaginary. Throughout, I attempt to consider the dialectic between those whose structures of power ground the imaginary and those subaltern groups "on the outs" that are ruled and regulated on the edges of the "rim."

## The "Asia-Pacific" Imaginary and the Geopolitics of Capital

At the risk of being identified with a "totalizing" intellectual position, I would argue that the "Asia-Pacific" or "Pacific Rim" can best be understood as the trope for a set of economic, political, and cultural processes creating relationships within a supraregion of Asia and the United States that have been under way since approximately the mid-1970s—processes arising from what the Marxist geographer David Harvey has called the "spatial displacements" or "spatial fixes" of contemporary capitalism (Harvey 1985, 1989). Harvey discerns that within the capitalist mode of production there exist processes that generate surpluses of capital and labor power. These processes—internal to the accumulation dynamic of capitalism—will lead, if unchecked, to crises of "overaccumulation," the incapacity of capitalism to absorb simultaneously the surpluses of capital and labor power, which in turn brings about the precipitous and calamitous devaluation or destruction of both (Harvey 1985: 133–36). Two principal means of confronting these processes and avoiding the crises they otherwise entail are temporal and spatial "displacements."

Temporal displacements absorb surplus capital and labor power in the form of investments in physical and social infrastructure within a long-term return. Railroads, roads, universities, research laboratories, airports, hospitals are examples (Harvey 1985: 135–36). Yet temporal displacements by themselves only postpone the day of reckoning, of crisis, since their "fictitious capital" represents a claim on future labor, and the heavy debt it generates must eventually be paid, and when this proves impossible, as is often the case, then devaluation of invested capital and labor power sets in with catastrophic results (Harvey 1985: 136–40).

According to Harvey, it is the combination of temporal displacements with "spatial displacements" or "spatial fixes" that has allowed postwar world capitalism to forestall the advent of profound crisis, at least until recently (Harvey 1985: 156; Harvey 1989). Spatial displacements occur when the surplus capital or labor power or both that are generated in one region are exported across (what are generally) international boundaries and invested in another region. These spatial "fixes," however, must accord with the internal dynamic of capitalism, which constains all capitalist enterprises not to exceed the socially necessary turnover time required to realize profits. Under these time constraints, what—paradoxically—makes such spatial displacements possible are the temporal displacements. These are of two kinds: direct displacements that embody transformations in transport and communications technologies, and indirect displacements that represent investments in productive technology and organization that free capitalists from place-specific constraints, such as localized labor skills and commodity markets and immobile fixed capital and productive materials (Harvey 1985: 135–36; Harvey 1989: Part 3).

These displacements and their associated technologies, taken ensemble, have over the last 150 years drastically reduced the time and cost of moving liquid capital, commodities, raw materials, and productive facilities and machinery for the capitalist, and they increasingly allow the flexible integration of production, exchange, and consumption markets. And it is over the last two to three decades, Harvey argues, that a quantum leap in the reduction of the friction of distance has taken place: space has now "imploded" with innovations in satellite telecommunications, air travel, miniaturization, containerization, and so on. This is but the most recent episode of "time-space compression," the recurrent transformation of the meanings of time and space in the direction of speeding economic processes and progressively overcoming spatial barriers that has been fundamental to the history of capitalism (Harvey 1985: 147–48; Harvey 1989: 240, 284–91).

Such temporal displacements make spatial fixes *possible*. But what makes spatial fixes *necessary*, or at least probable, is the condition of class struggle within an already developed region and its associated state. Both capital and labor within a region are caught in an endless dilemma: whether to "cut and run" to regions of higher profits or more favorable wages and working conditions, or to remain in more or less stable contest with each other within a region in which both capital and labor power have already been substantially invested in order to recoup embodied value (Harvey 1985: 150–53). What has occurred with the emergence of the "Asia-Pacific," one could argue, is a shift in the balance of regional class struggles such that capitalists specifically have sought recently to cut and run to peripheral regions and states with lower wages, more tractable labor, and higher profits, away from core regions and states where the prevailing strength of laboring classes and their supporters has been relatively great. Labor in these regions, being comparatively immobile, in contrast has remained behind and has begun to suffer catastrophic devaluation. Thus, for example, since about 1965 in the United States deindustrialization has proceeded apace, with an estimated net loss of about 15 million industrial jobs due to plant closures from 1968 to 1976 (Nash 1983a: ix; see also Bluestone and Harrison 1982); industrialization in our "Asia-Pacific" accelerated its increase in the same period (Snow 1979) and subsequently. On this account, the two trends are not merely connected, but are in fact different manifestations of the same process at work (Arrighi 1990). It is just such a process, together with its ramifications on a variety of fronts, that has been reified as the "Asia-Pacific"/"Pacific Rim" imaginary.

Applied to the spatial imaginary before us, capital transfers by transnational corporations and international lenders (e.g., the World Bank) to productive sites throughout the "Asia-Pacific" represent precisely such spatial displacements, which have proliferated since the mid-1970s. U.S. national and transnational corporations have shifted capital (and a small number of skilled laborers and managers) from the previously industrialized Northeast and Central United States to the South and Southwest and southern California, and to Mexico and Southeast Asia (Thailand, Malaysia, Singapore, Philippines); Japanese corporations have exported capital to Southeast Asia (Malaysia, Singapore, etc.), as have Korean and (most recently) Taiwanese corporations. It is equally important, however, to note that it was the existence of *prior* spatial displacements of surplus U.S. and European capital during the late 1940s, the 1950s, and the 1960s as an element of postwar "reconstruction" and the cold war that allowed Japanese, Korean, and Taiwanese capitalist enterprises, under strong state direction and encouragement, to develop their economies to become competitors with U.S. capital to begin with (Hamilton 1983; Haggard and Cheng 1987; Nolan 1990). This is not to deny that prior to World War II, Japan, Korea, and Taiwan already manifested (to various degrees depending on colonialism) "structured coherence" as regions internally dominated and organized by industrial and agrarian capitalist production."[4]

By invoking Harvey's analysis I mean neither to be economistic nor to make claims to comprehensiveness, but rather to point to underlying tendencies within transnational capitalism *that are both embodied in but are also constrained by* the economic, political, and cultural features of the regions and states defined as being within our "Asia-Pacific." In this vein, I want to discuss briefly some of the sequelae of *and* blockages to these spatial displacements as they bear on the theme of labor, gender, and ethnicity.

## Labor, Patriarchal Power, and the New Industrialism

Capital flight to the regions of the "Asia-Pacific" has, I suggested, been prompted by successful struggles by labor in preexisting core regions such as the United States to force capitalists to subsidize in part the social costs of economic growth in these regions—notably through high wages and taxes to support the welfare state. Such was the historic compromise between capital and labor prevailing from the end of World War II up to the 1970s that became known as Fordism (Harvey 1989; also see O'Connor 1984: 2–9). It is no surprise, then, that such capital export has been marked by the aggressive seeking out of sources of new inexpensive and tractable labor in order that the capitalist process of exploitation might continue through the production of commodities, but with the realization of higher profits. What this has led to has been the emergence and crystallization of what are called "segmented labor markets," with certain socially disadvantaged or stigmatized populations in Asia and the Americas—especially women and international labor migrants—channeled into "secondary labor markets" for poorly paid and relatively unskilled labor and excluded from "primary" labor markets for skilled laborers, technicians, and managers (Gordon, Edwards, and Reich 1982: 200–2; Green 1983).

Above all, these laborers have been the young unmarried women of Asia and increasingly the Americas, such as in the U.S.-Mexican border area. Thus we find the thousands of young Malaysian, Taiwanese, Hong Kong, Filipino, Mexican, and other young women working in export-oriented industries—in electronics assembly plants, textile mills, and garment factories owned and managed by transnational, indigenous, and state capitalists, working for extremely low wages, often under physically hazardous and stressful conditions (Nash 1983a, 1983b; Snow 1983; Southeast Asia Chronicle/Pacific Research 1978–79). In 1980, there were more than 600,000 workers in export processing zones in Asia alone (Pineda-Ofreneo 1987: 95), the vast majority young women—specific examples suggesting between 80 and 90 percent. The number has increased greatly since then. In some regions these women either reside in or are recent migrants from rural areas—such as those who work in the export processing zones and industrial estates of Malaysia, Indonesia, Thailand, Taiwan, and the Philippines (Ong 1983, 1987; Ackerman 1984; Jamilah

1984; Mather 1983; Charoenloet 1988, 1991; Bello, Kinley, and Elinson 1982: 127–64; Enloe 1983: 415); in other regions, such as in northern Mexico, they are migrants from highly urbanized areas elsewhere (Fernandez-Kelly 1983a, 1983b). Neither their physical distance nor nominal economic independence from their natal family and household necessarily means that these young women are socially cut off from them. To the contrary: the very physical and social infrastructures (roads, railways, telephone systems, etc.) that attracted transnational capital to these regions also facilitate workers' frequent communication and interaction with families, which in turn both allow and require these women to contribute to their natal household economy by direct payments or remittances (for examples, see Stivens 1986; Huang 1984; Strauch 1984). They are thus simultaneously "good daughters" and "good workers." One consequence, of course, is that whatever patterns of patriarchal power are in effect within these households—which generally hierarchically subordinate those who are female and young—reinforce the economic power of the new employers. Within such dual patriarchal regimes, the enhanced monetized contributions of these young women to their natal household budget may give them some personal leverage vis-à-vis their father and brothers in terms of new "freedom" and "independence" in making certain minor decisions (for this argument, see Lim 1983); however, the money these women earn can bind them even more closely, as in the case of Hong Kong parents who pressure their daughters to delay marriage so as to ensure that they will continue working in factories and maintain their financial support to their natal household (Grossman 1978–79).

Complementary to such rationalized factory production and also subject to patriarchal control, women's and children's waged labor has been employed "in the home" through extensive putting-out arrangements. Such contracted-out piecework to be done "at home" has preceded the advent of the new transnational factories, previously being common in such lines of production for the domestic market as garment manufacturing (for one example, see Nonini 1983: 173–75), but in some areas recently has become integrated with export-oriented factory production. Thus, for instance, on a visit one evening in 1990 to the home of a Chinese informant in Penang state in Malaysia, I witnessed his wife, mother, and three small children working energetically filling boxes with sports garments manufactured in a factory at a nearby industrial estate—a domestic assembly line in which women and children labored to earn a few cents per box on a piecework basis while my informant, his grown younger brother, and I all watched idly. Such "homework" has a definite place in the new "regime of flexible accumulation" (Harvey 1989), which is characterized by such innovations as subcontracting and "just-in-time" production (with concomitant "just-in-time" hirings and layoffs) as employers take advantage of the putting-out system to avoid paying pensions and other legally mandated benefits.[5] Too little is known about such women's (and children's) home labor—probably just because it is informal, its importance in the production trail is belittled, and it easily escapes official statistical attention—and there is a pressing research need to study it and its implications for working-class households in the "rim."

The placement of young women in these secondary labor markets, of course, is by no means merely an economic phenomenon. Indeed, the work tasks are themselves gendered, and in this sense these women's employment is surrounded by discourses, practices, and ideologies of "femininity" and by conditions of patriarchal social control. That the elements of the labor process are in some deep cultural sense gendered as well as classed is an important insight coming out of recent feminist theory (Weston 1990). Thus, there is the common mythic notion held fervently by factory managers—apparently widespread throughout our supraregion (e.g., from the U.S.-Mexico border region to the Philippines and Malaysia)—that it is young factory women in particular who show the "utmost patience and high dexterity for the delicate assembly job of fine connection" (Pineda-Ofreneo 1987: 96; see also Elson and Pearson 1981).[6]

Forms of patriarchal power that reinforce the employers' economic control within the workplace are common and take such forms as male factory managers and supervisors adopting the metaphorical roles of male family relatives (as "fathers," "brothers"); inciting rivalry between workers for their attention or affection (often linked to performance evaluations); organizing diversions such as athletic events, raffles, parties, and even "beauty contests" among women operatives; and exhorting workers to show such supposed "traditional" Asian female values as loyalty (to the corporation), hard work, honesty, deference to men, self-denial, and even piety. More punitive practices include sexual harassment of women workers; shaming of workers seen as recalcitrant or performing poorly through dressings-down before their peers; the making of invidious comparisons between the performance of the workers at a specific factory and of operatives in other offshore factories of the corporation, with the implicit threat of plant closures and "retrenchment" if quotas are not met; and petty Taylorist monitoring of workers' time use (Grossman 1978–79; Bello, Kinley, and Elinson 1982: 127–64; Mather 1983; Ong 1987; Pineda-Ofreneo 1987; Lin 1984; Arrigo 1984).

These forms of patriarchal power reinforce the constant pressures placed on these women workers by managers to intensify their labor and to meet continually increasing production quotas (see e.g., Lin 1984).

Such pressures, Harvey (1989: 229) argues, are a basic feature of the industrial labor process given individual capitalists' efforts to reduce "the turnover time of capital"—but have accelerated during the latest episode of time-space compression throughout our supraregion, with such innovations as "just-in-time" processing (Rajah 1981).[7] Despite the prevalent image of female passivity held by managers and government officials, women workers have resisted these pressures, at times with great militance, by overt means such as strikes (Pineda-Ofrenco and del Rosario 1988; Bello, Kinley, and Elinson 1982: 157–59), by more covert means such as work slowdowns and "mass hysteria" (Ong 1987), and by job hopping (Huang 1984; Deyo 1989).

Another stigmatized and socially disadvantaged population in the "Asia-Pacific" that is actively sought out and employed by offshore and indigenous capitalists in secondary labor markets is the "new helots" (Cohen 1987)—the various illegal and quasi-legal immigrant workers, *gastarbeiter,* or "guest workers." Here are included "undocumented aliens" from Mexico and Central America in the factories and sweatshop industries of southern California and the U.S. Southwest (Cohen 1987: 33–72; Davis 1989); Southeast Asian Chinese working in Taiwan and Japan, Indonesian laborers in Malaysia, Chinese and Malay Malaysians in Singapore (Rodan 1989), and many other groups. What distinguishes these groups is their distinctive ethnic and national identity, although their success in remaining in employment often depends upon their abilities to "pass" as citizens of the host regions. It is precisely their disadvantaged status as illegal or quasi-legal migrant laborers and their willingness to accept lower wages than local residents that permit employers within these regions to intensify their exploitation relative to local regimes of accumulation. The threat of deportation acts as a compelling form of industrial discipline. The conditions under which guest workers labor may in some instances approach involuntary servitude, as in the extreme case of one major Korean corporate contractor who imported Korean convict labor to work on the construction of a bridge in Malaysia. The presence of guest workers—and the requisites of capital accumulation that lead capitalists to seek them out and employ them—have as yet unexplored implications for the definitions of "nationality" and "citizen" within these regions, particularly in times of recession when these people are seen as threatening the jobs of indigenous workers.

It is worthwhile to consider how gender relations, patriarchal power, and the new forms of labor migration interact. Culturally specific local regimes of patriarchal power, reinforced by state regulation of women's bodies and actions, vary within and across the regions of the supraregion. These regimes constrain the geographic mobility of young women far more than that of young men. Young working-class women tend to remain at or near their place of natal residence under a regime of combined family and factory control—though highly modernized transport and communications infrastructure and technology in these regions, as noted above, allow social proximity to persist over long physical distances. Where young women do migrate over considerable distances to find work, it is often to live with kinfolk who have previously migrated (see e.g., Strauch 1984 for a Malaysian example). With some major exceptions, it is young working-class men who have become international labor migrants, working as illegal or quasi-legal laborers in countries where wages are higher, but whose indigenous laboring populations disdain to perform certain work because of its low pay (in local terms), "danger," and "dirtiness." Therefore working-class males far more than working-class females are able to respond to the differentiation in wealth and industrial technologies between countries within the supraregion; the specific exploitation of women workers in large numbers within their own country allows the differential generation of surplus-value that in turn over time provides an impetus that accelerates this international diversification. For example, young single working-class Chinese Malaysian males "jump from airplanes" (*tiao feiji*), "parachute in," that is, migrate to work illegally at factory, construction, and other relatively low-paid work in Japan and Taiwan. Their unmarried sisters remain in Malaysia to labor in petty self-employed enterprises, in their natal households in putting-out piecework, and in small-scale sweatshop industries in or near the cities or towns where their parents live. And at the same time young Javanese and other Indonesians, mostly men, migrate illegally into Malaysia to work in the housing construction and plantation sectors. Returning to Harvey's argument discussed above that both capital and labor within a region are caught in an unending dilemma whether to "cut and run" to other regions with higher profits and wages or to remain within a region, it should be pointed out that the dilemma is almost always a gendered one. In Southeast Asia, working-class men, like capitalists, are far more often allowed to cut and run, whereas working-class women tend to confront destabilization "at home" due to the class conflicts centered on their exploitation, created by the installation of new "offsource" capital imported from elsewhere in the supraregion.

There are, as stated, exceptions to this tendency. Thus, the recent histories of migration in both the Philippines and Thailand show trends in which women have migrated in greater numbers than men to the primate cities, respectively, Manila and Bangkok (Eviota and Smith 1984; Singhanetra-Renard 1987; Arnold and Piampiti 1984; Piampiti 1984). This also suggests that patriarchal regulation of these women migrants, to the extent that it exists, must take some form other than restraints on their geographic mobility. In some instances, the history of such experience for female migrants within a country may predispose them to become international labor migrants, as with rural-born Filipino women, who have a tradition of migrating to Manila to engage in domestic labor (Eviota and Smith 1984), but have also entered international labor circuits both across the cities of the supraregion and indeed beyond it, as the presence in large numbers of Filipino domestic workers trapped in Kuwait during the recent Persian Gulf War tragically illustrated. And on the eastern edge of the "rim," in contrast, a different tendency altogether appears to prevail, in which women migrate over long distances from central and southern Mexico to labor in the *maquiladora* factories of the U.S.-Mexico border region, whereas the men who accompany them remain largely unemployed and economically dependent on them (Fernandez-Kelly 1983b).

The fundamental points to be made are that instead of reifying "patriarchy," critical scholars must investigate the great variety of patriarchal controls within the supraregion in all their cultural and historical specificities; but that even then the working out of gender relations and the effects of patriarchal power must be accorded some autonomy in the making and the history of our supraregion. Similar points apply, as the discussion of guest workers suggests, to the variety of forms of state power that make persons "citizens" or not and members of one ethnic group or another, and confer or hold back rights of "nationality"—thus acting as a device to sort and classify workers throughout our supraregion as appropriate human materials for primary or secondary labor markets and the conditions of labor exploitation associated with them.

## Labor, Hegemony, and Domination

What makes the regions of the "Asia-Pacific" so attractive to the new transnational investors is not only the low cost of women's and guest workers' labor in these regions, but also its tractability; hence its articulation with patriarchal and state-nationalist forms of power. These forms of power represent the exercise of "hegemony," which on the cultural fronts of "civil society" conduces to consent on the part of working populations to the rule of national elites throughout the countries of the supraregion and to their arrangements with transnational and local capitalists (see Gramsci 1971).[8] Another hegemonic process provides an additional line of defense against the mobilization of the new workers against the new order: the romance of commodities, or what has been called "commodity aesthetics." As the highly transient transnational corporations penetrate the economies of the regions of the "Asia-Pacific," they also initiate new consumption markets—made possible again by representations in the media of television, videotapes, radio, and film—directed toward specific consumer populations, especially young adults and children. Commodities are offered that carry the cachet of certain "lifestyles," supposedly defining the good life in the preexisting core areas (especially the United States and Europe); thus we find McDonald's, Kentucky Fried Chicken, Levi-Strauss and Lee jeans, Rolex watches, Louis Vuitton luggage, Guinness stout, the music of the Beegees, and so forth. The inducement of desires for these commodities reinforces the emerging structured coherence of these new regional economies. The affirmation of such desires by the new industrial workers at whatever petty level they can afford to satisfy them also reconciles them to some extent to the oppressive conditions of their work (McGee 1987).

But if the gendering of production and the romance of commodities represent specific sites for the exercise of hegemony in regional class struggles,[9] then certainly hegemony's alter—"domination" (Gramsci 1971)—also makes its appearance, in its most extreme form of overwhelmingly repressive state power. Of course, outright resort to state coercion against recalcitrant laborers is a crude advertisement of weakness and creates friction between transnational capitalists and host states in the supraregion and therefore is resorted to only at times of perceived extreme crisis. Instead, there are a variety of intermediate stratagems that have been employed by transnational capitalists and their host states to regulate labor and ensure its pliability with the supraregion. The promotion of divisions between workers along ethnic lines within the same factories (Boulanger 1991; Wad 1989); the creation of house unions, as in Malaysia and the Philippines (Boulanger 1991; Pineda-Ofreneo 1987); the state incorporation of labor unions and their demands, as in Singapore (Rosa 1990) and the Philippines (Bello, Kinley, and Elinson 1982: 157–59); practices, laws, and regulations discouraging the registration of new unions or of federations of smaller unions, as in Singapore and Malaysia; the recent trend toward privatization, which effectively destroys previously powerful unions in the public sector; public intimations by political leaders that unions are Communist led, therefore threaten national security, and thus must be resisted in their demands—all are examples of options that fall short of the outright use of force. More extreme measures, a history of our supraregion suggests, also have been used and will be resorted to again on occasion. The violent breaking up of strikes; arrests and imprisonment of labor leaders, including women; and the decertification of labor unions, all are justified by various laws, regulations, and ad hoc fiats (Boulanger 1991; Pineda-Ofreneo 1987; Enloe 1983; Charoenloet 1991). Thus a range of state and capitalist stratagems are aimed explicitly against the formation of independent labor unions and seek to neutralize the collective gains of labor, both formal and informal. It has been argued that in the first tier of Asian "newly industrializing countries"—Hong Kong, Singapore, South Korea, and Taiwan—there has been a transition from earlier (1950s, 1960s) repressive state controls of laborers to recent corporatist strategems (Deyo 1987)—but this tendency, if general, is far less in evidence in other, peripheral regions within the supraregion.

With some exceptions, such as in the United States and Japan, these actions by the states of the regions of the "Asia-Pacific" make sense because the paramount political and military leaders and bureaucratic functionaries directing these states are of all groups those who most benefit from the accommodations reached with offshore capitalists to situate their operations locally. For example, the ruling bureaucratic and military elites of Malaysia, Indonesia, and the Philippines have aggrandized their economic positions by engaging in joint ventures with transnational corporations, and have received lucrative directorships, exclusive licensing privileges, and graft in return for the concessions of various kinds they have made to transnational investors—measures that discourage labor unions, offer tax vacations, provide free modern infrastructure, and so on (see Mehmet 1986; Robison 1986: 131–210; Bello, Kinley, and Elinson 1982: 1983–95).

## Petty-Commodity Production: Resistance to Exploitation?

I claimed above that certain features of the new regions did not facilitate but rather impeded the spatial displacements carried out by the capitalist order in the "Asia-Pacific" since the mid-1970s. What are these blockages? These obstacles to the successful realization of profits by offshore investments are connected to the fact that the regions are not completely capitalist in a variety of senses, although they are "dominated" by the capitalist mode of production. In particular, the existence of well-developed petty-commodity productive relations may provide an alternative to participation by young women and other disadvantaged groups as labor in the new capitalist enterprises, at least for some groups in some countries of our supraregion.

The new workers are drawn from substantial populations of past or continuing land-owning peasantries. The willingness of persons from these populations, women and men, to engage in production in the new export-oriented factories depends in large part on the preexisting economic, political, and social conditions prevailing in the countrysides and urban areas of the "rim" regions to which transnational capitalists have been drawn. Neither the seductive blandishments of commodities nor the exercise of local patriarchal power are per se sufficient to ensure that rural populations in these regions will be attracted to factory labor; other options may exist. One fundamental feature that determines the "willingness" of these populations is the history of the "primitive accumulation" process (Marx 1967)—of the changes in political economy that lead to rural proletarianization, marginalization, and displacement of peasants; in the course of this process, actions by colonial and postcolonial states against peasant cultivators have been crucial and decisive (see Arrighi 1973; Nonini in press). Here, of course, there has been much variation within and across the regions and over time within our supraregion. I would go so far as to argue that the presence of an advanced process of primitive accumulation is a necessary if not sufficient condition to "attract" rural laborers in sufficient numbers into the new factories.

A sober examination of agrarian conditions in the countries of Southeast Asia and East Asia in the "rim" does not lead one to sanguine conclusions about the alternatives to such "attraction." Most of the countries in capitalist Southeast Asia (i.e., ASEAN) show a long-standing and massive displacement of peasants out of agriculture due to Green Revolution innovations and the sociopolitical changes accompanying them, to stagnating rural productivity (often the result of past state policies), or to a colonial legacy of neglect of and discrimination against the masses of rural farmers; and in countries such as Malaysia, the Philippines, and Indonesia, there can be found large populations of marginalized and displaced peasants made "willing" to enter the gates of the new factories (Nonini in press; Limqueco, McFarlane, and Odhnoff 1989; Mather 1983; also see Pincus 1990).

But there are two sets of conditions under which rural farmers may prove more reluctant to take upon themselves the factory labor offered them by transnational capitalists. The first would be where the process of primitive accumulation has not sufficiently advanced and large populations of land-owning peasants still engage in petty-commodity production in *articulation* with large-scale capitalist enterprise, but not either directly employed by it as rural proletarians nor otherwise under its control.[10] Such may be the case in certain regions of contemporary Thailand. More promising for an alternative are the new mixed socialist/market economies of noncapitalist Southeast Asia, especially that of Vietnam, where rural decollectivization and the emergence of the "product contract system," devolving both productive responsibilities and incomes down to individual households, will increase peasants' commitment to maintain their cultivation, rather than leave their farms for city work, even as Vietnam has recently established special zones to encourage foreign industrial investment (Beresford 1990).

A second set of conditions prevails for Taiwan, where there was significant rural land reform in the 1950s, and for Hong Kong and the New

Territories, where British laissez-faire rule has not sought to disrupt but rather to rationalize rural land tenure (Chun 1991), leaving the rural population largely to develop on its own. In both countries, the peasantry combines agrarian petty-commodity production with family-based commercial ventures and small-scale industrial production (Hu 1983; Deyo 1987). Although both countries are known for their successful export-oriented industrialization, one could predict that in times of global recession, their still viable agrarian economy may provide enclaves of return to absorb retrenched ex-peasant workers and may confer a measure of protection against extreme wage reductions and intensified exploitation by the new factories of the transnationalists. This could allow workers to say to employers, in effect, "Lower than this we will not go, for we would rather go back to the rural natal household." Such at least has been the experience of earlier historical examples (see Loh 1988).

The forms of life associated with petty-commodity production thus represent a reservoir out of which oblique resistance to the exploitation unleashed by transnational capital can grow. The implications of this for the successful transplantation of offshore capital to the regions of "Asia-Pacific," and more generally for the theory of capitalist crisis discussed above, need substantial exploration, and soon.

## The State, Ethnicism, and Dominant Groups in the New Industrial Order

How the tendencies toward spatial displacements just discussed interact with pressures toward ethnic discrimination in the new capitalist regions is an interesting question. The mediating agency here is of course the states of these regions and the groups who control these states. In general, the political and administrative elites who assumed power with the end of colonialism brought with them specific ethnic allegiances (Thomas 1984; see also Geertz 1973). They have enacted state policies and practices that formally and informally label, segregate, discursively divide off, and structurally advantage or disadvantage specific ethnic populations within their territories. These forms of state ethnicism consistute and refashion ethnic differences more than any other factor.[11] Thus there have been, for example in Malaysia, the New Economic Policy of the state that discriminates against non-*bumiputera*, that is, ethnic Chinese and Indians; in Taiwan, Guomindang loyalties to "mainlanders" and the exclusion until recently of native Taiwanese from political leadership and from certain business sectors (Gates 1987: 50–67); in Singapore, the implicit practices of exclusion directed against non-Chinese (Li 1989); and in Indonesia, state bureaucratic favoritism toward Javanese and against non-Javanese—extended at one extreme to the point of ethnocide against recently conquered "West Irian" and East Timorese indigenous peoples (see e.g., Chomsky 1987).

One consequence of these forms of state ethnicism is that certain ethnic groups are systematically excluded from collaboration with the new off-shore capitalist enterprises and from participation in the side benefits (e.g., contracts for services) these generate. What began as a stigmatized civil status then becomes a matter of ecnomic disadvantage as well. In consequence, capitalists, technicians, intellectuals, and other members of these groups either attempt to change their ethnic identities to join dominant ethnic groups, out-migrate (and thereby engage in their own petty spatial fixes), or are relegated to the petty-commodity-producing sectors of these regions. In any event, over time these pressures of exclusion predictably lead to characteristic deformations in capitalist development, particularly in the "newly industrializing countries" of our supraregion. These need urgently to be investigated.

## Conclusion

I would like to conclude by merely asserting without demonstration the sense that the "Asia-Pacific"/"Pacific Rim" neologisms have been taken as seriously as they have been—in the symposium for which this chapter was originally written and elsewhere—because they stand as tropes of a certain kind. They are tropes of the obverse side to the multifarious constructed national identities and perceived national traditions that have heretofore divided off the regions within our supraregion from one another. These national identities and traditions have been, as has been repeatedly pointed out, invented and constituted *ab novo,* puffed up as it were by various "state-forming" elites aiming at power (see Robertson 1990). As Benedict Anderson (1983) so tellingly demonstrates, national communities are *always* imagined, limited, and sovereign—and specific elites are always implicated in these imaginings. But one problem with such factitious identities and traditions is that many people also come to take them very seriously—in a certain sense, through history, the imaginings take on a life of their own.

But what do those in power within the "Asia-Pacific" imaginary do when the contemporary connections of benign commerce and friendly investment aimed at "economic development"—rather than colonialism and war, as was so long the case previously—ostensibly define the economic relationships between regions, but these connections are in fact contradicted by fierce and at times desperate competition between increasingly mature capitalist regions and states—the United States, Japan,

Korea, Taiwan? They respond by finding a way of drawing everyone into a new ecumenism. They invent the "Asia-Pacific" and demand that we take it very, very, seriously.

## Notes

1. Were, for instance, Chinese communities in Hong Kong, Taiwan, and Southeast Asia parts of a "residual China," as claimed by the sinological anthropologist Maurice Freedman in the early 1960s (orig. 1969: 1979: 413–17), or did these communitities constitute a "residual China" only in the sense that although second best, they were still available for study at a time when Western social scientists had no access to the "real" unresidual China that had gone "Red" under Mao Zedong?

2. For instance, graduate programs have emerged in something called "Pacific Rim Studies," scholarly centers (e.g., the East-West Center in Hawaii) have appeared, and conferences such as the one for which this chapter was written have been held.

3. Thus much of contemporary anthropology since the 1960s has consisted of attempts to confront the many theoretical issues about the relationship between these small spaces and "systems" of region and nation—and how such articulation has changed over time. In this connection, see Skinner 1964, 1977; Smith 1976; and Lomnitz-Adler 1991.

4. "This structured coherence . . . embraces the forms and technologies of production (patterns of resource use, inter-industry linkages, forms of organization, size of firm), the technologies, quantities, and qualities of consumption (the standard and style of living of both labour and the bourgeoisie), patterns of labour demand and supply (hierarchies of labour skills and social reproduction processes to ensure the supply of same) and of physical and social infrastructures. . . . The territory within which this structured coherence prevails is loosely defined as that space within which capital can circulate without the limits of profit within socially necessary turnover time being exceeded by the cost and time of movement" (Harvey 1985: 146).

5. The evolutionary theorists who see the putting-out system as belonging to an earlier and "more primitive" stage of capitalism are of course completely refuted by the frequency of its contemporary use under the new regime of accumulation.

6. Tracing the sources and modes of diffusion of this notion through our imaginary would be a worthwhile research task. The costs to workers of the prevalence of this notion are great. For instance, of the 6,200 industrial accidents reported in the state of Penang in Malaysia in 1991, "about 60 percent . . . caused injuries to the fingers of female workers" (*Star* 1992: 20).

7. "The time of production together with the time of circulation of exchange make up the concept of 'the turnover time of capital.' This, too, is an extremely important magnitude. The faster the capital launched into circulation can be recuperated, the greater the profit will be. . . . There is an omnipresent incentive

for individual capitalists to accelerate their turnover time *vis-à-vis* the social average, and in so doing to promote a trend towards faster average turnover times" (Harvey 1989: 229).

8. By invoking Gramsci's concept of "hegemony," I do *not* mean to imply that resistance to hegemony or resistance to class exploitation are absent. However, it appears consistent with Gramsci's use of this concept to distinguish the former from the latter very clearly. Resistance to hegemony takes place in a variety of cultural sites (see Willis 1981 for an example of such resistance by working-class "lads" in British schools), whereas resistance to exploitation in the labor process is in general much more narrowly focused and more often than not manifested in "everyday forms of resistance" (cf. Scott 1985). This distinction is as valid for the "Asia-Pacific" imaginary as elsewhere. The issues involved are complex (see Nonini n.d.).

9. Other sites of exercised hegemony throughout the supraregion can only be noted in passing, but deserve separate treatment: state inculcation of industrial values of obedience, diligence, etc. through the primary and secondary schools; the claims of citizenship and nationality imposed by the state and envisioned to override class differences; and the appeal of consumption-oriented individualism, which would appear to make these differences irrelevant. These elements of hegemony are, I would argue, contra Gramsci (1971), not only ideologies, but also include discourses and their associated practices (Nonini n.d.).

10. For example, in the 1920s and 1930s, independent Malay peasant rubber smallholders in colonial Malaya were able to compete successfully with large-scale European rubber plantations on the international market—until the British rulers intervened with policies favoring the European plantation sector (Nonini in press).

11. By using the term "ethnicism" I wish to distinguish the discourses, ideologies, and practices that order everyday life in terms of ethnic group membership from racism or racialism, which is a sociopolitical and ideological transformation of physical differences between human beings into categories of humanity marked by ranked and incommensurate essences. Racism/racialism is in this sense a post-Enlightenment phenomenon largely unique to the preexisting core states of the "Asia-Pacific," though its effects have been widely disseminated abroad by colonialism.

# References

Ackerman, Susan. 1984. The impact of industrialization on the social role of rural Malay women: A case study of female factory workers in Malacca. In *Women: A Malaysian Focus,* edited by Nik Safiah Karim. Kuala Lumpur: Oxford University Press.

Anderson, Benedict. 1983. *Imagined Communities: Reflections on the Origin and Spread of Nationalism.* London: Verso.

Arnold, Fred, and Suwanlee Piampiti. 1984. Female migration in Thailand. In *Women in the Cities of Asia: Migration and Urban Adapta-*

*tion,* edited by James T. Fawcett, Siew-Ean Khoo, and Peter C. Smith, pp. 143–64. Boulder, CO: Westview.

Arrighi, Giovanni. 1973. Labor supplies in historical perspective: A study of the proletarianization of the African peasantry in Rhodesia. In *Essays on the Political Economy of Africa,* edited by J. Saul and J. Woods, pp. 180–234. New York: Monthly Review Press.

———. 1990. Marxist century—American century: The making and remaking of the world labor movement. In *Transforming the Revolution: Social Movements and the World-System,* edited by Samir Amin et al., pp. 54–95. New York: Monthly Review Press.

Arrigo, Linda Gail. 1984. Taiwan electronics workers. In *Lives: Chinese Working Women,* edited by Janet Salaff. Bloomington: Indiana University Press.

Bello, Walden, David Kinley, and Elaine Elinson. 1982. *Development Debacle: The World Bank in the Philippines.* San Francisco: Institute for Food and Development Policy/Philippines Solidarity Network.

Beresford, Melanie. 1990. Vietnam: Socialist agriculture in transition. *Journal of Contemporary Asia* 20(4): 466–86.

Bluestone, Barry, and Bennett Harrison. 1982. *The Deindustrialization of America: Plant Closings, Community Abandonment and the Dismantling of Basic Industries.* New York: Basic Books.

Boulanger, Clare. 1991. "Working the system": Constructive relations within the West Malaysian workforce. Unpublished Ph.D. dissertation, University of Minnesota.

Charoenloet, Voravidh. 1988. Factory management, skill formation and attitudes of women workers in Thailand: A comparison between an American and a Japanese factory. In *Daughters in Industry: Work, Skills and Consciousness of Women Workers in Asia,* edited by Noeleen Heyzer, pp. 209–36. Kuala Lumpur: Asian and Pacific Development Centre.

———. 1991. Thailand in the process of becoming a NIC: Myth or reality? *Journal of Contemporary Asia* 21(1): 31–41.

Chomsky, Noam.1987. East Timor. In *The Chomsky Reader,* edited by James Peck, pp. 303–12. New York: Pantheon.

Chun, Allen. 1991. La terra trema. Dialectical Anthropology 16(3–4).

Cohen, Robin. 1987. *The New Helots: Migrants in the International Division of Labor.* Aldershot, UK: Avebury.

Davis, Mike. 1989. *City of Quartz.* London: Verso.

Deyo, Frederic C. 1987. State and labor: Modes of political exclusion in East Asian development. In *The Political Economy of the New Asian Industrialism,* edited by F. C. Deyo, pp. 182–202. Ithaca: Cornell University Press.

―――. 1989. *Beneath the Miracle: Labor Subordination in the New Asian Industrialism.* Berkeley: University of California Press.

Elson, D., and R. Pearson. 1981. Nimble fingers make cheap workers: An analysis of women's employment in Third World export manufacturing. *Feminist Review* 7:87–107.

Enloe, Cynthia. 1983. Women textile workers in the militarization of Southeast Asia. In *Women, Men, and the International Division of Labor,* edited by June Nash and Maria Patricia Fernandez-Kelly, pp. 407–25. Albany: State University of New York Press.

Eviota, Elizabeth, and Peter C. Smith. 1984. The migration of women in the Philippines. In *Women in the Cities of Asia: Migration and Urban Adaptation,* edited by James T. Fawcett, Siew-Ean Khoo, and Peter C. Smith, pp. 165–90. Boulder, CO: Westview.

Fernandez-Kelly, Maria Patricia. 1983a. Mexican border industrialization, female labor force participation, and migration. In *Women, Men, and the International Division of Labor,* edited by June Nash and Maria Patricia Fernandez-Kelly, pp. 205–23. Albany: State University of New York Press.

―――. 1983b. *For We Are Sold, I and My People.* Albany: State University of New York Press.

Freedman, Maurice. 1979. Why China? In *The Study of Chinese Society: Essays by Maurice Freedman,* edited and introduced by G. William Skinner, pp. 407–22. Stanford, CA: Stanford University Press.

Galarza, Ernesto. 1971. *Barrio Boy.* Notre Dame, IL: University of Notre Dame Press.

Gates, Hill. 1987. *Chinese Working-Class Lives: Getting by in Taiwan.* Ithaca, NY: Cornell University Press.

Geertz, Clifford. 1973. The new integrative revolution. In *The Interpretation of Culture: Selected Essays.* New York: Basic Books.

Gordon, David M., Richard Edwards, and Michael Reich. 1982. *Segmented Work, Divided Workers: The Historical Transformation of Labor in the United States.* Cambridge, UK: Cambridge University Press.

Gramsci, Antonio. 1971. *Selections from the Prison Notebooks,* edited by Geoffrey Nowell Smith and Quintin Hoare. New York: International Publishers.

Green, Susan S. 1983. Silicon Valley's women workers: A theoretical analysis of sex-segregation in the electronics industry labor market. In *Women, Men, and the International Division of Labor,* edited by June Nash and Maria Patricia Fernandez-Kelly, pp. 273–331. Albany: State University of New York Press.

Grossman, Rachel. 1978–79. Woman's place in the integrated circuit. *Southeast Asia Chronicle 6/Pacific Research 9* (5–6).

Haggard, Stephan, And Tun-jen Cheng. 1987. State and foreign capital in the East Asian NICs. In *The Political Economy of the New Asian Industrialism,* edited by F. C. Deyo, pp. 84–135. Ithaca, NY: Cornell University Press.

Hamilton, Clive. 1983. East Asia's four little tigers. *Journal of Contemporary Asia* 13.

Harvey, David. 1985. The geopolitics of capitalism. In *Social Relations and Spatial Structures,* edited by Derek Gregory and John Urry, pp. 128–63. New York: St. Martin's.

———. 1989. *The Condition of Postmodernity,* Oxford: Basil Blackwell.

Horowitz, David. 1971. Politics and knowledge: An unorthodox history of modern Chinese studies. *Bulletin of Concerned Asian Scholars* 3(3–4): 139–68. (See esp. Appendix: Development of foreign affairs research centers: A selected chronology, pp. 167–68.)

Hu, Tai-li. 1983. The emergence of small-scale industry in a Taiwanese rural community. In *Women, Men, and the International Division of Labor,* edited by June Nash and Maria Patricia Fernandez-Kelly, pp. 387–406. Albany: State University of New York Press.

Huang, Nora Chiang. 1984. The migration of rural women to Taipei. In *Women in the Cities of Asia: Migration and Urban Adaptation,* edited by James T. Fawcett, Siew-Ean Khoo, and Peter C. Smith, pp. 247–68. Boulder, CO: Westview.

Jamilah, Ariffin. 1984. Migration of women workers in Peninsular Malaysia: Impact and implications. In *Women in the Cities of Asia: Migration and Urban Adaptation,* edited by James T. Fawcett, Siew-Ean Khoo, and Peter C. Smith, pp. 213–66. Boulder, CO: Westview.

Kingston, Maxine Hong. 1980. *China Men.* London: Pan Books.

Lefebvre, Henri. 1988. Toward a leftist cultural politics. In *Marxism and the Interpretation of Culture,* edited by Cary Nelson and Lawrence Grossberg, pp. 78–80. Urbana: University of Illinois Press.

Li, Tania. 1989. *Malays in Singapore: Culture, Economic and Ideology* (East Asian Social Science Monographs). Singapore: Oxford University Press.

Lim, Linda Y. C. 1983. Multinational export factories and women workers in the Third World: A review of theory and evidence. *Third World Studies Dependency Papers,* Series 51.

Limqueco, Peter, Bruce McFarlane, and Jan Odhnoff. 1989. *Labour and Industry in ASEAN.* Manila: Journal of Contemporary Asia Publishers.

Lin, Vivian. 1984. Productivity first: Japanese management methods in Singapore. *Bulletin of Concerned Asian Scholars* 16(4): 12–25.

Loh, Francis Kok Wah. 1988. *Beyond the Tin Mines: Coolies, Squatters* and New Villagers in the Kinta Valley, Malaysia, c. 1880–1980. Singapore: Oxford University Press.

Lomnitz-Adler, Claudio. 1991. Concepts for the study of regional culture. American Ethnologist 18(2): 195–214.

Marx, Karl. 1967. Capital: Vol. 1, A Critical Analysis of Capitalist Production. New York: International Publishers.

Mather, Celia E. 1983. Industrialization in the Tangerang Regency of West Java: Women workers and the Islamic patriarchy. Bulletin of Concerned Asian Scholars 15(2): 2–17.

McGee, Terry. 1987. Mass markets—little markets: A call for research on the proletarianization process, women workers, and the creation of demand. In Geography of Gender in the Third World, edited by Janet H. Momsen and Janet G. Townsend, pp. 355–58. Albany: State University of New York Press.

Mehmet, Ozay. 1986. Development in Malaysia: Poverty: Wealth and Trusteeship. London: Croom Helm.

Nash, June. 1983a. Introduction. In Women, Men, and the International Division of Labor, edited by June Nash and Maria Patricia Fernandez-Kelly, pp. vii–xv. Albany: State University of New York Press.

———. 1983b. The impact of the changing international division of labor on different sectors of the labor force. In Women, Men, and the International Division of Labor, edited by June Nash and Maria Patricia Fernandez-Kelly, pp. 3–38. Albany: State University of New York Press.

Nolan, Peter. 1990. Assessing economic growth in the Asian NICs. Journal of Contemporary Asia 20(1): 41–63.

Nonini, Donald M. 1983. The Chinese community of a West Malaysian market town: A study in political economy. Unpublished Ph.D. dissertation, Stanford University.

———. In Press. British Colonial Rule and Malay Peasant Resistance, 1900–1957. New Haven, CT: Yale Southeast Asia Monographs.

———. n.d. Beyond hegemony, beyond resistance: The dialectics of "disputatiousness" and "rice-eating money." Unpublished manuscript, University of North Carolina.

O'Connor, James. 1984. Accumulation Crisis. Oxford: Basil Blackwell.

Ong, Aihwa. 1983. Global industries and Malay peasants in Peninsular Malaysia. In Women, Men, and the International Division of Labor, edited by June Nash and Maria Patricia Fernandez-Kelly, pp. 426–39. Albany: State University of New York Press.

———. 1987. Spirits of Resistance and Capitalist Discipline: Factory Women in Malaysia. Albany: State University of New York Press.

Piampiti, Suwanlee. 1984. Female migrants in Bangkok metropolis. In Women in the Cities of Asia: Migration and Urban Adaptation, edited by James T. Fawcett, Siew-Ean Khoo, and Peter C. Smith, pp. 227–46. Boulder, CO: Westview.

Pincus, Jonathan. 1990. Approaches to the political economy of agrarian change in Java. *Journal of Contemporary Asia* 20(1): 3–40.

Pineda-Ofreneo, Roalinda. 1987. Women in the electronics industry in the Philippines. In *Technology and Gender: Women's Work in Asia,* edited by Cecilia Ng, pp. 92–106. Serdang, Malaysia: Women's Studies Unit, University Pertanian Malaysia and Malaysian Social Science Association.

Pineda-Ofreneo, Rosalinda, and Rosario del Rosario. 1988. Filipino women workers in strike actions. In *Daughters in Industry: Work, Skills, and Consciousness of Women Workers in Asia,* edited by Noeleen Heyzer, pp. 308–26. Kuala Lumpur: Asian and Pacific Development Centre.

Rajah, Rasiah. 1981. Reorganization of production in the semi-conductor industry and its impact on Penang's position in East Asia. In *Images of Malaysia,* edited by Muhammad Ikmal Said and Johan Saravanamuttu, pp. 203–23. Kuala Lumpur: Persatuan Sains Sosial Malaysia.

Roberts, Moss. 1971. The structure and direction of contemporary Chinese Studies. *Bulletin of Concerned Asian Scholars* 3(3–4): 113–38.

Robertson, Roland. 1990. After nostalgia? Wilful nostalgia and the phases of globalization. In *Theories of Modernity and Postmodernity,* edited by Bryan S. Turner, pp. 45–61. London: Sage.

Robison, Richard. 1986. *Indonesia: The Rise of Capital* (Southeast Asia Publication Series, 13, Asian Studies Association of Australia). North Sydney: Unwin Hyman.

Rodan, Garry. 1989. *The Political Economy of Singapore's Industrialization: National State and International Capital.* London: Macmillan.

Rosa, Linda. 1990. The Singapore state and trade union incorporation. *Journal of Contemporary Asia* 20(4): 487–508.

Scott, James C. 1985. *Weapons of the Weak: Everyday Forms of Peasant Resistance.* New Haven, CT: Yale University Press.

Singhanetra-Renard, Anchalee. 1987. Non-farm employment and female labour mobility in northern Thailand. In *Geography of Gender in The Third World,* edited by Janet H. Momsen and Janet G. Townsend, pp. 258–74. Albany: State University of New York Press.

Skinner, G. William. 1964. Marketing and social structure in rural China. *Journal of Asian Studies* 24: 3–43.

———. 1977. Cities and the hierarchy of local systems. In *The City in Late Imperial China,* edited by G. William Skinner, pp. 275–351. Stanford, CA: Stanford University Press.

Smith, Carol A. 1976. Regional economic systems: Linking geographical models and socioeonomic problems. In *Regional Analysis: Vol. 1, Eco-*

*nomic Systems,* edited by Carol A. Smith, pp. 3–63. New York: Academic Press.

Snow, Robert. 1979. Multinational corporations in Asia: The labor-intensive factory. *Bulletin of Concerned Asian Scholars* 11(4): 26–39.

———. 1983. The new international division of labor and the U.S. workforce: The case of the electronics industry. In *Women, Men, and the International Division of Labor,* edited by June Nash and Maria Patricia Fernandez-Kelly, pp. 39–69. Albany: State University of New York Press.

Southeast Asia Chronicle/Pacific Research. 1978–79. Changing role of the S.E. Asian women. Special joint issue of *Southeast Asia Chronicle 6/Pacific Research 9* (5–6): 1–27.

*Star.* 1992. Sosco: Industrial mishaps on the rise in Penang. *Star* (Penang), May 13, 1992, p. 20.

Stivens, Maila. 1986. Becoming workers: The social context of female labour migration in Rembau, Negri Semibilan. In *Women's Studies in Malaysia,* edited by Wendy Smith and Ariffin Jamilah. Singapore: Institute of Southeast Asian Studies.

Strauch, Judith. 1984. Women in rural-urban circulation networks: Implications for social structural change. In *Women in the Cities of Asia: Migration and Urban Adaptation,* edited by James T. Fawcett, Siew-Ean Khoo, and Peter C. Smith, pp. 60–80. Boulder, CO: Westview.

Takaki, Ronald. 1983. *Pau Hana: Plantation Life and Labor in Hawaii, 1835–1920.* Honolulu: University of Hawaii Press.

Thomas, Clive. 1984. *The Rise of the Authoritarian State in Peripheral Societies.* New York: Monthly Review Press.

Wad, Peter. 1989. Socio-cultural aspects of working-class formation: A study of industrial and labour relations in Malaysian manufacturing enterprises. In *Southeast Asia Between Autocracy and Democracy,* edited by Mikael Gravers et al., pp. 150–74 Aarhus, Denmark: Aarhus University Press.

Weston, Kath. 1990. Production as means, production as metaphor: Women's struggle to enter the trades. In *Uncertain Terms: Negotiating Gender in American Culture,* edited by Faye Ginsburg and Alma Tsing, pp. 137–51. Boston: Beacon.

Willis, Paul. 1981. *Learning to Labor: How Working Class Kids Get Working Class Jobs.* New York: Columbia University Press.

*Part Two*

# The Political Economy of the Pacific

# 6

# The Northeast Asian Political Economy

## BRUCE CUMINGS

East Asia today is the center of world economic dynamism. Japan in 1980 became number two in the world in gross national product (GNP). Its achievement is complemented by the "gang of four," South Korea, Taiwan, Singapore, and Hong Kong. These four East Asian developing countries now account for almost twice the export totals of the entire remainder of the Third World, and their growth rates are usually the highest in the entire world. Singapore and Hong Kong are difficult to categorize: are they nations? industrial platforms? city-states? My concern in this article will be with the northeastern portion of the East Asian basin: Japan, Korea, and Taiwan.

These four nations (including the two Koreas) in 1978, before the second oil shock, accounted for a combined GNP of about $1.06 trillion, a population of 190 million, an annual growth rate of 10 percent, and perhaps $232 billion of world trade. This compared to a U.S. GNP in 1978 of about $2 trillion, a population of 218 million, a growth rate of 4 percent, and world trade of $326 billion. Apart from the United States, no other region had a higher GNP—the combined GNP of the European Economic Community in 1978 was $1.95 trillion, less than double the Northeast Asian figure, and the average growth rate in the EEC was 2.9 percent. The Soviet Union had a larger population but a lower GNP, and a growth rate estimated at 3.1 percent.

Since the onset of export-led growth in the mid-1960s the GNPs of both Taiwan and South Korea have grown by an average of about 10 percent per year, with manufacturing expansion often doubling that figure. North Korea, according to official statistics, had the highest rate of agricultural growth in the entire world in the period 1970–78, and since the Korean War its industrial production has grown at the highest rate in the socialist world.[1] In the space of one generation these countries have transformed their economic structures such that the agrarian sector, including upwards of 60 percent of the population in 1960, now accounts for less than 20 percent of GNP. It is little wonder that American developmentalists speak of miracles in Taiwan and South Korea, or that socialist economists like Joan Robinson speak of a miracle in North Korea. For reasons of space, however, I shall limit this analysis primarily to South Korea and Taiwan.

A glance back before World War II suggests that we may need a longer perspective to capture the true dimensions of this growth. Japan's interwar annual growth rate of 4.5 percent doubled the rates of interwar Europe; colonial manufacturing growth in Korea, 1910–1940, averaged 10 percent per annum, and overall GNP growth was also in the 4 percent range, as was Taiwan's. No nation's heavy-industrial growth rate was steeper than Japan's in the period 1931–1940. In the textile sector, Japan's automation was ahead of Europe's in 1930. Yet new research now suggests that both Korea and Taiwan experienced higher GDP growth rates than Japan between 1911 and 1938 (Japan, 3.36 percent; Korea, 3.57 percent; Taiwan, 3.80 percent).[2]

In the past century Japan, Korea, and Taiwan have also moved fluidly through a classic product-cycle industrialization pattern, Korea and Taiwan following in Japan's wake. Japan's industrialization has gone through three phases, the last of which is just beginning. The first phase began in the 1880s, with textiles the leading sector, and lasted through Japan's rise to world power. In the mid-1930s Japan began the second, heavy phase, based on steel, chemicals, armaments, and ultimately automobiles; it did not begin to end until the mid-1960s. The third phase emphasizes high-technology "knowledge" industries such as electronics, communications, computers, and silicon-chip microprocessors.

Within Japan each phase, in good product-cycle fashion, has been, marked by strong state protection for nascent industries, adoption of foreign technologies, and comparative advantages deriving from cheap labor costs, technological innovation, and "lateness" in world time. Each phase involved a bursting forth into the world market that always struck foreign observers as abrupt and unexpected, thus inspiring fear and loathing, awe and admiration.

For Japan the product cycle has not been mere theory; it has melded with conscious practice to make Japan the preeminent example of upward mobility in the world system through successive waves of industrial competition. In the 1930s Kaname Akamatsu elaborated his famous "flying geese" model of industrial development in follower countries, predating Raymond Vernon's work by several decades.[3] Time-series curves for imports, import-substitution for the domestic market, and subsequent exports of given products tend to form a pattern like wild geese flying in ranks. The cycle in given industries—textiles, steel, automobiles, light electronics—of origin, rise, apogee, and decline has not simply been marked, but often mastered, in Japan; in each industrial life cycle there is also an appropriate jumping off place, that is, a point at which it pays to let others make the product or at least provide the labor. Taiwan and Korea have historically been receptacles for declining Japanese industries. Adding agriculture gives a pattern in which in the first quarter of this century Korea and Taiwan substituted for the diminishing Japanese agricultural sector, exporting rice and sugar in great amounts to the mother country (Taiwan was annexed in 1895, Korea in 1910). By the mid-1930s Japan had begun to export iron and steel, chemicals, and electric generation industries, although much more to Korea than to Taiwan. In the 1960s and 1970s both smaller countries have received declining textile and consumer electronic industries from Japan (as well as from the United States), and in the 1980s some Japanese once again speak of sending steel and autos in the same direction.

Thus if there has been a miracle in East Asia, it has not occurred just since 1960; it would be profoundly ahistorical to think that it did. Furthermore, it is misleading to assess the industrialization pattern in any one of these countries: such an approach misses, through a fallacy of disaggregation, the fundamental unity and integrity of the regional effort in this century. Yet ahistorical disaggregation is the most common approach; it is reinforced by the many differences between the three countries, and by the dominant modernization school in U.S. academic circles, which has produced by far the greatest quantity of literature on East Asian development. The three countries speak different languages, have different histories, different cultures (albeit all traditionally influenced by China), and, in Korea and Japan, two highly homogeneous but quite different ethnic constituencies. Modernization theory and these basic differences have reinforced a tendency, at least since 1945, to view each country apart from the others and to examine single country trajectories. Furthermore, critical and radical (or nonmodernization) developmentalists have tended to ignore East Asia, focusing instead on Latin America and Africa. Those that do study East Asia usually study the Chinese revolution, which produced many things but not stunning industrial development.

A country-by-country approach is incapable of accounting for the remarkably similar trajectories of Korea and Taiwan. Thus, specialists on Korea argue that its development success "is unique in world history";[4] Taiwan specialists make similar claims. Thus, Taiwan specialists cite the apparent "paradox" of Taiwanese development—that it developed in a fashion that contradicts the assumptions of dependency theorists—while not breathing a word about Korea.[5] Both groups of specialists omit the essential Japanese context of Korean and Taiwanese development. Conventional neoclassical economists attribute growth in Taiwan or Korea to specific attributes of each nation: factor endowments, human capital in the form of a reasonably educated workforce, comparative advantage in labor cost, and so on. Modernization theorists offer a diffuse menu of explanations for Taiwan or Korea, ranging from the discipline or "rationality" of traditional Confucianism, through various cultural arguments, the passion for education, U.S. aid and advice, and the presumed "natural" workings of the product cycle, to the diffusion of advanced education, science, and technology.[6] Political arguments about the alleged big power of small states, while addressing one facet of East Asian political development, beg the question why Korea and Taiwan but not Guatemala or Burma. Product-cycle arguments, unlike the others, do have the virtue of linking Japanese with Korean and Taiwanese development, but their proponents do not explain why the cycle has conformed to theory in Northeast Asia so much better than elsewhere.

This article asserts that an understanding of the Northeast Asian political economy can only emerge from an approach that posits the systemic interaction of each country with the others, and of the region with the world at large. Rapid upward mobility in the world economy has occurred, through the product cycle and other means, within the context of two hegemonic systems: the Japanese imperium to 1945, and intense, if diffuse, American hegemony since the late 1940s. Furthermore, only considerations of context can account for the similarities in the Taiwanese and South Korean political economies. Simultaneously, external hegemonic forces have interacted with different domestic societies in Korea and Taiwan to produce rather different political outcomes: this, too, has been characteristic throughout the century. Korea was more rebellious in 1910; it is more rebellious today. I seek, therefore, to explain both the similarities in economic development and the differences in political consequences in the three countries.

## Some Theoretical Considerations

The concept of the product cycle offers a useful way to understand change and mobility within and among nations. This theory of the middle range has the virtue of being compatible with liberal, neomercantile, and Marxist or world system theories. That is, the neoclassical liberal can make the Ricardian assumption that a system of open exchange (free trade) provides the structure in which nations maximize their comparative advantages and thus create a world-ranging and mutually beneficial division of labor. The mercantilist can make the Listian assumption that free trade is the ideology of the early-arriving hegemonic nation, and that to catch up the follower nation needs not laissez-faire but a strong state, not open systems but protectionist barriers. For a world system analyst the product cycle is one among several means of upward and downward mobility; the core assumption is the existence of a capitalist world economy that, at least in our time, is the only world-ranging system. Thus, the core power pursues an imperialism of free trade, and rising powers use strong states, protectionist barriers, or a period of withdrawal and self-reliant development (the Stalinist or socialist option) as means to compete within the world system.[7]

All three theories assume that the product cycle is a middle-range explanation for the waxing and waning of industrial sectors, and that it is imbedded in some larger structure—an international division of labor or a world economy. All likewise assume intense competitions—a race—for development; nations swim upstream, against the current, or are carried backward. Both Liberal and Marxist theory postulate a utopia to end the struggle: a world of free trade and the greatest good for the greatest number, or societies submitted to a rational plan under a world socialist government. Mercantilists are content to postulate a survival of the fittest, by whatever means necessary.

The world system perspective posits a tripartite division of the globe: core, semiperiphery, and periphery. A tripartite hierarchy appeals to many analysts: Aristotle was the first to note the social stability provided by a broad middle class, and Charles Kindleberger pointed out many years ago that in a hierarchy of top, middle, and low the middle functions "to discipline the third member in forms of behavior which he should adopt toward the first. The "relations of the middle class to the wealthy and to the working classes may partake of this character. . . ."[8]

Immanuel Wallerstein, a sociologist by academic origin, casts onto the global system the classic role of the middle class in providing social stability, disciplining and mediating those below to serve the interests of those above, and being an agency of change, through class or individual social mobility.[9] This is the role for the semiperiphery in the world; the means of upward mobility are wars, diplomacy, alliances, product cycles, and so on.[10]

What about the "world upper class," or core? I use the term *hegemony* to refer to core-state behavior. By hegemony I do not mean the Gramscian notion of class ethos, nor a crude Marxist notion of ruling class or imperial domination, nor the diffuse contemporary Chinese usage referring to bigpower domination in all its manifestations. Nor do I use it in Robert Keohane and Joseph Nye's sense "in which one state is able and willing to determine and maintain the essential rules by which relations among states are govemed."[11] I mean by hegemony the demarcation of outer limits in economics, politics, and international security relationships, the transgression of which carries grave risks for any nonhegemonic nation.

In the postwar American case, hegemony meant the demarcation of a "grand area."[12] Within that area nations oriented themselves toward Washington rather than Moscow; nations were enmeshed in a hierarchy of economic and political preferences whose ideal goal was free trade, open systems, and liberal democracy but which also encompassed neomercantile states and authoritarian politics; and nations were dealt with by the United States through methods ranging from classic negotiations and trade-offs (in regard to nations sharing Western traditions or approximating American levels of political and economic development) to wars and interventions (in the periphery or Third World), to assure continuing orientation toward Washington. The hegemonic ideology, shared by most Americans but by few in the rest of the world, was the Tocquevillean or Hartzian ethos of liberalism and internationalism, assuming a born-free country that never knew class conflict. Not a colonial or neocolonial imperialism, it was a new system of empire begun with Wilson and consummated by Roosevelt and Acheson. Its very breadth—its nonterritoriality, its universalism, and its open systems (within the grand area) made for a style of hegemony that was more open than previous imperialisms to competition from below. Indeed, we may eventually conclude that this was its undoing.

This form of hegemony establishes a hierarchy of nations, therefore, but not one that is frozen: it may render obsolescent the development of underdevelopment. Instead, far more than the German hegemony in Eastern Europe that Albert Hirschman analyzed or the Japanese unilateral, colonial hegemony, it is open to rising talent from below and particularly to disparities of attention (what Burke, speaking of England and the American colonial revolution, called "wise and salutary neglect") that give leverage and room for maneuver to dependencies. As Hirschman put it more recently, the dependent country "is likely to pursue its escape from domination more actively and energetically than the dominant country will work on preventing this escape."[13] Finally, this form of hegemony also fused security and economic considerations so inextricably that the United States has never been sure whether economic competition from its allies is good or bad for grand-area security. As a result, inattention often becomes catatonia (witness U.S. policy toward Japan in the past decade). A diffuse hegemony, then, it perhaps merits a diffuse definition: we know it in the doing, and we mark it more in retrospect. American postwar hegemony grew less out of specific human design (although Dean Acheson as architect would come close) than out of the long-term reaction of hegemonic interests to the flow of events.

These various terms and concepts are applicable to the international system. But Kindleberger notes in a seminal paper that foreign-policy actions and reactions are imbedded "deep in the structure of society." In one nation (e.g., Germany) class may be important in understanding foreign economic policy; in another (e.g., Britain) it may not.[14] Likewise, in nations the state may be strong or weak, and empirical investigation suggests that this bears little relationship to Wallerstein's strained argument that state power recedes as one climbs down the hierarchy from core to periphery. In Japan, Taiwan, and Korea, much of their success and their variance from one another may be explained by reference to state and society. For the strength of states, we can use Alexander Gerschenkron's sequencing argument and Stephen Krasner's simple scheme: strong states can formulate policy goals independently of particular groups, they can change group or class behavior, and they can change the structure of society.[15] (After all the inflated verbiage, this is fundamentally what Nicos Poulantzas had in mind when he referred to the "relative autonomy" of capitalist states.).[16] Japan, as Krasner notes, rates as very strong on this scale; so, in the later periods, do South Korea and Taiwan. Indeed, these three strong states go far toward explaining their product-cycle virtuosity.

Finally, there is society, by which I mean both the conventional notion of a system structured by groups and classes and Karl Polanyi's sense of society being the human web that reacts to market penetration, capitalist relations, and industrialization in varying but always critical ways around the globe.[17] Attention to society and its reactions can avoid the reductionism of some Wallersteinians who place inordinate emphasis on the structuring effect of the world system on national societies, as if they are putty to be shaped and molded. In fact, in the Northeast Asian case the three different societies deeply affect the development of the national and regional political economies.

## The Origin of the Northeast Asian Political Economy, 1900–1945

However much it may pain the majority of Korean nationalists and the minority of Taiwanese nationalists, the place to begin in comprehending the region's economic dynamism is with the advent of Japanese imperialism. Japan's imperial experience differed from the West's in several fundamental respects.[18] It involved the colonization of contiguous territory; it involved the location of industry and an infrastructure of communications and transportation in the colonies, bringing industry to the labor and raw materials rather than vice versa; and it was accomplished by a country that always saw itself as disadvantaged and threatened by more advanced countries. Japan was "weak and puny," Professor Eto Shinkichi has written, and this perception affected the entire colonial enterprise. All of these characteristics made themselves felt most strongly in Korea, the closest and always the most important of Japan's possessions.

Japan entered upon colonization late, in a world with hundreds of years of colonial experience and where, as King Leopold of Belgium said three years before the Meiji Restoration, "the world has been pretty well pillaged already." Most of the good colonial territories were already spoken for; indeed, for several decades Japan faced the possibility of becoming a dependency, perhaps even a colony, of one of the Western powers. With imperial attention mostly focused on China and its putative vast market, however, Japan got what E. H. Norman called a "breathing space" in which to mobilize its resources and resist the West. Its success was manifest in victories over China and Russia within the decade 1895 to 1905, but that should blind us neither to Japan's perception of its position as poised between autonomy and dependency in a highly competitive world system nor to the very real threats posed by the West. While the British and the Americans marveled at Japanese industrial and military prowess at the turn of the century, the Kaiser sent his famous "yellow peril" mural to the Tsar and the French worried about Japanese skills being tied to a vast pool of Chinese labor, posing a dire threat to the West. In such circumstances the Japanese were hardly prone to worry about the sensitivities of Taiwanese or Koreans but rather to see them as resources to be deployed in a global struggle; and, of course, Japan never lacked for Westerners (including socialists like Sydney and Beatrice Webb, and hardy Americans like Theodore Roosevelt) who were quick to justify Japanese aggression.[19]

The relative lateness of the endeavor imparted several additional characteristics: first, a posthaste, anticipatory quality in colonial planning; second, an extraordinary interest in and mimicking of previous colonial experience; third, a rather quick anachronism to the whole enterprise; last, little choice but to colonize contiguous neighbors.

Many have spoken of Japan's defensive reform and industrialization after 1868; and so it was with Japan's colonial expansion—offensive to Taiwanese and Koreans, it looked defensive to Japanese planners in a predatory world. And, much like reform at home, the colonial effort had an anticipatory, preconceived, planned aspect. The characteristic figure in this architectonic endeavor was therefore not an adventurous Cecil Rhodes type but an administrator and planner like Goto Shimpei, who played the architect in the Taiwan colony.

Like MITI in the Japanese economy today, the colonizers exercised sharp "administrative guidance" in shaping colonial society. These planners would both mimic the West and seek to avoid its errors. Thus, Ito Hirobumi discovered the secret of the German state, colonial administrators studied French policies of assimilation, architects designed railroad stations in the classic style for Seoul and Taipei. When Europeans witnessed Japanese behavior, they were looking into a mirror of their own behavior.

There was also something anachronistic about Japanese imperialism, perhaps not in the seizure of Taiwan but certainly by 1910 with Korea, and a fortiori 1931 with Manchuria. Japan since the 1880s has always seemed in some vague way to be about twenty years behind European and American developments, and therefore to be persisting in the lathered pursuit of things the West was tiring of; today, for example, an automobile boom runs in Japan some two decades after the boom began ending in the United States. By 1910 strong anti-imperialist movements had developed in England and the United States, and shortly therafter Woodrow Wilson was not only calling for self-determination in colonies but pursuing an American neoimperialism that envisioned organizing great spaces in the world for free trade and competition, thereby branding the exclusive possession of colonial territory as outmoded or immoral, or both. Another great power, Russia, emerged from World War I with an equally potent idea: self-determination and national revolution for colonial peoples. Wilson and Lenin both changed the rules of the game for latecomers like Japan. The swashbuckling, swordcarrying colonist suddenly looked like a museum exhibit to the modern world that Japan took as its constant reference after 1868. Thus, seeking to anticipate every eventuality, Japan met an unanticipated consequence: Progressives proclaimed Japan to be a backward exemplar of nineteenth century ideas.

In order to acquire colonies in the first place, Japan had to maximize its comparative advantages by seeking territory close to home. The West, always stretched in East Asia, could in judo-like fashion be dispatched in the near reaches of Japan. Thus, unlike most colonial powers Japan colonized neighboring countries, making feasible a close, tight integration of colony to metropole. Contiguity also facilitated the settling of colonial migrants, especially from among an insular, homogeneous people who abhor distance from the native source, and could raise the potential of extraordinarily rapid exchange time in market relations. Japan quickly enhanced this potential through laying railroads, opening ports, and making heavy investments in communications.

Lateral expansion also meant that Japan preferred the military, in the form of a land army resident in the colony, as its coercive force—not a navy or a tiny cadre of colonial ministers, a la Britain. As Hannah Arendt once suggested, lateral imperialism is usually more repressive, and this was true of Japanese colonialism.

In Korea and Taiwan the colonial power emphasized not only military and police forms of control but also development under strong state auspices. This was particularly true after the Depression, when Japan used a "mighty trio" of state organization, central banking, and *zaibatsu* conglomerates to industrialize Korea and parts of Manchuria. Although strong in both colonies, the state in Korea bulked even larger in the economy than in Taiwan, as figures on government capital formation show.[20] Much like its role in the decades after the Meiji Restoration, the state substituted for an absent or at most incipient entrepreneurial class. As David Landes writes of Japan, "it was the State that conceived modernization as a goal and industrialization as a means, that gave birth to the new economy in haste and pushed it unrelentingly as an ambitious mother her child prodigy. And though the child grew and developed its own resources, it never overcame the deformity imposed by this forced nurture."[21]

The deformations were even more marked in Korea and Taiwan, where the colonial state stood above and apart from societies that had not yet reached Japan's level of social, political, and economic development. Thus, a highly articulated, disciplined, penetrating colonial bureaucracy substituted both for the traditional regimes and for indigenous groups and classes that under "normal" conditions would have accomplished development themselves. The colonial state replaced an old weak state, holding society at bay so to speak; this experience goes a long way toward explaining the subsequent (post-1945) pronounced centralization of Taiwan and both Koreas, and has provided a model for state-directed development in all three.

Japan's administrative and coercive colonialism took two quite different societies and political economies, and molded them into look-alikes.[22] The first act was a major cadastral survey and land reform: 1898–1906 in Taiwan, 1910–18 in Korea. North-South trunk railroad lines were laid. Ports were opened. In Taiwan, cane sugar and to a lesser extent rice were promoted; by 1938 Taiwan was second only to Cuba in sugar exports. Korean rice exports expanded by leaps and bounds in the 1920s. Yet agricultural growth was stronger in Taiwan than in Korea; colonial administrators remarked that what could be done with economic incentives in Taiwan required coercion in Korea.

Here we have our first important societal reaction to hegemonic penetration. Whereas Taiwan had for the most part only an aboriginal population until the eighteenth century, and a small class of Chinese absentee landlords by the end of the nineteenth century, (the *dazuhu*), Korea had a powerful landed class of centuries' duration, in which property holding and aristocratic privilege were potently mixed.[23] The Japanese found it expedient to root landlord more firmly to the ground, as a means of disciplining peasants and extracting rice for the export market. The landlord class therefore persisted through to 1945, although by then it was tainted by association with imperial rule. In Taiwan, by contrast, land reform at the turn of the century eliminated absentee lords and fostered a class of entrepreneurial landowners, emerging "from below" as they had in Japan. By 1945 most Taiwan landowners held less land than their Korean counterparts and were far more productive. Whereas tenancy increased markedly in Korea, it actually decreased in Taiwan between 1910 and 1941. Samuel Ho has concluded that by 1945 agriculture in Taiwan was quite changed and change had occurred "without disrupting the traditional system of peasant cultivation."[24] Korea on the other hand, had frequent peasant protests and rebellions, guerrilla movements in the border region, and above all a huge population movement off the land that severely disrupted the agrarian political economy.[25] In other words, Korea betrayed most of the features associated with colonial underdevelopment, Taiwan did not. It may be that the very existence of Korea, and subsequently Manchukuo, gave Taiwan its own "breathing space" within the regional imperium. In any case, its experience did not conform to the predictions of dependency theorists. And, of course, Taiwan produced a weak nationalist impulse, Korea an extraordinarily strong one.

In the 1930s Japan largely withdrew from the world system and pursued, with its colonies, a self-reliant, go-it-alone path to development that not only generated remarkably high industrial growth rates but changed the face of Northeast Asia. In this decade what we might call the "natural economy" of the region was created; although it was not natural, its rational division of labor and set of possibilities have skewed East Asian development ever since. Furthermore, during this period, Japan elaborated many of the features of the neomercantile state still seen today. One prescient writer in the mid-1930s speculated that Japan's heavy industrialization spurt was so impressive that "if world trade were not restricted by tariff walls and import quotas . . . Japan might become the largest exporter in the world—and in a very short time." Guenther Stein saw in this spurt "the beginning of a new epoch in the industrialization of the world.[26] He was right on both counts. (This is not the usual dating: the watershed years of 1945–50 are presumed to have remade Japan, but, as we shall see, they did not).

The definitive work by Kazushi Ohkawa and Henry Rosovsky sees two "long swings" of Japanese industrial growth in this century, one in the 1930s and the other in the post 1955 period; the first was only marginally less successful. The 1930s' development rested on the "two sturdy legs" of cheap labor and "a great inflow of technology," followed by massive state investments or subsidies to *zaibatsu* investors. Exports were still mostly "light," mainly textiles; but iron and steel, chemicals, hydroelectric power, aluminum, and infrastructure (transport and communications) grew markedly in the imperium.[27] What is so often forgotten is that this spurt located industry in the colonies as well.

Japan is among the very few imperial powers to have located modern heavy industry in its colonies: steel, chemicals, hydroelectric facilities in Korea and Manchuria, and automobile production for a time in the latter. Even today, China's industry remains skewed toward the Northeast, and North Korea has always had a relatively advanced industrial structure. Samuel Ho remarks that, by the end of the colonial period, Taiwan "had an industrial superstructure to provide a strong foundation for future industrialization"; the main industries were hydroelectric, metallurgy (especially aluminum), chemicals, and an advanced transport system. By 1941, factory employment, including mining, stood at 181,000 in Taiwan. Manufacturing grew at an annual average rate of about 8 percent during the 1930s.[28]

Industrial development was much greater in Korea, perhaps because of the relative failure of agrarian growth compared to Taiwan but certainly because of Korea's closeness both to Japan and to the Chinese hinterland. By 1940, 213,000 Koreans were working in industry, excluding miners, and not counting the hundreds of thousands of Koreans who migrated to factory or mine work in Japan proper and in Manchuria. Net value of mining and manufacturing grew by 266 percent between 1929 and 1941.[29] By 1945 Korea had an industrial infrastructure that, although sharply skewed toward metropolitan interests, was among the best developed in the Third World. Furthermore, both Korea and Taiwan had begun to take on semiperipheral characteristics. Korea's developing periphery was Manchuria, where it sent workers, merchants, soldiers, and bureaucrats who occupied a middle position between Japanese overlords and Chinese peasants; as Korean rice was shipped to Japan, millet was imported from Manchuria to feed Korean peasants in a classic core-semiperiphery-periphery relationship. As for Taiwan, its geographic proximity to Southeast Asia and South China made it "a natural location for processing certain raw materials brought in from, and for producing some manufactured goods for export to, these areas."[30]

The Japanese managed all this by combining a handful of *zaibatsu*, several big banks, and the colonial state structures. They also foisted upon Koreans and Taiwanese an ideology of incorporation emphasizing a structural, family principle and an ethical filiality: the imperium was one (not-so) happy family with Emperor Hirohito as the father. Although the colonized peoples (especially Koreans) remember this period with intense loathing—the forced Emperor worship, the alien Shinto beliefs, the requirement to speak Japanese and take Japanese names—the fact remains that as Taiwan and Korea have industrialized in the postwar period they have fostered *zaibatsu-like* conglomerates, with extensive family interpenetration, and ideologies of familial hierarchy and filial loyalty (the "New Life" movement in Taiwan, the "New Spirit" movement in 1970s South Korea, a corporate familism in North Korea).[31]

Although Taiwan seemed to emerge from the last phase of colonialism relatively unscathed, with few disruptions, Korea was profoundly transformed. The period from 1935 to 1945 was when Korea's industrial revolution began, with most of the usual characteristics: uprooting of peasants from the land, the emergence of a working class, widespread population mobility, and urbanization. Because the Japanese industrialized from above, however, social change accompanying this revolution was greatest in the lower reaches of society. The social and regional conflicts that racked Korea in the 1945–53 period have their origins in the immense population shifts, agrarian disruptions, and industrial dynamism of the final phase of the Japanese imperialism. This was truly a decade-long pressure cooker; the lifting of the lid in 1945 deeply affected Korea.[32] But Japan, too, was deeply changed by the experience. Japan was remade in this period.

The modern Japanese state, well described in its contemporary features elsewhere,[33] was initially the great work of the Meiji oligarchs. But it was in the 1930s that it took on many of the neomercantile features that persist today: its virtuosity in moving through the product cycle, from old to new industries; the extraordinary role for the bureaucracy and key agencies like MITI, exercising "administrative guidance" throughout the economy; the peculiar vehicles for credit, which account for much of the mobility in and out of industries; the role of large conglomerates; the systematic exclusion of labor from most important decision making; and the high rates of exploitation of poorly paid female labor.

The imperatives of late development in a predatory world shaped more in the 1930s than in any other period, amid the general breakdown of the world system. Sharp competition precipitated remarkable unity at home. The militarist aggression and street politics of the young radicals blind us to the formidable coalition that came together within Japan during the decade. Chalmers Johnson argues that this period saw the emergence of three key features. The first was national planning and industrialist strategy that extended to most major industries in Japan. Its only American counterparts are isolated experiences like the Manhattan Project or the space program. The second was the structural features of the MITI function in the years 1939–43 (even though MITI had not yet appeared), including key managerial personnel ("old cadres") who persisted long into the postwar period. And the third was the role for the state and credit institutions that is by now the mark of the Japanese model.[34] G. C. Allen has argued that Japan owed industrial success in the 1930s to "structural adaptability" that came from systematic state subsidization and protection of new industries, and credit institutions that treated investment funds in very mobile fashion. Allen suggests that Japan's ability to centralize credit institutions and industry "under a single control" was a great comparative advantage at the time, although such concentration was also a measure of the immaturity of the Japanese economy: with capital weak and many producers still in traditional sectors, the state had to select and foster large industries and banks. Like Johnson, he finds "an identifiable thread of continuity" from this period to the contemporary era.[35] Ohkawa and Rosovsky also trace the practice of administrative guidance to the 1930s, with state planning agencies being central to the surveying of the foreign technology scene, the import of technology, licensing, allocation of foreign exchange to importers, and so on.[36] These early agencies, and their MITI successor, in effect were the directors of Japan's movement through the product cycle.

Behind everything in Japan there seems to have been a bank. In the 1930s the Big Four *zaibatsu* controlled four of the six biggest banks; their integrated financial power made it possible to mobilize and direct capital, achieving great and rapid adaptability. The banks, official and semi-official, along with the *zaibatsu*, "provided the chief means by which the government promoted industries of national importance."[37] Thus, the forerunners of MITI provided the goals, and the banks and corporations the means, for directing and riding the product cycle.

The prewar *zaibatsu* were family-interpenetrated conglomerates that used feudal-holdover ideologies to incorporate workers "as fellow clansmen who devote themselves to the services of their overlord." By the end of the 1930s, Mitsui, Mitsubishi, and Sumitomo controlled half the copper and coal production, half the total ship tonnage, 70 percent of flour milling, 90 percent of paper production, most of the aircraft industry, nearly all sugar refining, and, with some smaller and newer *zaibatsu*, nearly all of the colonial industrialization in Korea, Manchuria, and Taiwan.[38] The *zaibatsu* and the state combined to accomplish a thorough repression and incorporation of labor, leading in the 1940s to a forced military-style discipline in the factories that long left its mark on the working class. Women were particularly exploited: they received much lower wages than men for similar work, and predominated in the older textile sector. Finally, at the bottom were more than a million Korean laborers in Japan, men and women harshly regimented for the most difficult sorts of industrial work and subjected to invidious racial discrimination.

In the postwar period Japan was shorn of a few features of its 1930s political economy. But in Taiwan and later South Korea, the 1930s model reappeared in nearly all its aspects, including militarization and harsh repression of labor.

## The Postwar Settlement and the Emergence of a New Hegemony

In September 1945, as U.S. occupation forces filtered into Japan, an American officer walked into a Mitsui office in Tokyo and introduced himself. A man in the office pointed to a map of the Greater East Asian Coprosperity Sphere and said, "There it is. We tried. See what you can do with it!"[39] It was not until 1948 that the United States would seek to do much with it, however. In the period 1945–47 in Korea, Japan, and Taiwan, society reacted strongly against the effects of imperial militarism and industrial midwifery. American occupation in Japan led by a nineteenth century liberal also reacted strongly in the early years against the political economy of prewar Japan, seeking to destroy the Japanese Imperial Army, break up the *zaibatsu*, eliminate rural landlords, and bequeath to the world a reformed and chastened Japan that would never again mix aggression with economic prowess. Unions and leftist parties were unleashed and, with Occupation "New Dealers," mustered a challenge to the prewar system strong enough, at minimum, to establish the countervailing power that enables us to call postwar Japan a democracy. Although the main emphasis was on democratization and an end to militarism, narrower interests also asserted themselves. The first head of the Economic and Scientific Section of the Occupation, for example, was Robert C. Kramer, a textile industrialist; he and representatives of American textile, rayon, ceramics, and other industries threatened by Japanese competition opposed reviving Japan's economy, particularly in its potent prewar form.[40] American allies, especially the British, also urged that commitments to reform and reparations be carried through, thereby to weaken Japan's competitiveness in world markets.

From the early 1940s, however, one sector of American official opinion opposed a punitive ocupation, for fear that this would play into the hands of the Soviets and make a reintegration of Japan with the world economy impossible. In essence, such people, who included a Japanophile faction in the State Department,[41] wanted a Japan revived to *second-rank* economic status and enrolled in an American-managed free trade regime. Such recommendations remained in the background, however, while Japan's American emperor, General Douglas MacArthur, masterfully imposed a benevolent tutelage upon the Japanese people.

All this began sharply to change in late 1947, leading to what we might call the Kennan Restoration. George Kennan's policy of containment was always limited and parsimonious, based on the idea that four or five industrial structures existed in the world: the Soviets had one and the United States had four, and things should be kept that way. In Asia, only Japan held his interest. The rest were incontinent regimes, and how could one have containment with incontinence? Kennan and his Policy Planning Staff played the key role in pushing through the "reverse course" in Japan.

American policy in the mid-twentieth century resonated with Jacob Viner's description of British policy in the eighteenth: it was governed "by joint and harmonized considerations of power and economics."[42] Security and economic considerations were inextricably mixed. A revived Japan was both a bulwark against the Soviets and a critical element in a reformed and revived world economy. What is surprising, in the milti-tude of formerly classified American documents now available on early postwar Asian policy, is how powerful were the economic voices. In par-ticular, a cluster of bankers and free traders, now dubbed the "Japan Crowd," were instrumental in the ending of the postwar reforms in Japan and the revival of the regional political economy that persists today.[43] Economics bulked so large because, as Charles Maier points out, the de-feated Axis powers (Japan and West Germany) were to become world centers of capital accumulation and growth, not of political or military power.[44] Thus Japan's economy was reinforced, while its political and military power (beyond its borders) was shorn. The result is that in the postwar world economy Japan resembles a sector as much as a nation-state. Until the 1970s it was a distinctly secondary sector when compared to the United States, that is, it was returned to semiperipherality as (it was hoped) a permanent second-rank economic power.

The coalition that brought the reverse course to Japan has been well detailed elsewhere. In brief it included, in addition to Kennan, Dean Acheson, Dean Rusk, Max Bishop and others within the government, several journalists, and a powerful lobby of American firms and individu-als who had had large investments in prewar Japan: General Electric, Westinghouse, Goodrich, Owens-Libby, American Can, and others.[45] Percy Johnston, head of the pivotal Johnston Committee whose report in April 1948 was instrumental in the reverse course, was chairman of the Chemical Bank; the "Dodge Line" of fiscal austerity was run by a Detroit banker; many Wall Streeters, including the American maker of the Japan Peace Treaty, John Foster Dulles, supported a revival of Japan's economic prowess. As good free traders from the new hegemonic power, they had nothing to fear from Japan. The old hegemonic power, Great Britain, fought unsuccessfully against the changes.

As thinking about a revived Japan evolved in 1948–50, two problems emerged: first, how could Japan's vital but second-rate status be assured; second, how could a prewar political economy that got raw materials and labor from the Northeast Asian periphery survive in the postwar world without a hinterland? George Kennan raised these problems in a 1949 Policy Planning Staff meeting:

> You have the terrific problem of how the Japanese are going to get along unless they again reopen some sort of empire toward the south. . . . If we really in the Western world could work out controls . . . foolproof enough and cleverly enough exercised really to have power over what Japan imports in the way of oil and other things . . . we could have veto power over what she does.[46]

Thus, once the decision to revive Japan was made, two questions predominated: the hegemonic problem and the hinterland problem. The CIA in May 1948 suggested Northeast Asia as the new (old) hinterland:

> As in the past Japan for normal economic functioning on an industrial basis, must have access to the Northeast Asiatic areas—notably North China, Manchuria, and Korea—now under direct, indirect, or potential control of the USSR.[47]

A high official in the Economic Cooperation Administration, a few months later suggested the same hinterland, and a drastic method of recovering it. Without North China and Manchuria, he argued, Japan would have "no hope of achieving a viable economy"; it (and Korea) would be "doomed to military and industrial impotence except on Russian terms." Therefore, "Our first concern must be the liberation of Manchuria and North China from communist domination."[48] This rollback option, however, was delayed; the victory of Mao's forces throughout China and the possibility in 1949 that Washington might be able to split Moscow and Peking (Acheson's policy) combined to suggest a hinterland for Japan in Southeast Asia.

In July 1949, the CIA asserted that the United States had "an important interest" in "retaining access to Southeast Asia, for its own convenience and because of the great economic importance of that area to Western Europe and Japan." It argued that "the basic problem with respect to Japan is to recreate a viable economy. This in turn requires a stabilization of the situation in Southeast Asia and a *modus vivendi* with Communist China." The latter requirement might be satisfied if China could be drawn away from "vassalage toward the USSR."[49] Southeast Asia was the preferred candidate for Japan's hinterland. It would provide markets for Japan's textile and light industrial exports, in exchange for raw materials Japan badly needed. The problem was that France and Britain sought to hold the countries in the region exclusively, and nationalist movements resisted both the Europeans and a reintroduction of the Japanese. Thus, "Anglo-American consensus over Japan dissolved" as the United States played the hinterland option. Japan was a threat to sterling bloc trade and currency systems, and was "perforce in the dollar bloc"; the United States wanted Japan to earn dollars in the sterling bloc, which would have the dual virtue of supporting Japan's revival while encouraging Britain's retreat from empire.[50]

The Occupation also rearranged Japan's monetary and trade policies to support a revival of trade. The yen was fixed in 1949 at the rate of 360 to $1.00, from which it did not depart until 1971; the rate was artificially low to aid Japanese exports. The Dodge Line pursued a strict policy of fiscal restraint. In the same year (1949) the Occupation removed price floors on Japanese exports, raising fears of "dumping" in Southeast Asia.

Particularly important is the *triangular* structure of this arrangement: United States (core), Japan (semiperiphery), and Southeast Asia (periphery). This structure was clearly articulated in the deliberations leading up to the adoption of NSC 48/1 in late December 1949, a document so important that it might be called the NSC 68 for Asia. (With this the United States made the decision to send aid to the Bao Dai regime in Vietnam, not after the Korean War began.) The first draft argued the virtues of a "triangular" trade between the United States, Japan, and Southeast Asia, giving "certain advantages in production costs of various commodities"—that is, comparative advantage in the product cycle. It also called for a positive policy toward Communist-held territory in East Asia: the goal was "to commence the rollback of Soviet control and influence in the area." The final document changed this phrase to read, "to contain and where feasible to reduce the power and influence of the USSR in Asia."[51] The rollback contingency expressed both the fear of continuing communist encroachment, what with the fall of China in 1949, and the search for a Japanese hinterland.

The Korean War effectively drew the lines of the "grand area" in East Asia. When the war broke out, the Seventh Fleet was interposed between Taiwan and the mainland, suggesting once again an integration of Taiwan with Japan and the world economy. South Korea was almost lost in the summer of 1950. Then, after the Inch'on landing, the course of the fighting opened the realm of feasibility suggested in NSC 48/1; the "contain and reduce" phraseology was used in the State Department to justify the march north and, in passing, to wrench North Korea's industrial base away from the communists. Rollback met several hundred thousand Chinese "Volunteers," however, and that debacle froze the situation. The geopolitical lines, or hegemonic outer limits, were thus fixed and they have survived. Taiwan and South Korea were in, North Korea and Manchuria were out. It remained only to reintroduce Japanese economic influence, which the Kennedy administration did in the early 1960s in both Taiwan and South Korea.

Acheson would remark in 1954 that "Korea came along and saved us, and the we included Japan. The Korean War not only boosted the Japanese economy but provided MacArthur with justification for reviving police and military and for excluding labor and the left within Japan. The strategic lines of the new Northeast Asian political economy, however, brought the peculiar nature of American hegemony to the fore. There is a paradox at the heart of it: nonterritorial in contrast to Old World imperialism, organizing great spaces and knocking down barriers to trade, it has outer limits sufficient to keep countries in the system but not sufficient to protect the home economy against destructive competition, and not sufficient to maintain effective dependency relationships or a frozen hierarchy. The system permits upward mobility. The United States retrieved South Korea and Taiwan from oblivion in 1950, but invoking the threat of oblivion to keep them in line in later years was unthinkable. The United States keeps Japan on a food, oil, and security dependency, maintaining a light hold on the Japanese jugular; yet to squeeze would be disastrous. Outer limits are not enough to bring recalcitrant allies to heel. Furthermore, within those outer limits a dependent but strong state obtains leverage over the American "weak state," weak in the sense of competing centers of power and economic interest that can be played off against one another.[52] Thus, the postwar settlement simultaneously gave Japan, in particular, dependency and autonomous capability.[53]

Japan is ultradependent on the United States, or on American firms, for oil and security, and significantly dependent on the United States for food. During the Occupation, the Petroleum Board that set policy was made up of members mostly drawn from American oil majors, and even in the mid-1970s Japan was receiving about 70 percent of its oil deliveries from the majors.[54] In the 1960s and 1970s the United States also supplied 60 to 70 percent of Japan's food imports, and in the 1950s used the PL480 program to sell grain in Japan, Taiwan, and South Korea. All three have been protected markets dependent upon American grain. And since 1945 Japan has had no military capability remotely commensurate with its economic power. Even today analysts cannot decide if Japan is a superstate or a puny dependency. When Ezra Vogel began a Harvard seminar on Japan by saying that "I am really very troubled when I think through the consequences of the rise of Japanese power," Samuel Huntington responded that Japan has "these really fundamental weaknesses— energy, food, and military security." It is, he thought, "an extraordinarily weak country."[55] The paradox of the postwar Northeast Asian settlement is that both are right.

Within Japan, after the reverse course took hold, was a formidable political economy for competition in world markets. The *zaibatsu* were less smashed than reformed, prospering again by the mid-1950s if in less concentrated form. More important, they were now under *state* influence and control, something that prewar bereaucrats had longed for; the role of the big banks was also enhanced.[56] With the *zaibatsu* weakened, the military smashed, and the landlords dispossessed, but with the bureaucracy untouched (the Occupation governed through the existing bureaucracy with few reforms or purges), the Japanese state had more relative autonomy than in the prewar period. Indeed, it was the great victor of the Occupation. Autonomy enabled Japan to pursue neomercantile policies of restricting entry to Japanese markets, resisting the intrusion of foreign capital, and providing various incentives and subsidies to restructure the industrial base in the 1950s, and conquer foreign markets in the 1960s and 1970s.

T. J. Pempel and Jon Halliday both note the low level of internationalization of the Japanese economy. Total foreign assets in Japan in the mid-1970s were only about 2 to 3 percent of total assets, few non-Japanese multinationals operated there, and the major markets for foreign imports remained food and oil. Halliday argues that Japan's "successful isolation" has precipitated greater elite unity than in countries like the United States: Japan does not have major conflicts between firms with national and those with international interests, therefore foreign interests cannot invoke much leverage in domestic Japanese politics. Moving out of/declining into advanced sectors is much easier because powerful domestic business interests rarely clash, and a labor force lacking influence at the commanding heights can be eased out of old industries and retrained for new ones. Japan's monetary isolation lessens the influence of foreign lenders, while reliance on bank rather than share capital also promotes mobility and flexibility.[57] Finally, as in the prewar political economy, labor is corralled by docile unions, paternalism, and a large reservoir of workers in traditional sectors. Ohkawa and Rosovsky call Japan a businessman's "heaven on earth" in regard to labor, while Pempel says labor is "a fundamentally excluded sector. They also note that women continue to bear inferior and exploited positions in the workforce, and that the state still does not spend significant amounts on social welfare.[58]

## Postwar Korea and Taiwan

The immediate postwar settlement in Taiwan and Korea fundamentally expressed the differences in the two *societies*. Taiwan "drifted aimlessly" in the late 1940s, having to reorient its trade away from Japan and toward China (until 1949); it sold sugar, cement, aluminum, and food to this now enlarged periphery.[59] But it remained "an extremely well-ordered society," with "fewer signs of social disintegration" than any place on the Asian, mainland.[60] Like Japan, the state emerged stronger after the inflow of the Guomindang (GMD) and the China mainlanders in 1945–49. The potent colonial bureaucracy was preserved nearly intact; Japanese personnel in many cases stayed on well into 1946, training Taiwanese replacements, and native bureaucrats who had served in the colonial administration continued in office. When the mainlanders took over they added a powerful military component to give the state even more autonomy from society: the Guomindang had finally found a part of China where its bureaucracy was not hamstrung by provincial warlords and landlords. Thus, for the first time, the Nationalists were able to accomplish a land reform; they could, do so because none of them owned any land in Taiwan. The reform, in turn, aided the productivity of agriculture because redistributed land went primarily to entrepreneurial, productive, relatively rich peasants. Furthermore, a disproportionate number of experts, technicians, and well-educated professionals fled the mainland, adding to Taiwan's already significant human capital. The result, once the Seventh Fleet drew the outer limit in 1950, was a state with significant relative autonomy but now far more dependent on the United States than in any previous period of Nationalist rule.

Korea, of course, was divided in 1945. In the North a quick and efficient social and anticolonial revolution occurred under Soviet auspices, the ultimate (but also the predictable) societal response to nearly half a century of Japanese imperialism. The South, however, festered for five years through dissent—disorder, major rebellions in 1946 and 1948, and a significant guerrilla movement in 1948 and 1949. Southern landlords succeeded in recapturing the state in 1945 and 1946, under American auspices, and used it in traditional fashion to protect social privilege rather than to foster growth. They prevented major land reform until the Korean War began, and showed no interest in developing the economy. Instead, they ruled through draconian police and military organizations. As in Taiwan there was considerable continuity in the bureaucracy from the colonial period, but the Japanese officials had mostly fled when the war ended and those Korean functionaries who remained were largely unable to function, since they were often hated more than the Japanese overlords. The southern state entered a general crisis of legitimacy in the late 1940s: marked by the worst Japanese excesses but unable to carry forward colonial successes, the regime seemed doomed.

When civil war erupted in June 1950 the North had an easy time of it, sweeping the southern regime away until it met massive American intervention.

But paradoxically, the three-month northern occupation of the south, which included a revolutionary land reform in several provinces, cleared the way to end landlord dominance in the countryside and to reform landholding on the Taiwan model once the war terminated in 1953. By 1953 South Korea further resembled Taiwan. Its colonial heavy industry had been amputated by Korea's division, most of it now in the north and beyond reach; like Taiwan, southern Korea was the home of light industry and the best rice-producing provinces. During the war many northerners had fled south, also disproportionately including the educated and professional classes. By the war's end the South had a standing army of about 600,000 compared with 75,000 in 1950, so it approximated the distended Nationalist Army. Finally, Syngman Rhee, like Chiang Kai-shek, had won an ironclad commitment of American defense from communism. So, to put it concisely, by 1953 Taiwan and South Korea once more resembled each other, but what was accomplished with ease in Taiwan required a war in Korea.

## Import-substituting Industrialization

With the underbrush of the early postwar period cleared away, Taiwan and South Korea (ROK) once again began marching in tandem. The Korean War gave Taiwan a head start on postcolonial industrialization on the typical import-substituting pattern, but by 1953 the ROK was doing the same. Both were enmeshed in a system of American hegemony that brought them economic and military aid on an unheard-of scale, but Taiwan's low societal response and the GMD's high relative autonomy gave it more bargaining power with the United States. The Rhee regime, on the other hand, was penetrated from below by superannuated landlords who retained political influence and from above by a huge American political, economic, and military presence. In the years immediately succeeding the devastation of the war, society was quiet and Rhee ruled through a diffuse authoritarian system that was cruel in its domestic political consequences but incapable of mustering the autonomy to direct growth, and unable to withstand the social onslaught that came in 1960. The now-senile Rhee was toppled, the colonial-linked police and military came undone, and the way was clear for a dynamic authoritarian system.

Since 1945 South Korea has received some $13 billion in American military and economic aid, and Taiwan some $5.6 billion ($600 per capita in the ROK, $425 per capita in Taiwan).[61] To gauge the true dimensions of this munificence comparative figures are helpful. The ROK's total of nearly $6 billion in U.S. economic grants and loans, 1946–78, compares with a total for all of Africa of $619 billion and for all of Latin America of $14 billion; only India, with a population seventeen times that of South Korea, received more ($9.6 billion). U.S. military deliveries to Taiwan and the ROK in 1955–78 (that is, excluding the Korean War) totaled $9.05 billion. All of Latin America and all of Africa received $3.2 billion; only Iran got more, and most of that was pumped in after 1972 (the figure is $10.01 billion). Soviet economic aid to LDCs, 1954–78, was $7.6 billion in drawn aid, that is, little more than American aid to the ROK alone. Total drawn aid for all LDCs from all socialist countries, 1954–78, was $13.4 billion, about 25 percent greater than the total for Taiwan and the ROK since 1945. Soviet military deliveries to all LDCs,

1955–78, totaled $25.3 billion, about 280 percent of the total for Taiwan and the ROK.[62]

During the 1950s U.S. aid accounted for five-sixths of ROK imports. Aid was lavished on Japan as well, and special U.S. military procurements from Japan alone in the period 1952–56 totaled $3.4 billion, one-fourth of American commodity imports at that time.[63] Samuel Ho estimates for Taiwan that foreign savings, much of which was U.S. aid, totaled 40 percent of gross domestic capital formation.[64] This significant figure is low when compared to the ROK; Taiwan's higher rate of domestic savings can be accounted for by less postwar disruption and the Guomindang's having taken China's gold reserves to the island. Taiwan has also had an additional source of aid and investment unavailable to the ROK, overseas Chinese.

The United States, of course, did not just give military and economic aid to Taiwan and the ROK but deeply influenced economic programs and the societies themselves. Often it was difficult to know if natives or Americans were writing the plans and policies; the aid missions pushed through land reform on Taiwan and forced it through in Korea; here, in short, was by far the best example in the world of what Wallerstein has called "development by invitation." If the principle of upward mobility in this system is "many called, few chosen," Taiwan and the ROK were clearly part of the chosen few.[65] Japan, too, was chosen, if at a higher level in the system: not only were aid totals high, but the United States allowed a "simultaneous technological infusion" in the 1950s that brought backward Japanese industries up to speed and started new ones.[66] American hegemony also had an element of indulgence in the halcyon years of the 1950s—U.S. officials tolerated import substitution in Taiwan and the ROK while chiding both for having the state too involved in the economy (i.e., the typical policy of Republican administrations). Thus, the three Northeast Asian political economies had in the 1950s a rare breathing space, an incubation period allowed to few other peoples in the world. The period set the stage for the breakthroughs of the 1960s, and it may be a capitalist analogue to the radical tonic of withdrawal and reorientation by socialist state machineries and societies.

Taiwan and Korea pushed remarkably similar import-substitution programs, although the Taiwan program was less fitful. The key industries were textiles, cement, flat glass, and so on, protected by and nurtured behind a wall of tariffs, overvalued exchange rates, and other obstacles to foreign entry.[67] In both countries capitalist parvenus, usually mainlanders in Taiwan and northerners in the ROK, interpenetrated the state, official monopolies, and banks, making windfall profits in import-substituting industries through such connections. Both the GMD and the Rhee regime, after all, grew out of agrarian-bureaucratic traditional systems and had pursued so-called "bureaucratic capitalism," with its "total interpenetration of public and private interests.[68] Favored capitalists took over formerly Japanese-held industries in Taiwan and the ROK, laying the basis for many of the conglomerates that would appear in the 1960s and 1970s (especially in Korea). The phase of "easy" import substitution started two or three years earlier in Taiwan and came a cropper in 1958–59; it did the same in the ROK in 1960–62. In both countries a new export-led, industrialization began in the early 1960s.

In the 1950s both regimes had absurdly swollen military machines—about 600,000 soldiers in each army, ranking among the highest military/civilian ratios in the world. The United States footed much of the tab in Korea, less so in Taiwan because Americans opposed Taiwan's pretensions to retake the mainland. Thus, Taiwanese defense spending ran at about 12 percent of GNP, Korean at about 4 percent. These large militaries served two important purposes: first, as a perimeter defense for the hegemonic "grand area." Without such military machines and expenditures Japan would have had to spend much more than its less than one percent of GNP on defense. As Paul B. Simpson said of the U.S. aid program to the ROK in the 1950s:

> If we were to characterize the program simply, we would say that the Korean consumer has been subsidized by ICA and U.S. Military expenditures in return for the maintenance of a large military establishment. The attitude one adopts toward this Korean military program very largely determines one's attitude toward the U.S. aid program in Korea.[69]

Second, the military in both countries gave disciplined training and basic literacy to a mass of young people, the rearing officers and managers who later populated state bureaucracies and big corporations. Of course, both distended militaries have continually devastated democratic impulses.

In the Korean case the military also played a decisive role in the switch from import substitution to export-led growth. The downfall of Syngman Rhee carried the bureaucratic capitalists with it. After the military coup in 1961 those who had profited from import substitution were marched through the streets, carrying sandwich signs with slogans like "I was a parasite on the people." A transition that occurred with difficulty in several Latin American nations transpired quickly, if violently, in South Korea; managed from the top down, it cleared away social and political obstacles to the new program.

## The Export-Led Phase and the Emergence of BAIRs

Readers who know Latin America and especially the work of Guillermo O'Donnell will have noticed that Taiwan and Korea went through industrialization in phases that resemble the sequence in Brazil, Argentina, and other states, even though the import-substituting phase was much shorter in East Asia. It would have continued longer had it not been for opposition by American aid officials (which demonstrates their superior influence in this region of overwhelming American hegemony). But this phase did not have the political characteristics it had in Brazil and elsewhere. Politics did not stretch to include workers, peasants, or plural competition for power. The political sequence of inclusion followed by exclusion, as the "easy" phase ended and export-led development began, was absent.[70] Labor was excluded in the 1950s and remained excluded in the 1960s; nor did the squeezed middle class of bureaucrats and small businessmen achieve representation in either Taiwan or South Korea. It is possible to argue, however, that the Korean state was more penetrated by society in the 1950s, both because new capitalists gained some influence as the landlord interests receded and because the United States and a small stratum of Korean liberals insisted on a formal democratic structure that was occasionally implemented, if only through students massing in the streets. The democratic facade could occasionally be invoked. Taiwan, of course, has been ruled under martial law since 1947 in a single-party system; the GMD's internal organization principles were on Leninist lines. Its politics could easily translate into the new state requisites for export-led development and deepening import substitution. In Korea, however, such a state had to be reinforced: bureaucratic, secret police, and party power needed to be strengthened.

In both countries the export-led program was decided by the United States. Edward Mason and his associates say that in Korea the United States "basically dictated", the reform programs; Ian Little says that in Taiwan AID pressure was one of the "clearest castes in economic history of cause and effect."[71] Therefore, early 1960s' policies in Taiwan and the ROK tended to be very similar. Taiwan promulgated a nineteen-point reform package in 1960, containing extensive reforms of monetary, fiscal, taxation, and trade practices. Korea pursued the same package after Park Chung Hee's coup in 1961. It involved downward revaluation of currencies to cheapen exports, drastic lowering of tariff barriers that had protected native industries, tax holidays, exemptions, and reductions across the board for firms willing to export, and state guarantees for foreign investment and foreign loans. Implemented by 1963 or 1964, the package was followed by accelerated depreciation schemes, discounts and subsidies for transportation costs, and monopoly rights for certain firms, usually linked explicitly to export performance.[72] Taiwan established its big Free Export Zone (FEZ) at Kaohsiung in 1965, and Korea followed suit with its Masan FEZ. Both regimes developed long-range planning agencies and multiyear plans; American experts continued riding herd on the planning function (a sort of transnational planning). Both regimes pursued their comparative advantage in relatively well-educated and skilled, but low-paid, labor. Paul Kuznets notes that Korea's comparative advantage derived from these factors and that labor was "abundant and unorganized"; Wade and Kim estimate Korean labor productivity as higher than American in light industries such as textiles and electronics, at 20 percent the cost. In the FEZs, however, labor-cost savings for foreign firms may be substantially higher: one source puts Korean productivity at 2.5 times American at 10 percent of the cost, for a factor of 25 percent cost savings.[73] One Taiwan analyst has argued for the virtues of "splitting up the production process" on a worldwide basis, since capital has much greater mobility than labor.[74] This is, of course, the point. The result of the early 1960s' reforms was that Taiwan and the ROK became suppliers of labor to an increasingly far-flung division of production; in the mid-1960s multinational corporations, the World Bank, and the IMF replaced U.S. aid missions as the conduits to the world economy. This pattern, most marked in East Asia, is well known and need not detain us. More important were the political consequences.

By the mid-1960s both Taiwan and South Korea possessed strong states that bear much comparison to the prewar Japanese model, and to the bureaucratic-authoritarian states in Latin America. Termed NICs (Newly Industrializing Countries) in much of the literature, the Taiwan and Korean variants deserve a more accurate acronym. I shall call them BAIRs or Bureaucratic-Authoritarian Industrializing Regimes. These states are ubiquitous in economy and society: penetrating, comprehensive, highly articulated, and relatively autonomous of particular groups and classes. Furthermore, especially in Korea, state power accumulated considerably just as the ROK began a deepening industrialization program in steel, chemicals, ships, and automobiles. Taiwan has developed planning agencies and bureaucracies to go with its existing strong state, but with society weak the state has had neither the occasion nor the necessity to deepen or change its features: once strong for retaking the mainland and guaranteeing GMD power, it is today strong for economic development. The best Latin American analogy for Taiwan would be Mexico, where deepening industrialization occurred within the context of an established authoritarian system; Korea is closer to Argentina, where deepening required a much stronger state. In any case, by the mid-1960s Taiwan and South Korea had joined the world: we no longer need area-specific, idiosyncratic explanations for their politics. They now have the politics that their economies—and powerful external forces—demand.

In the creation of the Korean BAIR, there was a poignant moment for American political scientists. Amid Kennedy administration pressure to go civilian and respect human rights, the ROK promulgated a new constitution in 1963. Harvard scholar Rupert Emerson journeyed to Seoul and advised Koreans, in classic American fashion, to disperse power through a strong legislature, a two-party system, and various checks and balances. Five years later Samuel Huntington published a book that cited the ROK for precisely the opposite: he applauded the regime for its accumulation of central power and its stability amid rapid economic and social change. Huntington's concern for order transcended liberal categories: the problem was not to hold elections but to create organizations.[75] Although his preferred vehicle was the party, the logic fitted a strong state power by whatever means necessary. The book was translated into Korean and is widely read there. Huntington's logic was possibly the first piece of political advice from an American that did not fall on deaf ears in Korea.

Shortly after the coup, Park and his allies organized the Democratic Republican Party (DRP) and the Korean Central Intelligence Agency (KCIA). During much of the 1960s the DRP was the designated vehicle for a stable politics; its internal structure mimicked the GMD with its democratic centralism. But when Park's power was shaken in the period 1969–71 (he nearly lost the 1971 election to Kim Dae Jung in spite of manipulation), the KCIA emerged as the preferred organization of order. An arm of the executive, it penetrated nearly every arena of Korean life, with agents in factories, central and local government offices, and university classrooms. Organized with the help of the U.S. CIA, and always working in close liaison with the Seoul CIA station, it was an example of transnational politics to go with the transnational economics. Unfortunately for Park Chung Hee, the KCIA became so strong that every director came to challenge his power (Lee Hu-rak, Him Jae-gyu, Kim Hyong-uk) until finally its chief shot Park to death over dinner one evening in October 1979.

In the economic sphere the Koreans in the early 1960s set up an Economic Planning Board (EPB), which took on many of the functions of MITI. It took over from a previous ministry the entire budgeting function; it decides which industries and firms to promote, which to phase out; it closely supervises both the development and the implementation of planning; along with an official trade promotion agency (KOTRA) it surveys the world for needed markets, capital, and technology. The main difference from Japan is that the EPB brings in foreigners (Americans and Japanese) as "senior partners" in consultation and planning.[76] Many other state agencies are involved in export promotion, and in both Korea and Taiwan, the achievement of some export target is cause for patriotic hoopla and celebration (this has become the national pastime of these two BAIRS).

Until the mid-1970s, American analysts tended to deny that an authoritarian politics might have much to do with economic growth in Taiwan and the ROK. But more recent writing has discarded the previous assumptions of the modernization literature, that development could proceed amidst or would promote democracy. Kuznets, for example, argues that "because this [Korean] regime has been authoritarian and has no economic interest base, it could hold down wages and consumption, largely ignore rural interests, and concentrate on rapid development through industrialization."[77] He errs only in suggesting that the state has no base. The state's relative autonomy from particularistic economic interests, combined with the exclusion of workers and farmers, gives it the capacity to look after the whole in the interest of, but not necessarily at the behest of, certain of the parts. In this structural sense it resembles the relative autonomy of the Japanese state.

A Harvard project on the Korean economy also breaks with the assumption of inevitable democratic development. The authors find that "Korea, Inc." is "undoubtedly a more apt description of the situation in Korea than is 'Japan, Inc.' " The state is senior, the corporations lesser partners: "It is the government that is Chairman of the Board [of Korea, Inc.], with business holding a few directorships."[78] The Korean *zaibatsu* (the Koreans pronounce it *chaebol*, but the term is the same) have grown up with the new BAIR. Ten of them now appear on *Fortune's* international 500. Like prewar Japanese *zaibatsu*, there is great family interpenetration: the Harvard project found that of current *chaebol* chief executives, 61.4 percent are firm founders, 7.9 percent are direct descendants of founders, 12 percent are relatives of founders, and only 18.8 percent are unrelated to the founding family.[79] As a Gerschenkronian analysis would suggest, "feudal holdovers" have been an important aspect of late development in East Asia: in the case of prewar Japanese *zaibatsu, Korean chaebol,* and the Taiwanese state (the president being the son of Chiang Kai-shek), it is the traditional family structure that provides a basis for organizing industry. The power of this analysis is confirmed in the Northeast Asian socialist case, where the North Korean state is highly interpenetrated by Kim Il Sung's family and where his son has been chosen as successor.

As in Japan, Korean and Taiwanese big firms exercise paternalistic sway over workers with company dormitories, recreation and hospital facilities, uniforms, and company songs. The different labor markets in Korea and Taiwan mean, however, that there is no permanent employment, working hours are much longer (52 hours per week in the big firms, longer in small firms), and wages are much lower in relation to living cost.

Yet there is no question but that the state is the maker and at times the breaker of the conglomerates. They prospered and grew as the economy grew, in close consort with state support. They do not have the credit power of the Japanese *zaibatsu*. At the core of the latter was always a bank, but in Korea and Taiwan it is the state that provides credit. This is one of its greatest weapons. State bureaucracies like the EPB control domestic credit and favor certain export-oriented firms, and they mediate foreign credit through licensing schemes. Thus, they have almost total control over access to investment capital; the *chaebol* are all structured with very low equity and huge debt components.[80] Most are in technical bankruptcy at any given time. Thus, when the Yolsan conglomerate added to Park Chung Hee's difficulties by (reportedly) flirting with the opposition leader Kim Dae Jung in 1979, the president pulled the plug and Yolsan collapsed, taking several small banks with it. Samuel Ho notes the same sort of autonomy for the state in Taiwan: it can move in and out of sectors, promote this or that industry, because it is "relatively neutral to sectoral or regional interest."[81] It is this relative autonomy and promotion of sectoral mobility that makes these BAIRs resemble the Japanese model.

Another similarity with the Japanese model is the exclusion of labor, the exploitation of women, and the low state expenditures on social welfare—all three, of course, are bound to be more extreme in the periphery than in the core. Social spending is minimal in both countries. In 1973, expenditures on social insurance, public health, public assistance, welfare, and veterans' relief represented 0.97 percent of GNP in the ROK, 1.2 percent in Taiwan; this compares with 3 percent in Malaysia and 5.3 percent in Japan.[82] Such figures capture the trade-off between Japan and Korea and Taiwan: the latter two spend 4 to 10 percent of GNP on defense, and Japan can hold defense expenditures under one percent; but Japan, by virtue of its "New Deal" during the Occupation and its democratic system, must spend 5 percent on social prorams (still low by world standards). In any case both the ROK and Japan until recently escaped with spending about 6 percent of GNP on defense and welfare combined. Korean and Taiwanese workers pay the cost in the periphery.

Exploitation of labor, particularly females, is so marked that it is foolish to deny it (even though many American specialists continue to do so). In both the Kaohsiung and the Masan FEZs 80 percent of the workforce is female, and teenage girls are about 60 percent of that total. Most of the work is unskilled assembly, done by girls recruited from peasant families. Their wage rates are at the bottom of the heap in world scales—one-third of Japan's level, one-fifth to one tenth of the U.S. level, even one-half of the level in Hong Kong, where similar practices prevail. The state guarantees foreign firms not only various investment subsidies and profit remissions, but prohibition of union organization. In the Kaohsiung FEZ about 85 percent of the 150 or so firms are wholly or partially foreign-owned (including holdings by overseas Chinese).[83] FEZ products include light electronic assemblies (like calculators), textiles, and simple manufactured items like nuts and bolts. Thus these are basically platforms of world production located in countries that can provide cheap and controlled labor. In Korea and Taiwan strikes are usually prohibited (even though they may occur), and unions are company or state-managed in good corporate fashion.

All in all the BAIR provides a potent mix, fusing state and economic power in pursuit of comparative advantage in world markets. To the extent that hegemonic outer limits are not invoked, relative autonomy is at any given time greater in Taiwan and Korea than it is in Japan or the United States. Thus both states sought in the early 1970s to use their power to set transnational and free-trade interests by once again substituting, this time in heavy industry. Both sought not simply their industrial structures but to deepen their self-reliance and vis-à-vis their hegemonic partners. One key enabling factor was the massive reentry of Japanese capital (loans and investments) into the ROK and Taiwan in the mid-1960s. Accomplished relatively easily in Taiwan, in Korea, as we would predict, society reacted strongly and the "normalization" had to be rammed down the throats of protesting students and legislators in 1964–65. But Japan's reentry gave both regimes a strong proxy to play off against American power and capital: a single hegemony began to turn into a dual hegemony.

Park Chung Hee declared in 1972 that "steel = national power," a pitchy slogan that symbolizes the deepening industrialization of both countries. The third Five-Year Plan, 1971–76, inaugurated this phase. During 1969 to 1971 domestic capital formation rose markedly in the ROK, to account for 26 to 30 percent of gross domestic product, compared to 17 to 18 percent in the United States and 36 to 40 percent in Japan during the same years; the manufacturing sector rose from 11 percent to 30 percent between the early 1960s and the mid-1970s A similar and coterminous deepening occurred in Taiwan. Economist Anthony Michel has also noted that Korean economic nationalists were dominant in constructing the Third Five-Year Plan, bypassing the EPB, which is transnationally penetrated by Western economists with theories opposed to industrial deepening.[84] The ROK got a new integrated steel mill (developed and installed by Japanese technicians), supertanker shipbuilding capacity, heavy chemical factories and refineries, and an auto industry (with GM, Ford, and Japanese technology) that produced 38,000 cars by 1978. American planners and economists resisted these developments, arguing that heavy industry is unsuited to the factor endowments and small domestic markets of both countries; surplus, idle capacity would be the inevitable result.[85] In other words, Korea and Taiwan were violating a rational international division of labor.

The ROK and Taiwan were able to obtain needed financing and technology for these enterprises from the Japanese, in part because the new programs provided the structure necessary to receive declining Japanese heavy industry. This simultaneously increased Taiwanese and Korean autonomy in the world at large while deepening dependency on Japan. The United States was opposed and, indeed, during the same period the Nixon administration dealt the sharpest blows since 1949 to both countries by limiting shoe and textile imports, floating the dollar, recognizing People's China, and pulling a division of U.S. troops out of the ROK. This set the agenda of conflict for the present: would the Northeast Asian political economy continue as a joint hegemony or as an increasingly Japanese preserve?

By the early 1970s, Korea and Taiwan were both in transition between peripheral and semiperipheral status;[86] in a sense they had recovered their structural position of the last years of the Japanese empire. Vietnam was a periphery for both, as each sent contruction teams and other industrial personnel, and Korea sent some 300,000 soldiers over a seven-year period (1966–73). The Vietnam War played for the ROK the role that the Korean War played for Japan; labeled "Korea's El Dorado," it accounted for as much as 20 percent of foreign exchange earnings in the late 1960s.[87] Procurements for the war were also important for Taiwan, and, by the 1970s, Taiwan was exporting capital goods, technicians, and foreign aid to several Southeast Asian nations.[88] Both countries sent contruction teams to the Middle East to recycle petrodollars after the 1973 oil shock. By the late 1970s both nations were competing for an intermediate position in the world economy, continuing to export labor-intensive goods to advanced countries and capital-intensive goods to LDCs.[89] Firms in both countries sought to go multinational, looking for cheaper labor in Bangladesh, Mexico, and elsewhere, while continuing to supply construction to the Middle East. In these tactics Taiwan and the ROK have been more successful than other industrializing regimes such as Brazil and Argentina. Korea, however, had to bolster its state power and did so in dramatic fashion: the early 1970s were the period of the Yusin Constitution (Yuin in Korean is *isin* in Japanese, the same characters used to refer to the post-1868 Meiji reforms), KCIA penetration of society, a clump of "emergency decrees," and increasing use of vile tortures against dissidents.

Although Taiwan and Korea sought to escape dependency in the 1970s, what they succeeded in doing was exchanging one form of dependency for another, or enhancing one and reducing the other. The U.S. role has declined; experts no longer dictate to the regimes, as they did in the early 1960s, but "offer suggestions." The direct dependency of the 1950s and early 1960s has changed into an indirect dependency, increasingly like Japan's, within the U.S. hegemony.

Both countries remain captive grain markets for the United States, both continue to get much of their oil shipped in and refined by U.S. multinationals, and both remain highly dependent on the United States for security (with Taiwan moving into a less determinate position after the U.S.-China normalization). In both countries direct aid ended in the mid-1960s, but PL480 grain and other supports continue to flow as a trade-off for "voluntary" textile export restraint. In the period 1951–74 Korea alone received $8 billion in U.S. food shipments, most of it under PL480, and surplus American grain has been essential in keeping wages low in Korea and Taiwan.[90]

Japan, by contrast, lacking a military or resource component to foster peripheral dependency, has pursued a trade hegemony that could be a textbook example of Hirschman's schema for Germany in interwar Eastern Europe. Japan's trading practices toward Taiwan and the ROK fit almost perfectly with his outline of techniques a dominant country uses to create an "influence effect" dependency; create groups with vested interest in trade, direct trade toward poorer countries, trade with countries with little mobility of resources, induce discrepancies between production for export and for the home market, and so on.[91] Northeast Asia exemplifies Hirschman's rule that dependency will emerge where country A takes a large percentage of trade from country B, but country B's, trade is a small part of country A's total trade. He illustrates this by reference to Bulgaria's trade with Germany: 52 percent of its imports came from and 59 percent of its exports went to Germany, but that trade only amounted to 1.5 percent of German imports and 1.1 percent of German exports.[92] In the 1970s, Japan accounted for about 25 percent of ROK exports and 38 percent of its imports; Japan and the United States combined accounted for 70 percent of ROK imports and about two-thirds of its exports.[93] Direct Japanese investment in Korea ballooned after the 1965 normalization, which was itself accompanied by a munificent package of loans and credits totaling about $300 million. Within a few years Japanese direct investment outstripped the American total; in the period 1972–76, for example, Japanese investment was more than four times the American total ($396 million to $88 million). Japan's ten largest trading firms handled as much as 50 percent of exports and 60 percent of imports to and from Korea between 1963 and 1972.

Taiwan's trade is similarly skewed; but Taiwan is less dependent on financing from Japan and the United States, whereas the ROK's dependence on Japanese financing since 1965 is, according to Kuznets, "characteristic of Korea's earlier satellite role within the Yen Bloc."[94] Both countries remain almost entirely dependent on American and Japanese multinationals for foreign markets and technology transfer.[95] Although an indirect dual dependency continues to exist, the Japanese are more aggressive than the Americans: as Ezra Vogel argues, the Japanese try "to induce as much technological dependence on Japan . . . as possible."[96] In Taiwan and Korea this takes the form, for example, of letting them assemble color television sets while jealously guarding the technology necessary to make a color picture tube.

## Many Are Called but Few Are Chosen: Korea's Export-led Trap

Export-led development on the Korean and Taiwan model places four critical obstacles in the way of upward mobility in the world system. First, LDCs need to break into the system of economic exchange at a point other than comparative advantage in labor, that is, in marketing, better technology, or better organization. Yet multinationals provide most of the markets and use "steady-state" or obsolescent technologies—as Lin puts it, technology "is stable in the product-cycle sense."[97] Second, limited factor endowments and the small domestic markets that characterize such offshore prediction inhibit second-stage industrialization and cause early problems of surplus capacity. Third, rising competition from poorer states means that there is a critical but a short and slim lead over competing LDCs. Multinationals, especially the smaller textile firms, may simply move production facilities to countries offering better labor costs. Finally, core-country protectionism will arise to the extent that declining sectors have representation in the polity. In the late 1970s, Taiwan and Korea met all these problems compounded by inflated oil prices.

In any event, Taiwan was chosen but the ROK was not. Taiwan is beginning to manufacture computers for export (Atari moved a big factory there in 1983), while Korea suffered a loss of 6 percent of GNP in 1980, the first loss since the export-led program, began. In 1978, the Korean threat to advanced country industries seemed so palpable that Japanese newspapers were filled with wary editorials about "the Korean challenge," and a middle-level State Department official stated in my earshot that a prime goal of U.S. policy toward Korea was to "manage its articulation with the world economy so that we don't get another Japan there." According to some sources, the Carter administration put off its troop withdrawal plan both to maintain influence in Korea and to stave off ever-increasing Japanese dominance. In June 1979, Jimmy Carter visited Park Chung Hee and toasted him for his stable rule. Six months later Park was assassinated amidst a general political and economic crisis. The timing of the economic crisis may be explained by the second oil wave of early 1979, but the cause of the crisis lay deep in the structure of Korea's economic activity. The late 1970s saw increasing protectionism, declining technology transfer, and a greater need to borrow to meet oil expenses and service previous debt. Furthermore, in dialectical fashion, the remedy that Korea had used to ride out the first oil wave—dispatching construction teams to the Middle East—caused a skilled labor shortage that bid up wages within Korea, thus jeopardizing the ROK's comparative advantage. At the same time, an outward-turning People's China began eating into Korean textile markets. The big steel, shipbuilding, and automobile factories met the very obstacle that free traders had predicted: when ships and cars could not be sold abroad, the small domestic, market could not help out. Korean automobile production in late 1979 and 1980 came to a virtual standstill. Thus, as the economist Yung Chut Park stated, all these problems threatened to "bring the export-led industrialization to a rather abrupt end."[98] Korean EPB planners stated publicly that the economy was "uncontrollable" and in a "quandary."

The economic difficulties detonated a political crisis, beginning with vastly enhanced opposition power deployed around Kim Dae Jung. He in turn drew support from textile workers, small businesses and firms within national rather than international interests, and his native southwestern Cholla region, which, historically rebellious and leftist, had been left out of much of the growth of the previous fifteen years. Major urban insurrections occurred in the southeastern cities of Pusan and Masan in the autumn of 1979. Some 700 labor strikes were recorded in 1979–80, and in April 1980 miners took over a small town east of Seoul and held it for several days. In May, hundreds of thousands of students and common people flooded the streets of Seoul, leading to martial law, which in turn touched off a province-wide rebellion in South Korea and the capture of the provincial capital by rebels who held it for a week. Korea seemed to be on the verge of disintegrating as Iran had done, but unlike Iran the military did not fracture and a new general, Chun Doo Hwan, executed a multistage coup: within the military in December 1979, within the KCIA in April 1980, and throughout the state apparatus in summer 1980. Through withering repression the strong societal reaction was quieted, but at the cost of a deep radicalization of remaining protesters.

In the aftermath of this rebellious period, the Korean state intervened continuously to revive the economy's comparative advantage in the world system. The state sponsored the sectoral reorganization of several large conglomerates, on the principle of one *chaebol* for each industrial sector. For the first time the ROK publicly referred to the "organic" nature of its perimeter defense relationship with Japan, as justification for demanding at least $6 billion in Japanese loans and aid. (In early 1983 Korea and Japan agreed upon a $4 billion package of loans and credits, clearly marking Japan's increasing role as compared to that of the United States.) Finally, the state accomplished a thorough repression of labor in outlawing strikes and unions, closely watching any and all organizing activity, and driving down wages. Thus in 1981 labor productivity increased 16 percent while wages went down 5 percent in real terms. GNP growth of 6.4 percent recovered the loss of 1980.[99] Yet the period 1978–83 has seriously weakened the ROK in its struggle with Taiwan for advantageous position in the world economy.

In 1979, the World Bank reported that "the burden of external debt is being steadily reduced," and agreed with Korean planners that a growth rate for exports of 16 percent and for GNP of 9 to 10 percent per year could be sustained through the 1980s. It noted that "confidence in Korea's ability to meet its external debt service obligations is based on the continuation of rapid export growth."[100] Since the 1980 downturn the economy has grown only in the 5 to 6 percent range, debts have more than doubled since 1979 to a total external debt of $42 billion (third largest in the world), and export growth has tumbled badly. Growing by double-digit rates throughout the 1970s, and by 17 percent in the bad year of 1980 (to $17.2 billion), exports reached $21 billion at the end of 1981 and by mid-1983 were no higher than $22 billion on an annual basis. In other words, export growth has been flat since 1981. Taiwan's exports have not been booming either, but its external debt is no more than $7 billion and the slowing of export growth has had no apparent effect on internal politics.

Thus, in 1983 as in the rest of this century, Taiwan continues its smooth development, in spite of losing major security guarantees and in spite of structural obstacles to its development. South Korea, on the contrary, plays out its history of economic dynamism mixed with spasmodic social reaction. Today, its development program hangs in the balance.

## Conclusions

I have sought to demonstrate the shaping and conditioning effects of economic forces on three distinct societies, peoples, and cultures, and the effects of industrial product cycles on a regional political economy. Japan, Taiwan, and South Korea have come to have similar economic structures (although in different temporal sequences), and all three, with markedly different traditional polities, have adopted quite similar political models and roles for the state. The BAIR model—relative state autonomy, central coordination, bureaucratic short- and long-range planning, high flexibility in moving in and out of industrial sectors, private concentration in big conglomerates, exclusion of labor, exploitation of women,

low expenditures on social welfare and, in prewar Japan and comtempo-
rary South Korea and Taiwan, militarization and authoritarian repression—is found in all three nations. When one is compared to another the
differences will also be salient, but when all three are compared to the
rest of the world the similarities are remarkable.

I have also argued that industrial development in Japan, Korea, and
Taiwan cannot be considered as an individual country phenomenon; instead, it is a regional phenomenon in which a tripartite hierarchy of core,
semiperiphery, and periphery was created in the first part of the twentieth
century and then slowly re-created after World War II. The smooth development of Taiwan has its counterpart in the spasmodic and troubled development of Korea, and neither can be understood apart from Japan.
Not only was Taiwan's society less restive and its state less penetrated by
societal constraint, but it also had breathing space occasioned by Japan's
greater attention to Korea and Manchuria before 1945, and American
"development by invitation" after 1950. In short, the developmental
"successes" of Taiwan and Korea are historically and regionally specific,
and therefore provide no readily adaptable models for other developing
countries interested in emulation.

The evidence also strongly suggests that a hegemonic system is necessary for the functioning of this regional political economy: unilateral colonialism until 1945, U.S. hegemony since 1945. Today there is
increasing competition between American and Japanese hegemony over
semiperipheral Taiwan and South Korea, but as years pass there may well
be sharper competition over a new hinterland, People's China. Will the
United States or Japan, or both, organize Chinese labor in the world
system? And as Chinese labor-intensive exports increase, whither Taiwan
and South Korea? Past history suggests that a triangular structure works
best, and so Taiwan and the ROK should move into a middling position
between China on the one hand and the United States and Japan on the
other. The Chairman of the Korea Exchange Bank, Choon Taik Chung,
said in 1981 that "within ten years, Korea will be the bridge . . . between
mainland China and the United States." Already, some synthetic textiles
made in South Korea are being shipped to China for finishing, taking
advantage of cheaper labor cost; the finished product is then sold in
American markets. Within Japan, there are voices arguing that Japan
should slowly transfer its auto and steel industries to South Korea and
Taiwan, placing emphasis instead on high-technology "knowledge industries."[101] The continuing world competitiveness of Japanese auto and
steel exports in the early 1980s seems to have slowed this transfer, but it
will probably continue. Still, international politics and domestic social
forces (especially in Korea) complicate the replication and deepening of
this "natural" tripartite hierarchy.

The China connection comes to the heart of the problem. In a recent discussion Raymond Vernon said the Japanese capabilities for exploiting that opportunity are "some orders of magnitude greater than the capacity of the U.S." to deal with it. Jon Halliday argues that Japan is far better positioned than the United States to benefit from the economic opportunities of the 1980s in Northeast Asia.[102] In a situation of stable U.S. hegemony, such as existed from 1951 to 1970 in the region, Japan and the United States could profit equally from such opportunities. Today, in an era of limits, this is not the case. The world system does not provide open access for all. It can tolerate only one or two hegemonies, and only one or two Japans. For the smaller and weaker countries, core-power rivalry spells trouble in the intermediate zone. For Japan, the coming period, like the interwar period, will test its ability both to be successful economically and to live at peace with the world around it: tragically, in the past its striving toward core-power status resembled less flying geese than a moth toward a flame.

Americans, as Vogel suggests, "haven't begun to think about the implications of living in a world where Japan is the most powerful industrial power."[103] They must also decide if they can live at peace with a formidable Japan. And they must contemplate the obvious fact that, in the late twentieth century, the race is passing to those who are best organized for competition in a merciless world system. We see this reflected in a poignant observation by Raymond Vernon:

> The concept of free access of every country to every market and the gradual reduction of trade barriers and the openness of capital markets, served us well, given our internal political and economic structure, and given our position in the world from 1945 on. All my preferences, all my values argue for retaining this system, for as long as one can. But one observes the way in which Japan has organized itself. . . . with a certain unity of purpose, which can easily be exaggerated, but nonetheless at the same time should not be overlooked. One looks at the way in which state enterprises are being used somewhat . . . by the other advanced industrial countries and now by the developing countries in very considerable degree. Observing these various forms of interference with the operation of market mechanisms, I find myself reluctantly pushed back constantly to the question whether we have to opt for a set of institutional relationships and principles that reflect a second best world from our point of view. We have to somehow organize ourselves. . . .[104]

## Notes

1. U.S. Central Inteligence Agency (CIA), *Handbook of Economic Statistics 1979* (Washington, D.C.: National Foreign Assessment Center, 1980).

2. G. C. Allen, *Japan's Economic Policy* (London: Macmillan, 1980), p. 1; see also Kazushi Ohkawa and Henry Rosovsky, *Japanese Economic Growth: Trend Acceleration in the Twentieth Century* (Stanford, Calif.: Stanford University Press, 1973), pp. 74, 82–83. For the comparisons of growth rates with Korea and Taiwan see Mataji Umemura and Toshiyoki Mizoguchi, eds., *Quantitative Studies on Economic History of Japan Empire [sic], 1890–1940* (Tokyo: Hitotsubashi University, 1981), p. 64.

3. Kiyoshi Kojima, *Japan and a New World Economic Order* (Boulder, Colo.: Westview, 1977), pp. 150–51.

4. L. L. Wade and B. S. Kim, *Economic Development of South Korea: The Political Economy of Success* (New York: Praeger, 1978), p. vi.

5. See Susan Greenhalgh, "Dependency, Distribution and the Taiwan 'Paradox,' " and Denis Simon, "U. S. Assistance, Land Reform, and Taiwan's Political Economy" (both papers presented at the Taiwan Political Economy Workshop, Columbia University, New York, 18–20 December 1980).

6. For a good example of this line of reasoning se chap. 2 in Edward S. Mason et al., *The Economic and Social Modernization of the Republic of Korea* (Cambridge: Harvard University Press, 1980).

7. For references, see David P. Calleo and Benjamin M. Rowland, *America and the World Political Economy* (Bloomington: Indiana University Press, 1973), and Jacob Viner, "Power versus Plenty as Objectives of Foreign Policy in the Seventeenth and Eighteenth Centuries," *World Politics* 1 (October 1948), on mercantilism and neomercantilism; Raymond Vernon, *Sovereignty at Bay: The Multinational Spread of U.S. Enterprises* (New York: Basic Books, 1971), on the product cycle and free trade; Immanuel Wallerstein, "The Rise and Future Demise of the World Capitalist System: Concepts for Comparative Analysis," in Wallerstein, ed., *The Capitalist World-Economy* (New York: Cambridge University Press, 1979), for the world system approach.

8. Charles P. Kindleberger, "Group Behavior and International Trade," *Journal of Political Economy*, February 1951, p. 42.

9. Wallerstein, "Rise and Future Demise."

10. Like most interesting concepts, these categories of core, semiperiphery, and periphery have problems of definition and scope, but they are useful for locating nations in the world economy. A similar set of categories is Krasner's tripartite distinction between makers, breakers, and takers among nations. See Stephen D. Krasner, "US Commercial and Monetary Policy: Unravelling the Paradox of External Strength and Internal Weakness," in Peter J. Katzenstein, *ed., Between Power and Plenty: Foreign Economic Policies of Advanced Industrial States* (Madison: University of Wisconsin Press, 1978), pp. 51–52.

11. See C. Fred Bergsten, Robert O. Keohane, and Joseph S. Nye Jr., "International Economics and International Politics: A Framework for Analysis," in Bergsten and Lawrence B. Krause, eds., *World Politics and International Economics* (Washington, D.C.: Brookings, 1971), p. 14; also Keohane and Nye, *Power and Interdependence: World Politics in Transition* (Boston: Little, Brown, 1977), pp. 42–46.

12. The "grand area" was a concept used in Council on Foreign Relations

planning in the early 1940s for the postwar period. See Laurence H. Shoup and William Minter, *Imperial Brain Trust: The Council on Foreign Relations and U.S. Foreign Policy* (New York: Monthly Review Press, 1977), pp. 135–40.

13. Albert O. Hirschman, *National Power and the Structure of Foreign Trade* (1945; rpt. Berkeley: University of California Press 1980), pp. ix-x; Burke is quoted in Hirschman.

14. Kindleberger, "Group Behavior," pp. 43–44, 46. The *locus classicus* for such reasoning is now James R. Kurth, "The Political Consequences of the Product Cycle: Industrial History and Political Outcomes," *International Organization* 33 (Winter 1979), pp. 1–34.

15. Krasner, "US Commercial and Monetary Policy," p. 60; Alexander Gerschenkron, *Economic Backwardness in Historical Perspective* (Cambridge: Harvard University Press, 1962).

16. Nicos Poulantzas, *Political Power and Social Classes* (London: NLB, 1975), part 4.

17. Karl Polanyi, *The Great Transformation* (New York: Farrar & Rinehart, 1944).

18. See Bruce Cumings, *The Origins of the Korean War: Liberation and the Emergence of Separate Regimes* (Princeton: Princeton University Press, 1981), chap. 1. On Taiwan see Samuel Ho, *The Economic Development of Taiwan 1860–1970* (New Haven: Yale University Press, 1978), pp. 26, 32; he puts a similar emphasis on the role of the colonial state in Taiwan.

19. Jean-Pierre Lehmann, *The Image of Japan: From Feudal Isolation to World Power, 1850–1905* (London: Allen & Unwin, 1978), p. 178; J. M. Winter, "The Webbs and the Nonwhite World: A Case of Socialist Racialism," *Journal of Contemporary History* 9 (January 1974), pp. 181–92.

20. Umemura and Mizoguchi, *Quantitative Studies*, pp. 70–77.

21. David S. Landes, "Japan and Europe: Contrasts in Industrialization," in William W. Lockwood, ed., *The State and Economic Enterprise in Japan* (Princeton: Princeton University Press, 1965), p. 182.

22. Cumings, *Origins,* chaps. 1 and 2; Ho, *Economic Development,* pp. 28–57; also Chingyuan Lin, *Industrialization in Taiwan, 1946–1972: Trade and Import-Substitute Policies for Developing Countries* (New York: Praeger, 1973), pp. 13–28.

23. James B. Palais, *Politics and Policy in Traditional Korea* (Cambridge: Harvard University Press, 1975), pp. 1–19.

24. Ho, *Economic Development,* pp. 43, 57.

25. Cumings, *Origins,* chaps. 8–10.

26. Guenther Stein, *Made in Japan* (London: Methuen, 1951) pp. 181, 191.

27. Ohkawa and Rosovsky, *Japanese Economic Growth,* pp. 180–83, 197.

28. Ho, *Economic Development,* pp. 70–90; Lin, *Industrialization in Taiwan,* pp. 19–22.

29. Mason et al., *Economic and Social Modernization,* pp. 76, 78.

30. Lin, *Industrialization in Taiwan,* p. 19.

31. Bruce Cumings, "Corporatism in North Korea," *Journal of Korean Studies* 4 (1983).

32. Cumings, *Origins*, chaps. 1 and 2.

33. T. J. Pempet, "Japanese Foreign Economic Policy: The Domestic Bases for International Behavior," in Katzenstein, *Between Power and Plenty*, pp. 139–90.

34. Chalmers Johnson, "A Japanese Model?" (Paper presented at the Japan Seminar, University of Washington, School of International Studies, Seattle, May 1981); also Johnson, *MITI and the Japanese Miracle* (Stanford, Calif.: Stanford University Press, 1982), pp. 305–24.

35. Allen, *Japan's Economic Policy*, pp. 42–50, 119–20.

36. Ohkawa and Rosovsky, *Japanese Economic Growth*, pp. 221–23.

37. Allen, *Japan's Economic Policy*, pp. 50, 102, 128.

38. Ibid., pp. 51–54.

39. John Emmerson, *The Japanese Thread* (New York: Holt, Rinehart & Winston, 1978), p. 256. I am indebted to Michael Schaller for providing me with this quotation.

40. Jon Halliday, *A Political History of Japanese Capitalism* (New York: Pantheon, 1975), pp. 183–84.

41. Akira Iriye, "Continuities in U.S.-Japanese Relations, 1941–49," in Yonosuke Nagai and Iriye, eds., *The Origins of the Cold War in Asia* (Tokyo: University of Tokyo Press, 1977), pp. 378–407.

42. Viner, "Power versus Plenty," p. 91.

43. John G. Roberts, "The 'Japan Crowd' and the Zaibatsu Restoration," *Japan Interpretor* 12 (Summer 1979), pp. 384–415.

44. Charles S. Maier, "The Politics of Productivity; Foundations of American International Economic Policy after World War II," in Katzenstein, *Between Power and Plenty*, p. 45.

45. Halliday, Political History, p. 183.

46. See Kennan's remarks in "Transcript of Roundtable Discussion," U.S. Department of State, 6, 7, and 8 October 1949, pp. 25, 47, in Carrollton Press Declassified Documents Series, 1977, 316 B.

47. U.S. Central Intelligence Agency, ORE 43–48, 24 May 1948, in HST/PSF file, Memos 1949, box 255, Harry S. Truman Library, Independence, Missouri.

48. Economic Cooperation Administration, unsigned memorandum of 3 November 1948, in Dean Acheson Papers, box 27, Harry S. Truman Library.

49. Central Intelligence Agency, ORE 69–49, "Relative US Security Interest in the European-Mediterranean Area and the Far East," 14 July 1949, in HST/PSF file, Memos 1949, box 249, Harry S. Truman Library.

50. Calleo and Rowland, *America and the World Political Economy*, pp. 198–202.

51. Draft paper, NSC 48, 26 (October 1949, in NSC materials, box 207, Harry S. Truman Library. For a fuller elaboration see Bruce Cumings, "Introduction: The Course of American Policy toward Korea, 1945–53," in Cumings, ed., *Child of Conflict: The Korean-American Relationship, 1945–1953* (Seattle: University of Washington Press, 1983).

52. Krasner, "US Commercial and Monetary Policy," pp. 63–66; Hirschman, *National Power*, passim.

53. Jon Halliday, "Japan's Changing Position in the Global Political Econ-

omy" (Paper presented at the annual meeting of the Association for Asian Studies, 1979, Los Angeles).

54. See ibid.; also Martha Caldwell, "Petroleum Politics in Japan: State and Industry in a Changing Policy Context" (Ph.D. diss., University of Wisconsin, 1980), chap. 2.

55. Ezra F. Vogel, "Growing Japanese Economic Capabilities and the U.S.-Japan Relationship" (Summary of the 1st meeting of the American Discussion Group on U.S. Policy toward Japan, Harvard University, 13 December 1979; hereafter cited as Harvard Seminar 1979).

56. Johnson, "A Japan Model?" Also Allen, Japan's Economic Policy, pp. 108–9.

57. Pempel, "Japanese Foreign Economic Policy," pp. 163–64; Halliday, "Japan's Changing Position"; Halliday, Political History, p. 283.

58. Ohkawa and Rosovsky, Japanese Economic Growth, pp. 118, 235–36; Pempet, "Japanese Foreign Economic Policy," pp. 149–55.

59. Ho, Economic Development, p. 103; Lin, Taiwan's Industrialization, pp. 27–28.

60. Ho, Economic Development, p. 104.

61. CIA, Handbook 1979. Also Ho, Economic Development, pp. 108–11; also Mason et al., Economic and Social Modernization, p. 165.

62. CIA, Handbook 1979.

63. Allen, Japan's Economic Policy, p. 130.

64. Ho, Economic Development, p. 237.

65. Immanuel Wallerstein, "Dependence in an Interdependent World," in Wallerstein, Capitalist World-Economy.

66. Ohkawa and Rosovsky, Japanese Economic Development, p. 91.

67. On Korea, see Mason et al., Economic and Social Modernization, pp. 7–8; also Paul W. Kuznets, Economic Growth and Structure in the Republic of Korea (New Haven: Yale University Press, 1977), pp. 48–71; on Taiwan see Lin, Taiwan's Industrialization, pp. 3–4, and Ho, Economic Development, p. 106.

68. Alice H. Amsden, "Taiwan's Economic History: A Case of Etatisme and a Challenge to Dependency Theory," Modern China 5 (July 1979), p. 362.

69. Paul B. Simpson, "Report on the University of Oregon Advisory Mission," mimeo. (Eugene: University of Oregon, 1961), p. 49. I am indebted to Tony Michel for bringing this quotation to my attention.

70. Guillermo A. O'Donnell, Modernization and Bureaucratic-Authoritarianism in South American Politics (Berkeley: University of California Institute for International Studies, 1973); see also the articles by O'Donnell, Fernando Henrique Cardoso, Robert Kaufman, James Kurth, Albert Hirschman, and Jose Serra in David Collier, ed., The New Authoritarianism in Latin America (Princeton: Princeton University Press, 1979). Serra, Hirschman, and, in part, Kaufman challenge the O'Donnell theses.

71. Mason, et. al., Economic and Social Modernization, p. 47; Ian M. D. Little, "An Economic Renaissance," in Walter Galenson, ed., Economic Growth and Structural Change in Taiwan (Ithaca: Comell University Press, 1979), p. 474. See also Ho, Economic Development, p. 195.

72. Mason, et al., *Economic and Social Modernization*, pp. 96, 129–32; Kuznets, *Economic Growth*, pp. 73, 96–97; Lin, *Taiwan's Industrialization*, pp. 83–93.

73. Kuznets, *Economic Growth*, p. 10; Wade and Kim, *Economic Development*, p. 100; Suh Sang Chul, "Development of a New Industry through Exports: The Electronics Industry in Korea," in Wontack Hong and Anne O. Krueger, eds., *Trade and Development in Korea* (Seoul: Korea Development Institute, 1975).

74. Lin, *Taiwan's Industrialization*, p. 134.

75. Samuel Huntington, *Political Order in Changing Societies* (New Haven: Yale University Press, 1968), pp. 7, 25, 258–61.

76. Mason et al., *Economic and Social Modernization*, pp. 16–17.

77. Kuznets, *Economic Growth*, p. 85; see also pp. 105–7.

78. Mason et al., *Economic and Social Modernization*, pp. 16, 263, 485.

79. Ibid., p. 277.

80. Ibid., pp. 19, 486.

81. Ho, *Economic Development*, p. 251.

82. Mason et al., *Economic and Social Modernization*, p. 22.

83. Lin, *Taiwan's Industrialization*, pp. 139–44; Choe Boum Jong, "An Economic Study of the Masan Free Trade Zone," in Hong and Krueger, *Trade and Development*.

84. Kuznets, *Economic Growth*, p. 67; Mason et al., *Economic and Social Modernization*, p. 99; Greenhalgh, "Dependency, Distribution"; seminar paper by Anthony Michel, University of Washington, Seattle, 5 May 1983.

85. Kuznets, *Economic Growth*, p. 152; Lin, *Taiwan's Industrialization*, p. 137.

86. Daniel Chirot, *Social Change in the Twentieth Century* (New York: Harcourt Brace Jovanovich, 1977), pp. 218–20.

87. David C. Cole and Princeton N. Lyman, *Korean Development: The Interplay of Politics and Economics* (Cambridge: Harvard University Press, 1971), p. 135; also Kuznets, *Economic Growth*, p. 71.

88. Greenhalgh, "Dependency, Distribution."

89. Lin, *Taiwan's Industrialization*, pp. 131–32.

90. Wade and Kim, *Economic Development*, p. 10; Kuznets, *Economic Growth*, p. 103.

91. Hirschman, *National Power*, pp. 34–35.

92. Ibid., p. 30.

93. Mason et al., *Economic and Social Modernization*, pp. 138, 497; Kuznets, *Economic Growth*, p. 73.

94. Kuznets, *Economic Growth*, p. 81.

95. Lin, *Taiwan's Industrialization*, p. 173.

96. Vogel, *Harvard Seminar*, 1979.

97. Lin, *Taiwan's Industrialization*, p. 134.

98. A good summary of the recent economic problems of the ROK's export-led program can be found in Yung Chul Park, "Recent Economic Developments in Korea" (Paper presented to the Columbia University Seminar on Korea, 24 April 1981).

99. See "South Korea's New Leader. Off and Running," *Far Eastern Economic Review*, 30 January–5 February 1981; *Christian Science Monitor*, 5 January 1982; *Tonga Ilbo* (East Asia Daily), 26 December 1981.

100. World Bank, *Korea: A World Bank Country Economic Report*, Parvez Hasan and D. C. Rao, coordinators (Baltimore: Johns Hopkins University Press, 1979), pp. 8–9, 47. This is also a good source on World Bank criticism of Korea's deepening industrialization strategy during the third Five-Year Plan.

101. Lecture by Norman Thorpe, Seoul correspondent for the *Asian Wall Street Journal*, Seattle, Wash., 8 January 1982; also John Marcom Jr., "Korea Dents Japanese Dominance in Steel," *Asian Wall Street Journal*, 28 December 1981.

102. Raymond Vernon, in *Harvard Seminar 1979*, Jon Halliday, "The Struggle for East Asia," *New Left Review* no. 124 (December 1980), pp. 3–24.

103. Vogel in *Harvard Seminar 1979*.

104. Vernon in ibid.

# 7

# Global Sourcing and Regional Divisions of Labor in the Pacific Rim

## GARY GEREFFI

Most efforts to define the region variously known as Pacific Rim, Pacific Basin, Asia-Pacific, and so on, have been quite unsatisfactory. There is an inherent geographical bias in all these definitions, since they tend to view the region as a geographical given despite the difficulties of "delineating the boundaries of the region, determining its center(s), and deciding whom of all the people who inhabit the region to include within it as serious participants in its activities."[1] "Pacific Rim," one of the most commonly used terms, has the drawback of focusing too exclusively on the edges of the region, leaving out of the picture all that is inside the region. "Pacific Basin" has the opposite problem, since it suggests that the center of the region is somewhere in the ocean. "Asia-Pacific" has the advantage of referring not just to the region's location but also to one of its principal human components although the Asian peoples are so diverse that the term loses any social specificity. Finally, the term "Asian-American Pacific" might be preferred as descriptively more comprehensive, including the peoples on both sides of the Pacific, but this apparent egalitarian inclusiveness is misleading because it glosses over the historical problem of changes in the scope and structure of competing interests in the constitution of Asia and the Americas.

This chapter has not been written to defend any of these definitions of the region, nor to add a new one. The Pacific Rim is not just a geographical region nor is it solely the by-product of elite-centered, EuroAmerican "hegemonic ideologies" of expansion into the Pacific hinterland, although geopolitical factors undoubtedly have been important in shaping the internal dynamics of the region as well as its insertion into the world economy. Rather, I prefer to take a more inductive or grounded approach and look at the Pacific Rim as a geographical arena tied together by a variety of economic and social networks. My empirical focus will be a comparison of three global industries: garments, automobiles, and personal computers. During the post-World War II period, the trade, investment, and migration patterns associated with these industries have linked East Asian and Latin American nations with the United States in ways that have both consolidated and reshaped the Asian-American Pacific region. Furthermore, one of the important consequences of these transnational production networks has been a weakening of the role of individual governments in the formulation of national development policies, and in determining how these regions will be linked to the global political economy.

Evidence from the garment, automobile, and personal computer industries indicates the evolution of a pattern of global sourcing whereby the "national segmentation" that characterized the import-substituting industries of the past is being replaced by a new logic of "transnational integration" based on geographical specialization and tightly linked international supply networks. In other words, the shift from import-substituting industrialization (ISI) to export-oriented industrialization (EOI) in many Pacific Rim nations has ushered in a new international division of labor in the world economy.[2] The flows of goods, capital, and people within East Asia and North America serve to consolidate each region, as well as the trans-Pacific connections that link the regions on either side of the Pacific Basin, creating similar regional divisions of labor in East Asia and North America.[3] In addition, the trans-Pacific trade, investment, and migration flows are leading to a multilateralization of these regional blocs, with important consequences not only for the development strategies of the East Asian and Latin American nations involved, but also for the process of industrialization being carried out in the United States.

## Global Sourcing: Diverse Patterns in Three Industries

Industrialization today is the result of an integrated system of global production and trade, buttressed by new forms of investment and financing, promoted by specific government policies, and entailing distinctive patterns of spatial and social organization. International trade has allowed nations to specialize in different branches of manufacturing and even in different stages of production within a specific industry, leading to the emergence of a global manufacturing system in which production capacity dispersed to an unprecedented number of developing as well as industrialized countries.[4]

In the contemporary global manufacturing system, production of a single good commonly spans several countries and regions, with each nation performing tasks in which it has a cost advantage. This is true for traditional manufactures, such as garments, as well as for modern products, like automobiles and computers. In order to understand the implications of this worldwide division of labor for specific sets of newly industrializing countries (NICs) in East Asia and Latin America, it is helpful to analyze the distinct patterns of global sourcing that characterize each of these industries.

Three kinds of international subcontracting are used to promote global sourcing, but their relative importance varies across industries. *Export processing* production involves the labor-intensive assembly of manufactured goods, often in officially designated industrial zones that offer special incentives to foreign investors. This form of global sourcing has been significant in certain phases of all three of the industries considered below, since garments, certain auto parts (e.g., wiring harnesses), and the manufacture of semiconductors for use in personal computers all have assembly-intensive phases in the production process enabling major savings in low-wage countries. *Component supply subcontracting* refers to the manufacture of technologically sophisticated component parts for export to original-equipment manufacturers in the developed countries. This is an increasingly important feature of the automobile, computer, and household appliance industries. *Commercial subcontracting* of finished goods is based on specification buying by large-volume retailers who market the goods under private labels or in their own retail outlets. This is particularly common in the garment industry, but it also is of growing significance in the personal computer, replacement auto parts, and footwear industries.[5] Finally, there are *independent exporters* who do not utilize subcontracting relationships to sell their goods abroad. They assume the responsibility not only for production but also for overseas marketing utilizing their own brand names, as exemplified by auto producers in South Korea (Hyundai) and personal computer companies in Taiwan (Acer) and South Korea (Leading Edge).

These various types of global sourcing entail different sets of preconditions for the exporting countries. Export processing production is based on abundant cheap labor, political stability, and often a battery of official investment incentives. This is the easiest of the export roles for a developing country to adopt, but it also is inherently unstable as wage levels and political conditions change.

The component supplier role requires more highly skilled labor and investors willing to set up capital- and technology-intensive plants in the NICs. A nation's proximity to core country markets is an advantage for both the export-processing and component supplier forms of global sourcing, decreasing transport costs and increasing the speed of delivery for seasonal industries like garments and footwear.

Commercial subcontracting requires a local entrepreneurial class that has the capital and technological ability to supply large-volume, original-equipment manufacturer (OEM) contracts for developed country markets. Size of firms is not as important as the ability to flexibly shift output in response to the buyers' needs.

Finally, the successful independent exporters must control export and distribution networks in global commodity chains, in addition to attaining a high degree of productive efficiency. Large vertically integrated firms have a major advantage here, as do those with distinctive or technologically innovative products. So far, South Korea is the NIC that has made the biggest strides in this direction because the *chaebols* have the financial, technological and marketing resources needed to become fully internationalized.

## Garments

The garment industry was one of the first sectors in which developing nations achieved a rapid growth of manufactured exports to the industrialized economies. The Third World share in international trade in this sector nearly doubled from 22 percent to 41 percent between 1970 and 1981. In the mid-1980s, clothing accounted for 21 percent of all Third World manufactured exports, with Hong Kong, South Korea, and Taiwan being by far the largest clothes exporters.[6] Together, the East Asian NICs produced 60 percent of all clothing imports to the United States in 1988 ($13.6 billion), whereas the total share for Latin American nations was just under 10 percent ($2.2 billion). As we can see in Table 7.1, although the East Asian share of U.S. clothing imports declined by 14

TABLE 7.1
U.S. Imports of Textile and Clothing Products, 1980 and 1985–1988
(millions of U.S. dollars, customs value)

|      |          | Total  | Latin America[a] | | East Asia | |
|------|----------|--------|--------|-----------------|--------|-----------------|
|      |          |        |        | % of U.S. Imports |      | % of U.S. Imports |
| 1980 | Textiles | $2,676 | $239   | 8.9             | $929   | 34.7            |
|      | Clothing | 6,848  | 586    | 8.6             | 5,035  | 73.5            |
| 1985 | Textiles | 5,274  | 389    | 7.4             | 1,985  | 37.6            |
|      | Clothing | 16,056 | 1,070  | 6.7             | 10,727 | 66.8            |
| 1986 | Textiles | 5,768  | 446    | 7.7             | 2,177  | 37.7            |
|      | Clothing | 17,288 | 1,216  | 7.0             | 10,814 | 62.5            |
| 1987 | Textiles | 6,511  | 543    | 8.3             | 2,268  | 34.8            |
|      | Clothing | 20,490 | 1,627  | 7.9             | 12,606 | 61.5            |
| 1988 | Textiles | 6,748  | 567    | 8.4             | 2,225  | 33.0            |
|      | Clothing | 22,877 | 2,231  | 9.8             | 13,642 | 59.6            |

[a]Excluding Central America and the Caribbean.
*Source:* U.S. Department of Commerce, *Highlights of U.S. Export and Import Trade,* various years.

percentage points (from 73.5 percent to 59.6 percent) between 1980 and 1988, the Latin American nations (excluding Central America and the Caribbean) only increased their share of the U.S. market by 1 percentage point (from 8.6 percent to 9.8 percent) during this same period.

The manufacture of apparel traditionally has been a highly labor-intensive activity with low capital and technology requirements. The industry relies on a combination of dextrous, low-paid, and predominantly female workers, and sturdy, flexible, and relatively inexpensive sewing machines as the basic unit of production. Clothing manufacturing is a sequential, multistage activity that can be divided into three phases: (a) preassembly (the inspection, grading, marking, and cutting of the cloth); (b) assembly, which involves up to 100 sequential sewing operations; and (c) finishing, which basically entails pressing and packaging the completed garment.[7] Since the assembly of clothes from soft, limp fabrics requires considerable manual manipulation of the materials by machine operators at all stages of production, the industry has been highly resistant to automation.

The international organization of garment production basically is a response to three kinds of factors: (a) manufacturing costs, (b) national protective barriers, and (c) industrial flexibility. Materials and labor are the two primary manufacturing costs in garment production. Material costs are roughly the same for all producers. Labor costs, however, vary considerably from region to region and thus are the main determinant of international competitive advantage in the apparel industry. The hourly wage for textile workers in 1982, for example, was $5.20 in the United States, $1.80 in Hong Kong, $1.50 in Taiwan, $1.00 in South Korea, $0.40 in the Philippines, and $0.20 in mainland China.[8] Since labor costs are at least four times greater in the United States than in the Asian NICs and China, firms operating in the United States are at a considerable cost disadvantage. The large savings in labor costs thus has led U.S. apparel producers to invest heavily in offshore production.

Protective trade legislation (voluntary and involuntary export quotas, import tariffs, and other trade restrictions) continues to have a dramatic effect upon global sourcing in the garment industry. The consequences of tariffs generally are more straightforward than quotas because they directly increase the overall cost of imported products. Price sensitive retailers tend to source their garments from firms in nations with low tariffs because it lowers total costs. The effect of the U.S. export quota system on international sourcing is much more convoluted than that of tariffs, largely because the U.S. system itself is so complex. For example, the United States uses seventy-five narrow product categories for garment quotas, with many U.S. quotas based upon the quantity (or number) rather than the value of exports. To evade these quotas, exporting nations commonly switch their production to items or materials not yet subject to quotas. In the late 1970s, Hong Kong apparel producers began to export garments largely composed of ramie, a rough linenlike fiber that was not included in U.S. quotas at the time, and in the early 1980s some Hong Kong manufacturers started making jackets with zip-on sleeves since the quota on jackets was tight, but there were no quotas on vests or sleeves.[9]

Industrial flexibility refers to the ability of the industry to produce what buyers demand. In recent years, U.S. firms have started to become more responsive to retailers' demands in order to meet the challenge from foreign companies in a wide range of industries ranging from apparel to autos. Liz Claiborne, a major U.S. fashion company, began to source abroad less as a matter of price than because of the difficulty of finding capable domestic suppliers who were willing to give Claiborne the variety of fabrics and the careful tailoring she wanted.[10]

Technological innovations in the garment industry have begun to change the logic of global sourcing, however. Sophisticated computer-aided design (CAD) and computer-aided manufacturing (CAM) systems are now available to carry out the design, grader, and marking activities in the preassembly stage of production. In the assembly and finishing stages as well, numerical control and microcomputer-based sewing machines, robotic handling devices, and automated transfer systems are becoming more commonplace.[11] Garment producers in the United States thus can keep tariff duties to a minimum by performing the technology-intensive and high-value-added preassembly stage of apparel production in the United States; the more labor intensive assembly stage is still sourced offshore to low-wage nations. In addition, U.S. quotas based on quantity (rather than value) of exports have led some of the major East Asian garment-producing nations to make higher value-added clothes in order to increase the profitability of their fixed supply of exports. This strategy of climbing the value-added ladder has been hindered by the marked currency appreciations that have affected East Asian nations like Taiwan and South Korea.

## Automobiles

The international motor vehicle industry underwent a profound change in the 1970s and 1980s. The oil price rises of 1973 and 1979, coupled with the rapid growth of the Japanese automotive industry since the 1960s and the decline in demand for motor vehicles in the main producing countries, significantly advanced the internationalization of capital and fostered the creation of a truly global industry. The three regional blocs of North America, Europe, and East Asia are becoming much more closely linked in trade, cross-investments, and joint production arrangements.[12]

The leading automotive transnational corporations (TNCs) have transformed their global sourcing arrangements in two novel ways. First, the industry is integrating its production process on a global scale by the international sourcing of standard parts and engineering resources needed to design and build "world cars." In this way, certain countries have emerged as the key suppliers for basic components or even entire vehicles. Second, automotive TNCs are producing more complex components with advanced technologies in developing countries. This "world component supply strategy" entails a higher degree of technological sophistication and country specialization than the complementary "world car strategy," which emphasizes broadly based, and sometimes regional, production schemes of a more labor-intensive nature.

The trend toward regional integration within the global strategies of car makers is well illustrated by Toyota's recent agreement with members of the Association of Southeast Asian Nations (ASEAN) to begin a component-parts exchange program.[13] Diesel engines from Thailand, gasoline engines from Indonesia, steering gears from Malaysia, and transmissions from the Philippines are to be shipped among the participating countries for assembly of cars that eventually will be sent back to Japan for export to overseas markets. Such an arrangement will help Japan minimize tariffs within the ASEAN bloc and also avoid U.S. export quotas, since component supplies from the other Asian nations would not be counted as Japanese domestic content.

Mexico provides a good example of specialized component assembly for the U.S. market. Lured by low wages, a favorable currency exchange rate, close proximity to the United States, and favorable Mexican legislation, world automakers and parts suppliers have increased their exports from plants in Mexico.[14] Automobile engines are being manufactured by U.S.-based TNCs in high volume for incorporation into cars built in their U.S. plants. Mexican engine production is the epitome of global integration, combining "U.S. managers, European technology, Japanese manufacturing systems, and Mexican workers."[15]

The common pressures toward internationalization in both production and trade have produced distinct results in the Latin American and East Asian NICs.[16] Although South Korea and Brazil both have stressed exports of *finished vehicles*, these results stem from different kinds of corporate strategies and structures. The large integrated domestic auto companies in South Korea have been able to fund both long-term investment and product development at home and overseas, leading to the establishment of Korean automobile subsidiaries in major external markets like the United States and Canada. Brazil's exports of finished vehicles, however, reflect the desire of the U.S., Japanese, and European TNCs to use Brazil as a regional base to serve their customers in neighboring Latin American and other Third World countries.

Taiwan and Mexico have tended to emphasize the production of *auto parts* in the global motor vehicle industry, with close ties to the U.S. market. Whereas Mexico has implemented this component supplier strategy through the intrafirm networks of automotive TNCs, Taiwan has relied heavily on the efforts of 2,000 domestic auto parts companies, the majority of which are family businesses that are able to respond quickly to shifting consumer demand, but less able to invest in the research and expensive production machinery needed to improve their design capability and technological sophistication. Taiwan's auto assembly industry provided around 10,000 jobs in the mid-1980s; its parts industry employed 50,000 people. Nearly 60 percent of Taiwan's auto exports are sent to the United States. They are add-on accessories or spare parts sold in the after market; relatively few of Taiwan's auto parts exporters have major OEM contract.[17]

In summary, these diferences in the mode of incorporation of each of the NICs into the global motor vehicle industry are caused by national variations in industrial structure, the competitive strategies of the leading auto manufacturers worldwide, and the distinctive role of automobiles in advanced phases of ISI and EOI.

## Personal Computers

The production of personal computers consists of four different stages that can be separated in time and space: knowledge-based research and design, advanced manufacturing, unskilled assembly work, and final product testing.[18] Each stage has distinct labor requirements, which has led to the spatial segmentation of the global industry. Research and design activities require ready access to highly trained scientists and engineers, which is facilitated by proximity to universities and research institutes such as those found in the innovative centers of the United States, Europe, and Japan. Advanced manufacturing and testing functions require skilled manual workers, technicians, and quality control supervision. This phase of production has been dispersed to semiperipheral locations in East Asia and Latin America in recent years containing at a minimum isolated pools of skilled labor and an adequate industrial infrastructure. Increased automation in the advanced manufacturing and testing areas of production, however, has led to a gradual return of some of these jobs to the more developed countries. Finally, assembly activities continue to draw mainly on unskilled labor, and they overwhelmingly are located in the low-wage areas of East Asia, Latin America, and the Caribbean.

Three primary patterns of global sourcing are evident within the personal computer industry.[19] First, much like the garment and footwear industries, the personal computer industry depends to a considerable degree on the sourcing of semiskilled, labor-intensive production operations from low-wage locations offshore. Second, the global sourcing of components and "peripherals" is common in the personal computer industry because developing nations are able to manufacture components without necessarily having the technological capability to make complete computer systems. South Korean and Taiwanese producers have specialized in producing computer hardware on an OEM basis for computer TNCs.[20] Third, the sourcing of finished personal computers from the Third World into the United States is a relatively limited phenomenon since most developing nations lack the internal market needed to allow them to become efficient broad-line producers of completed personal computers. Mexico has an arrangement with IBM, however, to export finished computers to the U.S. market, and similar arrangements are being considered in other NICs.

## Regional Dynamics and the Reshaping of the Pacific Rim

The trend toward global sourcing arrangements and international subcontracting in the world economy has profoundly affected the regional dynamics in East Asia and North America. Even as the internal division of labor *within* each region has become more complex, the economic and social linkages *between* the two regions have increased. This has produced a simultaneous consolidation and multilateralization of these regional blocs. Changes in the flows of good (international trade), capital (direct foreign investment), and people (international migration) that link nations within the Pacific Rim illustrate these changes.

### Industrial Upgrading and the Consolidation of Regional Divisions of Labor

Manufactured exports from Japan and the East Asian NICs (Hong Kong, Taiwan, South Korea, and Singapore) have been a central feature of the so-called East Asian economic miracle of the past three decades. The level of these exports has skyrocketed throughout the 1970s and 1980s, as the East Asian NICs clearly established themselves as the Third World's premier exporters. Hong Kong topped the list in 1988 with U.S.$63.2 billion in exports, followed closely by South Korea and Taiwan with export totals of just over U.S.$60 billion each; Singapore had U.S.$39.2 billion in exports. Although quite successful by their own historical and regional standards, the Latin American NICs trailed their East Asian counterparts by a considerable margin. Brazil was the leading Latin American exporter at U.S.$33.7 billion, followed by Mexico with an export total of U.S.$20.7 billion.[21]

The East Asian and Latin American NICs' export promotion efforts have been centered on the U.S. market since their onset in the 1960s. Nonetheless, the degree of export reliance on the United States varies considerably among the NICs. In 1987, Mexico's dependence on the U.S. market was the greatest, at 65 percent, followed by Taiwan at 44 percent; South Korea, 39 percent; Hong Kong and Brazil, around 28 percent; and Singapore, 25 percent.[22] The United States was the leading export market for each of these nations.

The willingness and ability of the United States to continue to fuel the NICs' export growth in the future is very doubtful, however. The United States has had world-record trade deficits in the late 1980s. With the exception of Germany, most of the other West European nations are running trade deficits as well. The political pressures for protectionism in the developed countries are well documented and likely to grow. How the NICs respond to this challenge rests to a large degree on their ability to diversify their export markets, both geographically and through product specialization.

One way this diversification has occurred is through the process of industrial upgrading that has characterized many of the export-oriented industries in the NICs. Although the first significant wave of exports from the East Asian NICs in the late 1950s and the 1960s came from traditional, labor-intensive industries like textiles, apparel, and footwear that relied on low wages and an unskilled work force, there has been a very pronounced shift in the 1980s toward an upgraded, skill-intensive version of EOI. These new export industries include higher value-added items that employ sophisticated technology and require a more extensively developed, tightly integrated local industrial base. Products range from computers and semiconductors to numerically controlled machine tools, televisions, videocassette recorders, and sporting goods. This export dynamism in East Asia does not derive solely from introducing new products, but also from continuously upgrading traditional ones (such as garments).

The Latin American NICs also have developed a sophisticated array of exports on the basis of their earlier import-substituting industries. U.S. automobile companies are setting up world-class engine plants in Mexico, for example, partly to cope with Japanese competition.[23] Brazil too has developed state-of-the-art, technologically advanced, and increasingly export-oriented industries from an ISI base in fields like automobiles, computers, armaments, and assorted capital goods.

There are a variety of causes associated with this shift from labor-intensive to technology- and capital-intensive exports. One of the most obvious factors in the consumer goods industries is U.S. *protectionism*, which includes a battery of measures such as tariffs, quotas, and voluntary export restraints intended to protect U.S. firms from Third World manufactured exports. Ironically, these policies frequently have been counterproductive since they have encouraged overseas manufacturers (especially in East Asia) to develop more sophisticated exports to escape the protectionist barriers. Industrial upgrading also has resulted from the *rising wage rates* and recent *currency appreciations* within the East Asian NICs, which pushed them toward exports that were technology intensive and utilized better paid, skilled workers. This latter factor is coupled with the strong competition that has come from *relatively low wage neighboring Asian economies*, such as Malaysia, Thailand, the Philippines, Indonesia, and China.

From a regional perspective, one of the most important consequences of this industrial upgrading has been the emergence of a rather complex internal division of labor within the East Asian political economy. Japan is the technologically advanced core country of the East Asian region, with the East Asian NICs (South Korea, Taiwan, Hong Kong, and Singapore) playing the role of a semiperiphery with continuous industrial upgrading pushing them toward more technology-intensive, higher value added exports. Taiwan and South Korea also have taken in some of the energy-intensive and heavily polluting industries no longer encouraged to remain in Japan (such as chemicals, fertilizers, and mineral smelting operations). The periphery in East Asia is the resource-rich, lower wage countries such as the Philippines, Malaysia, Thailand, Indonesia, and China, which not only supply the region with raw material exports but also specialize in the labor-intensive manufacturing industries that were the export success stories of the East Asian NICs in the first stage of their EOI in the 1960s.[24]

A very similar regional division of labor is emerging in North America. Obviously, the United States is the core country in North America, both as a production center and a market. It has established tight transnational linkages with Canada and now also Mexico in a range of capital-intensive, high-technology industries such as automobiles, and electrical and nonelectrical machinery. Unlike the East Asian situation, however, all three of the main economies in North America also are rich in natural resources. Although Mexico traditionally has been the site for labor-intensive exports from its "old" *maquiladora* plants, many of these same export-oriented assembly operations are now springing up in a number of Caribbean nations, which may become the favored locales for these peripheral economic activities. One additional element in the North American situation is the growing importance of Asian investments in the region, with Japanese firms concentrating on the "new" technology-intensive export industries and Korean and Taiwanese companies investing in the "old" labor-intensive assembly operations.[25]

This latter feature moves us beyond the vertical integration of the regional political economies in East Asia and North America to the trans-Pacific linkages between the two regions. This can be seen most clearly if we focus on the growth of garment exports to the United States from countries in the Caribbean Basin.

## The Multilateralization of Regional Blocs

This cross-penetration of regional blocs in the world economy is fast making nations in the Caribbean Basin a preferred source of manufactured exports destined for the U.S. market. This is most readily apparent in the garment industry. Caribbean apparel exports to the United States more than quadrupled to nearly U.S.$1 billion in the four years following the passage of President Reagan's Caribbean Basin Initiative (CBI) in 1983, creating upwards of 100,000 jobs in the Caribbean.[26] The CBI allows U.S. apparel manufacturers to ship fabric for sewing to low-wage factories in the islands and reimport the finished goods with substantial tax breaks. The *maquiladora* factories in Mexico have a similar preferred status.

If we look more generally at garment exports into the United States that enjoy duty-free content under the Harmonized Tariff Schedule (HTS) subheading 9802.00.80 (formerly item 807 under the tariff schedules of the United States in effect prior to January 1, 1989), most of the foreign sewing operations are located in Mexico and four Caribbean countries: the Dominican Republic, Jamaica, Costa Rica, and Haiti (see Table 7.2). These nations have an abundant supply of low-cost labor, and their proximity to the United States provides U.S. and other foreign firms with greater control over production and shorter delivery lead times than goods shipped from East Asia. In addition, Section 936 of the U.S. Internal Revenue Code provides a tax break to U.S. companies operating "twin" or complementary plants in Puerto Rico and CBI beneficiary nations.[27]

Table 7.3 shows the cost of producing four typical garments in the United States, in the Caribbean Basin under HTS subheading 9802.00.80, and in Hong Kong, the major source of U.S. imported apparel. The figures show that assembly costs in the Caribbean are only one-third of U.S. assembly costs and three-fourths of Hong Kong's costs.

TABLE 7.2
Textiles, Apparel, and Footwear: Duty-Free Value of U.S. Imports for
Consumption under Harmonized Tariff Schedule (HTS) Subheading 9802.00.80,
by Principal Sources, 1985–1988 (millions of U.S. dollars)

| Source | 1985 | 1986 | 1987 | 1988 |
|--------|------|------|------|------|
| Mexico | 282 | 363 | 380 | 406 |
| Dominican Republic | 143 | 190 | 234 | 318 |
| Costa Rica | 62 | 84 | 92 | 131 |
| Haiti | 80 | 78 | 97 | 102 |
| Jamaica | 28 | 49 | 84 | 96 |
| Colombia | 22 | 26 | 30 | 50 |
| Honduras | 17 | 20 | 27 | 39 |
| Guatemala | 6 | 9 | 20 | 30 |
| South Korea | 4 | 4 | 7 | 27 |
| El Salvador | 6 | 6 | 13 | 17 |
| All other | 74 | 76 | 81 | 94 |
| Total | 723 | 906 | 1,065 | 1,312 |

Note: Because of rounding, figures may not add to the totals shown.
Source: U.S. International Trade Commission, *Production Sharing* (USITC Publication No. 2243, 1989), p. 6-3.

Even after subtracting the duties and other expenses associated with importing, the use of Caribbean assembled products still results in cost savings of between 15 and 30 percent.

East Asian garment makers, who are facing labor shortages and rising wages at home, are beginning to flock into the Caribbean Basin to circumvent quota problems and take advantage of lower production costs and faster reaction times.[28] The Dominican Republic provides a good example of this "reverse investment" by the East Asian NICs in the Caribbean. Although the majority of the 225 firms in the Dominican Republic's "Industrial Free Zone" are of U.S. origin, there already are fifteen South Korean companies, employing 6,000 workers, and nine firms from Taiwan.[29] Furthermore, East Asian projects usually contribute higher value added, more jobs, higher levels of investment, and a greater utilization of skilled labor than the 9802.00.80 sewing operations by other foreign firms.[30]

Despite these gains, one should be skeptical of the longer term role that labor-intensive EOI can play in the development of these Caribbean nations. Although export processing activities such as those that have grown so rapidly in Mexico and the Caribbean Basin in recent years have undeniable benefits in job creation, foreign exchange earnings, and the fostering of industrial experience, they do not constitute an appropriate

TABLE 7.3

Cost Comparison of Producing Selected Apparel Products among the United States, the Caribbean Basin, and Hong Kong under Harmonized Tariff Schedule (HTS) Subheading 9802.00.80, 1987

| | Materials | | Labor and Overhead | | Freight, Duty and Related Costs | Total Costs |
|---|---|---|---|---|---|---|
| | Fabric | Total | Cutting | Assembly | | |
| Women's Blouses[a] | | | | | | |
| Domestic | $2.91 | $13.33 | $0.29 | $4.75 | $0.04 | $8.41 |
| Caribbean | 2.90 | 13.33 | .29 | 1.66 | .77 | 6.05 |
| Hong Kong | 2.10 | 12.53 | .09 | 2.20 | 1.41 | 6.23 |
| Men's Sport Coats[b] | | | | | | |
| Domestic | $9.00 | $14.90 | $3.84 | $15.66 | $0.08 | $34.48 |
| Caribbean | 9.00 | 14.90 | 3.84 | 5.44 | 3.49 | 27.67 |
| Hong Kong | 7.20 | 11.63 | 1.26 | 7.24 | 8.12 | 28.25 |
| Brassieres[c] | | | | | | |
| Domestic | $0.55 | $2.19 | $0.18 | $1.79 | $0.01 | $4.17 |
| Caribbean | .55 | 2.19 | .18 | .73 | .45 | 3.55 |
| Hong Kong | .43 | 1.65 | .07 | .83 | .87 | 3.42 |
| Men's Casual Slacks[d] | | | | | | |
| Domestic | $3.03 | $3.59 | $0.16 | $4.46 | $0.02 | $8.23 |
| Caribbean | 3.03 | 3.59 | .16 | 1.50 | 6.57 | 5.88 |
| Hong Kong | 2.51 | 2.93 | .06 | 2.08 | 1.26 | 6.33 |

[a]Long-sleeved blouses, not ornamented, of 55 percent cotton and 45 percent polyester.
[b]Men's sport coats, not ornamented, of 100 percent polyester.
[c]Artificial-fiber underwire brassieres. The 9802.00.80 cost assumes finishing in the United States. The Hong Kong cost is for a finished package.
[d]Men's casual slacks, not ornamented, of 100 percent cotton canvas fabric.
Source: U.S. International Trade Commission, Production Sharing (USITC Publication No. 2243, 1989), p. 64.

basis for a long-term development strategy. Export processing industries may be a starting point for industrialization, but they are not a permanent solution for the countries of the region. They are best seen as a transitional phenomenon: the first stage in a process of moving to a higher level of industrial development when other, more secure jobs will be available.[31]

The major problems of labor-intensive export industries are that they typically have very shallow roots in the local economy and they contribute little to the technological progress of a nation. Mexico's *maquiladora* plants, for example, used only about 3 to 6 percent domestic content in the mid-1980s; well over 90 percent of the materials employed by the manufacturers were imported. This is one of the reasons why Taiwan and South Korea moved very quickly to increase the levels of local integration by export industries in their economies by allowing "bonded factories" to be established anywhere in the country as long as the majority of their output was destined for export.[32] In addition, even very small exporting firms in the East Asian NICs have been encouraged to use modern technology in their factories to enhance their industrial competitiveness. Although it usually takes a generation for a country's skill base to advance from garment work to electronics, both U.S. and East Asian electronics companies are beginning to establish new plants in the Caribbean to export electronics goods duty-free into the United States.[33] A favorable geographical location thus is a major positive factor that can help the Caribbean Basin nations spur their industrial development if accompanied by the right domestic priorities.

The proposed free trade agreement between the United States and Mexico, or a broader North American Free Trade Agreement (NAFTA) that would include Canada and perhaps the Caribbean as well, is unlikely to diminish the substantial transnational integration that already has been established in the region. Although NAFTA explicitly focuses on trade, the ongoing globalization of production in the world economy has produced a "silent integration" in North America that makes the strategic investment decisions by TNCs the prime determinant of new intraregional and interregional trading patterns.

In a formal sense, *maquiladora* industries will cease to exist in Mexico as a legal category if a zero-tariff NAFTA is put into place. Historically the main reason *maquiladoras* were set up was to take advantage of the U.S. tariff provisions (806/807) that allowed participating firms to receive duty-free inputs from the United States and thereby to pay tax only on the value added in Mexico. With no tariffs, *maquiladora* plants are an anachronism.

In reality, however, labor-intensive assembly industries tend to be established wherever low wages, adequate infrastructure, and political stability are to be found. Mexico remains a very attractive site for these investments, although there also is likely to be a sharp growth of "old"-style *maquiladoras* in the Caribbean and Central America where labor costs are as low as in Mexico and the "rules of origin" restrictions of NAFTA may not apply. If Mexico follows the example of the East Asian NICs, it will try to promote the "new" *maquiladoras* because of their added contributions to national development objectives and allow many of the "old" *maquiladoras* to migrate to other sites in the region.[34]

### Global Capitalism and Urban Restructuring in the United States

The dynamics of global sourcing and international subcontracting within and between East Asia and North America involve not only the flow of manufactured products and investment capital, but also of people. Migrant labor flows are significantly changing the spatial organization of production in global industries as core capitalist economies are becoming ever more dependent upon young migrant workers from the Third World. This is reflected in the urban restructuring that currently is under way in the United States. There has been a proliferation of turn-of-the-century-type sweatshops in the garment and electronics industries in large North American cities, especially Los Angeles, Miami, and New York City, that draw on vast pools of low-wage and in many cases undocumented immigrant workers from Mexico, Central America, the Caribbean, and Asia. Many of these U.S. plants have been set up by East Asian entrepreneurs to avoid U.S. trade barriers and to exploit low-cost labor, with the added advantage of direct access to the design and marketing centers in the United States.

Los Angeles County, for example, has become the largest manufacturing metropolitan area in the United States in the 1980s, and its heavy influx of Latin American and East Asian (especially South Korean) migrants has played a major role in this process.[35] Like New York City and Miami, whose resurgence is tied to diverse immigrant flows, Los Angeles combines manufacturing of the highest technical level and the lowest. For instance, garment manufacture in Los Angeles expanded by nearly 60 percent in the past fifteen years, while at the same time the industry contracted by 20 percent in the United States as a whole.[36] Over half of the 3,500 garment factories in Los Angeles County are owned by Asians, the three main groups being Korean, Vietnamese, and Chinese; another third of the factory owners are Latinos, primarily from Mexico.

If one takes a closer look at the bustling garment district near downtown Los Angeles, one finds a predominance of Korean subcontractors making clothes for manufacturers located all around the United States. The local subcontracting networks are exceptionally dense A single Los Angeles-based manufacturer of blue jeans sold under the brand name "Yes" employs 500 different ethnic subcontractors in Los Angeles alone.[37] It is not uncommon for Korean garment contractors to employ a mix of Asian and Latino workers, who battle many ethnic antagonisms as they struggle to make ends meet with several members of the family working in the area's needle trades. The most skilled and enterprising may save enough money to set up their own shops, using ethnic networks to entice their Mexican, Guatemalan, or Chinese compatriots to provide the labor and services needed to survive under conditions of cutthroat competition.

The garment industry in Los Angeles is but one example of the resurgence of domestic subcontracting in the United States, using local pools of immigrant workers and entrepreneurs to compete with the "runaway shops" that went to East Asia and Latin America in search of cheap and reliable labor. It draws the U.S. economy tightly into the Pacific Rim, not only as the world's largest market but also as a site for labor-intensive manufacturing in the tenement sweatshops of major U.S. metropolitan areas. And since many of these workers have come to the United States with the intention of staying as permanent immigrants, these new ethnically dominated industrial districts are likely to be stable domestic production alternatives to the overseas export platforms.

If development theory is to be relevant for the 1990s, it will have to be flexible enough to incorporate increased specialization at the product and geographical levels along with new forms of integration that link the core, semiperipheral, and peripheral nations of the Pacific Rim in novel ways.[38] The production and export networks of the garment, automobile, and personal computer industries illustrate the various modes of incorporation of the NICs in the world economy and the continuing geographical realignment of the location of core and peripheral economic activities in today's global commodity chains.

## Notes

A related version of this paper appears in Ravi Arvind Palat, ed., *Pacific-Asia and the Future of the World-System,* Westport, CT: Greenwood Press, 1992.

1. Arif Dirlik, "The Asia-Pacific Idea: Reality and Representation in the Invention of a Regional Structure," *Journal of World History* 3, no 1 (Spring 1992).

2. See Gary Gereffi and Donald Wyman, eds., *Manufacturing Miracles: Paths of Industrialization in Latin America and East Asia* (Princeton, NJ: Princeton University Press, 1990); Gary Gereffi, "International Economics and Domestic Policies," in Neil J. Smelser and Alberto Mertinelli, eds., *Economy and Society: Overviews in Economic Sociology* (Newbury Park, CA: Sage, 1990), pp. 231–258.

3. "North America" includes the United States, Canada, Mexico, and the Caribbean.

4. Gary Gereffi, "Development Strategies and the Global Factory," *Annals of the American Academy of Political and Social Science* 505 (1989): 92–104.

5. Regarding footwear, see Gary Gereffi and Miguel Korzeniewicz, "Commodity Chains and Footwear Exports in the Semiperiphery," in William Martin, ed., *Semiperipheral States in the World-Economy* (Westport, CT: Greenwood Press, 1990), pp. 45–68.

6. Kurt Hoffman, "Clothing, Chips and Competitive Advantage: The Impact of Microelectronics on Trade and Production in the Garment Industry," *World Development* 13, no. 3 (1985): 371.

7. Hoffman, "Clothing, Chips and Competitive Advantage," pp. 375–376.

8. Ashoka Mody and David Wheeler, "Towards a Vanishing Middle: Competition in the World Garment Industry," *World Development* 15, no. 10/11 (1987): 1, 281.

9. Michael L. Dertouzos, Richard K. Lester, and Robert M. Solow, *Made in America: Regaining the Productive Edge* (Cambridge, MA: MIT Press, 1989), p. 292; James Lardner, "The Sweater Trade," part 1, *New Yorker*, January 11, 1988, pp. 60, 62–65.

10. Lardner, "The Sweater Trade."

11. Hoffman, "Clothing, Chips and Competitive Advantage."

12. Rhys Jenkins, *Transnational Corporations and the Latin American Automobile Industry* (Pittsburgh, PA: University of Pittsburgh Press, 1987).

13. Charles Smith, "Parts Exchange," *Far Eastern Economic Review*, September 21, 1989, p. 73.

14. Gary Gereffi, "Big Business and the State," in Gereffi and Wyman, *Manufacturing Miracles*, pp. 90–109.

15. Harley Shaiken, with Stephen Herzenberg, *Automation and Global Production: Automobile Engine Production in Mexico, the United States, and Canada* (La Jolla, CA: Center for U.S. Mexican Studies, University of California, San Diego, Monograph Series No. 26, 1987), p. 2.

16. Gereffi, "Big Business and the State," p. 106.

17. Andrew Tank, "Made in Taiwan: Will Taiwan Be Asia's Next Automotive Powerhouse?" *Automotive News*, September 29, 1986, pp. 29–31.

18. Jeffrey Henderson, *The Globalisation of High Technology Production: Society, Space and Semiconductors in the Restructuring of the Modern World* (London: Routledge, 1989); Manuel Castells, "The New Industrial Space: Information-Technology Manufacturing and Spatial Structure in the United States," in George Sternlieb and James W. Hughes, eds., *America's New Market Geography* (New Brunswick, NJ: Center for Urban Policy Research, Rutgers University, 1989), pp. 43–99.

19. See David C. O'Connor, "The Computer Industry in the Third World: Policy Options and Constraints," *World Development* 13, no. 3 (1985): 311–332; Henderson, *The Globalisation of High Technology Production.*

20. Peter B. Evans, and Paulo Bastos Tigre, "Paths to Participation in 'High-Tech' Industry: A Comparative Analysis of Computers in Brazil and Korea," *Asian Perspective* 13, no 1 (1989): 5–35.

21. World Bank, *World Development Report* 1990 (New York: Oxford University Press; 1990), pp. 204–205.

22. United Nations, 1987 *International Trade Statistics Yearbook*, vol. 1 (New York: United Nations, 1989); Council for Economic Planning and Development, *Taiwan Statistical Data Book*, 1988 (Taipei: CEPD, 1988), p. 222.

23. Shaiken, *Automation and Global Production.*

24. Bruce Cumings, "The Origins and Development of the Northeast Asian Political Economy: Industrial Sectors, Product Cycles, and Political Consequences," *International Organization* 38, no. 1 (Winter 1984): 1–40; Henderson, *The Globalisation of High Technology Production.*

25. Gary Gereffi, "Mexico's Maquiladora Industries and North American Integration" (Paper presented at a conference titled "Facing North/Facing South: Canadian–United States–Mexican Relations," University of Calgary, Alberta, Canada, May 2–4, 1991).

26. Edward A. Finn, Jr., "Who Made Your Underwear?" *Forbes*, July 25, 1988, p. 56.

27. U.S. International Trade Commission, *Production Sharing: U.S. Imports Under Harmonized Tariff Schedule Subheadings 9802.00.60 and 9802.00.80, 1985–1988* (USITC Publication No. 2243, 1989), p. 65; Guillermo Hillcoat and Carlos Quenan, "Restructuración internacional y re-especialización productiva en el Caribe" (Paper presented at the Second Conference of Caribbean Economists, Bridgetown, Barbados, May 28–30, 1989).

28. Transit time by sea for U.S. clothing imports coming from East Asia is at least four weeks, compared to a matter of hours for goods flown to the United States from the Caribbean.

29. Hillcoat and Quenan, "Restructuración internacional y re-especialización productiva en el Caribe," p. 32.

30. U.S. International Trade Commission, *Production Sharing*, p. 65.

31. Sidney Weintraub, "The Maquiladora Industry in Mexico: Its Transitional Role," in Commission for the Study of International Migration and Cooperative Economic Development, ed., *Unauthorizaed Migration: Addressing the Root Causes*, vol. 2 (Washington, DC: U.S. Government Printing Office, 1990), pp. 1, 143–1, 155.

32. Gereffi, "Mexico's Maquiladora Industries and North American Integration."

33. Finn, "Who Made Your Underwear?" p. 58.

34. Gereffi, "Mexico's Maquiladora Industries and North American Integration."

35. Ivan Light and Edna Bonacich, *Immigrant Entrepreneurs: Koreans in Los Angeles, 1965–1982* (Berkeley: University of California Press, 1988).

36. Kevin F. McCarthy and R. Burciaga Valdez, *Current and Future Effects of Mexican Immigration in California* (Santa Monica: California Roundtable, Rand-R-3365-CR, 1986).

37. Author's interview with a Guatemalan garment subcontractor in Los Angeles, December 1, 1990.

38. Gary Gereffi, "Rethinking Development Theory: Insights from East Asia and Latin America," *Sociological Forum* 4, no. 4 (December 1989): 505–533.

# 8

# Market Dependency in U.S.–East Asian Relations

MEREDITH WOO-CUMINGS

The Argument of this chapter is that U.S.–East Asian relations are afflicted not just by trade tensions that have grown since the early 1970s, to which we have become accustomed, but also by a new cultural and rhetorical divide that increases friction at the same time that it obscures the continuing realities of the relationship. This divide in turn derives from asymmetries of power that have been consistent in U.S.-East Asian relations for decades. Whereas the United States increasingly looks toward East Asia with apprehension, Asians look to the United States much as they have since 1945, as a bigger, stronger, even dominating nation that is nonetheless essential to their continuing growth.

I will argue that certain aspects of this relationship are changing, like the single-market dependency that has characterized Japan, Korea, and Taiwan and the security situation, which is considerably relaxed from the troubled years of the cold war. East Asian moves toward diversifying markets—primarily in Europe—signal a growing departure from the previous structure (going back to the World War II settlement) whereby the United States interacted bilaterally with Western Europe and Japan, and Japan and Europe had little interaction. Additionally, the deepening of economic relations between Northeast and Southeast Asia heralds an interregional reorganization that will carve out more autonomy for all the Asian nations, and perhaps lead to changes in the security structure.

"I will also argue that this attenuation of bilateral relations across the Pacific—perhaps we can call it constructive disengagement—is not necessarily bad, and that it will afford the United States greater flexibility in its conduct of foreign economic policy.

While these changes occur, the deeper problem is the absence of an intellectual framework within which to understand the ongoing transition. I will suggest that Japanese and East Asian economic success has provoked both admiration and deep worry in the United States, giving rise to a "new Orientalism" that both honors and shames Asians too much; quick to find fault and exaggerate difference, this tendency is also quick to patronize and praise, the excessiveness in both directions being the index of the failure of the one to understand the alien Other.

In this chapter I will switch the optic to adopt the perspective of the "Other," to see how it all looks from a different shore—what we might call East Asia's America Problem. I will argue that the cultural constructs and contradictions by which Americans confront East Asian industrial prowess reflect not just an inability to apprehend a still-alien Other, but also the antagonistic currents in U.S. politics between protectionism and free trade, and deep conflicts in the U.S. orientation to the world between expansionism and imperialism, or between what used to be called Asia-firsters and Europe-firsters.[1]

If East Asia has an America problem, of course it is by no means only Americans who partake of it. Indeed, the United States has been more tolerant and open than several European countries, particularly Italy and France. These days it is the French above all whose well-known nationalism increasingly becomes the handmaiden of an appalling racism. The former Prime Minister Edith Cresson referred to "little yellow men" who stay up nights thinking about how to "screw" Europe. Japan is "another universe which wants to conquer," basing itself on a "hermetically sealed" system. "That's the way they are," she announced knowingly.[2]

## The New Orientalism

"Orientalism" is a term by Edward Said and others to connote a Western discourse about Asia that both projects Western hopes and fears onto Asia and fails to uncover the reality of Asia itself.[3] It is a species of prejudice, but one so deeply rooted that its practitioners are generally unaware of it. U.S. Orientalism in regard to East Asia today is Janus-faced and given to dramatic exaggeration: one face looks anxiously back, to find in the past a prelude to a new yellow peril shaking the edifice of Western civilization or even to find analogues in the decade of fascist political economy in the 1930s, whereas another looks forward euphorically to a Pacific Rim golden age in the next century, of "miracle" economies and budding East Asian postmodernity.

If Mark Twain's "innocents abroad" were non-Americans visiting the United States, one of the oddest cultural traits they might encounter would be the mysterious liberal probity of the United States: public utterance and private thoughts seem remarkably divorced, and voicing private thoughts is verboten. Yet racism appears to be on the rise on college campuses, on the far right, and elsewhere. We have heard much lately about a "politically correct" liberal United States in which ethnic jokes and racial stereotypes are forbidden in public discourse and uttering them can quickly get a college student expelled or a prominent person fired. Except in one's living room, or except with regard to one ethnic group: the Japanese in particular, Asians in general.

Some aspects of the problem are quite visible. It is still common on television, for example, to see crude stereotypes of rotund samurai made to masquerade as Japan's everyman, with concomitant bellowing and swordplay. Even the stalward critic of U.S. education and popular culture Allan Bloom feels free to refer to Asians as "yellows" in his recent best-seller.[4] The business of "making strange" in regard to the Japanese and other "Asiatics" like them is still visible in spite of liberal probity and it sells goods in the marketplace. Perhaps such stereotyping even acquires a patriotic halo in this age of perpetual trade deficits. But this realm of the visible is merely the tip of an iceberg.

If caricatures of East Asia in France are one aspect of inveterate French nationalism, we can argue that similar expressions in the United States are animated by the protectionist impulse of "Middle America" (or what Richard Nixon characterized as "mainstreams," or "Newark factory gate").[5] Historically this current has been the repository of U.S. nationalism and has conceived East Asia as a frontier for the United States, to be conquered, organized, and civilized. Today the East Asian countries are perceived to be in but not of the world, free riders in "defense" and predatory in economics—thus sapping U.S. strength such that it fast becomes, in Joseph Chamberlain's words, "a weary Titan staggering under the too vast orb of its fate," or just an amicable fool, taken advantage of at every turn. The contemporary rancor of representatives of this view (Lee Iacocca, for example) indicates a frustration about Asians getting off the reservation and "doing their own thing," so to speak.

The most influential book in the recent and growing genre of "Japan-bashing" literature is by Karel van Wolferen, a Dutch journalist stationed in Tokyo, who recently catapulted into the intellectual limelight in the United States when his book got rave reviews across the spectrum. *The Enigma of Japanese Power* both presents to us a cogent account of Japan's industrial growth and partakes of the new Orientalism. Van Wolferen shows how a long pattern of state-led "developmentalism," combined with a typical pattern of followership in industrial development (copying more advanced technology, adapting previously successful management skills), lies behind Japan's successes. But he also indulges in harmful stereotyping by explaining Japanese success to Americans in terms that only multiply misunderstanding by measuring Japanese deviance from what Westerners hold dear: the Japanese have no regard for "transcendental truths," are "less free than they should be," and are at odds with "one single command that has reverberated throughout Western intellectual development ever since the Greeks: [sic] 'Thou shalt not cherish contradictions.' "

The Japanese, the implication is, are not individuals, are not rational, not logical, and perhaps not "enlightened"; there seems to be no Eastern equivalent of the great Western caesura termed the Enlightenment. Some Japanese, of course, cherish rationality and individualism—van Wolferen has even "met quite a few who want to be taken for distinct persons." But the Japanese remain by and large indistinct to him. In any case his generalizations are so blanketed and opaque that they make refutatior difficult: that a people are "less free than they should be" can probably be said about any society in the world, the assertion rests on an unstated conception of freedom and morality.

When van Wolferen peered into the heart of the Japanese system of political economy, moreover, like Conrad he saw a horror staring back at him: not liberal pluralism, but an all-encompassing and mysterious "System" with no exit, one as "inescapable as the political system of the Soviet Union," only worse because it was more pervasive, and culturally legitimate.[6]

To see Japan as enigmatic, impenetrable, not individualistic, and run by a mysterious system of course recalls stereotypes that go back to the first Western encounters with Asians. What is more irresponsible, however, about the new Orientalism provoked by Japanese economic success is its dramatic exaggeration: not just indictment of Japan and its East Asian facsimiles—South Korea and Taiwan—as illiberal, run by subterranean "systems," and substituting strong states for the presumed natural workings of the market, but also hints that this might really be a kind of fascism.

Van Wolferen thus exhorts Americans to deal harshly with "the Japan Problem," as Europe had to in the past with "the German Problem,"[7] and Ian Buruma, the peripatetic observer for all of Asia for the *New York Review of Books*, compared the impressive Korean show during the opening ceremony of the Seoul Olympics to Hitler's Nuremburg extravaganza in 1936.[8] More recently Buruma has predicted a "Pax Axis" between Japan and unified Germany, pacifist and quiescent in the wake of the Persian Gulf War, but who knows what to expect from this "axis" in the future.[9] And now, perhaps, the inevitable title has appeared: *The Coming War with Japan.*[10]

Ishihara and Morita do little more than reflect back to and play upon these dark fears in *The Japan That Can Say No*. In their idiosyncratic Japanese way they also proffer a postwar replay of the prewar repertoire. Their ethnocentric view asserts Yamato superiority in empire building (as evidenced in the postcolonial performance of South Korea and Taiwan), over a slovenly Yankee imperialism (as seen in the mess in the Philippines). They indulge in a kind of epithet one-upmanship, seeing who can do best in previewing the contestation of the Pacific as a Japanese, and not a U.S. lake.[11] Perhaps Ishihara and Morita reveal more than they wish, however, because their book reads like the battered schoolboy finding a way to get back at the playground bully; it reeks of insecurity.

The new Orientalism thus has counterparts on both sides of the Pacific, and is contradictory and unsettled. For every dark worry about who the Japanese "really are," another U.S. genre looks happily forward to a budding Pacific Rim century in the offing. An admixture of Saint-Simonism and genteel Darwinism, this prophetic culture—and its gurus, such as Alvin Toffler and John Naisbett—privileges the denizens of the Pacific Rim as the mainstay of international capitalist utopia in the next century.[12]

To these prophets the Confucian culture incapable of "transcendental truths" is swell, even if it is non-Western, and indeed constitutes what Hofheinz and Calder call the "East Asia Edge," traditional culture being the background and driving ethic of the "miracle" economies. The old shibboleth that Confucianism stifled the entrepreneurial spirit, so prevalent in the "modernization" literature of the 1950s, is now replaced by a new shibboleth that equates capitalist spirit with hyphenated Confucianism: Post Confucianism, Aggressive-Confucianism, and even Samurai-Confucianism.[13] In other words, Confucianism is an all-purpose grab bag for both faulting and praising East Asia—but "as Confucius say," you can't have it both ways.

The cheerleaders for the Asia-Pacific capitalist utopia tour the internationalist line that nationalism is less important (or inconsequential) in an age of mobile capital and mobile labor. Pacific Asia is a manufacturing basin for consumer goods, and its wealthy class consumes Pacific America's high technology and agriculture: Cray supercomputers for the workaday world, California's mangoes for the dinner table. Meanwhile its poor labors for—anybody. The competitive edge of the United States, so this argument goes, likewise is bolstered through free trade, including free movement of capital, commodities, and people—especially fresh infusion of skilled labor and brains that the new immigration law promises: 600,000 Koreans in the Los Angeles area show that in the Pacific Rim era, you can bring the mountain to the prophet.

This is liberal imperialism at its finest, assuming that all are equal in the empyrean of free trade and ignoring the disparate power relations between the United States, now the only superpower, and Japan, South Korea, and Taiwan. From an objective point of view, Japan is an economic titan and a military wimp; South Korea is a rising economy, but still just half of a divided country with a semisovereign polity, its army still controlled by a U.S. general; Taiwan is a rising economy, a political midget, and a diplomatic nonentity.

The futurologists and the Japan bashers come together, however, in two ways: first, they both have difficulty grasping an East Asia that is neither a miracle nor a menace, but rather some hundreds of millions of people working hard to better their lot, coming along "late" to the task of industrial development and trying to make the best of it with a quite ordinary mixture of good and bad human traits. Second, they both tend to soft-pedal the remaining power asymmetries between the United States and East Asia, which severely constrain either the best or the worst out come, and which predict that for the next several decades we will have neither fascist political economy nor capitalist valhalla, but a persisting structure in which East Asia will continue to play second fiddle. Thus both they and the periodic outbursts of Japan's leaders conceal more than they reveal about the reality of power across the Pacific.

One would never know from the rhetoric of the new Orientalism that the Pacific is still a U.S. lake, where a dominant United States holds sway not just with the Seventh Fleet, myriad military bases, and a panoply of high-tech and nuclear weapons, but also with a U.S. presence that in all its forms—cultural, political, economic—remains pervasive. One would not know that Japan and the East Asian newly industrializing countries (NICs) largely retain a single-market dependency that has influenced their political economies for several decades and that this market is the U.S. one. Nor would one know that Japan and its East Asian neighbors still tend to interact with each other and with the rest of the world through a trilateral structure mediated by Washington.

The U.S. lake has opened, especially in the postwar years, a realm of opportunity for East Asia. But it has also been an albatross, denying the countries of the region their national agency and purpose. The U.S. market has been both a realm of vast opportunity and a drag on the flexibility of East Asian economic policy. Both of these aspects of the relationship, however, are mostly concealed in the U.S. discourse on East Asia, so that we end up either with the specter of authoritarian behemoth states chewing up U.S. industries or the international capitalist utopia.

These fundamental limitations, however, are rarely voiced. The East Asian counterparts of the United States tend to maintain silence on these points except for an occasional and predictably bigoted belch from the conservatives who rule Japan, people too often taken for all of Japan in the United States. The reason for this silence is that Japan, Korea, island China, and (increasingly) mainland China are "rule takers," and not "rule makers" in the international system. Perhaps more important, liberal free market discourse is *the* hegemonic discourse, with no challengers in the international realm.

No one stands for East Asia today and voices a distinctive regional perspective; rather its leaders tend to prefer a weak posture. (The last East Asian theorist of international politics was the now repudiated Mao Zedong.) The East Asian response is reactive, usually a mark of insecurity: an occasional riposte that often partakes of the same, visceral bias with which some Americans view newly risen Asian prowess.

Thus Japanese conservative leaders charge that the U.S. problem is indolence, selfishness, greed, or racial diversity, almost always in the burplike manner that reveals "what they really think," apart from surface politeness and diplomatic legerdemain. The liberals and internationalists of East Asia, on the other hand, plead that their politics is no different from that in the West: democratic and open, a pluralist mirror image (after all, the ruling party is called Liberal Democratic in Japan and Democratic Liberal in South Korea.) Their economies, too, are said to be open, with vast and impressive statistics on trade and investment deployed for the argument—and whatever trade barriers remain are on their way down, nothing more than a matter of time. This is a view of East Asia getting along and going along in the interstices of the international system, molding itself and being molded in the image of the Western creator.

Conservative response and liberal apologetics alike tend to obscure "private thoughts" that are increasingly strong, a growing nationalism in East Asia that lies behind a Japan trying to find a way to say No and a rising tide of self-assertion uniting right and left in South Korea, uniformly interpreted as anti-American by pundits and policymakers. The private thoughts cannot, however, gainsay the reality that the capitalist states of Northeast Asia are semisovereign in their politics and defense, and barely sovereign in their mass culture—the epicenter of the latter still being firmly in Hollywood and New York. They are regionally bereft of anything akin to the European Union, let alone a sense of Europeanness, or common adherence to the legitimacy of social democratic ideals. Japanese, Koreans, and Chinese barely talk to each other, if truth be known.

For all the talk about Japan as Number One, Japan remains utterly unable to fashion an alternative hegemonic discourse, one that can leap across civilizational boundaries to create a universal appeal and turn Japan's solipsism into everyone else's universalism. There is little indigenous weight to offset overwhelming U.S. influence, save the increasingly slim reed of "the East Asian tradition." Money can buy culture and ideology, as did Sony and Matsushita Columbia and MCA, but it has not—as yet—created any; as one literary critic put it, Japan can produce "the signifiers, but not the signified."[14]

This poverty of philosophy, I will argue, stems from the reality of postwar U.S. hegemony in East Asia, which has been overwhelming and unilateral, much more so than in Western Europe, and the reality of relations today, with the U.S. market remaining the engine of the world economy and the talisman of East Asian export success. Starting with MacArthur's suzerainty during the occupation of Japan, the United States has had mostly unilateral sway in the region, symbolized by its frequent apologetics for forgetting to "consult" with its East Asian allies—about opening relations with China, withdrawing troops from Korea, or forgiving debts to the Poles (a recent brouhaha with Japan). And however penetrated its market may be by Asian imports, that market remains the lifeline of East Asian economic success, giving the United States a reverse influence that it rarely acknowledges.

## The Political Economy of U.S. East Asia

Given all the heated rhetoric of recent years, it is useful to look at the basic structure of the East Asian region. In the postwar years, the United States has prevailed over the capitalist countries of East Asia through two historical compacts. One might be thought of as an international Brumairean compact[15] between the victor in the last world war on the one hand and the defeated and its colonial possessions on the other. Just as the bourgeoisie of Louis Bonaparte's France, prostrate before the rifle butt, traded its political rights for the right to make money, so did Japan—and in a curious working of the dialectic, its newly liberated colonies.

Through the "San Francisco framework" of postwar peacemaking, Japan essentially gave up its military power and its autonomy in foreign-policy making. South Korea did the same at the time of the Korean War. Elemental sovereignty over defense and security matters was and is mortgaged to the structure of U.S. defense policy in Japan and Korea, and the state's role in mediating the relationship between the domestic and the international spheres is decidedly weak, at least where the United States is concerned.

National defense, which would ordinarily be a primary task of any state, the Japanese included, was passed on to Washington, and to the U.S. bases in Japan and Korea. In the aftermath of the Korean War, moreover, Washington created under its nuclear umbrella a modified apparition of Japan's prewar military empire, with South Korea's massive military as a regional gendarme, not just to protect the Republic of Korea but to fight Communist insurgents in Vietnam in the 1960s. Vietnam's seventeenth parallel was to have been another cordon sanitaire. Thus former colonies and dependencies, not to mention the GIs in the bases in the Pacific, were to do their bit in protecting the big enchilada, the Japanese archipelago. This was not a bad deal for Japan, of course, and the compact was justified by a weird formula that reverberates today: the Japanese really had to be protected from themselves.

The result of this Brumairean compact was to place South Korea on the geopolitical fault line, with the Korean military as a backstop to Japan's defense—a political disaster for the Korean people. Korea's civil society came under the tight grip of the state, which was in turn thoroughly penetrated by the United States. Its formidable military force is one of the biggest and best in the world, but under the operational control of the United States: South Korea is a semisovereign state. It has a vast military establishment it does not fully control and a foreign policy that is essentially dictated from without. This was a great deal for the Korean military, which became the dominant force in political life, but it wasn't much of a deal for the South Korean people (not to mention the North Koreans). Even after the war, the Korean peninsula continued to be an armed-to-the-teeth tinderbox.

From 1948 to 1978 Taiwan had a similar "deal," with the Guomindang mainlanders dealt the best hand, native Taiwanese excluded from power, another huge military organization devastating democracy, but all the islanders free to make money. In 1978, of course, the United States demonstrated its ultimate trump hand by switching this China for the other one, leaving Taiwan to make the best of its very bad deal—the saving grace being that they were still free to make money, which they have done with a vengeance.

A virtual monopoly on the means of violence and the whip hand in important foreign policy decisions is one aspect of U.S. hegemonic politics in East Asia. The other compact shaping the region is economic, and this was the maintenance of a U.S. market open to the capitalist upstarts in East Asia. The history and the workings of this compact are complicated, but the upshot, I will argue, was to deny the states of the region national agency in the conduct of domestic politics and economics. We can call this the compact of *single-market dependence* and seek to understand its political logic.

In 1988 the United States absorbed more than a third of all of Japan's exports, about 40 percent of South Korea's, and 44 percent of Taiwan's exports. Even when Japan is excluded, U.S. imports from the four East Asian NICs, ASEAN, and China totaled U.S.$90 billion in 1989. The three Northeast Asian capitalist economies are thus remarkably dependent on the U.S. market. Canada and Mexico are the only other countries more singularly dependent on the U.S. market; no other West European, African, or Middle Eastern nation shows any comparable level of single-market dependence for its exports. It is a sobering thought that the only area in the world that is comparable in its trade pattern was the former

Eastern European bloc, with its single-market dependence on the Soviet Union.[16]

The political side of this economic coin is obvious. As Albert O. Hirschman once argued, a large economy that can accommodate a great portion of the exports of a small economy, with the latter having a relatively small fraction of import share, determines the relations of trade *and* political dependence for its trading partner. Germany, for instance, cultivated this pattern vis-à-vis smaller Eastern European nations in the interwar years.[17] Hirschman's argument, one of the first to articulate the logic of international dependence, gave grist to the mill of Latin American *dependencia* school, but has been mostly overlooked by students of East Asia.

This is quite a reversal from the turn-of-the-century open door policy toward East Asia; in fact, one might with some license characterize the situation today as a reverse open door. The open door was a modal foreign policy for a rising power like the United States, say, from the 1870s to World War I, seeking to penetrate markets in East Asia and Latin America that were held or influenced by European powers. Once hegemony was achieved, however, in the postwar period, the door also opened on the home turf, threatening weak domestic industries.

This did not happen without a struggle, of course. Some U.S. protectionist interests, mostly in declining industries, as well as big business that wished to invest behind the tariff barriers in the Third World, fought to encourage import-substitution industrialization as the strategy for foreign economic development in the 1950s and not export-led growth as economic pundits would have us believe.[18] Even the economic reconstruction of Japan, which was deemed necessary for closing the postwar dollar gap, had been predicated on restoring for Japan its colonial markets, not on opening the U.S. market.

Things worked out differently, however, in part because Japan's former colonies threw a monkey wrench into the plan for regional recovery. North Korea and China had their doors shut tight by 1949, recalcitrant South Korea all throughout the 1950s sabotaged U.S. attempts to recycle aid money by getting Koreans to procure goods from Japan, and even the Southeast market was difficult to penetrate because of competition from China and overseas Chinese. The only exception was Taiwan, which did welcome Japanese investment, but Japan did not want to touch it, looking nervously over its shoulders at China.[19] The major boost to the Japanese economy from the East Asian market—in fact, allowing Japan to "take off"—was the three years of the Korean War, "a gift of the gods," according to Prime Minister Yoshida Shigeru.[20]

With that boost Japan was able to sell in the U.S. market, and the United States opened its market to Japanese products in a big way. In the

1950s, however, this was no problem. As Dulles put it to Yoshida, "The Japanese [did] not make the things [the United States] likes." Taiwan and South Korea followed Japan into the U.S. market, which remained open as an essential component of U.S.-sponsored modes of "export-led growth" in the 1960s, and as a trade-off to South Korea for its contribution to the U.S. war effort in Vietnam. The U.S. market was also necessary to Korea and Taiwan because Japan remained mercantilist, closing its market to its former colonies. Even as of 1988, Japan, although the second largest export market after the United States for South Korea and Taiwan, takes in only 18 percent of Korea's total exports, and 13 percent of Taiwan's.

The deluge of commodities from East Asia to the Untied States since the 1960s did not occur without conflicts between the protectionist and internationalist camps, leading to periodic lifting and closing of the U.S. gate. Japan and South Korea, for instance, are comparable in the speed and structure of industrial development, but are by no means at the same level, with Korea remaining "behind" Japan by about fifteen years.[21] This has actually worked against the protectionists, enabling the United States to play one East Asian ally off against another (and U.S. protectionists and internationalists off against each other.) That is, to appease its protectionists, the United States has often stiff-armed Japanese firms after they flood the U.S. market in a given commodity, only to have the Koreans supply the same goods even more cheaply, thus satisfying consumers but still doing harm to domestic industries. There has ordinarily been an interval of about fifteen years between the entry of a Japanese commodity and protectionist measures directed against it, followed by the entry of Korean goods into the space where the Japanese goods had been. This process has occurred in textiles, color television, steel, automobiles, VCRs, and now computers and semiconductor chips.

Thus the United States has accommodated East Asian imports differentially and discriminately. But for all the East Asian economies, big and small, from the opposing shore the United States still looks like the only game in town, and this is where the United State has wielded a unilateral influence, making and breaking the essential fabric of political economy in the region. The logic of these exchanges is rarely articulated, however, beyond lots of rhetoric about supporting free trade. In fact the logic has often been solipsistically American and not without contradictions governed by shifting U.S. interests.

All throughout the 1950s, for instance, Americans urged the Japanese to reduce their trade barriers to conform to the General Agreement on Trade and Tariffs (GATT), only to turn around by the end of the decade and in violation of the spirit of GATT, pressure Japan to curb its increasing exports of textiles, Japan, to be sure, remained mercantilist despite the U.S. urging. But this was acceptable because the United States came to see Japan as a designated defender, so to speak, of the dollar: mercantilst Japan safely absorbed an immense quantity of exported U.S. dollars, and by supporting the dollar, helped to maintain the Bretton Woods order. In that sense, it is possible to argue that Japanese neomercantilist practice happened in part because the United States specifically *allowed* it to happen.[22]

By 1971, all that changed. Throughout the 1960s, the United States had supported a regime of fixed exchange rates and convertible currencies. But with inflation on the rise and the dollar heading for a fall, Richard Nixon resorted to the "New Economic Policy," a mercantilist revolution that suspended indefinitely the dollar's official convertibility into either gold or foreign currencies, leaving the Japanese and the Europeans holding the bag. Nixon also slapped a discriminatory 10 percent duty on Japanese imports. The hell with you, said Nixon and Connally; and Europe and Japan took it because they had nowhere else to go.

The Japanese commitment to GATT was slow in coming, but it has grown systematically over time; the problem is that at the same time, the U.S. commitment to the same GATT system, although still strongly defended by free traders and the administration in power, has gotten more capricious as protectionists make inroads on U.S. trade policy.

What we might call "hegemonic irresponsibility" continued through the 1980s, to the extent that the U.S. Treasury bill market came to be financed by Japan. The United States now combines selective closing of the U.S. market ("voluntary restrictions,") with mysterious codes—MOSS (Market-Oriented, Sector-Specific), SII (Structural Impediment Initiative), and Super 301—to restructure the way domestic politics and markets are organized in Japan. It has had more success than many observers realize.

Much the same can be said about U.S. pressure on the smaller East Asian countries. But these countries lack reciprocal leverage even more than Japan. Besides, their politics are much too brittle and their societies much too fragile to accommodate U.S. demands for liberalization, open markets, and democratized states without tidal waves of change. South Korea is one such country. With all its visceral animosity toward Japan, it nonetheless fashioned its political economy after Japan's—in part as a legacy of four decades of colonialism, but mostly because Japanese neomercantiist alchemy had industrialized the country rapidly and was there to be emulated. But the essential difference between South Korea and its much envied "mirror of the future" (that is, Japan) was that South Korea was a bulwark of containment; thus, instead of the "soft authoritarianism" of Japan, Korea ended up with hard-core military authoritarianism.

Another difference was that South Korea industrialized even later than the "late" developing Japan and thus was allowed—by the United States—a greater insularity in its conduct of political economy, so long as it occupied an innocuous place in the pores of the international market. The result was neomercantilism with vengeance, a developmental economy that was more tightly sealed and orchestrated from above even than Japan's.

In the 1980s when the United States began a frontal assault on South Korea to liberalize its commodity and financial markets, leading from the U.S. comparative advantage in agribusiness, high technology, and service industries, the authoritarian state went into a tailspin. Its power had been predicated on its ubiquitous ability to control developmental resources, to mold the investment pattern by selectively allocating credit, and to supplant and supplement the market and thus create and control a huge constellation of entrepreneurial forces. U.S. demands for economic liberalization helped to shift power from the state to the society and from the domestic to the international sphere. The military regime collapsed like a house of cards in 1987, as Korea's *haute bourgeoisie* sat on the side, silent spectators to a massive revolt begun by students and workers but swelled by members of the middle class. This was an unexpected outcome for a regime that had been so tightly embraced by the Reagan administration; it became a victim of the antinomies in U.S. foreign policy.[23]

The point here is not to argue the merits of this outcome, nor to say that the Koreans were mere puppets of the United States, but merely to point out the structural logic. The regime's demise came mainly because of widespread popular dissatisfaction, but U.S. pressure was a factor that helped shape the outcome. Hounding out a military dictator like Chun Doo Hwan may be a good thing in itself, but a situation whereby a hegemonic power undermines and compromises the political economy underpinning another society is profoundly problematic. This is a dilemma for the East Asian semisovereign states as they grapple with the U.S. hegemony in the region that still structures much of the political discourse by which we understand Asian politics.

The U.S. policy of restructuring East Asian economies is generally viewed as valid and enlightened, whereas Asian—especially Japanese—obstruction is seen as devious and self-interested. From the East Asian perspective, however, it looks very different. Why this is so requires some discussion of how Asians think about the question of national agency and purpose, and the role of the state in society. At bottom, as we will see, is a disparity over the purpose of politics and its agency, government.

## The State in the West and East

Liberal political theory has always seen state power as problematic, if not dangerous. The state in the United States is an imagined vacuity, a space in which interest groups contend and conflict. According to pluralist theory, the state is merely a referee that maintains rules and the political order and thus lubricates market and society. To the extent that the state is perceived to be autonomous of society, it has a negative image: a brooding presence that as it grows, threatens to expropriate the market and civil society. These assumptions are so strong that it is often difficult even to discuss alternatives to the U.S. political pattern; state intervention or state autonomy conjures in the liberal mind the European 1930s, and there discussion ceases and the shouting begins.

Alternative views of the state exist, however, apart from the extremes of fascism and Stalinism. The state, for instance, can be benevolent, protective, exemplary; it can be bountiful and generous, and it can be harsh and disciplinarian. Catholic cultures believed that and so did Confucian cultures. State and society do not compete in an adversarial relation or expropriate each other. Instead the state was an exemplary and meritocratic order that guided and educated the society. The Anglo-Saxon tradition of the minimal state is the exception, not the rule (rather than the other way around, as the Orientalist discourse would have you believe).

It would be fair to say that the peoples of China, North Korea, South Korea, Japan, and other Confucian cultures deeply believe that the state ought to provide not only material wherewithal for its people but moral guidance, and in that sense, the distinction between state and society is not one that is sharply drawn. By and large. Westerners have no way to understand this point except to assert a series of absences: no individual rights, no civil society, no enlightenment, and thus a weak or absent liberalism. In so doing they are saying little more than that northern Europe and North America had a different historical pattern than did other parts of the world. But too often this particular pattern presents itself as universal.

The state conceived by the East Asian Other is, furthermore, a practical necessity of development. Karl Polanyi, who was a Catholic socialist of a sort, thought of the modern state (however tragically flawed it was at times) as a prophylactic to protect society against the ravages of the world market. The resulting protected economy may have its inefficiencies—antique rice farmers and family store owners in East Asia, as well as the consumers who have to pay more for this "moral economy"—but who is to say, except the hegemonic power that believes in mammon and Adam Smith, that efficiency ought to reign as the only acceptable doctrine of political economy? And is it not true that the U.S. state might have done *more* in recent years to protect its people—especially blue-collar workers—against the vicissitudes of international competition?

Japan's habits of mercantilism are of long standing, of course. But from Japan's point of view this is a tried-and-true system that protected its domestic society from the ravages of the world market as Japan pursued "late" development, catch-up ball with the West. Viewed as narrow and irrational by liberal economists, this system has virtues that are rarely voiced in the United States.

For example, Japan is littered with small mom-and-pop stores of all types, with laws against major corporations absorbing them. Small business was a nineteenth-century ideal in the United States, too, but has suffered dramatically as national and international franchises, fast-food chains, K-Marts, and superstores have replaced family enterprises—late capitalism demolishing what some have called "moral economy." Japan's much-criticized protectionism also protects this valuable kind of business, and it now perceives that the United States will not be satisfied unless the whole world is turned into its mirror image of superstores and transnational economies of scale.

Simply to make this argument opens one to attack in the current climate in the United States, but U.S. pressure on the Japanese domestic market is a counterpart to the interior desires of U.S. Orientalists, who find the Japanese soul insular and unempathetic to the rest of the world and want to turn it inside out, into a gleaming reflection of the U.S. liberal Self: another triumph for "the end of history," the vanquishing of one more perceived nonliberal polity, after the demise of Stalinist systems in Eastern Europe.

## East Asian Solutions for the 1990s

If this analysis of growing tensions and misunderstanding in the East Asian-U.S. relationship is correct, what ought to be done about it? It is important to call attention to the gross bias and exaggeration in recent U.S. accounts of East Asia, but there is too much money and fame in Asia bashing to think that it will go away soon. Similarly, the more deeply rooted and contrary ways that Americans and East Asians think about the state and politics are likely to persist. It does appear, however, that the East Asian states are moving slowly to attenuate the economic Gordian knot that ties the region to the U.S. market, something that has been well known to policymakers in the region, but about which they have done little until the last few years.

The single-market dependency that characterized previous economic relationships now seems to have reached an impasse, partly because of U.S. protectionism, but also because, as I have argued, it leads to unwonted reciprocal pressures by the United States on Japan and Korea—in the first instance to "open markets," but in the last instance to give up domestic sovereignty and no longer protect the moral economy of small producers, that is, to give up national autonomy. Single-market dependency is something that policymakers can change, however, and they have recently begun to do so. Recent figures suggest that Japanese dependence on the U.S. market dropped from 33 percent of its total worldwide trade in 1986 to 27 percent in 1990 and an estimated 25 percent in 1992. Trade with Western and Eastern Europe is a particular target and has grown rapidly. Japan's imports from the United States climbed by 76 percent from 1986 to 1990, but they increased by 300 percent from France, and 133 percent from the EC (European Community) countries in general. South Korea and Taiwan have followed suit, actively reducing their shares of exports to the United States and aggressively cultivating markets elsewhere.[24]

To the extent that this pattern continues, it means a move away from the previous structure whereby the United States interacted bilaterally with Western Europe and Japan, with Japan and Europe having little interaction, toward a triangular structure, the base of which would be created through growing investment and commodity trade between Europe and Japan. East Asia's position in the world system continues to move toward a multiplicity of markets, away from "trilateralism" and toward a kind of triangulation and interregional reorganization. This implies also that Japan will have more direct relations with the other East Asian economies, rather than relations mediated by and through the United States, and that the smaller East Asian economies will also have stronger ties with Europe.

This revised North-North articulation is likely to be accompanied by a reorganization of North-South relations within the region. This would be achieved by greater cohesion among the region's more prosperous Northeast Asian economies, looking eventually toward something like the EC in East Asia, and deepened links with Southeast Asia, a region that is increasingly a good bet for the next round of rapid industrialization.

Trilateralism, Bruce Cumings argues, has characterized U.S. global policy since the late 1940s. Western Europe and Japan were the legs of the triangle, with the United States spending Marshall Plan and AID money to get war-torn economies going in the 1940s while maintaining for itself ultimate veto power over allied behavior—especially that of Japan and Germany, maintained on a U.S. defense dependency.[25] The lineaments of the triangle, however, ran through Washington back to Tokyo or Bonn, with little contact on the East Asian–European "axis" (I use the term gingerly). Communication was frequently mediated by Washington, especially on issues of critical importance, like the conflict with the Soviets or crises in Korea, Vietnam, or the Persian Gulf.

Richard Nixon was the best symbol of this, somehow forgetting to consult Japan's leaders about dramatic departures like the New Economic Policy and dealing with Brezhnev over the heads of European leaders. It was all too apparent that communication flowed through Washington, on its terms. During the heyday of "formal" trilateralism in the Carter administration, however, everyone still assumed that the initiative remained in Washington's hands, and there was little Japanese-European bilateral contact. This is a structure of one hegemonic power, reigning over regional associates.

A shift toward triangulation in the 1990s is likely to entail increased Japanese investment in Europe (as a way to break into post-1992 fortress Europe), as well as the beginning of such investment by the East Asian NICs. The United States seeks to do the same thing, so it is likely to support such Asian initiatives. European firms may welcome such investments, as a quid pro quo for technology transfer and for infiltrating into East and Southeast Asia, where returns on investment remain high. The announced collaboration of Daimler-Benz and Mitsubishi, and Kloeckner Werke and C. Itoh are moves in that direction.

To be sure, Japanese investment in Europe is still picayune in comparison to that by the United States: in 1990, Japanese direct investment in Germany remained, for instance, a paltry U.S.$1.1 billion against U.S.$32.5 billion made by the United States. Yet, the Japanese figure for that year was double what it was a year before, and the trend is on the rise, as it has been for Taiwan and South Korea.

Japanese interaction with the territories of its former empire has been tightly controlled by the United States, more so than the trilateral structure discussed above. This is widely misunderstood and thus requires some explanation. Despite much talk about the atavistic return of the "Greater East Asian Co-Prosperity Sphere," the only area in which ties were thick and thus easier to revive was in Northeast Asia. But even that took two decades and a war in Vietnam to make it into a reality; and when it happened it did so under U.S. auspices. Furthermore, the interaction between Japanese, Koreans, and Chinese was almost exclusively economic, rather than cultural or political, and it remains so today, nearly a half century after the "Co-Prosperity Sphere" met its demise.

Containment of communism in the mid-1960s required, among other things, placing East Asian and Southeast Asian nations on a sound economic footing. Japan was thus reintroduced to the region in the 1960s, as a U.S. partner and surrogate in developmental efforts. A critical year, 1965, saw the linking of the economies in the region, as the United States escalated its war efforts in Vietnam, in the normalization of the Japan-Korea relationship, which was with its big package of loans and credits, in part responsible for the Korean economic takeoff. Also inaugurated was the Asian Development Bank, which in addition to U.S. and Japanese aid, transferred vast amounts of loans, with priority going to Taiwan and South Korea and secondarily to the Philippines, Thailand, and Malaysia.

This task of linking Japan to other Northeast Asian capitalist economies in the 1960s is slowly coming to fruition. If we accept the forecast that by the year 2000 Japan's living standards will rise by 50 percent and that of the East Asian NICs will almost double—and this is not so unrealistic—the gap between Japanese living standards and the other East Asian economies will have narrowed from 4.3 times to 3.3 times. That is comparable to the gap in living standards between the richest member of the EC (Germany) and the poorest (Portugal), which is currently about five times. Should North and South Korea, and Taiwan and China reunify, that would expedite the process of regional interpenetration in Northeast Asia and help to offset Japan's dominance in the region.

Southeast Asia is a different story. Japan left no colonial imprint from which the region could create a political economy resembling Japan's. Southeast Asia was really a classic wartime occupation territory, existing only to "contribute resources to Japan," as Tojo put it. Before Pearl Harbor there was no blueprint for administration and development of Southeast Asia, and Japan's information on the region derived from existing "enemy" sources, usually meaning British sources; often Japan simply reestablished the former colonial government, relying on local personnel who had worked for colonial regimes. Thus, social systems in Southeast Asia remained by and large untouched.[26] Since the war, Japan and the Southeast Asian countries have had a less intense and more distant interaction than that between Japan and Northeast Asia, and again, the interaction is mostly economic.

Change is under way, however, and we might think of it in terms of the East Asian product cycle extending to Southeast Asia. Whereas the Northeast Asian economies represented an economic hierarchy created through transfer or labor-intensive industries from Japan to Taiwan and South Korea through the 1980s,[27] now the same process is being reproduced vis-à-vis ASEAN, with Japan and the NICs busily bequeathing their obsolete industries. Combined investment in ASEAN, for instance, by four NICs—South Korea, Taiwan, Hong Kong, and Singapore—exceeded Japanese investment in the area in 1988.

Thus we have the creation of a more lateral economic structure between Japan and the NICs, with a hierarchical structure stretching down from north to south in East Asia, from rich to poor countries. Economic activity within this dual structure has been bustling. Intraregional trade west of the Pacific is growing by more than 40 percent annually, amounting to U.S.$256 billion in 1989, representing a whopping 40 percent of the Pacific region's total worldwide trade. This ratio is anticipated to rise to 55 percent in ten years. Japan now invests upwards of U.S.$10 billion a year in Asia, engages in U.S.$126 billion worth of trade, and has dispensed a total of U.S.$4.4 billion in aid to the area, overtaking the United States in the mid-1980s as the largest aid donor in the area. More important, however, a high proportion of Japanese investment in Asia is manufacturing and thus is less sensitive to short-term factors. Whereas Japanese investment in the United States and Latin America is done primarily to defuse trade friction and thus tends to rise and fall with protectionist pressures, its investments in Asia tend to be driven by much longer term objectives.

Another force propelling change in the area is geopolitical. Anticommunism and containment were the rationale for organizing Pacific Asia after 1947, but that began to come apart with Nixon's overtures to China and the fall of Saigon. Since the early 1970s economic development replaced anticommunism as the defining trait in East Asia, with a sudden surge of euphoria around 1978 when the Chinese normalized relations with the United States and embarked on market-oriented reforms. Japan has moved into China in a big way, maintaining an embassy in Beijing that is second in size only to its Washington delegation. During the 1979–1989 decade of economic reform, Japan invested some U.S.$2.2 billion in China, compared to U.S.$1.8 billion invested by the United States. The Chinese government, for its part, insists that Japan invest and manufacture in China, so as not to repeat the all-too-familiar agony of a nation hooked on perpetual trade deficits vis-à-vis Japan. Thus, whereas China recorded U.S.$6 billion in trade deficit against Japan (36 percent of total Chinese imports) in 1985, it garnered U.S.$6 billion in trade surpluses from Japan, and imports from Japan were only a 15 percent share of the total Chinese imports in 1990.[28] Taiwan, South Korea, Hong Kong, Singapore, and others have also been investing in China with great alacrity.

The late 1980s, moreover, saw a number of socialist countries linking up with the capitalist orbit in the region, and agencies of Japanese expansion abroad, the so-called general trading companies, have lost little time in opening offices in Mongolia, Laos, and Vietnam. They came armed with tried-and-true methods successfully tested elsewhere: feasibility studies, followed by enunciation of Japanese "strategic interest," then signing of official aid to pay for infrastructure development, which leads to a tapping of inexpensive labor supply. Japan has been particularly quick to link Vietnam to its economy: Japan is now Vietnam's biggest oil customer and its second biggest trading partner after the Soviet Union, and business has been on the rise.

The East Asian NICs are also getting in on the act with alacrity. In the case of South Korea, there is more than a little triumphalism in its desire to push the North Koreans up against the wall: South Korea has normalized relations with the Soviet Union amid much talk about billions of dollars in aid to the Soviet Union and developing Siberia with South Korea's know-how in construction (and maybe North Korean labor). Meanwhile South Korea's *chaebôl* have been busily supplying Russia with consumer goods, computers, and other high-technology equipment, helping Boris Yeltsin to shore up his shaky rule. Taiwan's smaller firms have begun doing the same.

These trends harbinger an East Asia that wants to set itself free from the asymmetric and often smothering relations across the Pacific and wrest greater autonomy from the world system. This should be welcomed by the United States as it attempts to forge a "new world order," because it also affords the United States an opportunity for disengagement from hegemonic burdens.

## Conclusion

It would appear from our evidence that Japan and the East Asian NICs have made considerable progress in reducing their single-market dependence on the United States, and that they increasingly find ways of interacting economically that are different from the rules of the game since 1945. Growing economic integration and interregional trade will establish more latitude for East Asians in determining their own fate, not necessarily separate from the United States, but without the palpable U.S. pressures of past years. Substantial changes in the economic realm, then, are slowly dissolving the Gordian knot that has created both economic opportunities and a political albatross for the nations in East Asia.

The security situation is likely also to continue relaxing, thus diminishing U.S. leverage over the East Asian states. Tensions in East Asia have been significantly relaxed since 1985, the Soviets having withdrawn 200,000 troops from the Sino-Soviet border, and the Chinese having demobilized 25 percent of their total military strength. And the preponderance of U.S. and Japanese conventional air and naval power over Soviet military power in the North Pacific—as part of global strategy linked to the European situation—is an anachronism now that the Soviet Union does not even exist.

A relaxation of tensions, then, is clearly going on in East Asia. But unlike the economic realm, these changes have not begun to touch the basic security structure. As a result it is much harder to project what will happen to the international Brumairean compact—what will be the role of the United States in Asian regional security in the future? The United States is slow to let go in East Asia and vice versa. Japan has thus far been content to keep the postwar security arrangement, and Japan's neighbors feel safer with U.S. troops, certainly, than with Japanese.

As one Chinese strategist noted, Japan has 300,000 troops, of whom 70 percent are officers and noncommissioned officers, and is thus capable of quickly increasing the number of troops. Japan also possesses economic and technological potential to leap over several generations of weapons technology and develop intelligent or "smart" weapons as it pleases—a choice it has not yet made and is unlikely to make in the near future.[29] For the neighbors of Japan, this is not a proposition that they want to test. Regional security, then, is likely to remain in U.S. hands for some time to come. It is likely that the United States will seek to hold onto the levers of security as a way of continuing its influence in the region.

The change that will be the slowest in coming (if it comes at all) will be in regard to what one might call the hegemonic psychology in East Asia. The United States is still the world's greatest and most vibrant center of cultural and ideological production. Japan may slowly replace the U.S. lead in finance, manufacturing, and technology, but it does not begin to articulate a posthegemonic ideology, nor does its culture have a regional, let alone universal, appeal: at most it exports nintendo hardware (the signifier without the signified), maudlin songs, *karaoke* bars (where drunken males mimic pop hits), and the culture of sex tourism to East Asia.

Thus East Asia remains an area without an identity, a region incapable of imagining itself as a community, to borrow Benedict Anderson's conception. Former victims of Japanese aggression like Korea and China also partake of the either/or absolutes of the new Orientalism, projecting for the future either a dreaded neo-Co-Prosperity Sphere or the capitalist utopia of the Pacific Rim. That Alvin Toffler is listened to as a prophet throughout the region, including the PRC, is merely a token of the utter absence of any regional self-definition.

East Asia lacks the language and psychology for self-assertion, which is an artifact of its long domination by the West. This palpable absence is also testimony to the terrible difficulty of hegemonic transfer across a civilizational divide, something that has never before occurred. When Great Britain passed the hegemonic baton to the United States in the 1940s, it could do so in partnership with an ally sharing much of its culture and tradition. With Japan's meteoric rise, another such transition perhaps beckons on the horizon, but all too many pundits can only greet it with thoughts of conflict, eternal difference, the dire absence of (our) "transcendental truths," and even "the coming war with Japan." Surely our imaginations ought to do more than merely project into the future a past everyone—the Japanese included—would rather forget.

Japan's neighbors can hardly bear to watch Japan again assert itself as a superior, homogeneous nation uniquely fit among Asians to the tasks of the modern world. But then it isn't particularly comforting, either, to see Americans also "going nationalist" over the past decade, with huge displays of flag-waving that perhaps began at the Los Angeles Olympics in 1984 and certainly continued through the national celebration of the humiliation of Iraq. The first display—Japan's—is thought to be pathological, and the second—that of the United States—is accepted as normal. Yet both bespeak the attenuation of internationalism that occurred in the 1980s, caused by both Japan's competitiveness and the unilateralism of Reagan's foreign policy.

Orientalism coupled with East Asian aphasia does not make for happy prognostication on the future U.S.–East Asian relation. In the absence of a full airing of the issues that separate Americans and Japanese, public utterance becomes euphemistic, private thoughts run rampant, and slips of the tongue welling up from the viscera taint the relationship and poison the atmosphere.

It would be far better if we exclude antique conceptions of race and of Orient and Occident entirely from the ongoing debate and focus instead on what divides East and West—almost always some predictable and intelligible conflict of interest—and what unites East and West in a common endeavor of development.

Policies of "constructive disengagement" from the asymmetrical relations of the past can not only leave more room for Asian autonomy but also aid the United States by reducing security burdens and promoting a salutary period of "looking inward" that could help domestic U.S. industries revive and flourish—which after all is the best way to meet "the Asian challenge."

We need to think about a positive disengagement that prepares for truly equal and mutually beneficial relations in the future. We need to talk openly, if not "politically correctly," about what ties us together and what pushes us apart, what we really think about each other, how to build bridges of mutual understanding, and what American East Asia has truly been about.

## Notes

This chapter is a revised version of my article (under the name Jung-en Woo) "East Asia's America Problem" in *World Policy Journal* (Summer 1991), published by the World Policy Institute, New York.

1. Franz Schurmann, *The Logic of World Power* (New York: Pantheon, 1978).

2. *Newsweek*, May 20, 1991; *New York Times*, May 20, 1991.

3. Edward Said, *Orientalism* (New York: Random House, 1978).

4. Allan Bloom, *The Closing of the American Mind* (New York: Simon & Schuster, 1988), p. 34.

5. *New York Times*, April 4, 1991.

6. Karel van Wolferen, *The Enigma of Japanese Power: People and Politics in a Stateless Nation* (New York: Alfred A. Knopf, 1989), pp. 8, 10, 20, 23.

7. Karel van Wolferen, "The Japan Problem Revisited," *Foreign Affairs*, 69, no. 4 (Fall 1990), pp. 42–55.

8. Ian Buruma, "Jingo Olympics," *New York Review of Books*, November 10, 1988.

9. Ian Buruma, "The Pax Axis," *New York Review of Books*, May 22, 1991.

10. George Friedman and Meredith Lebard, *The Coming War with Japan* (New York: St. Martin's Press, 1991). Readers who want a sincere and thoughtful appraisal of racism in the last war with Japan ought to read John W. Dower's *War Without Mercy: Race and Power in the Pacific War* (New York: Pantheon Books, 1986).

11. Akio Morita and Shintaro Ishihara, *The Japan That Can Say No* (Washington, D.C.: Bootleg Edition, 1989).

12. See Alexander Woodside, "The Asia-Pacific Idea as a Mobilization Myth," Chapter 3, this volume.

13. Kent Calder and Roy Hofheinz, *The East Asia Edge* (New York: Basic Books, 1983); Michio Morishima, *Why Japan Has Succeeded: Western Technology and the Japanese Ethos* (New York: Cambridge University Press, 1982); Lucien Pye, *Asian Power and Politics: The Cultural Dimension of Authority* (Cambridge, MA: Belknap Press, 1982).

14. Remarks made by Massao Miyoshi at the Conference on the Asia-Pacific, Duke University, March 22–24, 1991.

15. The reference is to Marx's *Eighteenth Brumaire of Napoleon Bonaparte*.

16. T.J. Pempel, "The Developmental Regime in a Changing World Economy" (Paper presented at the meeting American Political Science Association in San Francisco, August 1990).

17. Albert O. Hirshman, *National Power and the Structure of Foreign Trade* (Berkeley: University of California Press, 1945).

18. Sylvia Maxfield and James Nolt, "Protectionism and the Internalization of Capital: United States Sponsorship of Import Substitution Industrialization in the Philippines, Turkey, and Argentina," *International Studies Quarterly*, Winter 1989.

19. Jung-en Woo, *Race to the Swift: State and Finance in Korean Industrialization* (New York: Columbia University Press, 1991), p. 56.

20. John Dower, *Empire and Aftermath: Yoshida Shigeru and the Japanese Experience*, 1878–1954 (Cambridge, MA: Harvard University Press, 1979), p. 316.

21. For discussion of Japanese and Korean industrial structures, see Peter A. Petri, "Korea's Export Niche: Origins and Prospects," *World Development*, January 1988, pp. 47–68.

22. David Calleo, *The Imperious Economy* (Cambridge, MA: Harvard University Press, 1982), p. 66.

23. Jung-en Woo, *Race to the Swift*, Chapter 7.

24. *Fortune*, May 6, 1991.

25. Bruce Cumings, "The Seventy Years' Crisis and the Logic of Trilateralism in the 'New World Order.' " *World Policy Journal*, 8, no. 2 (Spring 1991).

26. Akira Iriye, *Power and Culture: The Japanese-American War, 1941–1945* (Cambridge, MA: Harvard University Press, 1981), Chapter 2.

27. Bruce Cumings, "The Origins and Development of the Northeast Asian Political Economy: Industrial Sectors, Product Cycles and Political Consequences," *International Organization*, Winter 1984, pp. 1–40.

28. *Wall Street Journal*, December 13, 1990.

29. *Far Eastern Economic Review*, December 13, 1990, p. 28.

# 9

# China's Growing Integration with the Asia-Pacific Economy

## XIANGMING CHEN

### China's Growing Integration with the Asia-Pacific Economy

The great enigma in the Pacific area today is the future policy of China. The Korean War of 1950 showed that China was prepared to come to the rescue of a neighboring communist government threatened with military defeat. . . . Subsequent developments—notably the frontier disputes with India, Burma and Pakistan—showed that China has a long arm and a formidable punch. But for China, by tradition a land power, to challenge the American ascendancy in the Pacific would be more difficult than it was for Japan. It would run counter to her history. But history does not show what is possible in the future, only what has happened in the past.[1]

A historian writing about the great powers in the Pacific three decades ago, Morrell's prophecy is partially borne out by the developments in the Asia-Pacific region since the early 1960s. It was Japan, not China, that rose as an economic superpower to challenge the United States both globally and regionally. What was not foreseen, however, was that the newly industrializing countries (NICs) of South Korea, Taiwan, Singapore, and Hong Kong emerged as economic powers in both regional and global economies. The onset of the 1980s not only saw the rapid growth of the ASEAN nations, especially Malaysia and Thailand, into new NICs, but China's growing presence and new role in the Asia-Pacific region.

China's new role in the Asia-Pacific region differs qualitatively from its past one in exporting communist ideology and practice by either confronting the United States in Indochina or supporting indigenous communist insurgencies in the ASEAN countries. China also shifted from settling its border territorial disputes with neighboring India, Vietnam, and the former Soviet Union through military means to engaging in cross-border trade with those countries. Most important, China has focused development along its long eastern seaboard in order to maximize economic cooperation with the dynamic Western Pacific nations—Japan, the four NICs, and the ASEAN bloc.

## The Subregional Diversity of Pacific-Asia and China

The recent literature on the Asia-Pacific ranges between stressing the similarities and coherence within the region[2] and emphasizing its internal differences and diversity.[3] Between the two somewhat extreme ends are some of the best development studies[4] that integrate an East Asian regional and country-specific analyses in a broader comparative framework. The numerous case studies of individual Asia-Pacific countries have also contributed to our cumulative knowledge of the region. Despite the wide range of focuses in the literature, the primary unit of analysis tends to be either the entire region or an individual country in the region. But there are exceptions where the subnational systems (e.g., industrial sector) of Pacific countries are analyzed in a regional and global context.[5]

Given China's immense size and geographical location, a study of China's economic integration in the Asia-Pacific region involves different units of analysis based on a meaningful definition of the regional, subregional, and local boundaries and contexts. China's vast landmass borders on a number of countries in the north, west, and south, which are either landlocked (Afghanistan, Laos, Mongolia) or not on the Pacific Ocean (Burma, India). The geographical focus of this study implies excluding these countries from the analysis. This still leaves the relational construct of China and the Asia-Pacific region to be further defined. Even if Pacific Asia is taken to comprise the two major sociogeographical subsets of *East Asia* and *Southeast Asia*, East Asia may be subdivided into different parts. China and Inner Asia (i.e., Mongolia, Tibet) form one part, whereas Japan, the two Koreas, and East Siberia constitute another.[6] Segal used "Fringe East Asia" to include Japan, Taiwan, Hong Kong, and the two Koreas, while grouping China and the eastern portion of the former Soviet Union into a separate part of the Pacific.[7] Lardy's broader category of Northeast Asia included China with Japan, Mongolia, the former Soviet Union, Hong Kong, Taiwan, and the two Koreas.[8] Using the substantially overlapped parts of East Asia and the unambiguous designation of Southeast Asia (the ASEAN), I focus on China's economic links with Japan, the Soviet Far East, the ASEAN nations, Hong Kong, Taiwan, North Korea, and South Korea. While this suggests a focus on China and major Western Pacific countries (except Australia and New Zealand), the significance of the United States as an economic superpower in the Pacific Basin makes it necessary to include Sino-U.S. economic ties in the analysis.

Given the subregional diversity of Asia-Pacific and China, I have designed a two-tiered comparative case analysis. The primary comparison features a pair of economic subregions—the Greater South China Economic Zone (GSCEZ) and the Yellow Sea Economic Zone (YSEZ). The secondary analysis focuses on the Shanghai-Pudong Economic Zone (SPEZ) and China's open border areas involving the Soviet Far East. Within these Asia-Pacific subregions, I also examine the role of major cities, Chinese and foreign, in anchoring and channeling the economic activities that constitute the shape of the subregions. Three substantive and theoretical criteria guide this analytical design. First, the analysis is intended to cover China's economic links with all major Western Pacific countries and the United States at various areal levels. Second, there are relatively distinctive spatial boundaries that encircle and envelop parts of China and neighboring or geographically proximate countries into economic subregions, especially the GSCEZ and YSEZ. Most importantly, it is assumed that these geographically delimited subregions and areas not only contain internal flows of trade and investment, but constitute a division of labor reflecting economic dynamics at the global and Asia-Pacific regional levels. Ideally, this analysis will combine the advantages of *individualizing* comparison (contrasting specific instances of a given phenomenon as a means of grasping the peculiarities of each case) and of *encompassing* comparison (placing different instances at various locations to explaining their characteristics as a function of their varying relationships to the system as a whole.)[9]

## China's Growing Links with Major Asia-Pacific Economies

China's links with Asia-Pacific countries have been shaped by historical antecedents. Although China long had a dominating presence in the Pacific because of its size, rich civilization, and heavily populated eastern seaboard provinces, its role in the region was largely confined to cultural influence on Japan, the Korean peninsula, and Vietnam and outward migration of people to the Southeast Asian countries.[10] For several dynasties since the Tang (*circa* AD 600), China conducted most of its trade with West and Central Asian and European countries along the famous "Silk Road." It was only in the mid-1800s that the commercial penetration of China's ports by Western powers that brought about a major eastward shift to the Pacific Ocean. Even then China's primary trading partners at such key ports as Canton were European countries or South Asian countries like India. With a communist government coming to power in 1949 and implementing a self-reliant and closed economic policy through the mid-1970s, China remained disconnected with the rapidly growing and export-oriented Asia-Pacific economies, especially South Korea and Taiwan.

That China began an "open-door" economic policy in 1977–1978 has been a familiar story and much commented upon. The phrase "open door" does not simply mean trade liberalization in the conventional economic sense. The key elements of the policy instead were to be discriminate in imports (not importing things which China could make), to promote speedy entry of Chinese products into the world market, and to adopt the world's advanced technologies and equipment through attracting foreign investment.[11] The policy led to unprecedented growth of China's foreign trade, which has been documented sufficiently[12] as not to warrant a repeat here. Instead, I have compiled only data[13] on China's trade with the Asia-Pacific nations whose economic ties with China at the subregional and local levels will be examined later.

Although China's trade with all these nations grew during 1976–1995, the rate of increase varied considerably from case to case. China's trade with Hong Kong expanded very rapidly, surpassing Sino-Japanese trade in 1987, although it fell behind the latter from 1993 to 1995. The fastest growth of Sino-U.S. trade occurred in the late 1970s and again between 1992 and 1995, whereas trade between China and the former Soviet Union soared during 1982–1984, climbed up gradually through 1990, and rose further during the first half of the 1990s, with fluctuations. China's trade with the ASEAN nations grew most rapidly during 1979–1982, and surged continuously through 1995. While China's trade with North Korea fluctuated at basically the same level, its trade with South Korea and Taiwan grew astronomically, in spite of very small initial bases. During 1979–1989 China's trade with South Korea and Taiwan rose 32 and 45 times, respectively, and rose another fivefold through 1995. As certain proportions of China-South Korean trade and almost all of China-Taiwan trade have been conducted via Hong Kong, the huge volume of China-Hong Kong trade in the second half of the 1980s and the first half of the 1990s is somewhat overstated. (The increasing entrepôt role of Hong Kong in channeling South Korea and Taiwan's trade and investment flows into China will be further analyzed at the subregional and local levels.)

The dynamic differential growth of China's trade with the countries mentioned above has reshaped the patterns of trade with the Asia-Pacific region. In 1976 Japan was China's largest trading partner, with Sino-Japanese trade accounting for 22.6 percent of China's total trade. Hong Kong ranked as China's second largest trading partner, with 13.3 percent of China's total trade. No trade between China and any other country

TABLE 9.1

China's Trade with Major Asia-Pacific Nations, 1976–1995

(Million of U.S. Dollars in Current Price)

| Year | Hong Kong[a] | Japan | United States | Soviet Union[b] | ASEAN Six[c] | North Korea | South Korea | | Taiwan |
|------|------|-------|--------|--------|--------|--------|--------|--------|--------|
| 1976 | 1,787 | 3,039 | 317 | 415 | 390 | 395 | NE[d] | | 40 |
| 1977 | 1,913 | 3.465 | 294 | 329 | 478 | 374 | NE | | 30 |
| 1978 | 2,533 | 4,824 | 992 | 437 | 569 | 454 | NE | | 47 |
| 1979 | 3,328 | 6,708 | 2,452 | 493 | 762 | 647 | 19 | 100 | 77 |
| 1980 | 4,353 | 9,201 | 4,811 | 492 | 1,035 | 678 | 188 | 200 | 321 |
| 1981 | 5,174 | 9,978 | 5,888 | 225 | 1,592 | 480 | 353 | 400 | 467 |
| 1982 | 4,977 | 8,761 | 5,336 | 276 | 2,153 | 545 | 129 | 300 | 298 |
| 1983 | 5,382 | 9,077 | 4,024 | 674 | 1,807 | 493 | 134 | 260 | 265 |
| 1984 | 8,954 | 12,728 | 5,960 | 1,183 | 2,243 | 500 | 462 | 550 | 553 |
| 1985 | 10,844 | 16,434 | 7,020 | 1,881 | 3,964 | 473 | 1,100 | | 1,104 |
| 1986 | 15,395 | 17,217 | 7,349 | 2,640 | 3,350 | 509 | 1,282 | | 925 |
| 1987 | 22,215 | 16,472 | 7,868 | 2,519 | 3,433 | 513 | 1,679 | | 1,516 |
| 1988 | 30,242 | 19,429 | 10,011 | 3,258 | 5,854 | 579 | 3,100 | | 2,717 |
| 1989 | 34,458 | 18,897 | 12,254 | 3,997 | 6,650 | 563 | 3,200 | | 3,483 |
| 1990 | 41,540 | 16,550 | 11,640 | 4,370 | 6,692 | 483 | 3,800 | | 4,040 |
| 1991 | 49,600 | 20,283 | 14,202 | 3,904 | 7,959 | 610 | 4,500 | | 5,800 |
| 1992 | 58,046 | 25,361 | 17,495 | 5,862 | 8,468 | 697 | 5,028 | | 6,559 |
| 1993 | 32,496 | 39,065 | 27,652 | 7,673 | 10,695 | 900 | 8,221 | | 14,393 |
| 1994 | 41,821 | 47,894 | 35,432 | 5,077 | 13,208 | 624 | 11,721 | | 16,327 |
| 1995 | 44,575 | 57,467 | 40,830 | 5,463 | 18,438 | 550 | 16,983 | | 17,882 |

*Source:* See note 13.

*Notes:* a. Data for 1990 and 1991 also include Macao.

b. Data for 1991 onward include only Russia.

c. Brunei, Indonesia, Malaysia, the Philippines, Singapore, Thailand. Data for 1976–1980 include only Malaysia and Singapore. Since Brunei did not join the ASEAN until 1984, the figures for 1982 and 1983 include only five nations.

d. Negligible. The left column of figures for South Korea during 1979–1984 was from Chung, while the right column was from Lardy. Both were presented due to the differentials in the two estimates. As both estimates converged from 1985, only data from Lardy are presented.

exceeded 3.5 percent of China's overall trade. In 1983 Japan and Hong Kong held their respective rankings of trading partners and share of China's total trade. The more striking change was that U.S.-China trade rose to 9.2 percent of China's total trade, making the United States China's third largest trading partner. By 1989 Hong Kong surpassed Japan to become China's top trading partner, accounting for 36.6 percent of China's overall trade in 1991, while Japan's share dropped to 14.9 percent. Trade between the ASEAN countries and China increased to 6 percent of China's total trade, trailing behind only Hong Kong, Japan, and the United States. Both China-Taiwan and China-South Korean trade as a share of China's total trade rose to approximately three percentage points, making Taiwan and South Korea China's sixth and seventh largest trading partners after fifth place West Germany.

China's rapid trade expansion also improved its status in the international economic relations of these Asia-Pacific countries. In 1976 China was Japan's eighth largest trading partner. In 1985 China became Japan's second largest trading partner, behind only the United States. By 1985 China also became the fourth largest trading partner with both South Korea and Taiwan. China's role in the overall Pacific trade also grew steadily. By 1987 China contributed 6.4 percent of Pacific exports and received 5.9 percent of the region's imports, the fifth largest country in Pacific trade. Only one other socialist country (the former Soviet Union) in the region had over one (1.7) percent of Pacific trade.[14] China's growing trade with major Asia-Pacific countries also helped promote greater intraregional trade, which increased from 54 percent in 1977 to more than 60 percent of the total trade of the Asia-Pacific region in 1985.[15]

China's increasingly closer economic integration with major Asia-Pacific countries can also be measured by their direct capital investment in China. Official Chinese government data[16] show that Hong Kong has been the dominating overseas investor in China. Hong Kong and Macao (the latter with an insignificant share of the sum of the two) accounted for 49 percent of the total direct foreign investment (DFI) in China in 1985, 54.9 percent in 1990, and 54.6 percent in 1995. (Data by investing country prior to 1985 are not available.) During 1985–1990 Japan's direct investment as a proportion of China's total DFI averaged 13.1 percent, and stock at 8.5 percent in 1995. The United States provided 18.3 percent of China's total DFI in 1985, slightly ahead of Japan; the U.S. share dropped to 13.1 percent in 1990 and 8.2 percent in 1995. Investments from Taiwan and South Korea were not identified until 1990 for political reasons. South Korean sources, however, revealed that as of September 1990, 26 Sino-South Korean joint ventures were operating in China, with South Korean equity contribution amounting to $26 million.[17] Another Korean estimate put the amount of South Korean investment at $55 million as of December 1989. In 1995 alone, South Korean investment in China jumped to about $1 billion.[18] Taiwan's investment in China by the end of the 1980s was estimated as high as $3 billion. In 1991 Taiwan surpassed the United States to become the third largest supplier of China's DFI, behind only Hong Kong and Japan. By the mid-1990s, Taiwan's investment in China exceeded that of Japan.[19] The ASEAN countries' investment in China rose from 1.2 percent of the total in 1985 to 1.7 percent in 1990, and rose to 6.9 percent in 1995, ranking fifth collectively on the list of foreign investors. Of the ASEAN countries, Singapore stood out as the largest single-country investor.[20]

The data thus far have shown growing economic links between China and major Asia-Pacific countries through trade and investment. The aggregate statistics, however, mask the differential subregional and local dimensions of China's Asia-Pacific economic links, which will be closely examined in this chapter.

## The Spatial Dimensions of China's Asia-Pacific Economic Links

China's economic integration with the Asia-Pacific have been strongly conditioned by its spatially targeted open-door policy since the late 1970s. As there have been numerous accounts and assessments of this policy,[21] only a brief chronological recount is in order as a backdrop for the subregional and local analysis.

In 1979 China began an open and coast-oriented development strategy by granting special favorable policies to Guangdong and Fujian provinces. Of the four Special Economic Zones (SEZs)—China's first and most open areas to DFI, three (Shenzhen, Zhuhai, Shantou) are along Guangdong's coast and one (Xiamen) is a port city in Fujian. In 1984 China designated 14 coastal "open cities" to further attract DFI. SEZ status was also conferred to Guangdong's Hainan Island. In 1985 China opened three river deltas in its coastal region to DFI. In 1988 China extended the coastal development strategy to all coastal provinces, including Shandong and Liaoning penisulas, and upgraded the Hainan SEZ to a province.

The geographical distribution of DFI in China constitutes an indicator of the open policy's broad spatial consequences, as trade data at the subnational levels have not been reported.

Table 9.2 shows DFI in China by province and region during 1985–1995.[22] (Earlier data by province are not available.) At the provincial level, Guangdong received a disproportionately large share of China's total DFI. Besides Guangdong, only Fujian, Beijing, and Shanghai (central government municipalities with provincial status) took in close to 10 percent of China's total DFI during 1985–1995. Hainan, Jiangsu, Liaoning, Shandong, and Tianjin formed the third tier in attracting a large proportion of DFI. The data also show the overwhelming concentration (90 percent) of DFI in China's coastal provinces. In fact, 11 of the 12 coastal provinces and municipalities (except for Hebei province) ranked among the top 12 in attracting DFI during 1985–1995. The only inland province that sneaked into the tenth spot is Shaanxi (see Table 9.2), which hosted some heavily-capitalized resource extractive ventures.

The uneven geographical distribution of DFI in China, coupled with the state policy of encouraging some areas and localities to be more inte-

## TABLE 9.2
### Percent Foreign Direct Investment (FDI) in China, by Receiving Province and Region, 1985–1995
(Ranks in parentheses)

| Province and Region | 1985[a] | 1986[a] | 1987[a] | 1988 | 1989 | 1990 | 1991 | 1992 | 1993 | 1994 | 1995 | 1985–1995 Average |
|---|---|---|---|---|---|---|---|---|---|---|---|---|
| Beijing[b] | 6.80 (4) | 8.60 (2) | 6.58 (4) | 19.20 (2) | 10.42 (4) | 8.74 (3) | 5.93 (4) | 3.18 (8) | 2.44 (10) | 4.12 (7) | 2.90 (9) | 7.17 (4) |
| Shanghai[b] | 8.23 (3) | 8.55 (3) | 14.74 (2) | 8.91 (3) | 16.12 (2) | 5.49 (5) | 3.52 (5) | 4.48 (6) | 11.56 (2) | 7.44 (5) | 7.77 (4) | 8.80 (3) |
| Tianjin[b] | 4.28 (5) | 2.95 (6) | 8.79 (3) | 1.22 (12) | 0.92 (13) | 1.10 (12) | 3.20 (9) | 0.98 (15) | 2.24 (11) | 3.05 (9) | 4.09 (6) | 2.98 (9) |
| Anhui | 0.99 (14) | 2.02 (10) | 0.10 (21) | 0.44 (18) | 0.16 (22) | 0.30 (21) | 0.23 (20) | 0.50 (19) | 0.94 (18) | 1.11 (16) | 1.30 (17) | 0.74 (19) |
| Fujian | 9.08 (2) | 3.59 (5) | 3.54 (7) | 4.97 (4) | 10.76 (3) | 9.15 (2) | 11.30 (2) | 12.93 (3) | 10.51 (3) | 11.16 (3) | 10.87 (3) | 8.90 (2) |
| Gansu | 0.04 (23) | 0.07 (25) | 0.01 (23) | 0.08 (28) | 0.04 (24) | 0.03 (27) | 0.02 (26) | 0.003 (27) | 0.04 (27) | 0.26 (22) | 0.17 (24) | 0.09 (27) |
| Guangdong | 49.84 (1) | 49.53 (1) | 41.60 (1) | 36.58 (1) | 37.84 (1) | 46.08 (1) | 44.18 (1) | 33.62 (1) | 27.63 (1) | 28.45 (1) | 27.57 (1) | 38.45 (1) |
| Guangxi | 2.35 (8) | 2.83 (7) | 2.60 (9) | 0.79 (16) | 1.50 (11) | 0.90 (14) | 0.61 (15) | 1.65 (11) | 3.24 (8) | 2.51 (12) | 1.81 (11) | 1.89 (11) |
| Guizhou | 0.75 (16) | 0.70 (18) | — | 0.17 (24) | 0.24 (19) | 0.15 (24) | 0.18 (22) | 0.18 (24) | 0.16 (26) | 0.19 (24) | 0.15 (26) | 0.29 (23) |
| Hebei | 0.63 (18) | 0.65 (19) | 0.51 (16) | 0.64 (17) | 0.88 (14) | 1.24 (11) | 1.08 (12) | 1.03 (13) | 1.45 (15) | 1.57 (14) | 1.47 (13) | 1.02 (15) |
| Heilongjiang | 0.30 (20) | 1.41 (14) | 0.78 (15) | 1.53 (11) | 0.73 (16) | 0.77 (15) | 0.23 (20) | 0.66 (18) | 0.85 (20) | 1.05 (17) | 1.39 (15) | 0.88 (17) |
| Hainan[c] | — | — | — | 4.36 (6) | 3.11 (8) | 3.25 (8) | 4.27 (7) | 4.11 (7) | 2.59 (9) | 2.76 (11) | 2.85 (10) | 3.43 (8) |
| Henan | 0.63 (17) | 0.61 (20) | 0.31 (18) | 2.45 (9) | 1.40 (12) | 0.33 (20) | 0.92 (13) | 0.48 (21) | 1.12 (16) | 1.16 (15) | 1.29 (18) | 0.97 (16) |
| Hubei | 0.61 (18) | 0.71 (17) | 0.82 (14) | 0.85 (15) | 0.75 (15) | 0.92 (13) | 1.13 (11) | 1.85 (10) | 1.98 (13) | 1.81 (12) | 1.68 (12) | 1.19 (14) |
| Hunan | 2.09 (10) | 0.56 (21) | 0.16 (20) | 0.39 (19) | 0.21 (20) | 0.35 (18) | 0.55 (17) | 1.21 (12) | 1.60 (14) | 1.00 (18) | 1.36 (16) | 0.86 (18) |
| Jiangsu | 2.56 (7) | 1.94 (11) | 3.21 (8) | 3.93 (8) | 3.06 (9) | 3.92 (7) | 5.15 (5) | 13.29 (2) | 10.40 (4) | 11.31 (2) | 13.95 (2) | 6.61 (5) |
| Jiangxi | 0.80 (15) | 0.52 (22) | 0.27 (19) | 0.20 (22) | 0.19 (21) | 0.20 (22) | 0.47 (18) | 0.91 (16) | 0.76 (21) | 0.79 (19) | 0.78 (21) | 0.53 (21) |
| Jilin | 0.37 (15) | 1.39 (15) | 0.01 (23) | 0.24 (21) | 0.11 (23) | 0.56 (16) | 0.44 (19) | 0.68 (17) | 1.01 (17) | 0.73 (20) | 1.10 (19) | 0.57 (20) |
| Liaoning | 1.12 (13) | 2.77 (8) | 4.45 (6) | 4.40 (5) | 3.88 (6) | 7.69 (4) | 8.46 (3) | 4.69 (5) | 4.68 (6) | 4.33 (6) | 3.83 (7) | 4.58 (7) |
| Nei Mongol | 0.20 (21) | 0.43 (23) | 0.08 (22) | 0.13 (25) | 0.01 (26) | 0.34 (19) | 0.03 (25) | 0.05 (25) | 0.31 (24) | 0.12 (26) | 0.16 (25) | 0.17 (26) |
| Ningxia | — | 0.003 (27) | 0.002 (24) | 0.01 (29) | — | 0.01 (28) | 0.004 (28) | 0.003 (27) | 0.04 (27) | 0.02 (28) | 0.01 (28) | 0.01 (29) |
| Qinghai | — | — | — | 0.10 (27) | — | — | — | 0.006 (26) | 0.01 (28) | 0.007 (29) | 0.004 (29) | 0.03 (28) |
| Shaanxi | 1.19 (12) | 2.13 (9) | 5.02 (5) | 4.27 (7) | 3.18 (7) | 1.32 (10) | 0.77 (14) | 0.41 (22) | 0.86 (19) | 0.72 (21) | 0.87 (20) | 1.89 (11) |
| Shandong | 2.73 (6) | 3.77 (4) | 1.64 (10) | 1.65 (10) | 4.30 (5) | 4.76 (6) | 4.35 (6) | 9.12 (4) | 6.85 (5) | 7.67 (4) | 7.23 (5) | 4.92 (6) |
| Shanxi | 0.04 (23) | 0.01 (26) | 0.16 (20) | 0.25 (20) | 0.11 (25) | 0.11 (25) | 0.09 (23) | 0.49 (20) | 0.32 (23) | 0.10 (27) | 0.18 (25) | 0.19 (25) |
| Sichuan | 2.20 (9) | 1.83 (12) | 1.46 (11) | 0.90 (14) | 0.26 (18) | 0.51 (17) | 0.59 (16) | 1.02 (14) | 2.09 (12) | 2.77 (10) | 1.46 (14) | 1.37 (13) |
| Tibet | — | — | — | 0.001 (30) | — | — | — | — | — | — | — | 0.001 (30) |
| Xinjiang | 0.12 (22) | 0.80 (16) | 1.21 (13) | 0.19 (23) | 0.03 (25) | 0.17 (23) | 0.005 (27) | — | 0.19 (25) | 0.15 (25) | 0.15 (26) | 0.32 (22) |
| Yunnan | — | 0.22 (24) | 0.33 (17) | 0.12 (26) | 0.24 (19) | 0.08 (26) | 0.07 (24) | 0.26 (23) | 0.35 (22) | 0.20 (23) | 0.26 (22) | 0.21 (24) |
| Zhejiang | 2.04 (11) | 1.42 (13) | 1.61 (11) | 1.13 (13) | 1.70 (10) | 1.53 (9) | 2.22 (10) | 2.18 (9) | 3.77 (7) | 3.44 (8) | 3.38 (8) | 2.22 (10) |
| Total | 100.00 | 100.00 | 100.00 | 100.00 | 100.00 | 100.00 | 100.00 | 100.00 | 100.00 | 100.00 | 100.00 | 100.00 |
| Coastal[d] | 90.41 (1) | 86.59 (1) | 89.27 (1) | 87.78 (1) | 92.16 (1) | 94.96 (1) | 94.28 (1) | 91.27 (1) | 87.37 (1) | 87.83 (1) | 87.71 (1) | 89.96 (1) |
| Inland | 9.59 (2) | 13.41 (2) | 9.73 (2) | 12.22 (2) | 7.84 (2) | 5.04 (2) | 5.72 (2) | 8.73 (2) | 12.63 (2) | 12.17 (2) | 12.29 (2) | 10.04 (2) |
| Total | 100.00 | 100.00 | 100.00 | 100.00 | 100.00 | 100.00 | 100.00 | 100.00 | 100.00 | 100.00 | 100.00 | 100.00 |

*Source:* See note 22.

*Notes:* a. The figures for 1985, 1986 and 1987 include both FDI and other forms of foreign investment.

b. Central government municipalities with provincial status.

c. Hainan, formerly part of Guangdong province, did not become a separate province until 1988.

grated with the world economy than others, have either reinforced some existing regional and subregional economic differences or reshaped them into distinctively new economic subregions.

## The Greater South China Economic Zone (GSCEZ)

### Origin and Definition

The origin of the GSCEZ may be traced to some floating ideas in the mid-1980s about economic cooperation among South China, Hong Kong, and Taiwan, based on their comparative advantages: China's land, raw materials, and labor; Hong Kong's international financial services and transport hub, and Taiwan's capital, manufacturing technology, and management expertise. Scholars in China, Hong Kong, Taiwan, and the United States have proposed such concepts as the "Greater China Common Market" (presumably after the model of European Common Market) and the "Greater Chinese Economic Bloc" (implying the inclusion of the Chinese business communities in the ASEAN countries).[23] A recent *Business Week* article[24] clearly identified Greater China (referring to China's Guangdong and Fujian provinces, Hong Kong, and Taiwan) as a dynamic growth zone.

To delineate the distinctive spatial boundary of economic integration, I define the GSCEZ as an Asia-Pacific subregion that involves China's Guangdong and Fujian provinces, Hong Kong, and Taiwan (see Figure 9.1). Distinctive as it is, the GSCEZ should not be regarded as a closed system. Besides the triangular ties among Guangdong and Fujian provinces, Hong Kong, and Taiwan, the GSCEZ also involves DFI from the ASEAN countries, especially Singapore. The permeable boundary of the GSCEZ is also reflected in Hong Kong's entrepôt role in relaying trade and investment flows from other Asia-Pacific countries (e.g., South Korea) into China.

## The Nodes and Nexuses of Trade and Investment Flows

The city state of Hong Kong is the dominating node in this subregional network of commercial and industrial activities. South China, especially Guangdong, has had larger, stronger, and closer economic connections with Hong Kong than with Taiwan. South China was Hong Kong's primary hinterland until the 1920s, when the north-south railroad reached Guangzhou (Canton) and improved Hong Kong's access to central and north China. Although Hong Kong lost its vast hinterland as a result of

FIGURE 9.1

China's Open Coastal and Border Cities and Areas, Subregional Economic Zones
Along the Western Pacific Rim

the embargo against China during the Korean War in the early 1950s,
the opening of Guangdong in the late 1970s allowed Hong Kong to reas-
sert its key role in linking China with the global and regional economies.
While China-Hong Kong trade grew rapidly during the 1980s (see

Table 9.1), the volume of entrepôt (indirect) trade passing through Hong Kong to and from China increased five times faster than direct trade during 1980–1987.[25] China-Taiwan trade would not have been possible and growing rapidly without Hong Kong linking the flow of goods between the mainland and the island. Of China's $4.5 billion imports from Hong Kong in the first half of 1988, $890 million (20 percent) came from Taiwan, second only to Japan ($1.6 billion), and ahead of the United States ($540 million) and South Korea ($470 million).[26] Measured by the volume and form of trade flows, economic integration of China, Hong Kong, and Taiwan tightened in the 1980s.

Compared with trade, DFI is a stronger mechanism for integrating South China, Hong Kong, and Taiwan. Guangdong and Fujian were the first and fourth most attractive provinces to foreign investors during 1985–1991 (see Table 9.2). Of the DFI in Guangdong province, approximately 90 percent of the cases and 70 percent of the capital came from Hong Kong. In Fujian province about 60 percent of the DFI are from Hong Kong.[27] Given the government ban on direct investment on mainland China, Taiwan's companies, mostly small, have made a huge amount of investment on mainland China through Hong Kong. It is estimated that more than one third of Taiwan's investments in China are located in Fujian province.[28]

Below Hong Kong, a pair of cities in Guangdong and Fujian provinces serve as second-tier nodes for drawing DFI and spreading economic influence. For Guangdong, they are Shenzhen and Guangzhou, whereas Fujian has Xiamen and Fuzhou. Shenzhen, China's largest SEZ established in 1979, is on the border with Hong Kong (see Figure 9.1). During 1979–1985, Hong Kong and Macao, predominately the former, accounted for 98 percent of the DFI cases and 88 percent of contracted capital in Shenzhen. Japan, the United States, and the ASEAN group ranked a distant second, third, and fourth behind Hong Kong in DFI cases, while contracted capital was in the descending order of the ASEAN countries, the United States, and Japan. Singapore contributed 76 percent of the ASEAN DFI cases and 30 percent of contracted capital in Shenzhen. In 1989, when official reporting of Taiwan's investment in Shenzhen began, Taiwan emerged as the second largest investor to Hong Kong in terms of DFI cases, even though its average case was less capitalized than Hong Kong, Japan, and the United States. In 1990 Taiwan was ahead of Japan and the United States in DFI cases, contracted capital, and average capital intensity. In 1990 the ASEAN countries ranked third after Hong Kong and Taiwan in contracted capital.[29]

Guangzhou, named one of the 14 open cities in 1984, is located at the northern end of the Pearl River Delta (see Figure 9.1). It is the largest port in South China and the country's third largest industrial city behind Shanghai and Tianjin. Guangzhou has also been the site for China's national spring and fall trade fairs since 1957. Guangzhou attracted 15.6 percent of the total DFI in Guangdong between 1979–1984 and 18.3 percent in 1987.[30] Although there are no DFI data by nationality, the dominance of Hong Kong investment in Guangdong, especially in the Pearl River Delta, suggests that the bulk of DFI in Guangzhou has also been from Hong Kong.

Xiamen, one of the four SEZs created in 1979–1980, has long been an important seaport located across the water from Taiwan (Figure 9.1). By 1988 Hong Kong ranked first in both DFI cases and contracted capital. Taiwan, which began investing in Xiamen later than Hong Kong, was the second largest investor in both DFI cases and contracted capital. Singapore was third in both categories, followed closely by the United States, Japan, and the Philippines.[31] Of Guangdong and Fujian's cities, Xiamen has remained the primary site for Taiwan's investment. As of October 1991, Taiwan provided 42.4 percent of Xiamen's DFI cases and 42.1 percent of its contracted capital.[32] The evidence suggests that Taiwan is already surpassing Hong Kong to become the largest overseas investor in Xiamen.

Fuzhou, Fujian's capital and one of the 14 open cities designated in 1984, is an important seaport for foreign trade and a transport hub for distributing goods in southeastern China (Figure 9.1). Fuzhou is also Fujian's largest industrial center. Although detailed data are lacking, Fuzhou has attracted DFI from a number of countries such as Japan, the United States, the ASEAN, and South Korea. Since the mid-1980s, Fuzhou has become a favorable site for Taiwan's investment. As of May 1990, Fuzhou set up over 100 projects involving Taiwan capital, trailing behind only Xiamen and Shenzhen.[33]

Despite their dominant roles, the four cities above appear to have lost some appeal to Hong Kong and Taiwan companies, as the latter began to invest in other, often smaller inland cities in Guangdong and Fujian where labor costs are lower. As an indicator of this shift, the share of DFI in Guangdong and Fujian provinces accounted for by these four cities declined from 64 percent in 1987 to 51 percent in 1990.[34]

## Division of Labor in the GSCEZ

The spatial concentration of Hong Kong and Taiwan's investment in Guangdong and Fujian reflects a deeper economic transformation that can be characterized as a new subregional division of labor. It is shaped by the realigned niches of the Asia-Pacific countries as they have experienced mobility in the global and regional economic systems. As the East Asian NICs follow Japan's footsteps in moving up the industrial technology ladder, they began to shift their labor-intensive industries down to low-wage countries like China. The large number of small and medium-sized companies in Taiwan's most labor-intensive industries (e.g., textiles, footwear), which have been squeezed most severely by internal industrial upgrading and external competition, have taken the lead in relocating operations to closeby mainland provinces.

The shoemaking industry provides an illustrative case of the division of labor that is subregional, regional, and global simultaneously. Fujian province is known for its history and good skills in making shoes. The city of Putian, located between Xiamen and Fuzhou, has become China's major production site for athletic shoes. Recently, three China-Taiwan athletic shoe joint ventures, through which Nike Inc. places a lot of orders, moved from their original locations in Beijing and Shanghai to Fujian and Guangdong—the provinces closest to sourcing and marketing. Most of the raw materials come from Taiwan through Hong Kong to South China. Nike keeps at each shoe factory several Taiwanese resident managers who have been in the shoe business for years and speak the same local dialect. Nike's Hong Kong staff deal with designs, make sure the sample and raw materials reach the factory on time, and ship the finished Nike shoes out of China through Hong Kong toward their destined markets, mainly the United States.[35] This division of labor takes the form of a commodity chain that stretches across the Pacific Ocean through the United States, Taiwan, Hong Kong, and China.

### Explaining Economic Integration in the GSCEZ

The first major factor leading to economic integration among South China, Hong Kong, and Taiwan is the changing comparative advantages in the Asia-Pacific regional economies. High labor costs in Hong Kong, which are about five times that in Shenzhen (already the highest in Guangdong), coupled with the continued shift toward a high-service economy, have driven Hong Kong's labor-intensive manufacturing industries into Guangdong. It is estimated that Hong Kong companies now employ more than two million workers in Guangdong's Pearl River Delta, and the figure doubles to four million if jobs generated indirectly by Hong Kong investment are included. For Taiwan, the end of the 1980s saw rapidly rising labor costs and worsening labor shortages, the latter being caused by smaller birth cohorts of the 1960s entering the work force. Pay raises averaged 12.2 percent annually during 1987–1990, faster than productivity gains of 8.3 percent a year. Taiwan's labor force shrank slightly in 1990 for the first time, while labor force participation rate dropped to 58.2 percent, the lowest in five years.[36] And there is talk about importing workers from Thailand and even mainland China. Growing economic integration between Taiwan and Guangdong and Fujian is also a result of new state policies on both sides. A series of reciprocal policy moves from the mid-1980s created a favorable atmosphere for bilateral trade to grow, even though trade still has to go through Hong Kong due to the absence of formal political relations. The concentration of Hong Kong and Taiwan's investment in selected cities in Guangdong and Fujian also reflects the effect of location-specific policy implemented by China. In addition to such incentives as lower taxes associated with the status of SEZs and open cities, Shenzhen, Guangzhou, Xiamen, and Fuzhou offered competing preferential treatments specifically tailored to Taiwan businesses in the late 1980s.

Guangdong and Fujian's extensive kinship ties with Hong Kong and Taiwan provide convenient and encouraging opportunities for their companies to invest in South China. For example, an estimated 230,000 Hong Kong Chinese have family ties with Shenzhen residents. The proportion of Taiwan's population with ancestral roots in southern Fujian is estimated to be around 70 percent. Many residents in Fuzhou have kinship relations with the overseas Chinese living in Malaysia, the Philippines, and Singapore.[37] The fusion of kinship ties and shared subregional culture fosters close economic links among South China, Hong Kong, Taiwan, and the ASEAN countries.

Geographical proximity is the last but certainly not the least contributing factor, best exemplified by the closely integrated and increasingly open border between Hong Kong and Shenzhen. This phenomenon approximates what Herzog calls the "transfrontier metropolis," which is created by the frequent movement of population, industry, and capital across the increasingly porous international border.[38] Hong Kong businessmen now commute freely across the border to supervise production in Shenzhen and other Guangdong cities daily or weekly. Guangzhou is only three hours away from Shenzhen by rail and a recently completed highway. The cities clustered in the Pearl River Delta are reasonably accessible to Hong Kong and Taiwan investors through rail and roads. Physical distance, however, does not seem to inhibit the concentration of Taiwan's investment in Xiamen and Fuzhou, which are much farther away from the entry point of Hong Kong. A statistical analysis showed a consistently negative relationship between DFI in Guangdong and Fujian's cities and their distance to Hong Kong for 1984, 1987, and 1990, even though this association attenuated over time.[39] This suggests that with rare exceptions, Hong Kong and Taiwan's investment may continue to locate in cities closer to Hong Kong for some time to come.

# The Yellow Sea Economic Zone (YSEZ)

## Origin and Definition

The initial idea of an entity approximating the YSEZ was embedded in the broad discussion of potential economic cooperation among some Western Pacific countries (Japan, South Korea), on the one hand, and in the specific reference to China's Bohai Bay (the sea within China's territorial waters), on the other. As early as May 1986, the mayors and commissioners of China's cities and prefectures around the Bohai Bay held a conference to discuss ways of coordinating regional economic activities. But it was only in 1989–1990 that China's scholars and policy analysts began to explicitly propose developing the YSEZ in order to maximize economic cooperation with Japan and South Korea.[40] China's posture, coupled with rapidly growing Sino-South Korean trade in the late 1980s, helped sharpen the attention of overseas analysts on economic integration among China, Japan, and South Korea across, around, and beyond the Yellow Sea.[41] For this analysis, I define the YSEZ to include China's Liaoning and Shandong provinces, South Korea, and Japan (see Figure 9.1).

Like the "triple alliance" among Hong Kong, Taiwan, and China's Guangdong and Fujian provinces in the GSCEZ, the YSEZ comprises triangular economic ties among Japan, South Korea, and China's Liaoning and Shandong provinces, which ranked fifth and eighth in attracting China's DFI (Table 9.2). Of the 54 Sino-South Korean joint ventures either in operation or under contract as of January 1990, 30 (55.6 percent) were cited in Shandong, Liaoning, Beijing, Tianjin, and Hebei in that descending order. Shandong and Liaoning provinces were first and second in drawing South Korean capital into China, combining for 42.7 percent of all South Korean-invested projects in China during 1990–1991. The number of South Korean-invested ventures in Shandong province grew more rapidly, from 10 in 1990 to 34 in 1991, than any other coastal province.[42] Of the 26 China-South Korean joint ventures in operation as of October 1990, 15 (57.7 percent) were located in the major Chinese cities (e.g., Beijing, Dalian, Qingdao, Tianjin, Yingkou) rimming the Bohai Bay.[43] The Chinese press has reported Japanese companies' preference to invest in Liaoning, especially in the city of Dalian. From 1984 to October 1988, Japan set up 55 direct investment projects in Dalian, capitalized at $230 million.[44] Dalian also became a major Chinese seaport for trade with South Korea. In 1988 the volume of Sino-South Korean trade (all indirect) through Dalian amounted to $27.9 million, $21.4 million of which were exports to South Korea and $6.5 million were imports. During January–August 1989, indirect and direct

Sino-South Korean trade passing through Dalian rose to $63.6 million, $55.5 million for China's exports and $8.1 million for China's imports.[45] Dalian also plays a crucial role in Sino-Japanese trade. Of the total volume of trade leaving Dalian, 48 percent went to Japan.[46]

Dalian is not the only key Chinese port city with strong economic links to South Korea and Japan. With Dalian, the city of Qingdao on the Shandong peninsula and Tianjin midway along the Bohai Bay constitute a triangle of coastal nodes that anchor the investment and trade flows into that part of China. Dalian is China's second largest port, behind only Shanghai in total tonnage, but it ranks ahead of Shanghai in total foreign trade and in total exports. Tianjin and Qingdao are China's third and fourth largest ports in both freight and passenger traffic, with trade connections to over 100 countries and regions. By February 1992, South Korea and Japan ranked second and third (behind only Hong Kong) in investing in Qingdao, accounting for 13.8 and 10.8 percent of the ventures and 12.6 and 11.3 percent of the capital, respectively. In 1991 Qingdao's trade with Japan and South Korea made up 23.0 and 8.1 percent of its total foreign trade.[47] While data on DFI in Tianjin by all investing countries are not available, 7 percent of South Korean-invested ventures in China by 1991 were located in Tianjin.[48]

The concentration of DFI in these cities makes them key economic nodes, capable of spreading development benefits into their hinterlands of varying sizes. For example, Dalian's hinterland covers China's three northeastern provinces (see Figure 9.1). In 1986 they had 8.9 percent of China's population, but accounted for 14.6 percent of China's gross industrial output.[49] Constituting China's most dominating heavy industrial region, in 1986 the three northeastern provinces produced 51.8 percent of China's petroleum, 30.3 percent of China's automobiles, and 23.6 percent of China's steel.[50] This vast and productive hinterland is easily accessible through an extensive network of railroads and roads. A newly constructed highway between Dalian and Shenyang, the capital city (located away from the coast) of Liaoning province, allows the movement of people and goods within 4 hours, faster than train transport. Dalian's favorable transport system facilitated economic links with its hinterland and beyond. By year-end 1986 Dalian signed over 1,600 economic and technology agreements with interior cities and regions. Dalian-interior joint ventures and wholly interior-owned firms in Dalian amounted to 400 and were capitalized at $22 million.[51] A recently completed highway between Qingdao and Yantai has cut the travel time from about 5 hours to a little over 3. Construction is already under way to extend the highway to Jinan, the capital city of Shandong province, thus improving the transportation link between Shandong's coastal nodes and interior cities.

Facing China's coastal nodes across the Yellow Sea are several South

Korean coastal cities that are emerging as key points for economic interaction with China. The South Korean government has recently unveiled a spatially targeted plan for developing its relatively underdeveloped southwestern Chollar province. The plan included: (1) attracting capital investment for new industrial complexes to be located at Asan Bay and Kunsan Port; (2) building a 505 kilometers long highway from Inchon to Sunchon to link all major west coast cities; (3) giving Kunsan Port the key role in handling Sino-South Korean trade; and (4) upgrading other western ports, such as Inchon, Asan, and Mokpo (see Figure 9.1).[52] South Korea's initiation of its "west coast development strategy" was quickly reported by China's regional analysts[53] as a stimulus to further internationalize cities like Dalian for closer economic cooperation with South Korea.

### Division of Labor in the YSEZ

The emerging subregionalized division of labor in the YSEZ differs somewhat from that in the GSCEZ because of the different industrial structures of the national and regional economies involved in the two zones. On the one hand, South Korea has been imitating Hong Kong and Taiwan's strategy by setting up heavily labor-intensive projects in Liaoning and Shandong provinces. The 15 Sino-South Korean joint ventures in Chinese cities around the Bohai Bay as of 1990 were labor-intensive operations, such as toys, sporting goods (e.g., ski gloves), restaurants, and daily consumer products (e.g., lamps, brushes, souvenirs).[54] On the other hand, two South Korean companies (Korea Steel Pipe Co. and Pohang Iron and Steel Co.) have established in Shandong capital-intensive ventures to make steel pipes and other steel products. In addition, Kia Industrial Co. has agreed with a Chinese state enterprise in Yantai to manufacture passenger cars, microbuses, and trucks.[55]

The most "natural" division of labor in the YSEZ, however, still occurs in typical labor-intensive industries like toys. A Sino-foreign joint venture with multinational capital in Dalian has been making stuffed animals, especially Disney characters. The raw materials (e.g., flannel) were brought in from South Korea, while they are sewn and pressed by cheap Chinese labor into finished products, which are then sent to the U.S. market. Because these Chinese-made products are not as good as similar stuffed animals made with South Korea's own materials and labor, they are sold only at the middle rung of the overseas market.[56] Nevertheless, the sourcing, manufacturing, and marketing sections of this toy chain link the subregional division of labor to the global economy.

## Explaining Economic Integration in the YSEZ

The first explanation for the close economic links between China, particularly Liaoning and Shandong provinces, and South Korea is their complementary economies. Three specific economic factors contribute to close Sino-South Korean economic cooperation through trade and investment. First, some of South Korea's midlevel production and processing technologies may be more needed in and suited to China than Japanese or Western technologies. This is especially true of Liaoning and Shandong provinces, whose heavy industries like chemicals, steel, and shipbuilding are compatible with the same industries in South Korea. Second, China's lack of hard currency, coupled with the rising price of Japanese products and technologies due to the sharp appreciation of the *yen*, make the cheaper manufactured goods from South Korea more appealing to China.[57] Third, as labor costs in South Korea, especially manufacturing wages, have been rising rapidly, South Korea is eager to relocate its labor-intensive industries to nearby Chinese locales. With an average wage lower than that of China's Guangdong and Fujian provinces,[58] Shandong province is a logical target for South Korea's labor-intensive investment.

Economic complementarity is a necessary but not sufficient condition for close Sino-South Korean economic cooperation, which could not be established and strengthened without the changes in China and South Korea's state policies at the national and regional levels. China's adoption of the open-door policy and domestic reform in the late 1970s provided an initial opportunity for Sino-South Korean (indirect) trade to develop quietly. From 1983 on, both China and South Korea relaxed restrictions on travel in both directions, leading to reciprocal visits of athletes, businessmen, economic officials, scholars, and seamen. These policies facilitated more bilateral trade and South Korea's DFI in China. Between 1988 and 1991, 3,580 South Korean business groups with 8,600 people visited Shandong province, with 3,510 groups coming in the first half of 1992 alone.[59] The establishment of former diplomatic relations between China and South Korea in August 1992 would further promote and expand their business ties.

China's regional and location-specific policies, either intended or unintended, helped create favorable conditions for the emergence and growth of Sino-South Korean economic ties across the Yellow Sea. While consistent with its reform of decentralizing economic management, China designed a policy of "provincial contact only" toward South Korea to avoid angering North Korea. Both Liaoning and Shandong took advantage of this and established a provincial trade and liaison office in South Korea. Six major coastal cities in Shandong have recently been allowed to set up special trading companies for dealing with South Korean businesses.[60] In return, South Korea would open promotional missions in Qingdao and Beijing. Although not intended specifically as a policy toward South Korea, China's designation of 14 open cities in 1984, including Tianjin, Dalian, Qingdao, and Yantai, made the greater autonomy and lower taxes in these locations very attractive to South Korean investors.

Similar to the kinship ties that seal many business bonds between Taiwan and China, there is an ethnic component to Sino-South Korean economic integration in the YSEZ. It is estimated that South Korea has approximately 100,000 Chinese-Koreans of Shandong descent, many of whom became successful businessmen and had a strong desire to invest in their place of ancestry.[61] Some of the Chinese Koreans originally emigrated from Dalian and other parts of Liaoning, and are interested in promoting business relationships between South Korea and Liaoning.[62] Kinship ties between Shandong and Liaoning and South Korea, less extensive and deep as they may be than those connecting Guangdong, Fujian, Hong Kong, and Taiwan, are a contributing factor in Sino-South Korean economic cooperation in the YSEZ.

The last explanatory factor is geographical proximity. South Korea and Japan happen to be the two countries closest to China's coastal provinces around the Bohai Bay. Dalian is only 200 nautical miles from Inchon, with a one-way shipping trip taking a maximum of 13 hours. After direct air service to Tokyo began in early 1985, a jet flight from Dalian took less than four hours. As direct air services linking the key Chinese and South Korean cities across the Yellow Sea are currently under discussion, direct shipping between China and South Korea's ports around the Yellow Sea is still constrained. Although South Korean ships are allowed to carry goods directly to China, they have to register with a third country and often conclude the paperwork in a fourth country. It is estimated that direct shipping can save up to 20 percent on transport costs.[63] In September 1990 a shipping route was opened between Inchon and Weihai, an industrial port city on the Shandong peninsula closest to South Korea's west coast (see Figure 9.1). A South Korean ocean ship makes one round trip each week, carrying both passengers and cargo, and covers the 230 nautical miles in less than 17 hours. Other suggested direct shipping links are between Yantai, Mokpo, and Nagasaki, between Kunsan and Qingdao, and between Dalian, Tianjin, Inchon, and Nampo, the North Korean port closest to its southern neighbor.[64]

In spite of the continued transport barriers across the Yellow Sea, the relatively short physical distance between China and South Korea and between China and Japan provides a favorable spatial environment within which economic, political, and sociocultural factors interact to bring about close economic integration.

## China's Other Coastal and Border Economic Zones

China's long coastline and inland border, coupled with decentralized, spatially targeted, and location-specific open policies, have created other distinctive subregions that have developed strong economic ties with Pacific Rim countries. This section briefly examines two different cases.

### The Shanghai-Pudong Economic Zone (SPEZ)

The Shanghai-Pudong Economic Zone (SPEZ) began in 1985, when China designated Changjiang (Yangtze River) Delta as an open coastal region for DFI and international economic cooperation. More recently, scholars proposed a broader coast-oriented region—the East China Sea Economic Zone—that involves Shanghai, Jiangsu, Zhejiang, and Fujian provinces.[65] The East China Sea Economic Zone (with Fujian) overlaps with the GSCEZ discussed earlier. For this analysis, the Shanghai-Pudong Economic Zone is defined as the area covered by the Yangtze River Delta (see Figure 9.1). In April 1990 China's central government announced a grand plan for developing Pudong, a large suburban district of Shanghai municipality. Pudong, literally meaning "the east of Huangpu," refers to the large area east of the Huangpu River. It abuts Hangzhou Bay to the south, is closed in by the mouth of the Yangtze River to the northeast, and borders on the Huangpu River to the west. Pudong covers 2,000 square kilometers, about one-third of Shanghai's total land, and has about 1.4 million people, close to 10 percent of Shanghai's total population.[66]

The development of Pudong strengthens Shanghai's functions as the central node in linking the global, Asia-Pacific, and domestic subregional economies. Shanghai is China's largest port, carrying 30 percent of the country's international cargo. Shanghai's customs process and channel 20 percent of China's consumer goods.[67] With only 1 percent of China's population, Shanghai accounted for 10.6 percent of China's gross industrial output in 1984.[68] While this figure dropped to 6.8 percent in 1990, Shanghai's industrial weight was chipped away only by Jiangsu province (the city's immediate hinterland), Guangdong province (the core segment of the GSCEZ), and Shangdong province (a major part of the YSEZ), which ranked one, two, and three in provincial shares of China's total industrial output in 1990.[69]

Shanghai ranked third (behind Guangdong and Beijing) in receiving the proportion of China's total DFI during 1985–1991 (see Table 9.2). With regard to the nationality of investors in Shanghai, Hong Kong leads all countries. Of Shanghai's 160 foreign-invested ventures by the end of 1985, 92 (57.5 percent) had Hong Kong partners. With involvement in 26 of these ventures, the United States was a distant second, ahead of

Japan (20), the European Community (10), Thailand (4), and Singapore (3).[70] Shanghai, however, was the most favorable site for U.S. DFI in China. By year-end 1986 Shanghai had signed 34 investment agreements with the United States involving $600 million in U.S. capital. Beijing and Tianjin were the second and third choices for U.S. DFI, attracting 36 projects ($250 million) and 22 projects ($53 million), respectively.[71] Foreign companies have begun to invest in Pudong, especially after the latter was declared an open zone in 1990. By the end of 1990 Pudong approved 80 foreign-invested enterprises, including 70 Sino-foreign equity joint ventures, five Sino-foreign cooperative ventures, and five wholly foreign-owned firms. The capitalization of these ventures ranged between $3 and $6 million,[72] high by the average size of DFI projects in China.

The emergence and growth of the SPEZ result from the meshing of economic, political, and locational factors. Economically, Shanghai remains China's most dominant industrial center, and its labor force is among the country's best educated and most productive. An estimate shows that labor productivity in Shanghai was second only to Shenzhen in 1985.[73] These comparative advantages help overcome Shanghai's disadvantage of higher (than Liaoning and Shandong's) wages in attracting more capital-intensive DFI projects. Politically, Shanghai benefitted from being named one of the 14 open cities in 1984 and being given the right to approve DFI projects of up to $30 million, compared with the caps of $10 million for Guangzhou and Dalian, and $5 million for Qingdao. The SPEZ also includes the open cities of Nantong and Ningpo (see Figure 9.1), which can function as secondary growth centers for stimulating development of the surrounding areas. Geographically, located midway along China's eastern seaboard, Shanghai is more accessible to all foreign investors, which may account for the fact that Shanghai has a more evenly distributed nationality of foreign investors than key cities in the GSCEZ and YSEZ.

### Subregional and Border Economic Areas Involving the Soviet Far East

China's growing economic integration with Asia-Pacific nations is not restricted to market economies. The rapid growth of Sino-Soviet trade in the 1980s (see Table 9.1) indicates that both socialist states have tried to improve their bilateral economic relations. Like economic links with the Western Pacific countries, China's trade with the former Soviet Union has distinctive subregional and local dimensions. While a number of Chinese cities along the northeastern and northwestern Sino-Soviet border have been opened to trade, my analysis focuses on the border cities and areas in China's Heilongjiang province and the former Soviet Far East. This analysis will also be extended to the characteristics and conditions of broader economic integration involving Japan and the two Koreas around the Yellow Sea and the Sea of Japan (see Figure 9.1).

Sino-Soviet border trade in the Far East is mostly conducted through the two Heilongjiang cities of Suifenhe and Heihe (see Figure 9.1). Suifenhe is an inland port city sitting on Heilongjiang's southeastern border with the Soviet Far East. Opened to border trade in 1983, Suifenhe is linked by rail to the Soviet Pacific cities of Art'om, Vladivostok (the largest Soviet Pacific port), and Nakhodka (another major Soviet port city). Suifenhe is only 26 kilometers from the highway system connecting the Soviet cities. Internally, Suifenhe is a border terminal of a rail network that links all major cities in Heilongjiang, Jilin, and Liaoning provinces. Boosted by growing border trade, Suifenhe's revenue income rose from about $600,000 in 1987 to $5.2 million in 1991.[74] From the Soviet side, the state decided to set up a special economic zone at Nakhodka to attract Japanese and South Korean investments. This was only a small component of a larger development strategy for turning the resource-rich Far East into a strong economic subregion in the Pacific. The plan included modernizing and expanding the port facilities at Vladivostok, Nakhodka, and Ol'ga (see Figure 9.1).

Up north along the same border is the city of Heihe, which has emerged since 1985 as a competing center for Sino-Soviet border trade. With 145,000 people in 1990, Heihe is 5.4 times larger than Suifenhe.[75] Facing Heihe on the Soviet side is Blagoveshchensk, the third largest city in the Soviet Far East with 230,000 people. The two cities are separated by only 0.75 kilometers across the Heilong (Amur) River. The distance can be covered by a five-minute truck ride over the frozen river half of the year. In 1989 Heihe's border trade accounted for 25 percent of Heilongjiang's total trade with the Soviet Far East and 41 percent of the combined border trade passing through Heihe, Suifenhe, and Tongjiang,[76] a border city midway between Heihe and Suifenhe (see Figure 9.1).

Sino-Soviet border trade in Suifenhe and Heihe are only one dimension of growing economic integration in the northeastern Pacific. Guided by economic complementarity, geographical proximity, and pragmatic policies, countries based on either market or command economies and at different levels of development have begun to seek mutually beneficial opportunities in a regional context. The Soviets have already obtained loans and DFI from Japan and South Korea to harness their rich natural resources such as petroleum and natural gas.[77] As China and the former Soviet Union have gotten closer with South Korea economically, North Korea has no choice but to reach south for capital investment and other economic assistance. Neff and Nakarmi reported that South Korean companies planned to start joint ventures in North Korea in 1992, including a proposal to set up a ship-repair dock at the city of Wonsan on

North Korea's east coast (see Figure 9.1).[78] On the border with China and the Soviet Far East, North Korea was planning to open an economic development zone to lure Japanese investors. As early as 1986, China and the Soviet Union (at the time) negotiated to allow China to supply labor for Siberian projects in exchange for raw materials such as timber.[79] The South Korean press reported that Korean companies and some Chinese provincial governments discussed the use of Chinese labor, Korean-Chinese labor in particular, in third country construction projects.[80] These multilateral economic ties suggest the potential formation of a sprawling regional economy that extends southward to overlap with the YSEZ.

## China's Integration with the Asia-Pacific Economy: Implications

The preceding comparative analyses of four cases, two primary and two secondary, suggest that there has emerged increasingly distinct subregionalized and localized economic integration across the national boundaries within the Asia-Pacific region. This new reality strongly challenges the repeated multilateral efforts to create and promote regionally based cooperative organizations and bodies since the early 1980s, such as the Pacific Economic Cooperation Conference (PECC) and the Asia-Pacific Economic Cooperation (APEC).[81] The primary implication of this study is that the Asia-Pacific region should be reconceptualized as a network of multiple subregions connected and mediated by complex division of labor and commodity chains. That the Asia-Pacific is a homogeneous regional structure comprising politically defined and economically autonomous nation-states may be a rapidly fading perspective.

These Asia-Pacific subregions, as this chapter shows, are shaped by a multitude of factors. They have different combinations of effects on the formation of different subregions. Sociocultural similarity and kinship ties, for example, play a stronger role in integrating the economies of South China, Taiwan, and Hong Kong than in fostering economic integration among Northeast China, Japan, and South Korea. The dominating factor in the growth of trade and economic cooperation along the Sino-Russian border in the Far East is geographical proximity, rather than anything else. On the one hand, the comparison has revealed the peculiar characteristics of each subregion. On the other hand, the integration in the subregions is driven by the same basic economic determining conditions because they are all embedded in the global system of contemporary capitalism. The prevalent logic of global capitalism implies that the Asia-Pacific subregions are not self-contained. Just as South Korea's investment has flown into Fujian and Guangdong provinces in the

GSCEZ, Taiwan's investment has penetrated Liaoning and Shandong provinces in the YSEZ. Both zones have commodity chains stretching out to such distant markets as the United States.

By analytical design, China's various coastal parts and partial inland border form the spatial cores of the various Western Pacific subregions. The differential incorporation of a large socialist state into the capitalist world economy in the Asia-Pacific context carries many implications for China's national development and the countries in the region. As the cooperative aspects of China's integration with major Asia-Pacific countries have already been examined at length, I devote the concluding remarks to discussing contradictions with regard to China itself and the countries that have different economic ties with China in the Asia-Pacific region.

Within China at the intranational level, the most favorable economic policies granted to Guangdong and Fujian provinces, especially to their SEZs, through the 1980s and their effect on rapid growth in South China have created some economic gaps and policy conflicts with the northern portions of the coastal region. These were often subject to new interventions by the central government, which tended to reshape and realign the already differentiated regional and local interests. The Pudong development plan was intended to shift the policy focus away from the favored south to the central and northern parts of China. This new spatial orientation to Shanghai and surrounding areas was also interpreted as a victory of one party faction against another at the central level.[82] In 1989–1990 the central state also withdrew some export subsidies from Guangdong to curb that province's growing power and privileges. Although the purposes of these policies were to rebalance regional disparities and to recentralize some lost power, they may have strengthened the SPEZ as another regional competitor against other regions and the central government.

At a broader intranational level, the rapid development of the entire coastal region in the 1980s widened existing spatial inequalities with China's vast interior. From 1981 to 1988, the initial differential in gross industrial output between China's coastal provinces and its nine western provinces grew 2.7 times.[83] The rapid development of similar export-oriented processing industries in both the coastal and inland regions, especially the former, also generated fierce competition for raw materials, which tend to come from the western provinces. The shortage of domestic raw materials, coupled with double competition from labor-intensive processing industries in the interior and other low-wage countries (e.g., Indonesia, the Philippines), constrain the traditional export sectors of the coastal provinces, while giving them little time to diversify their industrial structure.

The increasing differentiation within the coastal region and across the coastal-interior divide constitutes a frontal assault on socialist China, which has historically taken some measure of national political unity, economic autonomy, and social integration as its premise for existence. The argument against uneven development between the coastal and inland regions in Chinese socialism goes back further than Mao's post-1949 ideology and practice to the 1920s.[84] One serious social consequence of China's spatially uneven insertion into global capitalism is growing class differentiation. Sklair identified three new social 'strata': the officials (many of them former communists) who deal with foreign capitalists as representatives of state agencies or managers of industrial enterprises; private entrepreneurs, many of whom do business with foreigners; and the so-called 'red capitalists'—a growing number of PRC Chinese who live and work in Hong Kong and abroad.[85] With the first and third groups developing into a global managerial elite with extensive international ties, the crucial question to be asked is whose interests will they represent: Chinese national, Chinese regional or local, or multinational across political and geographical boundaries.

Contradictions and conflicts have also emerged among the Asia-Pacific countries that compete for shares of China's national, regional, and local markets. In the GSCEZ, the recent surge of Sino-Taiwan trade and Taiwan's DFI in South China threatens to weaken the existing stronghold and influence of Hong Kong in that part of China. Taiwan also resents improved economic relations between China and South Korea for fear of losing its legitimate ideology against communism and some of the China market. Japan was reported to have obstructed Sino-South Korean business ties by disclosing a joint venture between Fujian province and the Daewoo Group in 1985. The subsequent objection by North Korea caused a delay in that project. Japan also encouraged South Korea to export cheap goods toward China and away from itself, thus driving China and South Korea to compete against each other, not with Japan. The suspicion of Japan's economic motive to dominate the region, coupled with economically integrated East Asia markets, prompt the United States to challenge Japan by facilitating Sino-South Korean economic cooperation.[86]

How do these contradictory and divisive forces affect the future shape of the Asia-Pacific region? The answer to this question lies in the present reality, as documented by this chapter. The fusion of economic comparative advantages, geographical proximity, sociocultural affiliation, and practical state policies has considerably weakened ideological barriers and territorial boundaries that defined and separated the nation-states in the Asia-Pacific region. The consequent emergence of subregional economic networks have already reshaped the entire Asia-Pacific region. The complex and intertwined division of labor within and between the subregions presents both cooperative opportunities and contradictory outcomes for the nations involved. The future welfare of each nation and the region as a whole hinges on how these opportunities are maximized and the contradictions minimized.

## Notes

*This research was supported in part by a grant from the Campus Research Board of the University of Illinois at Chicago. I am grateful to Arif Dirlik, Xiaoyan Hua, James Norr, and William Parish for suggestions and comments on an earlier draft and to Raymond Brod for his skilled production of the map.

1. W. P. Morrell, *The Great Powers in the Pacific* (London: Routledge and Kegan Paul, 1963), p. 34.

2. See David Aikman, *Pacific Rim: Area of Change, Area of Opportunity* (Boston: Little, Brown, 1986); Roy Hofheinz, Jr. and Kent E. Calder, *The Eastasia Edge* (New York: Basic Books, 1982); Staffan Burenstam Linder, *The Pacific Century: Economic and Political Consequences of Asian-Pacific Dynamism* (Stanford, CA: Stanford University Press, 1986).

3. See Gerald Segal, *Rethinking the Pacific* (New York: Clarendon Press, 1990).

4. See Frederic C. Deyo, ed., *The Political Economy of the New Asian Industrialism* (Ithaca, NY: Cornell University Press, 1987); Gary Gereffi and Donald Wyman, eds., *Manufacturing Miracles: Paths of Industrialization in Latin America and East Asia* (Princeton, NJ: Princeton University Press, 1990).

5. Gary Gereffi, "Global Sourcing and Regional Division of Labor in the Pacific Rim," this volume.

6. Mark Borthwick, *Pacific Century: The Emergence of Modern Pacific Asia* (Boulder, CO: Westview Press, 1992), p. 4.

7. Segal, *Rethinking the Pacific*, p. 10.

8. Nicholas R. Lardy, *China's Entry into the World Economy: Implications for Northeast Asia and the United States* (Lanham, MD: University Press of America, 1987).

9. See Charles Tilly, *Big Structures, Large Processes, Huge Comparisons* (New York: Russell Sage Foundation, 1984), pp. 81–83.

10. Borthwick, *Pacific Century*.

11. Samuel P.S. Ho and Ralph W. Huenemann, *China's Open Door Policy: The Quest for Foreign Technology and Capital* (Vancouver, Canada: University of British Columbia Press, 1984), p. 21.

12. See SSB (State Statistical Bureau), *China Trade and Price Statistics 1989* (New York: Praeger, 1991a), variables tables.

13. Data in Table 9.1 are adapted from Jae Ho Chung, "Sino-South Korea Economic Cooperation: An Analysis of Domestic and Foreign Entanglements," *Journal of Northeast Asian Studies*, Vol. IX (1990), p. 61; Qingguo Jia, "Changing Relations Across the Taiwan Strait," *Asian Survey*, Vol. XXXII (1992), p.

280; Won Bae Kim, "Yellow Sea Economic Zone: Vision or Reality?" *Journal of Northeast Asian Studies*, Vol. X (1991), p. 38; Lardy, *China's Entry into the World Economy*, p. 7; State Statistical Bureau, *Zhongguo Tongji Nianjian 1981* [China Statistical Annual 1981] (Beijing: China Statistical Press, 1981), p. 358; SSB, *Zhongguo Tongji Nianjian 1983* (1983), pp. 496–97; State Statistical Bureau, *Zhongguo Tongji Nianjian 1990* (1990), pp. 644–46; State Statistical Bureau, *Zhongguo Tongji Nianjian 1992* (1992), pp. 632–34; State Statistical Bureau, *Zhongguo Tongji Nianjian 1994* (1994), pp. 512–14; State Statistical Bureau, *Zhongguo Tongji Nianjian 1996* (1996), pp. 586–88; State Statistical Bureau, *China Trade and Price Statistics 1989*, pp. 144–49; UIC (University of Illinois at Chicago), *China Statistics Monthly*, February 1991a), p. 59, December (1991b), p. 58; Ken Yun, "Crossing the Yellow Sea," *The China Business Review*, January–February (1989), p. 40.

14. Segal, *Rethinking the Pacific*, p. 334.

15. Robert F. Dernberger, "Economic Cooperation in the Asia-Pacific Region and the Role of the P.R.C." *Journal of Northeast Asian Studies*, Vol. VII (1988), p. 6.

16. State Statistical Bureau, *Zhongguo Tongji Nianjian 1986* [China Statistical Annual 1986] (Beijing: China Statistical Press, 1986), p. 582; *Zhongguo Tongji Nianjian 1987* (1987), p. 604; *Zhongguo Tongji Nianjian 1988* (1988a), p. 656; *Zhongguo Tongji Nianjian 1990* (1990), p. 654; *Zhongguo Tongji Nianjian 1991* (1991b), p. 630.

17. Kim, "Yellow Sea Economic Zone," p. 40.

18. Chung, "Sino-South Korea Economic Cooperation," p. 63; State Statistical Bureau, *Zhongguo Tongji Nianjian 1996* (1996), p. 598.

19. Xiangming Chen, "The New Spatial Division of Labor and Commodity Chains in the Greater South China Economic Region," Chapter 8 in Garny Gereffi and Miguel Korzeniewicz, eds., *Commodity Chains and Global Capitalism* (Westport, CT: Greenwood Press, 1993); State Statistical Bureau, *Zhongguo Tongji Nianjian 1992* (1992), p. 642; State Statistical Bureau, *Zhongguo Tongji Nianjian 1996* (1996), p. 598.

20. Same as note 16 above; State Statistical Bureau, *Zhongguo Tongji Nianjian 1996* (1996), p. 598.

21. See Xiangming Chen, "China's City Hierarchy, Urban Policy, and Spatial Development in the 1980s." *Urban Studies*, Vol. 38 (1991), pp. 341–67.

22. State Statistical Bureau, *Zhongguo Tongji Nianjian 1986* [China Statistical Annual 1986] (Beijing: China Statistical Press, 1986), p. 583; *Zhongguo Tongji Nianjian 1987*, (1987), p. 605; *Zhongguo Tongji Nianjian 1988* (1988), p. 657; *Zhongguo Tongji Nianjian 1990* (1990), p. 655; *Zhongguo Tongji Nianjian 1991* (1991), p. 631; *Zhongguo Tongji Nianjian 1992* (1992), p. 643; *Zhongguo Tongji Nianjian 1994* (1994), p. 530; *Zhongguo Tongji Nianjian 1996* (1996), p. 600.

23. See Chaoming Lu and Tianxiang Zheng, "Yianhai Fazhan Zhanlue Xinjianyi" (New Proposals for the Coastal Development Strategy). *Tequ Yu Kaifang Chengshi Jingji* (Special Zone and Open City Economy), No. 5 (1990), pp. 45–48.

24. Dinah Lee, "Asia: The Next Era of Growth," *Business Week*, November 11, 1991, pp. 56–59.

25. Ezra F. Vogel, *One Step Ahead in China: Guangdong Under Reform* (Cambridge, MA: Harvard University Press, 1989), p. 67.

26. Kimiaki Taira, "Hong Kong-Ever Entrepôt," *China Newsletter*, Japan Export Trading Corporation (JETRO), Vol. 77, November–December (1988), p. 1.

27. Chen, "The New Spatial Division of Labor."

28. Hui Luo and Ming Chen, "Qiantan Xiamen Tequ Yinjin Taizi de Tezheng yu Qianjing" (A Preliminary Analysis of the Characteristics and Prospect of Taiwan's Capital Investment in Xiamen). *Tequ Yu Kaifang Chengshi Jingji* (Special Zone and Open City Economy), No. 10 (1989), pp. 31–34.

29. SSB, *Shenzhen Tongji Nianjian 1991* [Shenzhen Statistical Annual 1991] (Beijing: China Statistical Press, 1991c), pp. 284–94.

30. Computed from SSB, *China Urban Statistics 1985* (London: Longman, 1985b), p. 549; SSB, *Zhongguo Chengshi Tongji Nianjian 1988* [China Urban Statistical Annual 1988] (Beijing: China Statistical Press, 1988b), p. 443.

31. Fengqing Zhang, "Shixi Xiamen Tequ Waizi Laiyuan de Diqu Fenbu Wenti" (A Preliminary Analysis of Xiamen's Foreign Investment by Nationality). *Tequ Yu Kaifang Chengshi Jingji* (Special Zone and Open City Economy), no. 7 (1990), pp. 59–62.

32. *Tequ Yu Kaifang Chengshi Jingji*, "Taishang Chengwei Xiamen Jingji Tequ Fazhan de Zhongyao Liliang" (Taiwan Businesses Have Become an Important Force in Xiamen's Economic Development), No. 2 (1992), p. 41.

33. Mitchell A. Silk, "Silent Partners," *The China Business Review*, September–October (1990), p. 37.

34. Computed from SSB, (1988b), pp. 440, 443; SSB, *Zhongguo Chengshi Tongji Nianjian 1991* (Beijing: China Statistical Press, 1991d), pp. 509, 512.

35. See David Chang, "Speaking the Same Language," *The China Business Review*, September–October (1990), p. 39; Chen, "The New Spatial Division of Labor."

36. Julian Baum, "Taiwan's Building Block," *Far Eastern Economic Review*, May 2, 1991, pp. 36–37.

37. David K. Y. Chu and Xun-zhong Zheng, "Fuzhou: Capital of a Frontier Province," in Yue-man Yeung and Xu-wei Hu, eds., *China's Coastal Cities: Catalysts for Modernization* (Honolulu, HI: University of Hawaii Press, 1992).

38. See Lawrence A. Herzog, *Where North Meets South: Cities, Space, and Politics on the U.S.-Mexico Border* (Austin, TX: Center for Mexican Studies, University of Texas Press, 1990).

39. Chen, "The New Spatial Division of Labor."

40. Lu and Zheng, "Yianhai Fazhan Zhanlue Xinjianyi."

41. A group of researchers at the East-West Center in Hawaii has been studying economic cooperation and regional development issues in the Yellow Sea Rim and Northeast China. Recently, the East-West Center launched a new program for the Center on Northeast Asia Economic Development. The program would focus on the evolving relations among North and South Korea, the Russian Far East, Mongolia, Northeast China, Japan, and the United States. See *East-West Center Views*, Vol. 2, No. 3 (1992), p. 2.

42. Chung, "Sino-South Korean Economic Cooperation," p. 68; South Korean Trade Association, *The Current Status of the Chinese Economy and China-South Korean Business Ties* (in Korean), March (1992), p. 18.

43. Kim, "Yellow Sea Economic Zone," p. 40.

44. Yongle Fang, "Dalian Shi zai Dongbeiya Diqu Jingji Hezuo Zhongde Diwei Jiqi Fazhan Zhanlue Chutan" (A Preliminary Examination of Dalian's Position in Northeast Asian Economic Cooperation and Its Development Strategy). *Tequ Yu Kaifang Chengshi Jingji* (Special Zone and Open City Economy), No. 8 (1990), pp. 46–48.

45. Qian Tang, "Dalian Kouan due Taiwan he Nanchaoxian Maoyi Jiankuang" (A Brief Summary of Trade Between Dalian Port and Taiwan and South Korea). *Tequ Yu Kaifang Chengshi Jingji* (Special Zone and Open City Economy), No. 3 (1990), p. 58.

46. Hiroshi Tanimura, "Dalian Jingji Kaifa de Xianzhuang yu Wenti" (The Current Situation and Problems of Economic Development in Dalian). *Tequ Yu Kaifang Chengshi Jingji* (Special Zone and Open City Economy), No. 4 (1987), pp. 33–36.

47. Xingdi Li, "Jingji Quyu Jituanhua Chaoliu he Huanghai Jingjiqu" (The Trend of Regional Economic Conglomeration and the Yellow Sea Economic Zone), unpublished manuscript, 1992, tables 2 and 5.

48. South Korean Trade Association, *The Current Status of the Chinese Economy*, p. 18.

49. Computed from SSB, (1987), pp. 91, 268.

50. Tanimura, "Dalian Jingji Kaifa de Xianzhuang yu Wenti."

51. Xiangming Chen, *Some Social Aspects of China's Special Economic Zones as a Development Strategy: A Capitalist Means to Socialism* (Unpublished Ph.D. Dissertation, Department of Sociology, Duke University, Durham, North Carolina, 1988).

52. Yun, "Crossing the Yellow Sea."

53. Fangshuo Liu, "Shehui Zhuyi Zhidu Nei Zhengfu Hongguan Guanli Xiade Xinxing Kuaguo Jingji" (The New Cross-National Economy Macromanaged by Government Under Socialism). *Tequ Yu Kaifang Chengshi Jingji* (Special Zone and Open City Economy), No. 1 (1991), pp. 54–63.

54. Kim, "Yellow Sea Economic Zone," p. 40.

55. Pam Baldinger, "Deals Involving China and South Korea," *The China Business Review*, January–February (1989), p. 41.

56. Personal interview with a Chinese national who is involved in buying toys made by Sino-foreign joint ventures in China and selling them to U.S. wholesalers, April, 1992.

57. Borthwick, *Pacific Century*; Kim, "Yellow Sea Economic Zone"; Yun, "Crossing the Yellow Sea."

58. Xingdi Li, "Wuoguo Yianhai Fazhan Zhanlue he Shandong de Cilue Tantao" (Exploring China's Coastal Development Strategy and Shandong's Options). *Tequ Yu Kaifang Chengshi Jingji* (Special Zone and Open City Economy), No. 11 (1989), pp. 49–52.

59. Ralph N. Clough, "Political Implications of Sino-South Korean Trade,"

*The China Business Review*, January–February (1989), pp. 42–45; Information from personal interview with a high-ranking official of Shandong province, September 4, 1992.

60. Chung, "Sino-South Korean Economic Cooperation"; Same interview cited in note 59 above.

61. Li, "Wuguo Yianhai Fazhan Zhanlue he Shandong de Cilue Tantao."

62. Fang, "Dalian Shi zai Dongbeiya Diqu Jingji Hezuo Zhongde Diwei Jiqi Fazhan Zhanlue Chutan."

63. From the Chinese side, China National Foreign Trade Transportation Corp. has charted a Panamanian-registered container ship to go between Shanghai and Pusan via Japan. From the Korean side, Chungyung Shipping Co. Ltd., using a Hong Kong shipping company, began direct semicontainer shipping service between Pusan, Inchon, Shanghai, and Tianjin in July 1988. See Baldinger, "Deals Involving China and South Korea"; Yun, "Crossing the Yellow Sea."

64. It was reported that Dongnama Shipping and Hyundai Merchant Marine Co. Ltd. negotiated with China to launch direct shipping services between South Korea and China. See Baldinger, "Deals Involving China and South Korea"; Kim, "Yellow Sea Economic Zone."

65. Lu and Zheng, "Yianhai Fazhan Zhanlue Xinjianyi."

66. Zunwei Yan, "Pudong Xinqu 'Sanzi' Qiyi Fazhan Xianzhuang ji Jingrong Duice" (The Development of Foreign-Invested Enterprises and Its Fiscal Policy in the Pudong New Zone). *Tequ Yu Kaifang Chengshi Jingji* (Special Zone and Open City Economy), No. 9 (1991), pp. 44–46.

67. Chen, *Some Social Aspects of China's Special Economic Zones as a Development Strategy*.

68. SSB, (1985a), p. 327.

69. SSB, *Zhongguo Tongji Zhaiyao 1991* [China Statistical Abstract 1991] (Beijing: China Statistical Press, 1991d), p. 11.

70. Richard Pomfret, *Investing in China: Ten Years of the 'Open Door' Policy* (New York: Harvester Wheatsheaf, 1991), p. 86.

71. Baosen Chen, "Zhongguo Yianhai Diqu Jingji Fazhan Zhanlue he Meiguo Duihua Touzi" (The Economic Development Strategy of China's Coastal Region and the U.S. Investment in China). *Tequ Yu Kaifang Chengshi Jingji* (Special Zone and Open City Economy), No. 10 (1988), pp. 45–57.

72. Yan, "Pudong Xinqu 'Sanzi' Qiyi Fazhan Xianzhuang ji Jingrong Duice."

73. Pomfret, *Investing in China*, p. 88.

74. *People's Daily*, "Heilongjiang Bianjing Diqu Jingji Xunsu Fazhan" (The Economy of Heilongjiang's Border Areas Has Been Developing Rapidly), May 7, 1992, p. 2.

75. SSB, (1991d), p. 47.

76. Yan Zheng, "Guanyu Hehei Jingji Tequ de Yanjiu Baogao" (A Research Report on the Establishment of the Heihe Economic Zone) *Tequ Yu Kaifang Chengshi Jingji* (Special Zone and Open City Economy), No. 3 (1990), pp. 12–22.

77. The former Soviet Far East has half of the country's oil reserve, 70 percent of its coal and coke reserve, 75 percent of its timber, and 70 percent of its natural

gas, as well as over 70 different mineral resources. See Qiang Du, "Zhongguo Canyu Dongbeiya Quyu Jingji Hezuo de Qiaotoubao" (The Outpost of China's Participation in the Regional Economic Cooperation of Northeast Asia). *Tequ Yu Kaifang Chengshi Jingji* (Special Zone and Open City Economy), No. 12 (1989), p. 63.

78. Robert Neff and Laxmi Nakarmi, "Asia's Next Powerhouse: An All-But-United Korea?" *Business Week*, October 14, 1991, p. 63.

79. Lardy, *China's Entry into the World Economy.*

80. Kim, "Yellow Sea Economic Zone."

81. In 1980 the prime ministers of Australia and Japan advocated the formation of a government-supported private body, the Pacific Economic Cooperation Conference (PECC), based in Singapore. The PECC currently includes the ASEAN, Australia, New Zealand, the former Soviet Union, Japan, South Korea, China, Taiwan, Hong Kong, the Pacific Islands, Canada, the United States, Mexico, Peru, and Chile. There were already existing academic regional groups such as the Pacific Trade and Development Conference (PAFTAD) and the Pacific Trade and Development Conference (PBEC), but neither had government financial support and participation. In early 1989 the Australian Prime Minister proposed the creation of an intergovernmental forum called Asia-Pacific Economic Cooperation (APEC), which originally comprised twelve nations—the six ASEAN countries, Australia, New Zealand, Japan, South Korea, Japan, and the United States. In 1991 the APEC was enlarged to include China, Hong Kong, and Taiwan. See Borthwick, *Pacific Century*, pp. 526–28.

82. Elizabeth Cheng, "The East Is Ready," *Far Eastern Economic Review*, May 13, 1990, pp. 57–58.

83. Bing Sheng and Lun Feng, eds., *Zhongguo Guoqing Baogao* [China's State of Union Report] (Shenyang, Liaoning: Liaoning People's Press, 1991), p. 676.

84. See Arif Dirlik, "National Development and Social Revolution in Early Chinese Marxist Thought," *China Quarterly*, Vol. 58 (1974).

85. Leslie Sklair, "Problems of Socialist Development: The Significance of Shenzhen Special Economic Zone for China's Open Door Development Strategy," *International Journal of Urban and Regional Research*, Vol. 15 (1991), pp. 208–13.

86. See Chung, "Sino-South Korean Economic Cooperation"; K.A. Namkung, "The U.S. Role in Sino-South Korean Trade," *The China Business Review*, January–February (1989), pp. 45–46.

# 10

# Sexual Economies in the Asia-Pacific Community

NEFERTI XINA M. TADIAR

With the celebrated emergence of the Asia-Pacific community, the Philippines is confronted with the tensions of its historical identity and the political and economic crisis that is its persistent reality. As a region, the Asia-Pacific designates a political and economic constituency represented primarily by the United States, Japan, Canada, Australia, and New Zealand, a group known as the OECD (Organization for Economic Cooperation and Development) Five, and secondarily by newly industrialized countries such as South Korea, Taiwan, and Singapore. Such a representation and the excitement for regional prosperity that it generates, however, elide the contradictory Third World status of the rest of the Asia-Pacific—developing countries like the Southeast Asian nations that threaten to disrupt the congenial unity that the dream of "community" conjures. Once a dominantly geographical area composed of dispersed political territories, the Asia-Pacific is increasingly sold on the idea of constituting a purely economic network among its member nations. Indeed, the dream of "community" is steadily being realized as a transnational corporation with the power to regulate and determine national as well as individual lives. For the fantasy of the Asia-Pacific community is one that takes form and force within a particular global purview, namely, the First World fantasy of the Free World, or international community, that shapes international relations through the political and economic practices of individual nations. It is, in other words, the shared ground upon which the actions and identities of its participants are predicated—it is a field of orientation, an imaginary determining the categories and operations with which individuals as well as nation-states act out their histories. Among these categories is sexuality—in this fantasy, the economies and political relations of nations are libidinally configured, that is, they are grasped and effected in terms of sexuality. This global and regional fantasy[1] is not, however, only metaphorical, but real insofar

**219**

as it grasps a system of political and economic practices already at work among these nations.

Individuals as well as governments act not only as if a unified global community did exist, but as if nations were individual citizens who compose this community and who, like individuals, behave in particular (sexual) ways and act with particular desires.[2] That international community in effect works in the way it is imagined, but only because it is realized as this totality through the displacement of its constitutive contradictions onto Third World bodies; that is, capitalism is impelled by desire (visibly demonstrated by the endless processes of accumulation and consumption)—desire, in other words, for surplus wealth/pleasure, produced by and producing a fantasy of political-libidinal economies that regulate individual and national lives. The Asia-Pacific community is predicated on this fantasy of a global (Free World market) economy. Indeed, as a regional reproduction of an ideal international community, it reproduces the same sexual economies and relations at work in global capitalism, intensifying them to the greater profit of its main promoters and to the greater loss of the populations whose labor must pay for it. It is the logic of these libidinal processes that I would like to trace in this rendering of the fantasy of the Asia-Pacific community.

## Pacific Desires

Invoking the Asia-Pacific as a leader and symbol of an emergent international order, therefore, obscures the intensification of globalized capitalism to which this community is dedicated. It is, in effect, to invoke international cooperation without the competition and violence necessary to this global organization. I argue that the Asia-Pacific, as a dream and an actuality, functions as a locus of containment of the threat the region poses to the dominant powers who benefit from its promotion. With the Vietnam War and other anti-imperialist revolutionary struggles being waged in Southeast Asia (as well as in Africa, the Middle East, and Latin America) from the late 1960s to the mid-1970s, the Asia-Pacific region emerged as a threat to the global power of the United States, that is, to its political authority as well as economic superiority. The end of the cold war and the burgeoning economy of Japan and the newly industrialized countries only increased this economic and political threat and the necessity of its containment. Hence, the intensified efforts to push for the realization of the Asia-Pacific community, a dream dedicated to the greater dream of global capitalism.

Thus Prime Minister Nakasone could wholeheartedly claim: "In the Pacific we are witnessing the birth of a new kind of capitalism. Here the vigour and competitiveness of Western—particularly American—capitalism has been enriched by the Asian cultural heritage." Furthermore, "Asian free enterprise has shown itself capable of fostering a competitive dynamism of its own. The distinguishing mark of the Pacific Basin countries has been their commitment to free enterprise economics."[3] More than fifty years ago, Japan was advocating the founding of a very different Asian empire, a desire that all but ended in World War II. But forty years earlier, the United States had already set its sights on the very same region, which was to whet its appetite for global power: "The Pacific is the ocean of the commerce of the future. Most future wars will be conflicts for commerce. The power that rules the Pacific, therefore, is the power that rules the world. And, with the Philippines, that power is and will forever be the American Republic."[4] This desire to be a Pacific power has brought about these two wars: the "war of pacification," as Americans used to refer to the Philippine—U.S. war at the turn of the century, and the "Pacific war," as they called the war between themselves and Japan at mid-century. One might well argue, however, that this war over the Pacific continues to be waged today, but in a very different way. Global conflict is no longer envisioned in the fantasy of East-West relations (i.e., relations of the Orient and the Occident, or for that matter, of the two power blocs, the United States and the USSR); nor is it envisioned in the fantasy of the First and Third Worlds, or of North and South. These global unities have ceased to function in the same way in a decidedly post–cold war, post–Gulf War era. Japan and the United States are no longer up in arms over the Pacific or even over "the last land left in all the oceans," the Philippines; instead, they are now in cooperation. This new mode of relation realized through incorporation is libidinal/economic in character and thus can be truthfully described as a marriage of interests.

## The Pacific Marriage

It has been claimed that the idea of a Pacific community is "a baby whose putative parents are Japanese and American and whose midwife is Australian."[5] This marriage between Japan and the United States, however, masks as well as reveals the particular global desires and tensions still at play in the Free World. War has been consummated in a sexual relationship that stabilizes the tenuous unity of the international community. In this arrangement, sexual union is war through economic incorporation. Indeed, what this marriage evinces is an unequal and potentially antagonistic relation at the heart of the economic union, whether this union refers to the Asia-Pacific or to the larger international community. What it further reveals is the desire for incorporation into these global unions. Hence the Japanese initiative in proposing the formation of the Pacific community during the late 1960s, confirming what Nakasone could later admit as "Japan's need to become an '*international* nation'; that is to say, a nation that must bear a heavy share of international responsibilities in keeping with its international position."[6] The desire for incorporation might thus be seen as a desire for citizenship in the international community, a citizenship that entails more than an allegiance to the ideals of internationality, that entails also buying into the preconditions of the Free World. But the Japanese have only lately begun to see themselves as attaining this citizenship that persons in other nations, such as the United States, have long since held—with the idea that there are nation-citizens with more rights and responsibilities than others, that is, with more power than others. If there is such a thing as an international state, clearly the United States is seen to hold some kind of presidential power. Hence the uneasiness of the marriage. For in desiring inclusion, the Japanese show themselves to be lacking in political power in spite of their economic wealth (a condition secured with Japan's disarmament as a consequence of her losing to the United States in World War II). The Asia-Pacific community is, in this light, a way for Japan to marry into power and the United States to domesticate her desires for power. For in the transformation of this international community into a multinational corporation, the preoccupation with the balance of power becomes the participation in the bargain for power; that is, power becomes a matter of negotiating economic shares and political management or control.

I say "her," because in this scenario, Japan is the wife and the United States her husband. The antagonism that the fantasies of East-West, First World–Third World, and North-South relations have historically addressed (as frameworks of global contradictions) has been transmuted into libidinal cooperation, that is, into the fantasy of masculine-feminine relations. Deterritorialized, these global polarities are now predominantly enacted according to a prevailing mode of heterosexual relations. But the allies and partners that territories and possessions of a past age have been transformed into are not categories that pertain to particular nations at all times. As it is well known in the Philippines with reference to the United States, "There are no permanent friendships, only permanent interests." More than this wavering interest, the positions in partnerships, that is, of masculine and feminine, are continually in flux and dependent on what parties are in relation. In other words, masculine and feminine are defined against each other and function according to the specific historical relation at work. Hence, in relation to the United States, Japan may occupy a feminine position, but in relation to the Philippines, a masculine position. Since nations maintain simultaneous and crossing international relations, masculine and feminine should be seen not as essential features of even specific relations, but rather as diacritical marks of certain political practices and economic modes of operation within and between nations that are libidinal in character, such as investment of capital and extraction of interest.

The logic of this sociolibidinal economy at work among nations can be demonstrated in the "special relations" of the Philippines and the United States. The fantasy of this particular relationship is paradigmatic not only because of the intimate history shared by these two nations and the sexual form it has taken, but also because of the tremendous difference between them in national wealth and global power. In effect, they encapsulate two extreme positions within the Asia-Pacific community and thereby make more glaring the antagonisms it must contain. Furthermore, the role of the Philippines in relation to the United States and Japan evidences the costs entailed by the offspring of the latter's marriage of interests, that is, by the realization of the Asia-Pacific community.

## The Philippine-American Romance

The Philippines is second only to Bangladesh as the country with the worst growth rate in Asia.[7] She owes this position to a large extent to her enormous debt to and dependence on the United States, together with the World Bank and the International Monetary Fund, a relation that is "secured" through various policies and treaties, not the least significant of which is the U.S. military bases agreement. This "involvement" of the United States in the Philippines is as a territory to be invested in (whether in capital or in arms) in the name of national and regional *security*. Although "security" has long been touted as being an issue of military defense of political sovereignty, the end of the cold war and the move to steer clear of "politics" in the promotion of the Asia-Pacific community have brought out the full implications of its economic and financial significance. As an economic arrangement, "security" also has its romantic overtones, inasmuch as it means the cementing of a relationship or the insuring of its stability. But the question to be asked of the international arrangements being made in the Asia-Pacific is: Who is getting off on this? Who is getting screwed and by whom?

In the case of Japan, clearly some leverage, that is, some bargaining power, is gained in her marriage of interests with the United States. In the case of the Philippines, that "security" is at least questionable. For the "special relationship" of the Philippines and the United States is no marriage, and the Philippines is no wife; she is, rather, the mistress of the United States. Feminized in this relationship of debt and dependence, the

Philippines produces the surplus pleasure (wealth) that the United States extracts from her bodily (manual) labor. It is indeed her inexhaustible labor and her abundant natural resources that draw the United States to her, that is used to "attract" the latter's interest and investments. Philippine security therefore comes to mean the political stability necessary to attract foreign investors, the source of capital. An advertisement the Philippine government took out in the *New York Times* (July 28, 1974) demonstrates the sexual marketing of the country's domestic attractions:

> We've put our house in order. . . . There are attractive investment packages for you if you want to explore, develop and process mineral resources. . . . Easy entry for expatriate staff. . . . Doesn't that sound like an offer you can't refuse? We like multinationals. Manila's natural charms as a regional business center have been enhanced by a special incentive package. . . . your expatriate-managers will enjoy Asia's lowest living costs among the most outgoing people in the Pacific. . . . Accountants come for $67, executive secretaries for $148. Move your Asian headquarters to Manila and make your cost accountants happy. . . . The country is lovely. And loaded. Beneath the tropical landscapes of our 7,000 islands lies a wealth of natural resources. . . .[8]

The prostitution of the Philippines that is attendant upon such rhetoric is made possible by and perpetuates a logic in which certain divisions of labor and patterns of sexual relations converge and collaborate in the driving of the national economy. Those who are at the wheel of the nation are its representatives, and the behavior they exhibit bespeaks the character of the nation. Thus does the Philippine-U.S. relationship appear as a romance-fantasy that has each government courting and manipulating the other for his or her security and happiness:

> Philippine presidents, out of tradition but more of necessity, have always had a love-hate relationship with the Great White Father in Washington. Cory Aquino is no exception. Right now, she is displaying the classic behavior of a spurned lover, one who not too long ago was playing beautiful music with no less than George Bush himself.
>
> What explains this cyclical and all too predictable behavior of virtually everybody who has ever lived in Malacañang? First, there is the realpolitik aspect. Nobody gets to be president of this country without, more or less, the imprimatur of whoever happens to call the shots in the White House. Second, Washington tends to keep a tight leash on Philippine presidents, especially on the matter of keeping American bases in this part of the world. Third, America's love is never constant, never enduring; Filipino presidents come and go, but American interest in this country is eternal. Or so it seems.[9]

The article from which this extract was taken goes on, relating the "tragic pattern of presidential love-hate for America" in which the various presidents experienced "the sweet love of American support, followed by an acrimonious parting of ways," sharing "the common fate of being at the mercy, if not in the physical custody of America." This custody that makes Filipinos a kept people, however, is actively pursued by those who in their desire to share in the rights and privileges of the international community buy into this economic arrangement (free enterprise, free love)—this open relationship that economically means the letting down of protectionist barriers and "liberalization" of imports, that is, easy entry and exit.

This "special relationship" is the manifestation and consequence of an imperialistic dream that at the turn of the century was steeped in sacred tones. As Senator Beveridge exclaimed:

> We will not repudiate our duty in the archipelago. We will not abandon our opportunity in the Orient. We will not renounce our part in the mission of our race, trustee under God, of the civilization of the world . . . of all our race He has marked the American people as his chosen nation to finally lead in the regeneration of the world. This is the divine mission of America, and it holds for us all the profit, all the glory, all the happiness possible to man. We are trustees of the world's progress, guardians of its righteous peace. The judgement of the Master is upon us: "Ye have been faithful over a few things; I will make you rule over many things."[10]

The religious rhetoric of U.S. colonization has become today the libidinal action of U.S. capitalism. The goal of economic and political conversion was also zealously expressed by Senator Beveridge:

> American soil is producing more than Americans can consume. . . . The trade of the world must and shall be ours. American law, American order, American civilization and the American flag will plant themselves on shores hitherto bloody and benighted but by the agencies of God henceforth to be made beautiful and bright.[11]

This process of evangelization has today become explicitly the process of seduction. But although the form has changed, the dream yet seeks the same coveted object, the Philippines—a body resistant to its desire and to its ideals of democracy and freedom, that is, free enterprise. The Philippines needs to be converted and seduced because she is a contradiction to these ideals to the extent that she is residually feudal or precapitalist and threatening to become communist or anticapitalist. As a colony she therefore had to be "emancipated" and granted independence, converted to that U.S. order that has become today a global order in order to contain the potentially eruptive antagonism that could develop from the contradiction she poses (by serving as a locus for her displacement), a contradiction that is nevertheless necessary for the motoring of capitalism. What one might glean from this history of decolonization is the same logic at work in the granting of autonomy to the Asia-Pacific region. Now constituted as a self-governing unit, it could thereby be more efficiently engaged in the global economy.

The coveting of former colonies, however, did not cease with "liberation." These recalcitrant bodies, now members of an independent region, must continually be lured into feeding the desires of power. As Luz del Mundo observed:

> The Western powers are now reaping the effects of their ignoring "nationalist" aspirations of Arab countries and their greedy grabbing of spheres of influence on Arab oil resources in the past several decades, thus triggering retaliatory moves from OPEC. Now they turn their attention to the Asia-Pacific region. ASEAN is now at a stage where it has more countries from Europe, the Middle East and Latin America interested in entering into partnership with ASEAN. Japan sees this and wants to preempt the ASEAN as its own preserve; a prize and plum to be won permanently by persuading its other OECD partners, particularly the US and Australia, that through the creation of a Pacific community, Japan will be certain to remain an ally of the West.[12]

Part and parcel of this "prize and plum to be won" that is the ASEAN is the Philippines. Thus, the Philippines plays a curious role in the marriage of Japan and "the West"—"won" back from Japan in World War II by the United States, she must now be shared as the price of alliance and as insurance of Japanese fidelity. But this price is paid neither by the United States nor Japan, that is, neither by "the Great White Father" nor his recent spouse—but by the Philippines, mistress-infant to one, stepdaughter-servant to the other, the body that keeps the two in relative harmony by acting as a membrane for the coursing of their desires and as a locus for the playing out of their antagonism. Such is a typical international triangle: an incestuous ménage a trois as well as a perverted oedipal affair.

## A Model Asian-Pacific Family

As Aida Fulleros Santos and Lynn F. Lee show in their analysis of the Philippine Aid Plan (PAP), a current project of the United States and Japan, the marriage of the two powers is convenient but uneasy. There are obvious tensions in this "triangular relationship between institutions in the United States, Japan and the Philippines": Japan has not agreed entirely that aid to the Philippines be conditioned by the U.S. perception of their common regional interests, and that Japan be "guided by the United States while giving the bulk of ODA [Official Development Assistance] funds. . . . Japan sees its strategic interests as similar to the United States but does not have exactly the same view on the best ways of furthering these mutually shared interests. For the United States, the PAP concretises a political strategy for the U.S. and Japan to work together to further their mutual interests in the Asia-Pacific region and globally. . . . PAP shows the U.S. strategy—U.S. political direction and Japanese funding."[13]

In spite of the tensions, however, the U.S.-Japan cooperative effort is bound to make the Philippines pay, for aside from giving the two more leverage with the Philippine government in defining and determining "regional security," it also increases the Philippine foreign debt. "In the long term, foreign investment that may flow on from PAP will contribute to the net outflow of money from the Philippines."[14] Indeed, what the PAP scheme shows is that such marriage of powers only augments their individual exploitation of the country of their desires.

In her relationship to the United States, the Philippines is an exploitable body, an industry hooked up to the U.S. desiring machine through a system of flows of labor and capital in the guise of free exchange (export oriented, capital and import dependent), but functioning in the mode of dialysis, which gives one the strength and life depleted from the other. As such, the Philippines is the hooker of the United States who caters to the latter's demands (ostensibly demands of global production and consumption); in other words, a hospitality industry, a hostess to U.S. desires, a prostitute. As the greatest of her foreign investors, that is, the most powerful of her multinational clients, the United States establishes free trade zones on the body/land of the Philippines over which he exercises a considerable degree of monopoly (the way he derives his pleasures) by obtaining free entry and exit rights (investment of capital and repatriation of profits). This mode of relations between the Philippines and the United States operates according to a fantasy of relations between masculine and feminine ideals that has become dominant in economically advanced nations—a sexual masquerade in which the Philippines serves as a feminine ideal for the United States, servicing his power the way the Philippine prostitutes service U.S. military men, symbols of U.S. national (masculine) strength. The fantasy is shared, of course, and the United States in turn becomes a masculine ideal for the Philippines, determining the kind of desires expressed by this "bar waitress" who might speak for the Philippines as well: "Sure I would like to marry an American! I want to help my family. If I marry a Filipino, it will be the same; but if I marry an American, maybe it will be better."[15] The fulfillment of the prostitute's desire to marry into a better life (i.e., foreign, American), however, is not forthcoming, as it has been preempted by other partners of the United States.

New investment flows in the Philippines are dominated by Japanese as well as Taiwanese capital. "For both Japan and Taiwan, the motives for investment are primarily the need to recycle trade surpluses and the exploitation of advantages offered by the Philippines, e.g., a cheap labour force, natural resources, trade preferences vis-à-vis the developed countries, as well as a location for polluting industries."[16] In other words, the interest Japan and Taiwan take in the Philippines is not very different in form from the interest the Untied States takes in her, for the attractions the Philippines holds are all the same for these capital-bearing nations. In this scenario, speaking of interest and involvement is the same as speaking of investment, and to speak of any of these things is to use the language of politics and economics as well as the language of love and sexual exploitation. Thus with the increase of Japanese loans and grants to the Philippines, Japan joins in the feminization of the Philippines: "As Japan chalks up more trade surpluses, Japanese penetration of the country's economy will, no doubt, increase."[17] Adopting the Free World fantasy of the advanced nations of the West in order not only to enter the international community but also "to step out of the shadow of the U.S."[18] and exercise equal if not greater power in a new global order, Japan is yet determined by the threat of an emasculation similar to that which she participates in effecting on developing nations such as the Philippines. Thus the protectionist measures she adopts in the form of high tariffs on processed or semiprocessed products are in effect a successful defense against getting screwed, that is, penetrated.[19] Who is penetrating whom—in translated terms, which countries export capital, technology, and finished products to which countries—hence becomes a gauge by which to measure economic strength. It is no surprise then that even those in developing nations who want to get in on the action that the Asia-Pacific community promises point out the necessity of correcting the uneven trade among member nations—demonstrated, for example, by the fact that "tropical products from the Pacific Developing Countries (PDCs) suffered from low import penetration into the American, Japanese, Canadian and Australian markets"[20]—a problem whose proposed solution lies merely in an equalization of flows through political reform ("national goodwill") rather than in a transformation of the mode of relations among these nations. Furthermore, development is always seen in terms of inside and outside, feminine and masculine, domestic and international. Hence the possibility of critiquing the economic growth registered by the Philippines in recent years in the following way: "One finds that most of the permanent or 'structural' features of the growth have originated from the outside. These have come in the form of loans, official assistance, and the expansion in world markets. . . . the impetus has come mainly from without."[21]

Thus subjected to extensive and intensive penetration of her economy by powers such as the United States, Japan, and the rest of the OECD Five, as well as the newly industrialized countries, the Philippines finds herself hyperfeminized in her relations. It is not an accident that the U.S. expression "to fuck someone over" means to exploit or abuse someone. The way in which this dominant fantasy of sexual relations has developed as an essential condition of advanced capitalism might be traced through the history of imperialism up to the present. Indeed, one could show that the hyperfeminization of certain countries signifies their condensation of the contradictory symptoms of patriarchy, colonialism, and imperialism. Thus the hyperfeminization of the Philippines is a historically new phenomenon, which is not to say that this process of objectification did not exist earlier, for it might be argued that the production of the prostitute as a feminine ideal is a cultural corollary to commodity fetishism in the age of capitalism, and feminization is the process of management through investment (such was the new mode of control of the colonies in the age of imperialism). But what is new is the way in which prostitution has become a dominant mode of production of neocolonial nations in late capitalism—that is, neocolonial nations are now like prostitutes to be invested in for the extraction of surplus pleasure (wealth)[22]—and the extent to which this feminizing process has intensified on a global scale since the mid-1970s. Indeed, it is the intensification of global capitalism that has led to the visible manifestation of its internal contradictions in the catastrophe of developing nations—the sexual fantasy is henceforth literally realized on the bodies of women. That is to say, this hyperfeminization is not merely metaphorical, but translates into the concrete exploitation and abuse of actual women.

## Sexual Labor and Commerce

In the case of the Philippines this phenomenon is most clearly seen in the feminization of exploited labor. "The export-oriented, debt-propelled strategy has given rise to the global commodification of Third World women in the form of female labor export, exploitation of their cheap labor power and their utilization through sexual trade, whether it be in the legitimate 'tourism' or hospitality and mail-order bride business or in prostitution which has phenomenally spread."[23] Indeed, what the case of the Philippines and other Southeast Asian nations demonstrates is the veritable feminization of the Third World of Asia (rather than simply the

Third World, which was once synonymous with Asia). In these countries the sexuality of commerce thus necessarily means the commerce of feminine sexuality, that is, the selling and trading of women forced into prostitution through poverty or physical abuse, not only within these countries but internationally as well.

In the Philippines, there are 300,000 to 500,000 prostitutes,[24] working not only in the areas surrounding the U.S. bases servicing U.S. military men on leave, but also in Japanese-owned hotels catering to Japanese businessmen on vacation. The "boom of the sex industry" is only the necessary consequence of the "development" of a larger hospitality industry, that is, one that hosts the capital and arms of touring men[25] and multinationals. In fact, the establishment of the Ministry of Tourism in 1973 was a key achievement of the Marcos state in its revitalized efforts to transform the nation into a lucrative business beginning with the declaration of martial law:

> Before 1973 the Philippines was not much of a tourist spot. The combination of street crime and well-organized demonstrations against American imperialism and the Vietnam war created a less-than-friendly environment for a fun seeker. When President Ferdinand Marcos declared martial law on September 21, 1972, a lot of that changed. Criminals were rounded up and the political opposition jailed. In 1973 the Ministry of Tourism was established with former Marcos press agent Jose Aspiras in charge, and the number of visitors rapidly increased from less than 150,000 in 1971 to more than a million in 1980.[26]

With the military imposition of stability in an otherwise crisis-ridden country, the number of hotels and tourists, multinationals and investors increased rapidly. Martial law was not, however, merely the whim of a dictator in pursuit of power (although that was undoubtedly at work as well), but part of the engineering of a new economic order necessary to meet the intensified demands of global capitalism. Marcos's indebtedness to the World Bank and the IMF, for which the Filipino people are still paying dearly, is only the logical consequence of the latter's instrumental role in this cooperative prostitution of the country through "authoritarian modernization":[27]

> The Bank set in motion in the Philippines a development program with two key objectives: "pacification" and "liberalization." The pacification component consisted of rural and urban development programs aimed at defusing rural and urban unrest. Liberalization referred to the drastic restructuring of Philippine industry and external trade strategy to open up the country more completely to the flow of U.S. capital and commodities. To implement this strategy of "technocratic modernization," the Bank encouraged the for-

mation of an authoritarian government and carefully cultivated a technocratic elite.[28]

Mostly educated in the United States, this elite was heavily influenced by the Keynesian revolution in economics during the 1950s and the principles of technocracy "fine-tuned" during the 1960s. Thus the technocrats who replaced the industrial elite in the 1970s could be said to share "a strong sense of fraternity with their World Bank and IMF counterparts."[29] As one columnist wrote in 1981, "Now we're completely under the thumbs of the IMF because our principal planners are IMF boys."[30]

This situation hardly changed when Aquino came into power in 1986—the fraternal identification with these governing bodies of international finance transcended national changes. Hence Aquino's finance minister, Jaime Ongpin, could sincerely claim, "I don't blame the IMF for what they did. If I were in their shoes, I would have been tougher."[31] Such are the outstanding young men of the nation whose consolidation with the government and fraternal bonding with international economists, financiers, and other managers of nations was the single-handed, multiarmed achievement of martial law. Part of the legacy of martial law is the desire for authoritarian (masculine) rule evidenced in the repeatedly expressed desire on the part of many Filipinos for a "strong leader" (in complaints, for example, that Aquino is not "man enough" for the position), a desire stoked not only by the absence of Marcos and fueled by the tradition of patronage politics, but now especially attractive in light of the ostensible success of authoritarian regimes in newly industrialized countries.

With Marcos and his boys and cronies manning the nation, modernization and militarism went hand in hand in restructuring the economy, now characterized by import liberalization, privatization, foreign capital dependency, and export orientation. Free trade zones and tourist belts were essential components of the government's "incentive packages" to attract capital to the Philippines and thus similar in constitution. Both relied on a predominantly female and wholly feminized labor force. Both employed a "get laid or get laid off" policy. In the case of the tourist industry, labor and raw material were the same: women. It is not an accident that "Sin-city," Manila, the "sex-capital of the world,"[32] was touted and fashioned by Imelda Marcos as "the City of Man." The "beautification" projects meant to raise Manila to the level of a modern metropolis to compete for international attention and capital only evidences the veritable prostitution of the Philippines. This means not only the selling of women but the feminization and parceling out of the land: in Ermita, the red-light district in Manila, different zones of bars and clubs are owned and primarily patronized by different nationalities, so that one could identify, for example, an Australian strip, a German one, and so forth—a free trade zone that makes Manila into a multinational brothel.[33] Thus one could in all truth declare, "The government is not only selling women to foreigners, but also the sovereignty of the nation itself."[34]

## Imperial Sons, National Pimps

The rise of a "strong-man" regime was a World Bank-endorsed response to the growing and intensifying crises felt in the nation as a result of the political and economic system installed by United States colonization being pushed to its limits by the acceleration of global capital. Other developing countries underwent similar postwar crises and responded with similar "strong-man" regimes.[35] The nationalist tenor of these Third World dictatorships only made manifest that in the age of imperialism, nationhood is figured and operates in masculine terms. The early experience of the Philippines with nascent nationalism in the late nineteenth century evidences this form of masculinization, a masculinization that found its symptomatic expression in the militarism of interimperial rivalry. Given these conditions and the infantilization of the colonies that predominated in an earlier age, early anti-imperialistic nationalism could only be articulated as a son's demand for independence and sovereignty:

> The nation is gendered and domesticated within the circle of sacrifice and the idealization of loss that binds the child-patriot to this motherland. By doing so, the patriot not only expresses his love but also reverses the relationship of dependency between mother and child. He posits his future authority over her, imagining himself and others like him as potential patrons, "bequeathing" to the *patria* the legacy of freedom. In this way, the motherland inherits from her sons an "immense fortune"—a surplus of symbolic wealth with which to nurture future sons. Offspring and lover, the patriot is now also father to the nation. It is thus wholly without irony that Filipinos have regarded Rizal as the "father" of Philippine nationalism and that one of his biographers has referred to him as the "first Filipino."[36]

The infantilization of the Philippines continues to be felt. Senator Estrada expressed it when he spoke against the presence of the U.S. bases: "Our current relations with the U.S. is not untarnished. It's not the relation of two friends, but the relation between the master and a ward who is forcibly being suppressed to remain a child."[37] The representation of this relation is the result of the general mode of exchange between the Philippines and the United States; it is a discourse built up also from an exchange of representations that is most evident in the media. The *New York Times*, for example, recently wrote:

> Even among Filipinos who want the United States military to stay, it is commonly said that this is a nation that has never been allowed to progress beyond adolescence, beyond an immature need to hide behind someone or something else for protection. . . . many Filipinos admit that too often they seek out godfathers rather than take responsibility for their own actions.
> Led by several fierce, hard-headed nationalists, who say with a touch of pride that they are willing to buck popular opinion, the Philippine Senate seems poised to try to end the country's dependence on what is being portrayed as the biggest godfather of them all, the American military. . . .[38]

The patronizing recognition of that "touch of pride" is then explained (and thus legitimated) by a Filipino political analyst whose understanding of the significance of rejecting the bases affirms his identification with this infantilized image: "It will be therapeutic, a national primal scream that may mature us."[39] In all such attempts to articulate the problems of the Philippine national identity, the motherland seems, however, to have disappeared; the maternal has vanished, leaving only traces of a feminine body transposed over the national territory.

Thus are the national resources configured for exploitation—as raw material for processing or export. With the government's model of development necessarily bolstering "domestic industrialization" and other economic activities considered "productive," that is "infrastructure and other capital investments that have long-term impact on the economy," women-dominated activities have to suffer. "There is no budget support for women's subsistence and income substitution/generation economic activities, the budget makes their work, and contribution to the local and to the national economy, effectively invisible."[40] In effect, their productive capacity is erased and their increasingly bodily labor must henceforth function as raw material for the national industries. Small-scale industries and firms, subsistence agricultural production, education, the "underground economy," all of whose labor force is predominantly comprised of women, these are activities that must be sacrificed in the name of development. The destruction of domestic income-generating activities results in the effective dispossession of the female and feminized labor force, thus making it more accessible for exploitation and circulation as commodified products. At the same time that the feminized labor force is deterritorialized—forced to seek employment abroad, pushed out of the country by the sheer absence of means of living, pulled into advanced countries by the spaces of demand for cheap and tractable labor—it is also further grounded in the female body.

With the erasure even of the reproductive function of the nation, all its resources are extricated from any organic life or vital community of their own, processed and packaged, and made ready for circulation and unimpeded exploitation. Thus is labor produced for the export-oriented policy of authoritarian modernization. In the export processing zone, there is not much distance between human labor and raw material. Furthermore, the replacement of manual strength by machines eliminates unskilled males from the newly tailored definition of human labor, since within an already patriarchally divided society, unskilled females are the preferred operators of those unfulfilled functions of the machines requiring physical dexterity, patience, tractability, and long periods of immobility, all learned in the domestic sphere. As one manager explained, "We hire girls because they have less energy, are more disciplined, and are easier to control."[41] Supervisors and managers, on the other hand, are male, thus reinforcing the configuration of industrial, technologically advanced countries where the necessary intangible services and skills, education and information technology for such positions are produced, as masculine. This gender division of symbolic capital and bodily labor into, respectively, masculine and feminine, thus results in a diaspora of unemployed, unskilled men.[42] It also enables the "sons of the nation," that is, the technocratic and political elite at the hub of the nation, to cooperate fraternally with internal capital in the stimulation and regulation of trade flows, thereby at once becoming supervisors and pimps of the nation.

In the actual export of women forced into the "entertainment industry," there is no more difference between raw material and labor, for the prostitute applies her labor power to her own body in the production of herself as a commodity. A testament to the ever-increasing efficiency of multinational capital, prostitutes are at once the raw material, labor, and machines of new national industries in advanced countries such as Japan: "Filipino women in Japan are grist to Japan's 10-trillion-yen-a-year sex mills. The boom in the sex industry in Japan is an indication of the economic prosperity enjoyed by that country."[43] One might add that it is this economic prosperity without military prowess that has made Japan the leader among national sex industries. Sex takes on a crucial role in the domestic staging of political fantasies and economic realities of nations.

Global conditions have taken another shift. With the increase of hostilities in the Philippines, not only in the sense of antagonism to Japanese sex tours and to the presence of the U.S. bases, but also in the sense of military and insurgent fighting, the climate has become largely unfavorable or at least precarious for foreign investments of any kind. Hence the necessity of drawing labor and raw material into the developed countries that now employ the strategy of import liberalization. Nowhere is this strategy more clearly visible than in the case of Japan; Japan, however, cautiously confines her definition of imports to "non-traditional semiprocessed products" meaning, labor material—in other words, women. The increase of hostilities within the Philippines is also symptomatic of the World Bank—determined economic strategies for development reaching their effective limits. The depletion of natural resources and destruction of the productive capacity of outmoded economic forms, especially those that have been female dominated, have forced the transformation of an already feminized labor force into the semiprocessed products that await final processing for the realization of surplus value. In this sense, women are the last abundant resource of the nation—they are like the surplus products they themselves sell for subsistence, now sold themselves by their own feminized nation. Free floating, they are "excess liquidity" that is "mopped up" in "stream-lining operations" at the injunction of "international capital,"[44] their mobility now regulated by their sex (more accurately, their sexual function, which is their penetrability[45]) and their passport. Sexuality and nationality thus become deterritorialized indicators of vulnerability to exploitation, as well as instruments of such exploitation.

## Export Oriental Labor

The fate of Filipino women exported to other countries as domestics and prostitutes demonstrates the logic that subjects their own feminized nation to the same treatment. The cruel scenario that becomes typified from the accumulation of recounted individual experiences presents itself as the same operations that have cohered through the process of history into a system of exploitation of the Third World. Yayori Matsui, a Japanese journalist, reports that in 1988 there were 7,000–8,000 Filipinas who were working as domestic helpers in Singapore and 30,000 working in Hong Kong.[46] She also reports that nearly 100,000 Asian migrant women working as "entertainers in the booming sex industry" enter Japan each year, 90 percent of whom come from the Philippines, Thailand, and Taiwan, and 80 percent of that total coming from the Philippines.[47]

> Usually they are picked up by recruiters in their own countries and sent to Japan with a promise or contract stating that they will work as waitresses, models or ordinary hostesses (not engaging in prostitution). However, in reality, they are sold out by the recruiters to promoters in Japan. . . . The women are then sold again, by the Japanese promoters, to clubs or other

sex business owners, at double the price. Sometimes they are simply rented at a monthly charge of US$1,600 to US$6,400. In order to cover such expenses, the owners force the women into prostitution, taking advantage of their vulnerability, the prime cause of which is their illegal visa status. Without the protection visa status affords, there is no limit to the abuse and exploitation that these women may have to face.

The sexual relations that marked the political and economic links of the Philippines with the United States have become literally realized in the case of Japan—military prowess and domination has in Japan become masculine prowess and domination, international politics acted out by male sexual violation, military arms translated into raping penises. As one reporter described:

> I visited the tiny theater where Maria was working. On the stage of the smoke-filled room, just big enough for 40 people, she stood naked. Then an announcement was heard; "We have something special tonight, a direct import from the Philippines! Come and get it, quick!" An office worker type climbed up to the stage, and dropped his pants. I saw Maria raped again and again, in full view of the audience.[48]

But the international economy of forced prostitution is not merely a symptom of Japan's repressed political fantasies—it is in fact a constitutive part of the current mode of relations between Japan and the Third World populations[49] from which she derives her economic prosperity. The series of transactions between recruiters, promoters, and sex business owners are analogous to the series of transactions between national and multinational bodies regulating trade flows of capital, goods, and labor. With intangible services, information, and technology dominated by multinational production, nations such as the Philippines and other Southeast Asian countries are reduced to providing physical labor, which makes the national government no more than a recruiting agency for the sale of its feminized labor to markets in more advanced economies. Indeed, it is the government that does the "mopping up of excess liquidity" for smooth transfers and expedient profits. To the extent that it functions as a multinational corporation, the Asia-Pacific community acts as the promoting agency that secures the uninterrupted flows between the recruiters and the business owners by functioning as a regional membrane managing individual national interests. Finally, multinational companies and industries function like the sex business owners—the employers of feminized labor from various developing countries.

The women are kept in physical and financial bondage—locked in cells, their passports and airline tickets confiscated, desperate to earn money for their families as well as for themselves (if only to buy a ticket home); they are in no position to resist the brutally enforced prostitution for which they were imported. In fact, those who do resist are physically and sexually abused—raped, beaten, and starved, often to the point of critical or fatal injury. The irony of this situation is that their bodies abroad are worth more than their skills and education at home. Produced as physical commodities, they cease to be treated as humans. They are indeed what they are advertised (on T-shirts around the U.S. bases) to be: "little brown fucking machines powered by rice." More than a hundred years ago, Gustave Flaubert observed that "The oriental woman is no more than a machine: she makes no distinction between one man and another man."[50] The equivalence of the oriental woman and a sexual machine was already functioning then in congruence with the relations of imperial nations and their colonies. It only took a global shift in those relations in the age of neocolonialism to equate the two terms with the entire economy of the colony, now an "independent" developing nation. But it is precisely because of the historical development of these colonies from political appendages to economic dependents that developing nations, particularly their labor, now serve their developed "masters" (the word used to designate the club owners).

Like the women who are rented out to clients, developing nations operate through the subcontracting of their properties, whether buildings, facilities, land, or labor, to client companies. In the words of Finance Minister Ongpin: "We are paying special attention to . . . international subcontracting, where we provide facilities for large multinationals to come in and do the more labor-intensive aspects of their operations in this country."[51] What this provision of facilities entails, however, is a specialization that destroys the nation's productive capacities and reduces it to a field of operations, a place "to come in and do . . ."—very much as these women are reduced to a sexual function. Short-term investments and limited time horizons are merely economic equivalents of the "short-times" clients enjoy with their prostitutes, a practice that belies the promise of permanent friendships and financial security. This is a lesson the United States continually teaches because he has epitomized the practice in the actions of his servicemen. As one bar waitress asserted: "While they are here, they love you very much. Then they return to the States and you are forgotten. They take no more notice of you. They might support you for one year, but they tire of that and see someone new in the States."[52] The difference between this relation, however, and that of transnational corporations and their feminized labor is in the latter there is neither pretense nor hope of love. The relations have been streamlined into efficient versions of what they always were: strictly economic transactions. Corporations are not personified in the same way nations are, hence their operations manifest more blatantly the mode of relations they are founded upon. Again this is demonstrated by Japan's sex industry.

Although transnational corporations seem to transcend the ideologies and boundaries of nations, their existence and prosperity nevertheless do depend on them. The possibility, for example, of extracting and enslaving labor rests on the nation-state and its institutions. Passports and visas become both a means of protection and a means of exploitation. National differences also become a means of disempowerment. Immigrant women in Japan are imprisoned in the confines of their national languages and cultures. At the same time, however, national unities also function as a means of empowerment. Thai women in Japan are apparently more victimized than Filipino women because the Thai community is smaller than the Filipino community and therefore its members have less access to organized efforts to address their problems.[53] Nevertheless, nationalities are used as instruments of exploitation. The fact that Filipino girls are imported in Japan to replace the Japanese prostitutes who used to service U.S. soldiers in Okinawa demonstrates that certain national ideologies of discrimination are at work.

It is curious that although the Japanese have historically been referred to as "orientals" by Westerners, it is other Asians, specifically people from developing nations within Asia, who are referred to by the Japanese as "orientals." Statements in the Japanese press like "Asian women are favorite goods with 'Oriental Charm' and an exoticism for Western and Japanese men" and "Japan's sex industry has need of Asian women, especially Filipinas"[54] shows the extent to which Japan has come to distinguish herself from Asia. The feeling of racial superiority is not new to Japan, nor is the culture of patriarchy. What is new is the merging of these discourses of race, sex, and capital in multinational industries and in the production of a new species of inferior beings:

> There is a general feeling among the Japanese that they are superior to other races, but especially to the peoples of the Southeast Asian region. A Japanese priest confessed in a meeting with Filipino priests that Japanese Catholics looked down on Filipinos in Japan, who as a rule are Catholics, as "the kind of people who would do anything for money."
> "Most Japanese are allergic to Filipinos who scare them as bearers of some infectious disease," said the Japanese priest.[55]

Indeed, what in the prevailing fantasy defines prostitutes and orientals in their inferiority is financial parasitism, moral depravity, sexual proclivity and communicable disease. And since the political weakness and economic dependence of nations marks them as inferior, it is not difficult to see how the equivalence between developing nations, orientals, and prostitutes can be made. Japan herself has not been immune to this hierarchic configuration of nations. Thus at another time, "In order to convince the West that it was really in earnest and civilized enough to be treated as an equal, Japan had to fight and win a war."[56] One might hence explain the heavily-documented Japanese bestial treatment of imported prostitutes in part by the historical emasculation of Japan, for equality in the international community requires proof of a certain kind of masculinity and the debasement of a certain kind of femininity or, better, feminization. However, one must also bear in mind that for Japanese women the imported prostitutes are not merely feminine but altogether a different species. As Matsui describes:

> Men buying prostitutes is never socially condemned, nor is women's acceptance of it condemned—women often say: "If my husband goes to a 'professional' woman, it's not a problem, but if he is attracted to an ordinary woman, I get hurt and jealous." Such a double standard of women is still deep-rooted among the Japanese and they consider the prostitute as a special kind of woman, and fail to treat them as human beings and to accord them their human rights.[57]

The double standard is a result not only of Japan's patriarchal structure, feudal history, and tradition of prostitution, but also of the new configuration of these systems of relations within an advanced capitalist economy. The elevation of women's status in Japan in areas not traditionally open to them necessitates the displacement of the contradictions of capital, which they have historically borne, on other peoples. At the same time, women in Japan can find their place in society by either joining the white-collar work force, the masculine sphere, or remaining in the home as housewives and mothers, the feminine sphere; in other words, in this economy there are two paths that are open for those who have the means of staying human whether one is male or female: to act productive or to be reproductive, to act masculine or to be feminine. Anything outside of this dichotomy becomes relegated to the less than human, reduced to the "professional" animal or thing.

## Familial and Pedophilic Exploitation

So far I have been speaking of the feminization of developing labor. But as the relations of the Philippines with the United States and Japan (as paradigms of power) show, in this context feminization also necessarily means dehumanization, and emasculation necessarily means debasement. Within a Japanese-style management system in which the company takes on a feudal familial structure, those who are not seen as productive sons or reproductive daughters are food for machines. Feminized objects can have no human role in this system. Increasingly multinational corporations are adopting this family mode—hence the call for "families of nations." Soon the international community will be dominated by "first families" of the world. The Asia-Pacific community is one such bid to becoming a first (world) family-corporation, one that will rival the other family-corporation building up in Europe. But within this family are collectives of labor that embody all the historical contradictions of international capital and therefore cannot "mature" and compete with or equal the nations that have established themselves as their parents. At the same time they are rendered incapable of producing or reproducing their own means of subsistence, like children or things. This is the condition of the Philippines within the Asia-Pacific family—subject to a sociolibidinal economy that deploys deterritorialized relations of power through sex and money.

Ward, child, mistress, commodity—the Philippines is a historical condensation of these different relations tending toward equivalence, an equivalence that does not rest easy but which must continually be secured through systematic violence. But the tendency toward equivalence is evident in the mass production of a new commodity, the child prostitute. The phenomenal scale of forced prostitution of children in Southeast Asian nations is yet another testament to the subordination, infantilization, and feminization at work in the production of labor material necessary to maintain the level of prosperity attained by advanced economies such as Japan and the NICs. Lured by promises of prosperity and familial security and forced by the dire circumstances of their lives if not by their own desperate parents, children are turning into the raw material of an intensified prostitution industry. In Japan the average age of imported prostitutes is decreasing rapidly due to several related factors: the increasing fierceness of competition in the sex industry, the increasing organized resistance of women, and the increasing risk of AIDS.[58] Hence the great demand for young, tractable, virgin boys and girls.

What this phenomenal explosion of forced child prostitution demonstrates is the constant need for capital to produce new commodities and the desire to consume them. The debt-servicing policy of developing nations is using up all traditional and nontraditional (such as feminized labor) resources and is now exploiting new nontraditional products: children. Hence in 1990 the United Nations Children's Emergency Fund (UNICEF) could truthfully report that "the heaviest burden of the debt crisis is falling on the growing minds and bodies of children in the developing world."[59] UNICEF's concern, however, only reveals itself as a concern for capital. As a deputy executive of UNICEF put it: "Human capital is a far more important factor in economic growth than physical capital.

Investment in a human capital in the form of nutrition, basic education, and health cannot be postponed. . . . The underemphasized tragedy of the disinvestment in human capital in the 1980s is that the results will be carried forward in stunted bodies and deficient educations well into the 21st century."[60] In other words, children are another resource for multinational capital to invest in. But as child prostitution attests, children need not be long-term investments—they are marketable now. If the price of production of a prostitute is minimal, the cost to produce a child prostitute is even less. Such is the cold logic of the Free World.

Within the Free World, therefore, pedophilic exploitation is only an intensified mode of the relations already prevailing between multinational corporations and their developing labor. With these international pedophilic tendencies in mind it is difficult to see how any familial harmony can be achieved within the Asia-Pacific community. For the regional security it promises means the abuse and exploitation of weaker, dependent, feminized, and infantilized collectives—the poor Southeast Asian relations of the OECD Five and the NICs. The call for privatization in the current movement toward global incorporation is therefore a call for the privatization of the antagonisms and crises of nations. It is, in effect, a privatization of the violence endemic to global capital. With the effacement of nations in the creation and incorporation of new global families emerges a deterritorialized Third World—a new race of infantilized, feminized, commodified peoples distributed over the world, motoring globalized production. It is no longer, therefore, a matter of nations acting like people, but of people embodying their nations. The libidinal character of national economies makes it easier for the crises of nations to become at once deterritorialized and grounded in the bodies of people. Those who occupy the masculine ranks of global management are free to move and accumulate profit like capital, but those who remain in the feminized terrain of labor must passively bear the burden of their nations.

Such is the prospect of the laboring populations of developing nations such as the Philippines. It is indeed a dim prospect. And yet the existence of other such collectives leaves space for hope, for other desires to emerge within this already overdetermined region. Hence the efforts to redefine the community, to seek alliances with the collectives that share the burden of capital's contradictions. Instead of the desire for "security," which prostitutes nations like the Philippines, condemning them to an increasingly oppressive existence, alternative voices are calling for solidarity among Third World collectives—solidarity based not on a shared region or a common investment in the Free World, but on common interests and a cooperative political strength yet to be founded. As one such voice expressed:

There is an international network in Asia and the Pacific of advocacy for a wide range of social, economic, and political issues heretofore unimagined, much less articulated: denuclearization, demilitarization or disarmament, rights of indigenous or ethnic peoples to their ancestral domain, human rights as guaranteed by international covenants to individuals and groups, development with consultation and consent, environmental protection (which daily grows into a universal concern of critical proportions), and increasingly, women's and children's rights and welfare.

It is incumbent upon the governments of ASEAN and the Pacific community of island states to seriously consider the possibility of a continuing dialogue with these advocates, whose rallying cry has been "regional solidarity" based on common causes and shared problems, instead of the more unstable and potentially more volatile ideal of "regional security" which has traditionally drawn strength from the realpolitik of confrontation, containment and the balance of power.[61]

This is the challenge that the concept of the Asia-Pacific poses—not as an economic network of dominant classes, but as an emergent political constituency composed of peoples desiring an alternative community. Instead of a nonaligned movement that only secures the citizenship of these countries in the Free World, laboring populations within the Asia-Pacific (and not their representative governments) must engage in a movement of alliances not for aggression but for the assertion of shared desires for self-determination and for the strength to forge an alternative international community that does not buy into another fantasy of the Free World. In other words, we must struggle against the practices that reproduce the political-libidinal relations of our present lives and engage in alternative modes of production to realize a more just form of community. But we can only begin working for this if in our actions we are already dreaming other worlds in other ways.

## Notes

1. The concept of fantasy that I employ here derives from Slavoj Zizek, for whom a fantasy construction "serves as a support for our 'reality' itself: an 'illusion' which is structuring our effective, real social relations and which is masking thereby some insupportable, real, impossible kernel" ("The Real of Ideology," *PsychCritique* 2, no. 3 [1987], p. 265). In the global fantasy, that impossible kernel would be the Third World, that is, the nonindustrialized, residually feudal, pre- or anticapitalist sectors of the world.

2. The possibility of grasping the actions of nations as citizens or international subjects is founded precisely on the historical colonization and decolonization of the world. The entire debate on imperialism since the turn of the century might be seen to turn on the issue of world citizenship, that is, whether the colo-

nial peoples were fit for self-government and thus inclusion in the world community of nations. As present global divisions show, however, inclusion did not in any case mean equality with imperial nations. The divisions of the world into First, Second, Third also signify a hierarchy among nations in the eyes of the Free World. There is no room for me here to elaborate on the historical process of oedipalization of nations, that is, in the creation of nations as modern subjects. But the strong identification peoples have with their nation and the state actions and popular movements that are predicated upon this identification should point to a shared process of identity formation for individuals and nations as subjects in the modern world. Hence there is more than metaphorical truth in the observation not only that nations act like men and women, but that men and women act like nations. Inasmuch as sexuality is a central axis of subject identities, nations are configured sexually. Sexuality is endemic, however, not only to the individual modern subject, but to the modes of production that have produced him (the modern subject is configured as masculine) as such, other individuals who do not quite qualify as modern subjects (women, colonials, ethnic and sexual minorities, the masses), as well as all modern nations, and countries that do not qualify as international subjects. These modes of production of modern identities to which sexuality is endemic include patriarchy, colonialism, orientalism, imperialism, and global capitalism.

3. "The New Asia-Pacific Era: A Perspective from an International Nation Building for the 21st Century," *Britannica Book of the Year 1986* (Chicago: Encyclopedia Britannica, 1986), p. 14.

4. Senator Alfred J. Beveridge, "Our Philippine Policy," in *The Philippines Reader*, ed. Daniel B. Schirmer and Stephen Rosskamm Shalom (Boston: South End Press, 1987), p. 24.

5. Purificacion Valera-Quisumbing, "Towards an Asia-'Pacific Community': Varying Perceptions," in *The Pacific Lake*, ed. Jose P. Leviste, Jr. (Manila: Philippine Council for Foreign Relations, 1986), p. 81. Abrino Aydinan also asserts this U.S.-Japanese parentage of the Pacific idea: "The idea of organizing the nations lying along the basin or rim of the Pacific is a Japanese and American notion which has been embraced by the Association of Southeast Asian Nations (ASEAN), with the United States and Japan only too willing to yield the cares of paternity" ("Doubts Plague Pacific Basin Organization" in Leviste, ed., *The Pacific Lake*, p. 119). It is interesting to note that this expression of lineage or history is one used in the discourse of law (Valera-Quisumbing is a law professor) as well as in the discourse of business (Aydinan is a writer for a business-economics review).

6. "The New Asia-Pacific Era," *Britannica Book of the Year 1986*, p. 14.

7. Edgardo B. Maranan, "Peace, Development and Solidarity through Initiatives from Below," in *Diliman Review* 37, no. 4 (1989), p. 21.

8. Philippine Government, "*New York Times* Advertisement," in Schirmer and Shalom, eds., *The Philippines Reader*, pp. 227–229.

9. Nelson Navarro, "Accidental Saints of Filipino Nationalism," *Malaya* (13 May 1990). The fantasy is one maintained by Americans as well. George Bush's ludicrous toast to Marcos after the latter effected his reelection in 1981 ("We

love you, sir") attests to this. U.S. government support of the popular ousting of
Marcos five years later also attests to the inconstancy of that love.

10. Schirmer and Shalom, eds., *The Philippines Reader*, pp. 23–26.

11. Quoted in Epifanio San Juan, Jr., *Crisis in the Philippines* (South Hadley,
MA: Bergin and Garvey, 1986), p. 18.

12. Luz del Mundo, "Disadvantages of a Pacific Community," in Laviste, ed.,
*The Pacific Lake*, p. 116.

13. Aida F. Santos, *The Debt Crisis: A Treadmill of Poverty for Filipino
Women* (Manila: Kalayaan, 1989), p. 16.

14. Ibid.

15. Lolita, quoted in Joseph Collins, *The Philippines: Fire on the Rim* (San
Francisco: Institute for Food and Development Policy, 1989), p. 271. This was
her response to the question whether she wanted to marry an American, which
was posed to her during a discussion of her illegitimate child whose father is
American. Two significant things come out of this contextualization: first, the
option of marriage is a question posed to Lolita by an American, that is, the form
of her desire is predetermined by a dominant logic; second, the wish expresses
the need for legitimation and financial support, both of which mean the same
thing and are the result of a preexistent relation. In other words, the desire to
marry is the consequence of already being fucked.

16. Emmanuel S. de Dios, "The Philippine Economy: A Conspectus of Recent
Developments," *Diliman Review* 37, no. 2 (1989), p. 5.

17. Raffy Rey Hipolito, "Japanese Economic Power, Philippine Setting," *Diliman Review* 37, no. 2 (1989), p. 23.

18. This possibility is one that Aydinan ("Doubts Plague Pacific Basin," p.
121) sees as necessary if Japan is to serve as a model for other Asian countries.

19. This successful defense has, however, roused Japan's international partners to action, into forcing her open: "The yearly trade surpluses of Japan with
the U.S. and European Economic Community members have angered the latter.
Japan has been subjected to strong-arm tactics by her Western allies to open her
economy" (Hipolito, "Japanese Economic Power," p. 22). The leverage that the
United States and the EEC have, of course, is the "international community," a
global superego over which they exercise dominant control through ownership
of greater symbolic shares. As a U.S. political economist asserted: "If there is one
country that is criticized for not playing by these emerging global rules, it is
Japan. But the logic of the global web is so powerful that the Japanese will either
be forced to comply over time or else face a stiff penalty from the marketplace,
the talent pool, and competitors and governments" (Robert B. Reich, "Who Is
Them?" *Harvard Business Review* (March–April 1991), p. 81.

20. Jose P. Leviste, Jr., Introduction, p. 19.

21. de Dios, "The Philippine Economy," p. 5.

22. As Walker, the character in Pontecorvo's film *Burn* who argues for and
effects the transformation of the fictional colony Quemada into a neocolony (that
is, the transformation of a slave-labor economy into a wage-labor economy), asks
its colonizers, "Gentlemen, which would you rather have? A wife whom you
must clothe and feed even when she is no longer of any use to you? Or a whore
who you need only pay for so long as she pleases you?"

23. Liza Maza, "Equity in the Philippines: Development Strategies and the Impact on Philippine Women," *Gabriela Women's Update* 7, no. 3 (July–September 1990), p. 15.

24. Santos and Lee, *The Debt Crisis*, p. 36.

25. In the 1970s, about 200,000 Japanese visited the Philippines annually, 90 percent of whom were male (*Japan Christian Activity News* [29 August 1980]).

26. A. Lin Neumann, "Tourism Promotion and Prostitution" in Schirmer and Shalom, eds., *The Philippines Reader*, p. 182.

27. Walden Bello, David Kinley, and Elaine Elinson, *Development Debacle: The World Bank in the Philippines* (San Francisco: Institute for Food and Development Policy, 1982), pp. 13–39. The authors argue that the World Bank emerged as a central influence in Philippine affairs as a consequence of an economic and political crisis. "In the late 1960s and early 1970s, Philippine society underwent a fundamental crisis. In its economic dimension, the crisis was precipitated by the intersection of three developments: the failure of the strategy of import substitution as a path to sustained industrialization, the increasing inability of agriculture to meet the country's basic food needs, and the growing pressure from foreign capital to 'open up' the economy more completely." Added to this was a growing class and national consciousness, the breakdown of patronage politics, and the intensified competition within the oligarchy for political power. With the declaration of martial law and the blessing of U.S. businesses whose interests the World Bank represented, Marcos reconsolidated his position and centralized power, commandeering the state for the desires of capital.

28. Ibid., p. 198.

29. Ibid,. p. 28.

30. Quoted in Ibid., p. 14.

31. Quoted in Paul A. Gigot, "Manila's Economic Revolutionary," in Schirmer and Shalom, eds., *The Philippines Reader*, p. 375.

32. "Under Marcos, promotion of tourism resulted in Manila's competing with Bangkok for the title of 'International Sex City'; Manila's reputation has become well-known, particularly to the Japanese." (Yayori Matsui, *Women's Asia* [London: Zed Books, 1987], p. 70.)

33. This division of the land into prostitution colonies also occurs with beach resorts, a practice that might be traced as a libidinal-economic practice to the mistresses' salons in late-nineteenth-century Europe. In the Philippines, these brothels and other owned land and businesses are generally acquired by expatriate men marrying a Filipino wife or adopting a Filipino child, under whose name the property is registered.

34. Karina David, quoted in Neumann, "Tourism Promotion and Prostitution," p. 185.

35. "In the Philippines, Chile, and Uruguay—all countries renowned for long-standing democratic traditions—there emerged from the wreckage the same formula pioneered by the Brazilian junta in the late 60s: a military or presidential-military dictatorship 'sanitizing' the social situation with massive repression, justifying its existence with the ideology of controlled modernization with the indispensable participation of foreign capital, and resting on a social coalition of

technocrats, officers, local bureaucrat-capitalists, and foreign investors" (Bello, Kinley, and Elinson, *Development Debacle*, pp. 35–36).

36. Vicente L. Rafael, "Nationalism, Imagery, and the Filipino Intelligentsia in the Nineteenth Century," *Critical Inquiry* (Spring 1990), p. 602.

37. Schirmer and Shalom, eds., *The Philippines Reader*, p. 453.

38. Philip Shenon, "How Subic Bay Became a Rallying Cry for Philippine Nationalism," *New York Times* (15 September 1991), p. 2.

39. *New York Times*, (15 September 1991), p. 2e.

40. Santos and Lee, *The Debt Crisis*, p. 23.

41. Sr. Mary Soledad Perpiñan, "Philippine Women and Transnational Corporations," in Schirmer and Shalom, eds., *The Philippines Reader*, p. 239.

42. Many of these men find employment and the opportunity to regain lost masculinity in the army or vigilante groups, both running rampant over the countryside. Extreme militarization is evidenced by the creation of the Citizens Armed Forces Geographical Units in 1987 by the executive order of President Aquino and other vigilante groups (Arnel de Guzman and Tito Craige, "Counterinsurgency War in the Philippines and the Role of the United States," *Bulletin of Concerned Asian Scholars* 23, no. 2 [1991], p. 41). The armed forces of the Philippines plans to have 80,000 "combat-ready forces" in the CAFGUs when the master plan is fulfilled. The human rights abuses (including torture, mutilation, and cannibalism) of the 600 vigilante groups that exist at the present are well documented. Given that the insurgency movement is also growing steadily, absorbing the dispossessed, the unemployed, and the abused—all refugees of the state of political and economic war being waged to motor international capital—the military is a secure occupation. The regional community proposed by the Asia-Pacific can only exist in its present form through the maintenance of this war. That "the United States provides 83 percent of the procurement, operations, and maintenance budget (excluding salaries) of the Philippine military" (p. 46) attests to its interests in this community.

43. M. Dueñas, "Filipina as Japayuki-San," *Philippines Free Press* (April 4, 1987), p. 40.

44. " 'Mopping up excess liquidity' was the term Central Bank (CB) Governor Jobo Fernandez, currently the CB head and former Marcos government official, used to justify an increase in domestic rates, which made credit hard to come by. Small companies and factories with little capital had to close down and hundreds of workers were laid off. By IMF standards, but with extreme hardship for the people, the 'mopping up' resulted in improved financial capacity so the Philippine government could better service its foreign debt obligations" (Santos and Lee, *The Debt Crisis*, p. 9). The analogy is accurate inasmuch as the export of women is directly tied to the debt-servicing policy of the government—not only as an outcome but also as a necessary function of this policy. Not only does the policy result in inadequate funding for local income-generating activities, which forces the women to seek employment abroad, but also the earnings abroad that they remit are used for debt payments (p. 40).

45. This qualification is important when we consider the phenomenon of forced child prostitution, which manifests that feminization cuts across biological

and age differences and depends more on the tractability and economic dependence of the feminized subject.

46. Matsui, *Women's Asia*, p. 52.

47. "Asian Migrant Women Working at Sex Industry in Japan Victimized by International Trafficking," *In God's Image* (June 1990), p. 6.

48. Mainichi Shimbun, quoted in *Philippines Free Press* (4 April 1987), p. 15.

49. The economic and ideological contradictions of the harmonious Asia-Pacific community become most visible in the fate of the Third World, an appellation that increasingly refers to peoples marked by poverty, infantilization, and feminization; in other words, in the fate of the poorest of the global poor, notably indigent, nonwhite women and children. The feminization and infantilization is unambiguous and intensified in the case of Third World Asian nations because of the combination of two independently feminized units, that is, Third World and Asia.

50. Quoted in Edward Said, *Orientalism* (New York: Vintage Books, 1979), p. 187. Flaubert was one of the more notable writers who contributed to the simultaneous idealization and debasement of prostitution in nineteenth-century France. I discuss elsewhere the relation between this representation and the role of France in the age of imperialism. Suffice it to say that prostitution as a mode of discourse of international relations was already evident in France at the time because of the latter's particular "sentimental relations" with the colonies until then—relations defined more by capital investments than by physical and military presence.

51. Quoted in Bello, Kinley, and Elinson, *Development Debacle*, p. 153.

52. Marlyn, quoted in Brenda Stoltzfus, "The Sale of Sexual Labor in the Philippines: Marlyn's Story," *Bulletin of Concerned Asian Scholars* 22, no. 4 (1990), p. 19.

53. Matsui, "Asian Migrant Women," p. 8. Compare this with another assessment: "Filipinos, mostly women, accounted for about 70 percent of all offenses committed by Asians in Japan in 1985, followed by Thais, 20 percent, and Koreans, 9 percent, a dubious distinction consistently maintained by Filipinos since 1982—a phenomenon which a top official of the Japanese immigration office perceived as an indication of the depressed Philippine economic condition." (Tono Haruhi, quoted in *Philippines Free Press* [4 April 1987], p. 15).

54. Matsui, "Asian Migrant Women," p. 12; and Tono Haruhi in *AMPO*, quoted in Schirmer and Shalom, eds., *The Philippines Reader*, p. 15.

55. Dueñas, "Filipina as Japayuki-San," p. 42.

56. V. G. Kiernan, *The Lords of Human Kind* (New York: Columbia University Press, 1986), p. 182. In other words, Japan had to show it was man enough to be treated like an imperial nation.

57. "Asian Migrant Women," p. 9.

58. Compare this with the perception of Filipinos as bearing diseases. It is not merely coincidental that AIDS has been represented as having spread in the Philippines mainly through the U.S. bases. The "tainted" relation between the Philippines and the United States only legitimates and aggravates the system of exploitation that Japan engages in. This is achieved, however, through not only

representation but actual practice. For Japan's mode of relation with the Philippines is built upon or made possible through the system of exploitation that the United States had already established in its "special relations" with the Philippines.

59. Quoted in "Debt Crisis Burden Heaviest on Children," *Daily Globe* (30 December 1989).

60. Ibid.

61. Maranan, "Peace, Development, and Solidarity," p. 4.

*Part Three*

# Pacific Social and Cultural Formations

# 11

# Latin America in Asia-Pacific Perspective

## EVELYN HU-DEHART

Although Latin America enjoys a long Pacific coastline, because of its relative economic and political insignificance in the late twentieth century, it can be overlooked easily in discussions of the Asia-Pacific region. In point of fact, from Mexico to Peru, and across the South American continent to Brazil, there has been a long and continuous historical connection between this large region of first Iberian America and Asia, and later Latin America and Asia. Asians established small communities in Mexico already at the beginning of the seventeenth century, and most recently in 1990, a Peruvian of Japanese descent, Alberto Fujimori, was elected president of his adopted homeland.

Here I sketch out a history of the relationships between Latin America and societies across the Pacific, especially China. The discussion focuses on the most prominent aspect of these relationships: Chinese immigration into Latin America beginning in the mid-nineteenth century, first as coolies, then from the late nineteenth century, as free labor. Labor migrations, I argue, were initially tied in with developments in Latin America as part of a larger world economy, specifically, the need for labor in plantation economies once the abolition of slavery cut off sources of labor in the Atlantic region. The migrations themselves contributed to the formation of a "Pacific" and encouraged further flows of population. By way of conclusion, I will say a few words on Asian immigrants' contributions to Latin America in spite of a social and cultural environment that was frequently hostile to their presence.

## Spanish America and the Initial Formation of the Pacific

In 1513, Spanish explorer Vasco Núñez de Balboa's "discovery" of the Mar del Sur (the Southern Sea), the first European name for the Pacific Ocean, set in motion Spain's "discovery" and exploration of the Pacific coast of South America. By mid-century, Spanish conquistadores had conquered the Inca empire, renaming it the colony of New Castille, or Peru.

In 1518, Hernán Cortés arrived on the Atlantic coast of Mexico near present day Veracruz, sailing not directly from Spain but from the already established Spanish foothold in Santiago de Cuba. Three years later, the Aztec empire collapsed from the combined weight of internal disintegration and external pressures; from its ashes arose the Spanish colony of New Spain, or Mexico. Together, the silver-producing colonies of Peru and Mexico constituted the core of the extensive and long-lasting Spanish empire in the New World.

In 1540, the Spanish Crown sent its first viceroy to New Spain, which extended from today's U.S. Southwest to today's Central America. During the preceding two decades, Cortés and other early conquistadores sent expeditions north from Acapulco and other points along the Pacific coast to Baja California and California, culminating with Vázquez de Coronado's exploration (1540–1542) of the Colorado River and the Gulf of California (then known as the Sea of Cortés) and Juan Rodríguez de Cabrillo's long voyage to present day San Francisco in 1542.

By the end of the sixteenth century, the Spanish finally figured out how to accomplish what Columbus had failed to achieve—finding a way to the Orient by sailing westward. Spain established the Manila galleon trade, which lasted some three centuries, linking China and Japan via the Philippines (which Spain had also acquired as a colony) to Europe in an exchange of Mexican silver for Oriental luxury goods. Acapulco on Mexico's Pacific coast was developed specifically for this purpose.

Not long after the Manila trade was established, the first Asian colony in the Americas appeared. In 1635 a group of Spanish barbers in Mexico City complained about excessive competition from Chinese barbers in that colonial capital city. They petitioned the viceroy to remove these bothersome Asian barbers to special quarters at the outskirts of town, so that they, the Spaniards, would not have to compete with the *chinos de Manila* for business.[1] Although this early settlement of Asians never grew into a large colony during the colonial period, it left legacies now firmly entrenched in Mexican folklore, notably the embroidered blouse known popularly as the *china poblana*, worn by Mexican women in central Mexico.[2]

Thus, it can be said that long before any North Europeans laid eyes on the Pacific coast region of what is now the United States, the "Spanish-Pacific" was already a well established geographical and political entity. Moreover, the Spanish-Pacific was the result not only of Spanish settlement along the Pacific coast from California to Chile, a settlement sparse at both ends but dense and intense in the middle (Mexico and Peru)—it established early a continuous link with Asia through trade and some migration across the Pacific.

## Asian Labor in Latin America

After Mexico and Peru's independence from Spain in the early nineteenth century, the reality of a Spanish-Pacific, though briefly interrupted by the cessation of the Manila galleon trade in the late eighteenth century, was renewed by first Peru and Cuba, and later Mexico. In the creation of a "Latin American-Pacific" in the nineteenth and twentieth centuries, material trade continued to play a role, but this time it was secondary to international labor migration and other forms of population movements from Asia across the Pacific. Chinese labor was initially most prominent in these population movements, starting around the turn of the twentieth century and later joined by Japanese labor. Peru, among the countries of Spanish America, took the lead in attracting Japanese labor, but the largest number of Japanese immigrants in Latin America would end up not in Spanish America but in Brazil on the Atlantic coast.

## Chinese Coolie Labor in Cuba and Peru

In the middle of the nineteenth century, Peru, which had become independent of Spain, and Cuba, which remained a Spanish colony in the Caribbean, both actively promoted the importation of Chinese coolies or contract laborers to work on sugar plantations. Known in Spanish as *la trata amarilla* (the yellow trade), it bore remarkable resemblance to the African slave trade, which both countries, especially Cuba, had practiced extensively. From 1847 to 1874, as many as 250,000 Chinese coolies under eight-year contracts were sent to Peru and Cuba, with 80 percent or more destined for the plantations. In Peru, several thousand coolies also helped build the Andean railroad and worked in the offshore guano mines south of Lima. In the 1870s escaped coolies and free Chinese were among the pioneers who penetrated the Peruvian Amazon building settlements; introducing trade activities; cultivating rice, beans, sugar and other crops; manufacturing on a small scale; and brokering communication between the native Amazonian peoples and later European arrivals. Finally, although demand for cheap plantation labor remained high, international outcry against this brutal human traffic abruptly terminated the coolie trade in 1875, with the last contracts expiring by the 1880s.[3]

The British were the first to experiment with the exporting of Chinese, then East Indian, laborers under contract to their overseas colonies. As early as 1806, at precisely the time when the British ended the slave trade, 200 Chinese were sent to Trinidad. Although this experiment was a failure, British entrepreneurs continued to press for the export of Asian labor, turning from China to India by the 1830s. By 1838, some 25,000 East Indians had been exported to the new British East African colony of Mauritius and successfully adapted to the plantation system there. In 1845, the first cargo of East Indians was shipped to British Guiana, Trinidad, and Jamaica in the West Indies. They were under contract to the plantations for five years, a period known euphemistically as "industrial residency," after which they could presumably ask for passage home or remain in the colonies as free men and women. During the same time, the French also acquired East Indians who were indentured to French colonies in East Africa and the Caribbean.[4]

Between 1763—the year the British captured Havana, occupied the city for ten months, and opened this Spanish colony to international trade and the emerging North American market—and 1838, when the Cuban industry mechanized significantly, Cuban society was transformed from "the relatively mixed economy based on cattle-ranching, tobacco-growing, and the small-scale production of sugar" to the "dominance of plantation agriculture based on the large-scale production of sugar and coffee."[5] Cuba surpassed its British West Indian neighbors to become the preeminent sugar producer in the world. Along with new markets; improved technology; capital availability; a responsive political climate; a modern, entrepreneurial spirit among the planters; and other factors, African slave labor was crucial to the success of the plantation economy. The slave population had grown from 38,879 (22.8 percent of the total population) in 1774, to 436,495 (43.3 percent of total population) by 1841. Despite British efforts already under way to end the international slave trade, Cuba continued to import large numbers of Africans during the early nineteenth century, as many as 25,841 in 1817.[6]

The transformation of Cuban society was not just an economic phenomenon, it was social as well, for the population became not only increasingly slave and colored, but the planter class—often *hacendado* (landowner), *esclavista* (slave owner) and *negrero* (slave trader) all in one—reigned supreme, with its interests driving most policymaking, and its authority, particularly on the estates, largely unquestioned.

In Peru, the coastal sugar economy declined after independence due to the ravages of war and the labor shortage brought on by the end of African slavery. The slave trade to Peru ended in 1810, and slavery itself was formally abolished in 1854. But the guano trade of the 1840s generated new capital, some of which was transferred to agriculture, and revitalized the agrarian economy. Referring to the rise of this new *burguesía agraria*, Peruvian historian Jorge Basadre stated:

El poderlo económico de la nueva plutocracia costeñia tuvo su base en parte en contratos de individuos aislados con el Estado enriquecido por el guano, en especulaciones bursátiles o en dividendos en honos, as como también en propiedades urbanas y, a la vez, en el auge que supieron dar a sus haciendas trabajadas principalmente por los chinos.[7] (The economic power of the new coastal plantocracy had its base in part in isolated individual contracts with the state, enriched by guano, stock market speculations, and dividend earnings, as well as in urban properties, and at the same time, in the economic surge that they knowingly gave their plantations as worked principally by the Chinese [my translation].)

Together with the guano merchants, coastal planters went in search of cheap labor overseas, unable to find it among the small coastal peasantry or the faraway *serranos*. When slavery was officially abolished in Peru in 1854, there were only 17,000 slaves left. Even if willing to remain as salaried workers, they were hardly enough to meet the growing labor demand. Between 1839 and 1851, the Peruvian government paid 450,000 pesos in premiums to encourage importation of foreign labor to replace slaves.[8] Two-thirds of this money was directly invested in labor for the sugar plantations.

In Cuba, planter interests were represented by the powerful Real Junta de Fomento y de Colonización, presided over by the eminent landowner and international businessman Julián Zulueta. An agency of the junta was the Comisión de Población Blanca, charged at first with promoting the immigration of free European workers to Cuba, as these farsighted planters were already preparing for the imminent end of Africa as their source of labor and the need to adjust to free white labor. But free men and women in Europe were not attracted to a plantation society with slave labor. So, in 1844, when the British coolie trade was in full swing, the junta sent an agent to China to study the possibility of importing Chinese coolies. The Spanish government was also familiar with Chinese agricultural labor in the Philippines. An agreement was concluded in 1846 between Zulueta in London and the British in Amoy, a treaty port in Fujian province, South China. On June 3, 1847, the Spanish ship *Oquendo* docked in Havana with 206 Chinese on board, after 131 days at sea. Six died at sea and another seven shortly after arrival. Nine days later, a British ship, the *Duke of Argyle*, arrived with 365 Chinese on board, after 123 days at sea.[9] Thirty-five persons had died at sea. Both human cargoes were consigned to the Junta de Fomento, which proceeded to distribute the coolies in lots of ten to the island's most prominent planters and a railroad company.

Shortly after the Cubans initiated the Chinese coolie trade, Peruvian planters emulated their Cuban counterparts. An immigration law of November 1849 granted exclusive license (called *asiento* as in the African slave trade) for four years to two planters, Domingo Elias and Juan Rodriguez, to introduce Chinese into the departments of Lima and La Libertad after they had imported an initial experimental group of 75 Chinese *colonos* in October 1849. During the Elias-Rodriguez license period and continuing until 1854, 4,754 Chinese were imported.[10]

Initial response to the Chinese as workers in both Cuba and Peru was not enthusiastic. The Peruvian government suspended the trade in 1856, although a few hundred more trickled in between 1857 and 1860. Cuba also suspended the trade after the first contract with Zulueta and spent the next few years promoting other forms of immigrant labor, including Yucatecos (Mayan Indians) from Mexico and Gallegos, Catalans, and Canary Islanders from Europe. But these failed to meet the ever-growing labor demand. The Chinese trade was officially resumed in 1853 to Cuba and in 1861 to Peru. By then, in response to harsh international criticism of an already infamous human experiment, the British prohibited their subjects from participating in the particularly notorious passage to Cuba and Peru, forcing the trade to the Portuguese colony of Macao off the China coast, where Portuguese colonial authorities for the right price fully cooperated with the European coolie traders until 1874, when even Portugal succumbed to international pressures to end it. By then, over 200,000 Chinese had been sent from Macao, although of course, the ultimate origins of the Chinese remained in South China, in Guangdong and Fujian provinces. Table 11.1 summarizes the figures for the duration of the trade to Cuba and Peru, correlated with slave importation for Cuba and sugar production for both Peru and Cuba.

In the case of Peru, about half of the total number of coolies arrived during the first twenty years of the trade, 1849–1869. The other half arrived during the last five years, 1870–1874. This was also a time when sugar production mounted rapidly, from 13,475 metric tons in 1870, to 31,940 metric tons in 1874—more than doubling. It skyrocketed to 56,102 metric tons in 1875. Although the trade had ended by then, most of the Chinese were still under contract. During this time, the Chinese constituted almost the exclusive labor force on the plantations, as Peru had no slaves and few other forms of labor. It is undeniable, therefore, that coolie labor was a significant factor in the growing success of sugar production.

A similar correlation can be observed in the case of Cuba. As the African slave trade wound down and ended with the last shipments in 1865 of just 145 and in 1866 of 1,443 slaves, the size of the coolie imports rose markedly, reaching as many as 12,391 and 14,263 in 1866 and 1867. From 1865 to the end of the coolie trade in 1874, 64,500 coolies

TABLE 11.1
Coolie Imports and Sugar Production in Peru and Cuba, 1847–1878

| | Peru | | Cuba | | |
|---|---|---|---|---|---|
| Year | Coolies | Sugar (metric tons) | Slaves | Coolies | Sugar (metric tons) |
| 1847 | | | | 571 | |
| 1848 | 4,754 | | | | |
| 1853 | | | 12,500 | 4,307 | 391,246 |
| 1854 | | | 11,400 | 1,711 | 397,713 |
| 1855 | 2,355 | | 6,408 | 2,985 | 462,968 |
| 1856 | 4,220 | | 7,304 | 4,968 | 416,141 |
| 1857 | 405 | | 10,436 | 8,547 | 436,030 |
| 1858 | 300 | | 19,992 | 13,385 | 426,274 |
| 1859 | 321 | | 30,473 | 7,204 | 469,263 |
| 1860 | 1,092 | 618 | 24,895 | 6,193 | 429,769 |
| 1861 | 2,116 | 885 | 23,964 | 6,973 | 533,800 |
| 1862 | 1,691 | 1,257 | 11,254 | 344 | 454,758 |
| 1863 | 1,620 | 1,615 | 7,507 | 952 | 445,693 |
| 1864 | 6,562 | 2,864 | 6,807 | 2,153 | 525,372 |
| 1865 | 5,943 | 1,463 | 145 | 6,400 | 547,364 |
| 1866 | 6,725 | 5,111 | 1,443 | 12,391 | 535,641 |
| 1867 | 3,360 | 3,431 | | 14,263 | 585,814 |
| 1868 | 4,307 | 9,352 | | 7,368 | 720,250 |
| 1869 | 2,861 | 12,479 | | 5,660 | 718,745 |
| 1870 | 7,544 | 13,175 | | 1,227 | 702,974 |
| 1871 | 11,812 | 13,141 | | 1,448 | 609,660 |
| 1872 | 13,026 | 14,022 | | 8,160 | 772,068 |
| 1873 | 6,571 | 21,696 | | 5,093 | 742,843 |
| 1874 | 3,827 | 31,940 | | 2,490 | 768,672 |
| 1875 | | 56,102 | | | 750,062 |
| 1876 | | | | | 626,082 |
| 1877 | | | | | 516,268 |
| 1878 | | | | | 553,364 |

Sources: Peru, coolies—Humberto Rodríguez Pastor, *Hijos del Celeste Imperio en el Perú (1850–1900): Migración, Agricultura, Mentalidad y Explotación* (Lima: Instituto de Apoyo Agrario, 1988), Table 4 and Anexo I, pp. 27, 296; Peru, sugar—Rodríguez Pastor, *Hijos del Celeste Imperio,* p. 296; Cuba, slaves—Rebecca Scott, *Slave Emancipation in Cuba: The Transition to Free Labor, 1860–1899* (Princeton, NJ: Princeton University Press, 1985, p. 10; Cuba, coolies—Scott, *Slave Emancipantion,* p. 29; Cuba, sugar—Scott, *Slave Emancipation,* pp. 36, 240.

arrived, constituting over 50 percent of the total number imported. During this period, sugar production climbed steadily, reaching a high of 768,672 metric tons in 1874. Coolies constituted the source of labor replenishment, delaying the crisis that would have set in with the end of the slave trade and making it possible for the plantation economy to continue to prosper. It is also noteworthy that after 1875, when both the slave and the coolie trade had ended, sugar production displayed a pattern of general decline, a crisis brought on certainly in large part by the shortage of labor.

When the coolie trade was cut off to Cuba and Peru in 1874, many of those already in these two countries still had to work off their terms of servitude. Moreover, in both places mechanisms were put in place to extend the term of service by forcing or enticing the Chinese to continue working under some kind of contract primarily on the plantations, where demand for labor continued to be high.

In Cuba, forced recontracting began early, with the *Reglamento* of 1860, which obligated those coolies who had completed their first eight years to recontract (for an unspecified period of time) or leave Cuba at their own expense. Only those whose contracts expired before 1861 were exempt. To critics such as Cuban historian Juan Pérez de la Riva, recontracting simply further confirmed his conclusion that the coolie system was slavery, in that compulsory and successive recontracting perpetuated servitude to the point that the legal distinction between indenture and slavery became blurred in practice.

There is no doubt that the Cubans issued the recontracting regulation in order to keep as much as possible of this captive foreign labor force on the plantations, knowing full well that very few of the coolies could have saved enough from their meager wages to pay for their passage home. Equally undeniable a factor was racism, for the question of race definitely figured in this decision to keep the Chinese unfree. Cuban slavers and abolitionists alike had trouble dealing with a free nonwhite population and were concerned about the further mongrelization of Cuban society with the admission of another undesirable colored race—more on this point later. Recontracting succeeded well as a device to keep Chinese labor in agriculture. The 1872 Cuban census noted 58,400 Chinese, of whom 14,046 were "free," that is, had completed their original contracts. Nevertheless, of this number, 10,044 remained in agriculture.[11] Records uncovered by historians in the People's Republic of China, reveal that from 1880 to 1885, a period when many of the coolies sent to Cuba and Peru during the height (also the last thrust) of the coolie trade in the first half of the 1870s would have completed their original contracts, only 1,887 Chinese managed to make their way back home to

China. This was an insignificant number, given that over 100,000 left China in the 1870s for Cuba and Peru.[12]

In Peru, recontracting began in the early 1870s, a time of many expired and expiring contracts. No law *per se* forced the coolies to recontract, although compulsory recontracting was proposed by a Peruvian lawmaker in 1870. The planters resorted to debt or other forms of coercion. One frequent practice was the *sobretiempo*, or *yapa*, an extension attached to the original term on grounds that the coolie had not worked all the days due the *patrono* (some planters argued that work was due them on Sundays, in spite of the contracts consistently exempting Sunday work) or owed money to the *patrono*, which then had to be paid off by more work. The debt could have been incurred as a result of loans, advances, or even costs involved in recapturing coolies who ran away.[13] More likely, however, the wages offered and the short term of the recontract—ranging from as short as six months to no more than one or two years at the most, with the option of recontracting several times under these terms—enticed many coolies to recontract voluntarily in their desire to accumulate more savings and ultimately break free from the plantations. What made savings more feasible under the recontracting system was the planter's offer to pay the wages in advance, up to year's worth, as incentive. In the late 1870s and 1880s, as the trade came to a close but demand for labor remained high, planters offered other concessions to lure the Chinese to remain longer on the estates. As early as 1870, in Santa Province, in the labor force of twenty haciendas that relied almost exclusively on Chinese labor, 930 laborers or 77.1 percent, were under contract; 117 (9.7 per-cent) were recontracted, and 160 (13.2 percent) were *libres* (free), living and working in nearby pueblos.[14]

In both Peru and Cuba, recontracting took a significant new turn, beginning as early as 1870 in Cuba and appearing around 1880 in Peru. Although the original recontracts were between the individual coolie whose contract had just expired and the planter or estate administrator; usually the same persons who made the original contracts, a new contracting system involved a free Chinese—operating as an *enganchador* (labor contractor or broker)—who engaged and organized fellow free Chinese (*chinos libres*) into *cuadrillas*, or gangs. This entire group of *cuadrilleros* was then hired out to a plantation for a specified period of time or a specific piece of work, such as the evaporating room (*casa de calderas*) in the *ingenios* (sugar factory on the estate) of Cuba.[15]

In Peru, the Chilean invasion in 1880 during the War of the Pacific created chaos along the coast and led to the destruction of numerous estates. The displaced Chinese, both those still serving out contracts and those already freed, became readily available clients of the Chinese *enganchadores*. The Chinese *enganchador* negotiated all terms of work for a squad and handled all aspects of employment for the workers, including obtaining advances from the planters to pay them; handing out tools; and arranging for lodging and food and was responsible for discipline, control, and supervision. The *enganchador*, who also assumed the risks of all losses and damages, was likely once a coolie, now an independent merchant trading in goods and people. Michael González, who studied the Aspillaga planter family and their estate Cayalti, found that the Aspillagas also offered their Chinese contractors the right to operate small stores on site to cater to the needs of the Chinese workers, who were each paid sixty centavos per day without rations.[16]

In Cuba, by the census of 1872, 14,064 coolies had completed their original contract and naturalized or registered as foreign residents. Under contract were 34,408 coolies; 7,036 were runaways still missing, 864 were captured runaways, and 684 were sentenced criminals. Awaiting recontracting in the *depositos* (pens where slave were held, awaiting sale) were only 864.[17] Thus, the planters welcomed the Chinese *cuadrillas* in 1870 as an innovative device to keep the Chinese working on the estates after their contract expired. But the planters also realized that the presence of these *chinos libres* posed a severe problem of control over slaves and especially coolies still under contract. An editorial in the *Boletin de Colonización*, an official organ of the colonial government that represented sugar interests, concerned about the high rate of *marronismo*, or runaways, charged that the *cuadrillas* were the principal cause of flight. The writer asserted that the runaways could easily hide among the *cuadrilleros*, and that their presence "demoralized the workers."[18] Thus, the colonial authorities banned the use of *cuadrillas*, seeing the need for control as more important than economic flexibility. But the system was revived in 1879 at the end of the Ten Years' War, when the coolie trade as well as slave imports had been terminated for several years and labor was in short supply.[19]

For the Chinese, given the 1860 regulation forcing them to recontract or leave the island, joining one of these *cuadrillas* was one way to stay in Cuba without resorting to the much-hated individual contract with a planter. And as in Peru, the Chinese contractor accumulated capital for business through this process.[20]

As the decade of the 1880s drew to a close, both Peru and Cuba saw the end of dependence on slave and coolie labor on the plantations. Very simply, after 1885, an aging Chinese population whose ranks were not being replenished by younger immigrants, was increasingly replaced by Peruvian *peones libres*; Chinese disappeared almost entirely from the plantations by the end of the century. By then, Peruvian *hacendados* had learned how to entice and keep native Peruvian workers with the use of advance wages and debts, much the same way they had enticed and coerced free Chinese to work for them. In Cuba, the old plantation system gave way to the *colonos*, or independent small farmers, who cultivated and supplied the newly modernized mills with the raw canes. Many of these *colones* were new immigrants, mostly Canary Islanders and Gallegos.

During the chaos of the War of the Pacific, when the invading Chilean army sacked a number of Peruvian coastal haciendas and liberated coolies (whether under original contract or recontracted), other *hacendados* eagerly hired the Chinese, usually by agreement with a Chinese contractor, "incorporating them as peones," or wage workers, to supplement the coolies that remained under contract on the estates. "It would not be exaggerated to say that for a period of time, very short to be sure, the great sugar estates depended on these Chinese contractors and those Chinese engaged by them, that is, the same people who years before had worked as forced laborers and been treated like slaves." These outside-contracted Chinese workers (*chinos enganchados*) became an "embryo" of Peru's "rural proletariat," and an initial form of peonage" or wage labor.[21]

The *enganche* system in Peru gave way entirely to a free, or wage labor system, involving many Chinese until these died or moved out of agriculture into commerce and other urban occupations. They were succeeded in the field by Peruvian *serranos* contracted by labor brokers emulating the example of the Chinese.

An official inspection of the coastal provinces of 1887 located 8,503 Chinese, of whom the vast majority, 6,245, were ex-coolies now free, who worked in agriculture, and whose condition "was similar to that of the *peon libre nacional*." They received the same wages and rations as other workers, although wages varied from hacienda to hacienda. Another 1,182 Chinese on the coast were individually recontracted, and only 838 were tied to a labor contractor. There were also 40 *yanaconas*, or sharecroppers, 193 *arrendatarios*, or renters, 5 shopkeepers and innkeepers. The commission of inspection even located one ex-coolie who had become an *hacendado* himself, and who hired eighty or ninety free Chinese to work for him.[22] The work force of one important plantation as early as 1883 had become predominantly Peruvian and Chinese wage laborers—373 of the total of 550, or 68 percent.[23] The transition to an authentic free labor system was clearly in progress. If coolies—that is, Chinese workers during their eight-year term—were more slave than free in the way they were treated, ex-coolies earning a wage did become the country's early free workers, paving the way for other *peones*.

Although the major imprint of the Chinese in Peru was unquestionably on the coastal export economy (guano and sugar) and later in retail commercial development, they also ventured into the largely Indian *sierra* as well as joined the pioneer efforts into the Peruvian Amazon.[24] It is for their contribution to Amazon settlement and resource development that the Chinese have been least known, most neglected, and as one new study suggests, deliberately suppressed in official Peruvian historiography due to a prevailing nineteenth-century Peruvian attitude that only European pioneers were capable of bringing "civilization" to the jungle.[25]

As early as 1873, Chinese colonies were established in the Amazon. By the end of the century, Chinese had built colonies in major towns such as Inquitos, Huánuco, Chanchamayo, and Pucallpa, as well as scattered all over the Amazon region. Some of these first pioneers and settlers very likely were fugitives from coastal masters, joined later by coolies who had completed their contract and were free immigrants.

These early colonies were small—around one hundred persons each—but prosperous, and in the sparsely populated underdeveloped Amazon region, assumed a significance above their size. The Chinese acquired urban lots as well as rural land; they manufactured basic consumer items as well as growing food to provision the towns. In the towns and regional markets, as itinerant peddlers (muleteers) and shopkeepers, they not only sold their own crops (principally rice, but also beans, peanuts, sugar cane) and manufactured goods (clothing and shoes), but also took on an intermediary role in the exchange of natural, artisanal, and agricultural products between the highland and the jungle. When cash was not available, they bartered.

In these activities, the Chinese covered a lot of territory, occasionally suffered Indian attacks, and also became much sought after as expeditionary guides and interpreters. Not only did the Chinese adapt with alacrity and facility to the Amazon environment, but as early pioneers and trailblazers, they acted the role of cultural broker between the "uncivilized" Indian natives and the Peruvian and European settlers.

Rubber and gold in Loreto Province, with its capital in Iquitos on the Amazon River, attracted Chinese from all over Peru, directly from China, and from California. They spread over the vast jungle to tap wild rubber trees; they washed for gold in the tributary rivers; and they established themselves in business in Iquitos. By 1899, the Chinese community of Iquitos, numbering 346, was the largest of many foreign groups in that most cosmopolitan of Peruvian cities, isolated to be sure from the national capital of Lima, but well connected to Europe, the United States, and especially Brazil.

## Chinese Immigrants in Mexico

After the coolie trade, some Chinese continued to go to Peru and Cuba, now as free immigrants, but a much larger number voluntarily migrated to Mexico, particularly to the northern frontier zone bordering the United States. Not coincidentally, this new migration occurred just when the United States enacted the first Chinese Exclusion Act in 1882, by which the Chinese became the first group specifically designated by race to be barred from entering the country.

Chinese immigrants, mostly young males, began arriving on the west coast of Mexico in 1876, coinciding with the military coup of Porfirio Diaz, who ruled Mexico with an iron hand for thirty-five years and promoted its rapid economic development by foreign investors. This immigration accelerated following the passage of the Chinese Exclusion in the United States. Entering through the Pacific coast ports of Mazatlán and Guaymas, the Chinese spread throughout Mexico but primarily the northern border states, no doubt attracted by their proximity to the United States. An initial tendency to cross illicitly into the United States abated, however, as the Chinese perceived and moved swiftly into a widening economic space in the rapidly developing frontier region, where the bulk of U.S. investment in Mexico was concentrated. Unlike the Chinese north of the border, those in northern Mexico did not take up laboring jobs, which were filled by Mexicans, but rather entered commerce as small independent entrepreneurs or occasionally in partnership with U.S. mine and railroad owners in the company towns. Chinese shopkeepers followed the trail of Yankee capital.

Nowhere was this pattern clearer than in the northwestern state of Sonora, which bordered the then territory of Arizona. Astutely avoiding competition with established European and Mexican merchants in old towns such as Guaymas and Hermosillo (the state capital), the Chinese ventured into some remote villages of the interior, but mostly into new working-class settlements that sprang up along railroad and mining sites, and later, modern agricultural colonies. These were the new towns that grew in the wake of foreign, mainly U.S., investment in northern Mexico during the last quarter of the nineteenth century. The Chinese were often the first *comerciantes* to reach these new localities, thus the first shopkeepers to cater to the needs of the workers.

Within two generations, they succeeded in monopolizing the small commercial sector of the state's economy. Far from being a hindrance, the Mexican Revolution of 1910–1917 actually furthered their commercial growth in several ways. First, with most Mexicans engaged in the civil conflicts, the revolution retarded the emergence of Mexican small businesses to compete with the Chinese. Second, even during these turbulent times, towns, including mining and railroad centers that continued to operate, needed to be supplied with goods and services. Third, the various revolutionary armies needed to be provisioned. As aliens, the Chinese remained officially "neutral" and willing to do business with all revolutionary factions. Although some of the sales were on "forced loan" bases, whereby Chinese merchants were given a credit slip for future payment by revolutionary generals who commandeered goods and supplies, the Chinese figured these inconveniences to be part of the cost of doing business in the midst of chaos. Fourth, further solidifying the Chinese position in Sonoran commerce was the weakening of traditional commercial links between Mexico and Europe during World War I, which coincided in time with the Mexican Revolution. Some of the departed German, French, and Spanish commercial houses were replaced by Chinese firms, which turned to U.S. suppliers, thereby forging new Mexican-U.S. commercial ties. This in turn strengthened the existing symbiotic relationship between Chinese merchants and U.S. interests in Sonora, and explains the actions frequently taken by U.S. consuls to protect Chinese persons and businesses when they came under violent attack by Mexicans.

Most of the Chinese immigrants were young males, who arrived in Mexico nearly penniless, armed with only a willingness to work long and hard. However, a small number of Chinese capitalists also went early to Mexico to set up merchant houses in Guaymas and Hermosillo, with branches in important new towns such as Magdalena along the Sonoran railroad and Cananea of the Greene Consolidated Copper Company. In some cases, they added factories next to the stores to manufacture cheap shoes and clothing. These large merchants hired almost exclusively fellow Chinese in the stores and factories. They also, significantly, extended goods on credit to enterprising but poor compatriots to peddle in small, remote mining towns and to set up new stores throughout the state. By the twentieth century, the Chinese controlled the trade in groceries, dry goods, and general merchandise. Some Chinese truck-farmed on land they leased, then carted the fruits and vegetables to local markets, which were often dominated by Chinese-owned stalls. Other Chinese worked as artisans and small-scale manufacturers, producing shoes, clothing, brooms, *masa* for tortillas, pasta, and sweets. In these multiple ways, the Chinese succeeded in creating a production, purchasing, supply, and distribution network among themselves, a closed system with characteristics of vertical integration that in effect became the state's first commercial infrastructure. This remarkable system endured until early 1931, when most of the Chinese were expelled from Sonora and their businesses nationalized.[26]

By the end of the Porfiriato, in 1910, the Chinese population in Sonora had reached 4,486, in a total population of 265,383, making them the largest foreign colony in the state, surpassing the 3,164 U.S. nationals by over a thousand and well above the 259 Spaniards and 183 Germans. In 1910, according to Mexico's official census, there were 13,203 Chinese throughout Mexico, in every state except Tlaxcala. Table 11.2 summarizes demographic data for Chinese immigration to Mexico, by state, from 1900 to 1930.[27] The Chinese colony in Sonora—as in all of Mexico—was almost exclusively male. Even as late as 1930, the census noted only 412 women among the 3,471 Chinese recorded for Sonora. Not even all these four hundred or so women were necessarily Chinese, for Sonoran law had begun to strip Mexican women married to Chinese men of their citizenship and nationality, consigning them to their husband's ethnic group.

The highest number of Chinese in Sonora was recorded in 1919, when the Chinese colony itself supplied the county of 6,078. The sharp drop to the 3,571 noted for 1930 can be explained in a number of ways, aside from unreliable statistics. It reflected declining new immigration into the state at a time when Sonora had begun expulsion proceedings against established residents, many of whom were nationalized Mexican citizens. During the 1920s, as anti-Chinese campaigns mounted in intensity and frequency, many Chinese fled the state—back to China, illegally across the border to the United States, south to Sinaba, and it appeared, especially across the gulf to Baja California, which recorded 5,889 Chinese in 1927 compared to 3,785 for Sonora.

When the Chinese first began arriving in Sonora in the last quarter of the nineteenth century, they congregated in Guaymas, the port of entry, and in the capital of Hermosillo. Then they moved to newer towns, notably the railroad hub of Magdalena north of Hermosillo, and to the state's leading mining town of Cananea on the northeast corner of the state close to the U.S. border. By 1904, Chinese could be found in all nine districts of the state, although unevenly distributed. Still prominent in Guaymas, Hermosillo, and Magdalena, by far the largest number had gone to Arizpe district, which included Cananea as well as a number of smaller mining camps and border towns. Of Arizpe's 1,106 Chinese, 800 resided in Cananea. By contrast, the districts of Altar, Sahuaripa, and Ures, which had no significant mining or railroad activities, had only a few Chinese residents each. The informative 1919 census, the data for which was provided by the Chinese Fraternal Union to the federal Department of Labor, noted 6,078 Chinese distributed across all nine districts and in fifty-eight of the state's sixty-two municipalities. Only four very small towns in Sahuaripa and Ures districts had no Chinese at all.

The 1919 community was composed overwhelmingly of young to middle-aged men, that is, men of working age. Eighty-four percent were between twenty-one and forty-five, the percentage increasing to an astonishing 91 percent if the upper limit is raised to fifty. Only 33 individuals, or 5.4 percent, were under twenty, and only 170, or 2.8 percent, were older than fifty-one. In years of residency in Mexico as of 1919, 41 percent had been in Mexico for ten to fifteen years, and another 37 percent

TABLE 11.2
Chinese Population in Mexico, 1900–1930

| State | 1900 | 1910 | 1921 | 1927 | 1930 |
|---|---|---|---|---|---|
| Aguascalientes | 102 | 21 | 14 | 31 | 47(18) |
| BC Norte | 188 | 532 | 2806(14) | 5889 | 2982 |
| BC Sur | | 319 | 175(3) | | 139(3) |
| Campeche | 5 | 70 | 61(1) | 108 | 113(38) |
| Coahuila | 197(5) | 759(14) | 523(16) | 707 | 765(153) |
| Colima | 5 | 80(2) | 32(1) | 43 | 38(14) |
| Chiapas | 16 | 478(1) | 645(30) | 1261 | 1095(238) |
| Chichuahua | 328(2) | 1325(9) | 533(16) | 1037 | 1127(229) |
| Méx.D.F. | | 1482(5) | 607(18) | 1062 | 886(141) |
| Durango | 147(1) | 242(2) | 46 | 197 | 229(33) |
| Guanajuanto | 11 | 102 | 21(3) | 37 | 37(12) |
| Guerrero | 3 | 27 | 3 | 7 | 10(3) |
| Hidalgo | | 38 | 50(1) | 98 | 70(18) |
| Jalisco | 20 | 70(1) | 53(1) | 192 | 151(48) |
| México | 15 | 58(1) | 25 | 78 | 24 |
| Michoacán | 4 | 26 | 5 | 8 | 12(1) |
| Morelos | 5 | 18 | 3 | 9 | 3 |
| Nayarit | | | 152 | 164 | 170(27) |
| N. León | 90 | 211 | 89(2) | 216 | 165(4) |
| Oaxaca | 81 | 262 | 158(6) | 254 | 158(50) |
| Puebla | 11 | 31 | 17(1) | 22 | 44(12) |
| Queretaro | 1 | 5 | 1 | 1 | 2 |
| Quin.Roo | | 3 | 3 | 2 | 10(4) |
| San Luis P. | 32 | 109 | 105(2) | 288 | 271(18) |
| Sinaloa | 233(1) | 667(4) | 1040(4) | 2019 | 2123(438) |
| Sonora | 850(9) | 4486(37) | 3639(66) | 3758 | 3571(412) |
| Tabasco | 2 | 36(1) | 48(4) | 67 | 64(23) |
| Tamaulipas | 38 | 213(2) | 2005(21) | 2916 | 2117(242) |
| Tepic | 29 | 173 | | | |
| Tlaxcala | | | | | |
| Veracruz | 116 | 434(1) | 847(10) | 1908 | 1238(162) |
| Yucatán | 153 | 875 | 773(5) | 1726 | 972(153) |
| Zacatecas | 19 | 41 | 19 | 113 | 142(25) |
| Total | 2,719 | 13,203 | 14,498 | 24,218 | 17,865 |
| | (18) | (80) | (185) | (1,772) | (2,522) |

Note: Women in Parentheses.
Sources: Mexican Censuses for 1900, 1910, 1921, 1930. For 1927, see "Extranjeros residentes Estados Unidos de México. Resúmen del censo practicado por la Sría. de Gobernación en 1927, y extranjeros, distribución por estados, 14 marzo 1928," Archivo Histórico del Gobierno e Estado de Sonora (AHGES), vol. 50, 1930.

for five to ten years. Thus the vast majority, almost 80 percent, had at least five years experience in Mexico. The data also suggest that a significant number, 1,459 or 24 percent, had entered Mexico during the active revolutionary years of 1912–1915.

The first year for which there is good commercial data on the Chinese was 1913, published by the International Chinese Business Directory.[28] For Sonora, 279 Chinese businesses were noted, most of them in general merchandise or groceries, located in twenty-six towns. There were also 40 restaurants, 16 laundries, 4 hotels, 2 dry goods businesses, 2 clothing factories, 1 shoe factory, and 2 pharmacies (probably Chinese herbal goods).

In 1919, of the 6,078 Chinese residents in Sonora, 70 percent (4,258) were listed as *comerciantes* by occupation, which probably included store owners, partners, and clerks (see Table 13.3). Common or day laborers, *jornaleros*, were a distant second, with 12.8 percent. There were very few cooks or launderers. Artisans and craft workers of various kinds—tailors, shoemakers, jewelers, carpenters, bakers, tanners constituted another 2 percent.

By 1925, although the Chinese population had declined sharply as noted above, the Chinese maintained a solid hold on local small businesses throughout the state.[29] Only a handful of traditional communities

TABLE 11.3
Chinese Occupation in Sonora, 1919

| District | (1) | (2) | (3) | (4) | (5) | (6) | (7) | (8) | (9) | (10) |
|----------|-----|-----|-----|-----|-----|-----|-----|-----|-----|------|
| Moctezuma | 514 | 25 | 75 | 5 | 6 | 8 | 2 | 4 | 5 | 75 |
| Guaymas | 1156 | 50 | | 5 | 15 | 8 | 2 | 1 | 9 | 65 |
| Sahuaripa | 46 | 2 | | 1 | 1 | | | | 1 | 6 |
| Altar | 146 | 15 | 1 | 4 | 2 | 1 | 1 | | 3 | 15 |
| Alamos | 492 | 2 | 15 | 5 | 6 | 5 | 2 | | 2 | 100 |
| Ures | 51 | 3 | | 1 | 1 | | | 1 | 1 | 8 |
| Arizpe | 758 | 20 | 120 | 15 | 18 | 15 | 8 | 6 | 10 | 287 |
| Magdalena | 516 | ⸗3 | | 15 | 12 | 8 | 4 | | 7 | 147 |
| Hermosillo | 579 | 24 | | 7 | 8 | 24 | 4 | 3 | 1 | 75 |
| Total | 4258 | 207 | 196 | 58 | 69 | 69 | 23 | 15 | 39 | 778 |

(1) Merchants (fixed or traveling); (2) Truck farmer; (3) Mine worker; (4) Cook; (5) Launderer; (6) Shoemaker (or repairer); (7) Tailor; (8) Confectioner, butcher, tanner; (9) Baker; (10) Day Laborer. In addition, there were 8 "industrialists" (probably meaning someone who owned some kind of manufacturing business); 3 jewelry maker/repair, carpenter; 100 "minors"; and 255 "vagrants (probably meaning someone without a fixed or stable occupation).

*Source:* Departamento de Trabajo. Sección de Conciliación. "Informe que rinde el Jefe de la Sección sobre la situación República," 1919 (E. Flores, Commissioner). Archiva General de la Nación/Trabajo. México, D.F.

in Ures, Altar, and Sahuaripa districts had no Chinese presence. What is important is that these towns had *probably no stores whatever.* In other remote communities, such as Atil, Tubutama, and San Pedro de Cueva, with only one or a few commercial outlets, *all* were Chinese owned and operated. Even more significant, the commerce of certain mining towns, such as Nacozari de García near Cananea, was also exclusively in Chinese hands. The same was true for rapidly developing commercial agricultural towns in the southern part of the state, such as Cócorit in the Yaqui Valley, with 42 Chinese merchants, and Etchojoa and Huatabampo in the Mayo Valley.

The widespread distribution of Chinese businesses must also be noted in the context of their capitalization. In 1913, only 15 Chinese businesses were capitalized at $20,000 pesos or above, for a total of $721,830, compared to 238 non-Chinese businesses, with a total of $18 million.[30] The average Chinese in this group had capital of $48,789, compared to $75,630 among the others. Only 3 of the Chinese had over $50,000; by contrast, 98 non-Chinese firms were capitalized at over $50,000. If this group can be characterized as Sonora's "grande bourgeoisie," then the Chinese were only an insignificant part of it. Chinese participation at this level of economic activity did not grow with time. From 1917 to 1920, Chinese entrepreneurs formed some eighty "mercantile societies," or companies.[31] The vast majority of the eighty were capitalized under $5,000 pesos. Mexican, European, and U.S. companies, by contrast, were typically capitalized at $25,000, $50,000, in the hundreds of thousands, and up to one or two billion for the big mining, railroad, land, and agricultural enterprises.

The detailed report prepared by the Mexican Labor Department on capital invested in the Sonoran economy in 1919 further confirms the low Chinese presence among the large enterprises and the fundamentally petit bourgeois nature of the Chinese business community. Total Chinese-owned capital did not lag far behind all other capital combined, $2,186,935 pesos compared to $2,813,540 (see Table 11.4). However, there were almost twice as many Chinese establishments as all others combined—North American, German, French, Arab, Japanese and other foreigners, and Mexican. The average Chinese business capital was $2,644, compared to $6,482 for others. Of the 827 Chinese businesses distributed over sixty communities, 740 were capitalized under $5,000.

Finally, in 1925, in the midst of a vigorous anti-Chinese campaign that called for their expulsion from Sonora, the state government once again took stock of the Chinese business profile, this time comparing it to Mexican industrial and commercial holdings.[32] By this time, it should be noted, a Mexican industrial and large commercial bourgeoisie had firmly established itself in Sonora, home to President Plutarco Elias Calles and

TABLE 11.4
Commercial Establishments and Capital in Sonora, 1919

| District | Chinese | | Mexican and All Others | |
|---|---|---|---|---|
| | No. | Total Capital | No. | Total Capital |
| Moctezuma | 81 | $220,520.00 | 28 | $522,270.00 |
| Guaymas | 248 | 854,110.00 | 54 | 936,805.00 |
| Sahuaripa | 6 | 27,000.00 | 29 | 40,550.00 |
| Altar | 30 | 61,404,00 | 42 | 73,810.00 |
| Alamos | 102 | 185,100.00 | 44 | 104,400.00 |
| Ures | 25 | 48,900.00 | 28 | 45,400.00 |
| Arizpe | 110 | 196,320.00 | 67 | 546,555.00 |
| Magdalena | 107 | 320,621.00 | 54 | 168,400.00 |
| Hermosillo | 118 | 272,960.00 | 88 | 375,350.00 |
| Total | 827 | 2,186,935.00 | 434 | 2,813,540.00 |

Source: Departmento de Trabajo. Sección de Conciliación. "Informe que rinde el Jefe de la Sección sobre la situación de las colonias asiáticas en la Costa Occidental de la República," 1919. Archiva General de la Nación/Trabajo. México, D.F.

former President Alvaro Obregon as well as many other revolutionary leaders who all laid claim to land and other properties in the state except for what the Chinese still held. Mexican-owned enterprises can be characterized as falling within the medium to large range: 27 capitalized at $5,000 to $10,900 pesos; 28 at $11,000 to $99,000, and 5 over $100,000. Among the Chinese, a considerable 41—fell in the $5,000 to $10,900 range, but only 4 between $11,000 and $99,000, and only 1 above $100,000. The vast majority of Chinese businesses were capitalized under $5,000, with most of them actually worth $1,200 to $2,500. There was only 1 Mexican-owned business in this modest category. Moreover, the 517 Chinese businesses were spread over sixty-five of the state's seventy municipalities; the 61 Mexican firms were to be found in only fourteen towns.

In short, this commercial/industrial survey conducted by the state government conclusively demonstrated the Chinese monopoly of the small commercial sector, to the practical exclusion of Mexicans. The situation was not particularly alarming to the large Mexican capitalists who in turn controlled the large commercial industrial sector of the economy, but it would provide fodder for the average Mexican who could, and did, aspire to the small commercial sector that was firmly in Chinese hands. The ubiquitous nature of these Chinese comerciantes, although providing a necessary service to all Sonorans, also became a thorn on the side of middle- and working-class Mexicans. Modest in fact, but prosperous in comparison to ordinary Sonorans still struggling to improve their lives well after the revolution in which many of them fought in the name of social justice, the Chinese also reminded Sonorans just how much foreigners had historically controlled their destiny, and how much farther they would have to go to reclaim Mexico for the Mexicans. Understandably, Mexican workers, landless peasants, and their families formed the backbone of the campaigns to remove the Chinese from their midst.

Where did the expelled Chinese go? It is hard to trace their steps. Some tried to enter the United States surreptitiously; some returned to China; and others resettled in more hospitable parts of Mexico, notably Baja California Norte, a territory and Mexico's last frontier.

Like Mexico's other frontier and border regions, such as Sonora in the north, the Yucatan and Tapachula in the south, Baja California also experienced an influx of Chinese. But well before Sonoran Chinese fled to Baja California in the late 1920s and early 1930s, Chinese workers had been brought there under rather unique circumstances at the beginning of the twentieth century to develop the virgin land of the fertile Mexicali Valley. U.S. landowners and entrepreneurial Chinese formed partnerships to clear this rich valley, an extension of California's Imperial Valley, for large-scale cotton cultivation. U.S. landowners leased land to California Chinese merchants and labor contractors who brought in the workers to do the backbreaking work. By 1920, Chinese lessees and their Chinese workers were raising 80 percent of Mexicali's cotton crop. Details of the relationships between U.S. landowners and Chinese lessees, and between Chinese labor contractors and workers have been recounted elsewhere.[33]

## Other Asia-Pacific Labor in Latin America

My concern in this discussion is primarily with Chinese immigrants. I would like to note here, however, Chinese were not the only Asia-Pacific people to end up in Latin America. Equally important in numbers and activity have been Japanese immigrants. In contrast to Chinese labor, the emigration of Japanese labor into Latin America, as into the United States, was much more closely regulated and supervised by the Japanese government. The first Japanese laborers began to arrive in Latin America—in Mexico and Peru—just about the turn of the twentieth century and increasingly after 1908, in Brazil. By the second and third decades of this century, Peru and Brazil were the foremost recipients of Japanese labor in the Western hemisphere. By 1940, there were 234,574 immigrants of Japanese origin in Latin America, nearly 48 percent of all Japanese living abroad outside of Asia. By far the largest number were in Brazil (around 200,000), followed by Peru and Mexico. Also noteworthy is the fact that among Japanese immigrants to Latin America were large numbers of Okinawans and Ryukyu Islanders.[34]

The majority of Japanese immigrants to Latin America arrived initially also as contract laborers on coffee plantations in Brazil, sugar plantations in Peru, and rubber plantations in Bolivia. Although the Japanese, like the Chinese in Peru, Cuba, and Mexico, would gradually move into urban small businesses (and after World War II, the professions), in Brazil in particular they were to achieve prominence as independent landed proprietors ("middle-class farmers," as historian James Tigner describes them) pioneering settlement in frontier regions, which made them a crucial sector of the agrarian economy in Brazil.[35]

One other group must be mentioned here not because it played any significant part in the development of Latin America, but because of what its presence in Latin America reveals about the underside of an Asia-Pacific formation. These are the Easter Islanders, who were nearly exterminated by labor needs in Peru. In 1862–1863, for a period of a few months, private entrepreneurs "recruited" by force and guile Easter Islanders (among other Polynesians) to work in the guano fields in Peru. In the end, the islanders proved not to be suitable for the job. Many perished on the voyage or of disease and suicide after arrival. In a few months, the population of Easter Island came to the verge of extinction, about to follow in the wake of the Arawaks of the Caribbean and the Tasmanians of the Pacific. Luckily for the Easter Islanders, their labor proved "useless," and the trade created such disgust in Peru that it came to an end while some of them still lived.[36]

Asian laborers contributed in significant ways to Latin America's development. As coolies and workers, they provided much needed labor in mines, guano fields, and plantations. As free laborers and small entrepreneurs, they opened up new frontiers of settlement and contributed to the vitality of urban economies.

As the earliest modern agriculturists in Baja California who cleared the land for commercial crops, as coolies who moved progressively from semi-slavery to wage labor in Peru, the Chinese in Latin American agricultural and labor history have not been adequately recognized and fully documented. Yet the prosperity of both Baja California Norte and the Peruvian coast could not have been realized without Chinese sweat. The exact relationship of various categories of Chinese workers to production needs further research and more in-depth analysis.

As free immigrants to northwest Mexico and the Amazon, the Chinese proved adaptable to strange physical and cultural surroundings as well as harsh work regimens. They demonstrated an uncanny ability to detect and move swiftly into new economic spaces, often in "untamed" and underdeveloped frontier and border regions, where they usually found little or no competition from locals. They also tended to avoid conflict with entrenched, more powerful white or European interests. Rather, they were instrumental in both Mexico and Peru's frontiers in clearing land to grow food for local consumption and crops for export. And with their production and distribution system and their widespread retail network, they in effect helped create in both countries a modern commercial infrastructure.

## Latin America and the Asia-Pacific

The fragility of the small Easter Island population nearly drove it to extinction in a short period of recruitment for labor in Peru. There was no such danger for Chinese and Japanese. The experiences of immigrant laborers from China and Japan, however, were also revealing of the economic exploitation, racist discrimination, and cultural suppression of Asia-Pacific peoples that attended the formation of the Asia-Pacific region.

Although the coolie labor of the nineteenth century must be distinguished from slavery, it is quite clear that Chinese laborers were imported to Cuba and Peru to substitute for African labor that was lost with the abolition of slavery, and at least initially, they were barely distinguishable from slaves in the conditions of labor as well as in the treatment to which they were subjected.

The eventual success of Chinese in converting themselves into small urban business proprietors and the influx of free Asian immigrants to Latin America in ensuing decades were accompanied everywhere by anti-Asian agitation and mob action, as well as more organized state campaigns and persecution. In emulation of the U.S. Exclusion Act, Latin American governments in the early twentieth century enacted laws to severely limit further Asian, especially Chinese, immigration.

In Mexico, again echoing what had occurred earlier in California, anti-Chinese persecution culminated in 1929–1931, the onset of the Depression, with mass expulsion from Sonora and to a lesser extent Baja California. The once ubiquitous and relatively prosperous Chinese community of Sonora never recovered, although the Chinese have continued to be a viable commercial force in Baja California.

In Peru at the end of the twentieth century, Chinese Peruvians remain a visible minority, their presence illustrated by the numerous and popular *chifas*, or Chinese restaurants, in Lima and other Peruvian towns big and small. Shortly after the triumph of the Cuban Revolution of 1959, a large number of the Cuban Chinese left the island as part of the massive exodus of the Cuban middle class.

Although Japanese communities in Latin America survived more intact than Chinese communities, in some ways anti-Japanese persecution in Latin America reached even greater heights. In Peru, anti-Japanese sentiments led to the government's willingness to allow the U.S. government during World War II to round up and transport 1,429 Japanese Peruvians to the United States for internment in special concentration camps. In spite of this infamy, Japanese immigration resumed after World War II to Peru and especially Brazil. Significantly, from the beginning and throughout its history, Japanese migration to Latin America included more women and children. New immigration and natural reproduction allowed Japanese communities in both Peru and Brazil to continue to grow, until in both countries they came to constitute the largest immigrant community in the postwar period, numbering over 50,000 in Peru and 700,000 in Brazil by the 1970s.[37]

Against this historical background, Alberto Fujimori's election to Peru's presidency is truly extraordinary. On the other hand, the Japanese Peruvians are only cautiously proud of their fellow son of immigrants, fully aware that in the extremely difficult economic condition and volatile political situation of the country, Fujimori could well fail to govern effectively. Should that happen, another round of anti-Asian violence would not be beyond question.

In sum, the Latin American Pacific from the mid-nineteenth to the late twentieth century has been a mixed and often bitter experience for most Asian immigrants. Until Fujimori's election in 1990, Asian Latin Americans led a mostly quiet existence, trying hard not to call excessive attention to themselves.

For the past 150 years, from the California Gold Rush days on, the Pacific has been defined by another kind of Latin American migration. Led by Mexicans, but since the 1960s increasingly joined by Central and South Americans, a stream of legal but mostly undocumented Latin Americans have been streaming across the Mexican border into the United States. Largely in search of better economic opportunities, they also come to escape from civil war and political persecution at home.

At the time of Mexican independence from Spain in 1820, both the United States and Mexico had wide and sparsely settled frontiers rich in natural resources and open land. Both frontiers were also inhabited by hostile indigenous peoples determined to protect their distinctive way of life, land, and environment, and whose resistance to white encroachment made colonization difficult for EuroAmericans in both countries.

With a series of disastrous territorial losses by Mexico (amounting to three-fifths of its national territory) to the United States in the mid-nineteenth century—Texas independence in 1836, the Treaty of Guadalupe Hidalgo in 1848, the Treaty of La Mesilla (Gadsden Purchase) in 1853—

the U.S. frontier expanded greatly at the expense of Mexico, and the U.S. government increasingly assumed responsibility for pacifying this broad zone. The long and violent process culminated with the pacification of the Apaches in the 1880s, opening up the final chapter of U.S. conquest of the west and Mexico's colonization of its by then much reduced north. When the two frontiers finally met along the Rio Grande, they were also transformed into an international border.[38] But far from separating two countries, this border has functioned to integrate Mexico and the United States far more closely than they had ever been before. For twentieth-century Mexicans, this border and the land beyond is known as *El Norte*.[39] The *El Norte* phenomenon has created in Los Angeles the second largest Mexican city in the world, second only to Mexico City.

Driven from their homeland by landlessness and unemployment, twin results of dependent capitalist development, and by revolutions and civil wars, Mexicans have been going north since the days of the California Gold Rush. They continued crossing the border when mining gave way to agriculture, factories, manufacturing. assembly, and service industries in the late nineteenth and throughout the twentieth century. With jobs and economic opportunities constantly beckoning on the other side of the border, Mexicans have become the reserve labor force of the U.S.-Pacific. For Mexicans, this border has always been porous, a legal fiction never intended to keep them out permanently, but merely to control their movement to conform to vicissitudes of the U.S. economy and its changing labor demands.[40]

Although population movements back and forth across the border have involved mostly Mexican laborers, equally significant since the 1880s has been the massive flow of U.S. capital investment into Mexico and the resultant trade with Mexico. Initially concentrated in mining and railroads, since the 1940s it has diversified into commercial agriculture—culminating in the highly technified Green Revolution—and manufacturing. More recently, since 1965, U.S. capital has erected labor-intensive border plants known as *maquiladoras*, which utilize mostly young female labor to assemble products from parts imported duty-free into Mexico; the finished products are then shipped back into the United States, also duty-free. Touted as an ingenious mechanism to contain surplus Mexican labor within Mexico and hence stem the flow of Mexican workers across the border; the *maquiladoras* have actually served to integrate the Mexican economy even more closely with that of the United States and further consolidate Mexico's dependent status.

Any current and future conceptualization of the Asia-Pacific must contend with the *El Norte* phenomenon and integrate at least Mexico, if not the rest of the Pacific Rim of Latin America, into its configuration. With an equally massive post-1965 migration from Asia, Mexicans and Asians have transformed the demographic makeup of the U.S.-Pacific. According to the 1990 census, these two ethnic/racial minorities already exceed 35 percent of California's total population of nearly thirty million. Through continuous immigration and high reproductive rates, their growth will continue to outstrip that of other EuroAmericans, and their presence severely challenge the preservation of the dominant ethnic composition of U.S. society.

## Postscript: Latin America and the Asia–Pacific in the 1990s

On January 1994, the Indian peasants of Chiapas, Mexico's southernmost province, rose up in rebellion, timing their action to coincide with the first day of implementation of NAFTA, the North American Free Trade Agreement eagerly signed by the governments of the United States, Canada, and Mexico to consolidate neo-liberal economic policies and practices in the hemisphere. Grandiosely named the Zapatista National Liberation Front (FZLN, for *Frente Zapatista de Liberacion Nacional* in Spanish) and quickly popularized as Zapatistas, the rebels aimed their protest directly at outgoing President Carlos Salinas de Gotari and against NAFTA's certain acceleration of immiseration for the country's rural poor.

Dubbed the world's first postmodern uprising because the rebels professed no interest in seizing state power while demonstrating uncanny sophistication in generating and maintaining international media interest in their just cause, the Zapatistas have been joined less than two years later by other indigenous and peasant insurgencies in at least six other poverty-stricken states in southern and central Mexico loosely organized under the banner of the Popular Revolutionary Army (EPR, or *Ejercito Popular Revolucionario*, organizationally distinct from the EZLN).

What all these rural rebels have in common is their vociferous objection to one of Salinas's most controversial preparatory moves for NAFTA: undoing Article 27 of the constitution of the Mexican Revolution, which had created thousands of pueblos with inalienable community land holdings called *ejidos*, the centerpiece of Mexico's postrevolutionary land reform and primary symbol of social justice for the peasants. Much to the shock of observers in Mexico and worldwide, Salinas violated an unspoken, sacrosanct principle that even his most corrupt and venal predecessors had kept, when he allowed the communal land holdings of the ejidos to be broken up, sold off and privatized.[41]

This fateful decision indicated just how far Salinas and Mexico's governing elite in the official party PRI (*Partido Revolucionario Institutional*) were willing to go to mortgage Mexico's most vulnerable citizens to neo-liberalism's New World Economy. For over eighty years, peasants were assured of at least a minimum safety net; now even this thread-bare net was yanked out from under them, leaving Mexico's forty-plus million already living in poverty (half of Mexico's total population) to sink deeper into misery. In the ten years of neo-liberal policies that preceded the formal implementation of NAFTA in 1994, more than two million new rural poor were produced in the countryside.[42]

Nowhere is the poverty more visible or more entrenched than in Chiapas, Mexico's poorest state, where the insurrection has been converted into an "armed critique" of Salinas's neo-liberal policies, designed to modernize Mexico through international economic integration based on export-oriented production and removal of all trade barriers, protective tariffs and central government regulation of the economy. To demonstrate his commitment to the free market, Salinas also had to maximize privatization of Mexico's wealth, her resources and infrastructure. Not even communally owned land was immune to this onslaught.[43]

While the Zapatistas launched their protest in Mexico's south, all was seemingly quiet on the northern front. The maquila-driven border economy has been recently embellished and enhanced by capital investment from Asian "tigers" big and small—Japan, Korea, and Taiwan. In March 1996, Samsung of Korea opened a new $212 million TV assembly plant. Together with Daewoo, Sony and Matsushita, these three giant conglomerates employ 24,000 Mexican workers in the Tijuana area (border with San Diego), producing nine million TV sets a year, 90 percent of which are sold in the U.S. Also operating in Mexico are some sixty Taiwan plants, soon to be joined by many more.[44] Given its abundant, increasingly disciplined and still cheap work force of mostly young women, and its gateway location to both the U.S. and Pacific markets, Mexico's advantage as the manufacturing center of the continent was firmly sealed in place by NAFTA.

Never explicitly stated but increasingly obvious is that Asian capital has become an unnamed partner of the North American Free Trade project. Salinas's secret plan was to diversify Mexico's economic relations with the world while lessening her dependence on U.S. capital and markets. To do so, Mexico needs to attract more capital from Asia and even Europe. For this to succeed, Mexico must be seen as an equal partner with Canada and the United States in the North American regional economy. By the same token according to this "trilateral strategy," expanded relations with industrial powers such as Japan may enhance Mexico's negotiating leverage with its powerful northern neighbor.[45]

By early 1990s, Japan had become Mexico's second largest international economic partner. This relationship actually took off in the late 1970s, when Japan turned Mexico into a key supplier of her petroleum needs. During this past decade, Mexico saw a three-fold increase of Japanese manufacturing investment in Mexico. Almost 180 Japanese maquiladoras were doing business in Mexico in 1990, most in automobile and electronics. Japanese firms are investing in Mexico for a variety of reasons. Nissan, for example, moved some operations to Mexico initially to survive the contraction of its domestic market. By contrast, Sanyo (electronics) and Yasaki (automobile) invested in Mexico as part of their globalization strategy within the larger North American market. By 1989, Mexico was exporting over $3 billion worth of auto parts, engines and automobiles, mostly to the United States.

What has attracted Japanese investors to Mexico is Mexico's abundance of cheap labor and its close proximity to the United States. The maquiladora program allows plants to import raw materials, components, and capital equipment to Mexico duty-free, while assembled products exported to the United States are subject only to duties on value added. The aggressive growth of the Japanese maquiladora sector can be further explained by Japan's policy of linking production in Mexico more to their U.S. investments than to the Mexican market. In other words, when Japanese auto makers opened plants in the United States to counter charges of U.S.-Japan trade imbalance, the Japanese concurrently established plants in Mexico to produce parts and components for the U.S.-based factories. For example, Honda opened a parts plant in Jalisco, Mexico, in the mid-1980s for $41 million; the operation has been exporting goods to the United States worth $100 million annually.[46]

In recent years, neo-liberalism has been spreading beyond Mexico and the confines of NAFTA to Central America, where labor is even cheaper. In the San Marcos Free Trade Zone of San Salvador, capital of the densely populated, extremely poor country of El Salvador, Taiwanese businessmen such as David Wang have been setting up sweatshops to take advantage of cheap female labor. President of Mandarin International, Wang's Salvadoran plants have been sewing for such well-known U.S. clothing brands such as the Gap, J. Crew, Eddie Bauer, Liz Claiborne, among others. When women workers tried to organize, Wang apparently fired them.[47]

We can now make abundantly clear that far from being unconnected, the Zapatistas and other peasant rebels in Mexico on one side, and the maquiladora workers on the other, actually weave together one narrative, the underside of NAFTA. This narrative, furthermore, has an Asia-Pacific dimension. If in the distant past of the Spanish colonial period, Europeans went via Mexico and Central America across the "Mar del Sur" to extract the Orient's luxury goods for export, and if in the more recent past of the nineteenth century Latin American and Caribbean economies imported Asian coolie and family labor for plantations and factories, today, in the twilight of the twentieth century and the dawn of neo-liberalism's New Global Economy, these critical relationships have reconfigured. Today, Latin America *imports capital* from Asia, and *exports parts* as well as finished products to the United States, in turn *supplying cheap labor* to Asian entrepreneurs. Bearing the brunt of the cost are the poorest of the poor in Mexico, for whom NAFTA is, in the words of the enigmatic Zapatista leader, Subcomandante Marcos, "a death certificate for the Indian peoples of Mexico."

## Notes

1. H. H. Dubs, "The Chinese in Mexico City in 1635," *Far Eastern Quarterly* 1 (1942): 387–89.

2. The popular historian Stan Steiner asserted that a Chinese from Mexico City helped found Los Angeles in the eighteenth century. A seductive idea undoubtedly, but I believe he made a mistake, based on a misreading of colonial Spanish terminology, specifically a reference to a *chino* named Antonio Rodrigues who was a member of a motley crew of marginalized, mostly mixed-race individuals—8 Indians, 3 mulattos, 2 Blacks, 1 mestizo and 2 Spaniards—seeking their fortune on New Spain's far northern frontier and founding a settlement they named "Ciudad de Los Angeles" (City of Angels). In colonial Spanish terminology, the term *chino* by itself did not refer to a Chinese or an Asian, but rather; a dark-skinned person of mixed racial heritage. To refer to a Chinese or a person from Asia, the colonial records used the term *chinos de Manila*. Stan Steiner, *Fusang: The Chinese Who Built America* (New York: Harper & Row, 1979).

3. Watt, Stewart, *Chinese Bondage in Peru: A History of the Chinese Coolie in Peru, 1849–1874* (Durham, NC: Duke University Press, 1951); Evelyn Hu-DeHart, "Coolies, Shopkeepers, Pioneers: The Chinese of Mexico and Peru (1849–1930)," *Amerasia* 15 (1989): 91–116. During this period, about 1.5 million Chinese went overseas, to Southeast Asia, North America, as well as South America and the Caribbean, and other parts of the world. See Arnold Joseph Meagheir, "The Introduction of Chinese Laborers to Latin America and the 'Coolie Trade,' 1847–1874" (Ph.D. dissertation, UC Davis, 1975), p. 55. (This is an excellent piece of research that should have been published as an important contribution to an aspect of the international migration of labor in the nineteenth century.)

The approximately 225,000 Chinese who went to Cuba and Peru were almost exclusively males. So few women went under contract that they were statistically insignificant. A few women went as prostitutes (possibly sent from California by enterprising California Chinese) or free women. The Cuban census of 1872 noted 58,400 Chinese, of whom only 32 were females, 2 under contract, and 30 free. Of the 34,650 noted in the 1862 census, 25 were females. Of the 24,068 in the 1877 census, 8 were females (some possibly born in Cuba and Peru). These figures taken from C. M. Morales papers, vol. 3, no. 19, Biblioteca Nacional José Martí, Havana: Vidal Morales y Morales, "Inmigración de chinos en la Isla de Cuba. Datos que ha proporcionado el que suscrita a Mr. Sanger, Inspector General del Censo" (Collection of clippings, n.d.). The Peruvian census of 1872, which is incomplete, notes 12,849 Chinese in the four coastal provinces of Pacasmayo, Trujillo, Chiclayo, and Lambayeque where the Chinese population was concentrated; only 15 of them were females (Censo de 1872, Archivo General de Peru [AGP]).

4. After experimenting briefly with Chinese coolies in the early nineteenth century, the British exported massive numbers (1–2 million) of East Indian coolies to the West Indies and East Africa; for a comprehensive study of this coolie trade, see Hugh Tinker, *A New System of Slavery: The Export of Indian Labour Overseas: 1830–1920* (London: Oxford University Press, 1974).

5. Franklin Knight, *Slave Society in Cuba during the Nineteenth Century* (Madison: University of Wisconsin Press, 1970), p. 6.

6. Ibid., p. 22.

7. Cited in Humberto Rodriguez Pastor, *Hijos del Celeste Imperio en el Perú (1850–1900): Migración, Agricultura, Mentalidad y Explotación* (Lima: Instituto de Apoyo Agrario, 1988), p. 32.

8. Michael J. Gonzáles, *Plantation, Agriculture and Social Control in Northern Peru, 1875–1933* (Austin: University of Texas Press, 1985), p. 23.

9. Archivo Nacional de Cuba (ANC), Junta de Fomento, 147/7278. Also, Juan Jiménez Pastrana, *Los Chinos en la historia de Cuba, 1847–1930* (Havana: Ed. Ciencias Sociales, 1983), pp. 13–17.

10. Watt Stewart, *Chinese Bondage in Peru*, pp. 13–17; he gives the number of Chinese imported in 1849–1854 as 2,516. The figure of 4,754 was taken from Rodriguez Pastor, *Hijos del Celeste Imperio*, p. 27, Cuadro no. 4.

11. *Boletín de Colonización*, 1: 18, 15 Octobre 1873. The Boletin, published in 1873 and 1874, was the official organ of the powerful Junta (or Comisión) de Colonización, which had jurisdiction over the coolie trade and the coolies, whom it always and consistently termed *colonos* or *inmigrantes*. The president of the junta was the prominent planter and international businessman, Julián Zulueta, the same who introduced the first coolie cargo to Cuba in 1847. Zulueta exemplified what might be termed vertical integration in the sugar industry of Cuba.

12. Zhang Kai, "Guba Huagong yu ZhongGu jianjiao shimo" (Chinese Labor in Cuba and Establishment of Sino-Cuban Diplomatic Relations), *Huaqiao Huaren Lishi Yanjiu* (Overseas Chinese History Review) 4 (1988): 3–11.

13. Rodriguez Pastor, *Hijos del Celeste Imperio*, p. 39; Stewart, *Chinese Bondage in Peru*, pp. 117, 123.

14. "Actas de la comisión inspectors de asiáticos en la provincia de Santa," *El Peruano*, 29 April 1870; Rodriguez Pastor; *Hijos del Celeste Imperio*, p. 52. Many examples of recontracts in Cuba can be found in the ANC, Misc. de Exp., e.g. 4193/Cs, which contains several for 1868. The Archivo del Fuero Agrano account books for Peruvian plantations also contain much information on recontracted Chinese in the 1870s and 1880s.

15. Antonio Chuffat Latout, *Apunte histórico de los Chinos en Cuba* (Havana: Molina y Cia., 1927), p. 93; *Boletín de Colonización* 1:9, 30 May 1873, contains an editorial on the *cuadrillas*, describing them as dedicated "colectivamente a las faenas de la finca."

16. Gonzáles, *Plantation, Agriculture and Social Control*, pp. 71, 93.

17. *Boletín de Colonización* 1:18, 15 October 1873. By law, anyone residing in Cuba but not naturalized must be registered as an alien or foreign resident. As most Chinese in Cuba embarked from Macao, they registered generally with the Portuguese consul in Havana. Besides, there was no representation of the Chinese government in Havana at the time of the census (1872).

18. *Boletín de Colonización* 1:9, 30 May 1873 (Editoria); Denise Helly, *Ideólogie e ethnicité. Les Chinois Macao a Cuba, 1847–1886* (Montreal: Les Presses Universitaires de Montréal, 1979), pp. 231–37.

19. Rebecca Scott, *Slave Emancipation in Cuba: The Transition to Free Labor, 1860–1899* (Princeton, NJ: Princeton University Press, 1985), pp. 99–100, 110, 120.

20. Helly, *Ideólogie e ethnicité*, pp. 237–40.

21. Rodriguez Pastor, *Hijos del Celestre Imperio*, pp. 108, 121.

22. "Expediente sobre la averiguación practicada por la Comisión China asesorada por funcionarios del gobierno, respecto a la situación de sus connacionales que prestan sus servicios en las haciendas," Lima, 9 de mayo 1887–diciembre 1888. Biblioteca Nacional, Lima, Peru. This document, also based on testimonies taken from the Chinese (in this case, mostly ex-coolies, given the late date), is the Peruvian equivalent of the Chinese Commission to Cuba.

23. Rodriguez Pastor, *Hijos del Celeste Imperio*, pp. 145–46, 165.

24. A study of a small but important Chinese community in a sierra town is contained in Isabel Lausent, *Pequeña propiedad, poder y economía de mercado. Acos, Valle de Chancay* (Lima: Instituto de Estudios Peruanos, 1983).

25. Lausent is also the one who has published on the Chinese in the Peruvian Amazon: "Los inmigrantes chinos en la Amazonía Peruana," *Bulletin Institut François d'Etudes Andines* 15 (1986): 49–60.

26. Elsewhere I recount more fully the establishment of the Chinese community in Sonora and Mexican reaction: "Immigrants to a Developing Society: The Chinese in Northern Mexico, 1875–1932," *Journal of Arizona History* 21 (Autumn 1980): 49–86; "Racism and Anti-Chinese Persecution in Mexico," *Amerasia* 9 (1982): 1–28. See also Charles Cumberland, "The Sonoran Chinese and the Mexican Revolution," *Hispanic American Historical Review* 40 (1960): 191–211; Leo H. D. Jacques, "The Anti-Chinese Campaign in Sonora, Mexico, 1900–1931" (Ph.D. dissertation, University of Arizona, 1974).

27. The demographic discussion is based on the following sources: Mexican censuses for 1900, 1910, 1921, 1930; "Extranjeros residentes Estados Unidos de Mexico. Restimen del censo practicado por la Sría de Gobernación en 1927; y extranjeros, distribución por estados, 14 marzo 1928," Archivo Histórico del Gobierno e Estado de Sonora (AHGES), vol. 50, 1930; Consul A. Willard to State Department, Guaymas, 31 December 1887, U.S. National Archives, General Records of the Department of State, Record Group 59, M284, Roll 4, no. 851; Willard to State, 8 May 1890, RG59/M284/Roll 4, no. 983; Ramon Corral, *Memoria de la administración pública del estado de Sonora* (Guaymas, 1891), vol. 1, pp. 586–602; "Comisión oficial encargado del estudio de la inmigración asiática en México, 18 noviembre 1903," reports submitted by district prefects

in 1904, AHGES, vol. 1900; Sonora State Government, Census of Chinese residents, submitted by municipal presidents, 1919, AHGES, vol. 3345; "Estado de Sonora, Sección de Estadistica, Ailo de 1925, Censo Chino," AGHES, vol. 3741; Departamento de Trabajo. Sección de Conciliación. "Informe que rinde el Jefe de la Sección sobre la situación de las colonias asiaticas en la Costa Occidental de la Republica," 1919, Archivo General de la Nación/Trabajo, México, D.F.

28. International Chinese Business Directory, 1913.

29. Estado de Sonora. Sección de Estadistica. Año de 1925. "Censo Chino," AHGES, vol. 3741.

30. "Lista de los causantes sujetos a la contribución directa ordinaria que tienen capitales de $20,000 en adelante," AHGES, vol. 2968.

31. "Sociedades civiles y mercantiles en Sonora, 1912, 1917, 1918, 1919, 1920," taken from the Registro Público de la Propiedad (property registration) of each district, AHGES, vol. 3432.

32. "Noticia estadística comparativa de los giros comerciales e industriales con especificaciones de su capital invertido, de Nacionales y Chinos establecidos en el Estado de Sonora," 2 junio 1925, AHGES vol. 3758.

33. For a fuller discussion of the Chinese in Baja California Norte see my article "The Chinese of Baja California Norte, 1910–1934," Baja California and the North Mexican Frontier, Proceedings of the Pacific Coast Council on Latin American Studies, vol. 12 (San Diego, CA: San Diego State University Press, 1985–1986). This pattern of Chinese leasing land from U.S. landowners and contracting Chinese labor gangs to work the land is similar to what happened in California as described in Sucheng Chan, This Bittersweet Soil: The Chinese in California Agriculture, 1860–1910 (Berkeley, CA: University of California Press, 1986).

34. James L. Tigner, "Japanese immigration into Latin America: A Survey," Journal of Interamerican Studies and World Affairs 23, no. 4 (November 1981): 457–82. Despite their number and importance little has been published in Spanish or English on the Japanese in Brazil and Peru (though more may be published in Japanese). Among available works, in addition to Tigner are the following José Tiago Cintra, La Migración Japonesa en Brasil (1908–1959) (México. El Colegio de México, Centro de Estudios Orientales, 1974); C. Harvey Gardiner, The Japanese and Peru, 1873–1973 (Albuquerque: University of New Mexico Press, 1975); Amelia Morimoto, Los Inmigrantes Japoneses en el Perú (Lima: Taller de Estudios Andinos, Universidad Nacional Agraria, 1979); C. Harvey Gardiner, Pawns in a Triangle of Hate: The Peruvian Japanese and the United States (Seattle: University of Washington Press, 1981).

35. Tigner, "Japanese Immigration," p. 476.

36. Grant McCall, "European Impact on Easter Island: Response, Recruitment and the Polynesian Experience in Peru," Journal of Pacific History II, pt. 1 (1976): 90–105. See also H. E. Maude, Slavers in Paradise: The Peruvian Slave Trade in Polynesia, 1862–1864 (Stanford, CA: Stanford University Press, 1981).

37. Evelyn Hu-DeHart, "Asians in Latin America," Encyclopedia of Latin American History (forthcoming).

38. For an elaboration of this thesis on the two frontiers becoming an interna-

tional border; see Friedrich Katz, *The Secret War in Mexico: Europe, the United States and the Mexican Revolution* (Chicago: University of Chicago Press, 1981), Chapter 1.

39. Since the 1960s, Mexicans have been joined by increasing numbers of Central Americans going to *El Norte*. A good depiction of this migration is the film *El Norte*.

40. For a fuller discussion of Mexican labor immigration into the United States and the idea of the border as legal fiction, see James D. Cockcroft, *Outlaws in the Promised Land: Mexican Immigrant Workers and America's Future* (New York: Grove Press, 1986).

41. Andrew Reding, "Rebellion in Mexico," *The Washington Post*, January 11, 1994; Reding, "Chiapas is Mexico: The Imperative of Political Reform," *World Policy Journal* (Spring 1994), pp. 11–25; "Nafta and the Chiapas Crises," *Latin American Labor News*, Issue 9/1993–94, pp. 1 and 4; Greg Campbell, "The New Manifest Destiny: NAFTA and Oil Threaten Future of Chiapas Indian," *Boulder Weekly*, July 4, 1996, p. 8.

42. Julio Moguel, "Salinas's Failed War on Poverty," in Fred Rosen and Deidre McFadyen, eds., *Free Trade and Economic Restructuring in Latin America*. New York: Monthly Review Press, 1995, p. 210.

43. Gerardo Otero, "Mexico's Political Future(s) in a Globalizing Economy," *The Canadian Journal of Sociology and Anthropology* 32:3 (August 1995), pp. 315–339. See also Otero, ed., *Neo-Liberalism Revisited: Economic Restructuring and Mexico's Political Future*. Boulder: Westview Press, 1996.

44. Anthony DePalma, "Economic Lesson in a Border Town," *New York Times*, May 23, 1996, p. C1; Kelly Her, "Mexico's Luring Taiwan Investors," *The Free China Journal*, September 13, 1996, p. 8.

45. Barbara Stallings and Gabriel Szekely, "The New Trilateralism: The United States, Japan, and Latin America," in Stallings and Szekely, eds., *Japan, The United States, and Latin America: Toward a Trilateral Relationship in the Western Hemisphere*. Baltimore: Johns Hopkins, 1993, pp. 33–34.

46. Gabriel Szekely, "Mexico's International Strategy: Looking East and North," in Barbara Stallings and Gabriel Szekely, eds., *Japan, the United States, and Latin America: Toward a Trilateral Relationship in the Western Hemisphere*. Baltimore: Johns Hopkins, 1993, pp. 159–160.

47. Bob Herbert, "In Deep Denial," *New York Times*, October 13, 1995, p. A15.

# 12

# The Asia-Pacific in Asian-American Perspective

## ARIF DIRLIK

In this chapter, I discuss some issues arising from the conceptualization of an Asia-Pacific regional formation from an Asian-American perspective—by which I mean not just the perspective of Asian Americans, but a perspective on the Asia-Pacific region that recognizes an Asian-American presence within its field of vision. The issues are derivative of questions that writers on the Asian-American experience (themselves mostly Asian Americans) have raised in the course of elucidating and defining that experience. It is a fundamental assumption of Asian-American historiography that the locus of Asian-American history is imbedded in the history of the United States. I am quite aware that carrying these questions over into a discussion of the Asia-Pacific region idea takes them into a realm unintended by their authors and in some cases contrary to their intentions.

It is my contention, however, that problems of Asian-American history are also problems in the history of an Asia-Pacific regional formation. Although studies of the Asian-American experience do not usually relate their subject matter to an Asia-Pacific *problematic* (with the notable exception of migration studies), an Asia-Pacific context is unavoidably implicit in much of the writing on Asian Americans, and the relationship of Asian-Americans to their trans-Pacific origins is a matter of urgent, sometimes acrimonious, controversy. I suggest here that in an almost trivial sense the presence of Asian Americans (and the very term itself) invokes an Asia-Pacific regional formation—as both its condition and its effect. Rendering the regional dimension explicit is intended not to deny Asian Americans an integral part in the national history of the United States, but rather to re-view the national history within the context of a broader regional perspective and to question the ways in which it has been conceived and written. Conversely, the fact that Asian Americans have suffered racist subordination and cultural denial for their regional affiliation is revealing of a deep-seated contradiction that historically has characterized attitudes toward the Asia-Pacific region on the part of the hegemonic culture in the United States and problematizes the part the United States has played (or might play) in the regional formation. Finally, the efforts of Asian Americans to cope with their situation have produced cultural forms that may have much to tell us about Asia-Pacific as social and cultural construct—that point at once to a regional formation with its own social and cultural features, and local formations that resist their ingestion into a homogeneous national or regional identity.

My discussion is of necessity illustrative rather than comprehensive. Although I do my best to be circumspect with generalizations, the very term "Asian Americans" implies important blind spots that need to be spelled out from the beginning, especially in a discussion that conjoins the Asian-American experience to an Asia-Pacific regional formation. First, the "American" side of the term, which identifies a continental notation with a national entity. Although this usage has the sense of an almost unalterable convention, it is necessary to note, especially in a discussion considering human motions as a fundamental constituent of a regional formation, that the flow of Asian peoples to the United States has been only part of the flow to the Americas, which include not only Canada but Latin American societies; the latter are barely included in discussions of Asia-Pacific in our day, even though the relationship between Spanish America and East and Southeast Asia played an important part initially in the formation of a Pacific region. In the middle decades of the nineteenth century, the Chinese (the primary group of Asians at the time) populations of Cuba and Peru exceeded in numbers that in the United States.[1]

The "Asian" component is even more problematic, as it encompasses people of diverse national, cultural, linguistic, and racial origins who would seem to share only two things in common: origins somewhere in Asia and a common experience of oppression and discrimination peculiar to Asians at the hands of a hegemonic culture that imposed a racist and culturalist homogeneity as "Asiatics" or "orientals" on otherwise vastly different peoples.[2] The term "Asian Americans" is a product of the radical movements of the late 1960s, when different groups of U.S. citizens of Asian descent sought to counter such oppression and discrimination by establishing coalitions of those who shared in the experience of this particular form of oppression—the goal being less to assert their identity as "Asians," although that was inescapable, than to underline that in spite of its particular form, the oppression of U.S. citizens of Asian descent had much in common with the oppression of other "Third World" peoples, within and outside the United States (within the United States, these included Native Americans, Afro-Americans, Latino Americans, and others).[3] The term, in other words, was not so much a descriptive term as a product of a coalition-building political discourse; but as such, it was to enter the intellectual and academic discipline of "Asian-American studies," which was itself a product of the radical movement for social and cultural emancipation. Asian Americans themselves have been quite aware of the question of diversity ("Is there such an ethnic group?" queried a Filipino-American activist in the subtitle to a book on the subject)[4] as well as of the fact that different groups of Asians have been at odds with one another at different times. Viewing Asian Americans in Asia-Pacific perspective underlines this diversity, although the reverse is also true: common experiences in the course of a regional formation have brought together peoples originally quite remote from one another. Most important, the term requires sensitivity in light of the continued racist confounding of one Asian group for another. Finally, the term "Asian Americans" does not explicitly recognize the growing presence in the United States of peoples of Pacific origin, which has led one author recently to speak of "Asian Pacific Americans." It is not surprising that the author, Stephen Sumida, is of Hawaiian origin.[5] Once again, this is a reminder that is especially important in discussions of Asia-Pacific, which are on the whole oblivious to the Pacific islands around which, ironically, Asia-Pacific as a regional formation first took recognizable shape.

## Asian Americans and Asia-Pacific as Regional Formation

Writers on the Asia-Pacific region as a rule point to the intensity of capital and commodity flows, or political and military relationships to argue the reality of a regional construct. What is missing from most discussions of the subject is what may be the most fundamental—and enduring— element in an Asia-Pacific regional formation: the motions of people that have produced human networks that endow the region with a social reality and inscribed upon it the cultural features of trans-Pacific experiences. Asian Americans are prominently visible in these motions. Although the Asian-American experience bears upon it the stamp of its particular context in the history of the United States, it is important to note here that this experience shares certain common features with the experiences of Asian and Pacific peoples moving in alternative directions across the Pacific, for all these motions shared a common context in an Asian-Pacific regional formation, of which they were at once a product and an integrative ingredient.

I say "product," because a regional formation was the premise of Asian and Pacific peoples' migration to the United States. Asian and Pacific migrations coincide with the development of a capitalist world economy in the Pacific, which from the late eighteenth century on integrated the region economically (we might say *produced* the region as we know it today), gathering force by mid-nineteenth century with the development of the west coasts of the United States and Canada, of Australia and New Zealand, and of the plantation economies of Hawaii, Peru, and Cuba. This is not to say that there were no migrations in the region before capitalism. The Americas were initially populated by peoples from Asia (as were the Pacific islands). There were localized migrations and trade in the South Pacific. And of course, Chinese migrated to Southeast Asia in numbers from the fifteenth and sixteenth centuries onward, although that movement already coincided with the arrival of Europeans in the region. But the Pacific as we know it today did not exist until the late eighteenth century, and it was not until the nineteenth century that Asian migrations assumed a large scale and coherent direction: toward areas that with sustained economic development were emerging as economic cores.

Recent studies have adopted a world system approach as the most comprehensive framework for understanding Asian and Pacific migration to the United States. In the ground-breaking volume edited by Lucie Cheng and Edna Bonacich, *Labor Immigration Under Capitalism: Asian Workers in the United States Before World War II*, the editors described their theoretical framework "schematically" as follows:

> Capitalist development leads to imperialism, which in turn distorts the development of colonized territories. As a result, many people were displaced from their traditional economic pursuits, becoming available for emigration. Meanwhile, as the original capitalist society develops, its requirements for labor, especially cheap labor, increase. These two conditions, the displacement of colonized peoples and the requirement of more labor in the capitalist economy, arise out of the logic of capitalist development. And both result in pressure for people to migrate as workers to the more advanced capitalist countries. In other words, migration is a product not of discrete and unconnected factors in the sending and receiving societies but of historical connections between the countries. It is not fortuitous; it is systemic.[6]

A more recent study of migration patterns in the Pacific, *Pacific Bridges: The New Immigration from Asia and the Pacific Islands*,[7] although retaining a world system approach, introduces refinements into the analysis to account for complexities that have become evident in Asian migration since World War II (although the complexities were there before then), especially since 1965 when changes in the United States immigration laws led to a flood of Asian and Pacific immigrants to the United States. The dynamics of migration are still rooted in a world capitalist system and the motions of people from the peripheries to the core(s) of this system. In this more complex understanding of the world system, eschewing economistic reductionism, migration is no longer a direct function of the activities of capital, but is intermediated by the structures (not merely economic, but political, military, social, and cultural as well) of the capitalist world system. The approach also (implicitly) takes into account changes in structure that have accompanied the transnationalization of capital, which include the emergence to core status of formerly precapitalist states that have introduced considerable confusion into earlier notions of core and periphery. What Alejandro Portes describes in his contribution as the "relational dynamics within a global order" include in addition to labor flows induced by the motions of capital, international relations (among which political and military relationships are prominent), refugee movements spawned by wars and revolutions, and students, all of which may be accounted for by reference to the capitalist world system, but also have an autonomous dynamic of their own that is not reducible to capital-labor relations within the world system.[8]

Unlike "push-pull" analyses of migration (with factors "pushing" people out of the country of origin and factors "pulling" them to the country of arrival treated as if they were isolated from one another), the world system analysis of migration presupposes a regional formation. Factors of "push" and "pull" appear in this kind of analysis, therefore, as related outcomes of the regional formation. Even more important, perhaps, the regional formation provides the medium (through networks of interaction, organized formally or informally)[9] that makes migration possible. In this perspective, then, the very existence of an Asian-American population presupposes a regional formation rooted in the capitalist world system.

"Push-pull" analyses of migration stress local conditions in sending and receiving societies as if these conditions were independent of one another; world system analysis posits ties between these localities as parts of a broader regional formation. The contributors to *Labor Immigration Under Capitalism* do not deny differences between localities, but argue only that differences must be perceived within the context of a system dynamized by capital and the needs it creates for labor, which implies that large-scale migration is not fortuitous but is a product of those needs. Differences between localities in this approach are as likely to be creations of the regional formation as they are legacies to the regional formation of the precapitalist past.

The world system approach successfully explains a number of basic features of the motions of people across the Pacific, including the direction of these motions—which by the very premises of the analysis is from the less developed peripheries to the advanced core areas—and the timing of migration. The analysis shows that large-scale Asian migration to the United States coincides with the economic development of the North American West in the nineteenth century and the labor needs created by such development—mining and railroads on the continent and the plantation economy in Hawaii even before it became a part of the United States.[10] Incidentally, the situation was similar with Asian flows to other parts of the Pacific, such as Latin America and Australia.

This world system approach points to an important element in understanding the fate of Asian immigrants in the United States, which was bound up with conflicts between labor and capital. Labor opposition to Asian immigration was largely responsible for exclusionary policies toward Asian labor, beginning with the Chinese exclusion law of 1882 and culminating in the 1924 immigration law prohibiting the immigration to the United States of "aliens ineligible to citizenship." Although this opposition was most striking for the racist language in which it was expressed (of which more later), it is important nevertheless that the opposition was part of the struggle of labor against big business and the exploitation of Asian labor by the latter to hold down labor in general. In Hawaii, the competition took the form of competition among different Asian populations, with the plantation owners playing one against another to undercut labor resistance to exploitation; hence the importation successively of Chinese, Japanese, Koreans, and Filipinos to deal with labor problems.

Finally, a world system analysis also helps account for changes over the years in the *kind* of labor immigrating to the United States. In the early years of immigration to the United States, manual laborers predominated, although not all immigrants were manual laborers. By contrast, Asian immigrants to the United States over the past twenty-five years have included an increasingly significant number of professionals of one kind or another, reflecting changes both in Asian societies and in labor needs in the United States. The change, I might add, seems to correspond to changes in the capitalist world system as a whole and the increasing dependence of core countries on the importation of professional labor from peripheral societies.[11]

Two aspects to the Asia-Pacific regional formation do not appear in these studies with the importance they deserve, and I would like to stress them here. First, because they tend to employ world system analysis at a high level of abstraction, the authors show insufficient regard for differences between different regions of the globe. Neither study emphasizes what seems to me to be a peculiar feature of the Asia-Pacific regional formation: that although it was EuroAmerican capitalism that produced the region as an economic region, the people who filled out the region with their motions (and their labors) have been predominantly Asian and

Pacific peoples.[12] The conflict between capital and labor (or core and peripheral societies for that matter) appears in this region therefore simultaneously as a racial and cultural conflict, which has determined the language in which social and political relationships are expressed. To complicate matters, given the racial and cultural diversity of the inhabitants of the region, such conflict has not been restricted to conflicts between labor and capital, or peripheral versus core societies, but has extended to conflict among the inhabitants of the region themselves, undermining, against the reality of economic integration, the possibility of a regional formation. I will return to this question below.

Second, in their preoccupation with the motive forces of migration, these authors do not emphasize with sufficient force that people's motions across the Pacific were not just a product of regional formation, but were themselves an integrative ingredient of the region, because in the ties that migrant societies retained to their societies of origin, they contributed both to the formation of the region and to its consolidation at a fundamental, social level. In this perspective, the Asian-American presence is not merely an expression of an Asia-Pacific regional formation, but a fundamental constituent of such a formation because Asian Americans' relationships to their society of origin provide, to use a commonly encountered metaphor, "bridges" across the Pacific. Herein lies the Asia-Pacific element in Asian-American history.

This question is not unrelated to the first question above. There may be good reasons why Asian-American history has downplayed this Asia-Pacific aspect of Asian-American historiography. Regarded as "strangers" from the beginning because of their cultural and racial affinities, Asian Americans have suffered discrimination, oppression, and exclusion, which makes for a certain reluctance among Asian-American scholars to speak of this Asia-Pacific dimension of Asian-American history, emphasizing instead the "Americanness" of the Asian-American experience.[13] Further contributing to this reluctance, I suspect, is the diversity of Asian Americans that an emphasis on their Asia-Pacific affinities underlines, undermining the coalition-building political discourse to which I referred above. Sympathies for societies of origin that have been in conflict with one another on and off over the last century have also brought different groups of Asian Americans into violent conflict with one another, on occasion playing into the hands of the hegemonic culture of which they were all victims. The question nevertheless is important not only for understanding Asian-American history, but also for appreciating the role Asian Americans have played both in the constitution of an Asia-Pacific region and for what their diversity may reveal concerning the tenuousness of such a regional formation.

In the remainder of this section I will illustrate briefly Asian Americans' ties across the Pacific that justify a perspective that places their experiences within an Asia-Pacific context. I will return in later sections to the problems Asian Americans have faced because of these ties and what those problems may reveal about the relationship of the United States to Asia-Pacific, and the Asia-Pacific idea itself.

Most important among these ties are kinship and other social (such as regional) ties, which bound Asian immigrants to their society of origin and to some extent shaped their behavior in the United States. Portes has emphasized the role in migration of "network structures of migration," which he describes as structures that stabilize people's motions "by adapting to shifting economic conditions and by generating new opportunities apart from the original incentives."[14] Among these networks, kinship networks have played an especially significant part in the migration of Asian and Pacific peoples to the United States. It is easy to exaggerate the strength of such ties due to stereotyped notions about the "clannishness" of Asians, which long served as a reason for discrimination against Asian Americans (overlooking that "clannishness" might have been a product of discrimination). In their investigations among Chinese in Chinatown, San Francisco, Victor and Brett deBary Nee found that even among those who had come to the United States as "sojourners" (as was typical of early immigrants from Asia—and other places as well), memories of home faded with the passage of time and the realization that there would be no going back.[15] Nevertheless, where emigration abroad was not so much a matter of individual choice but of family survival strategy (as it was in most of these cases) by adding to the income of the family through the labor of members abroad, family ties retained considerable strength. It was even possible for families to exert pressure on wayward sons through formal or informal social networks when they failed to perform their duties, such as failing to send home the remittances that were expected of them.[16] These ties were reinforced by discriminatory laws against Asians in the United States. The prohibition of marriage between whites and "Mongolians" in many Western states forced Asian immigrants to look "home" to find mates. Such discrimination perpetuated the practice of arranged marriages and therefore the hold of the family on the individual.[17] Conversely, kinship ties provided a medium that facilitated further immigration. As June Mei has written of Chinese-Americans:

> It was well-known in Guangdong that a few Chinese emigrants did indeed "strike it rich" during their stay abroad. Some used their money to extend loans to others who needed funds to cross the Pacific. The most likely recipients of such loans would be people known either directly or indirectly to the creditor—in other words, people from his own district. Conversely, with

a number of their kinsmen already in the United States and returning as lenders to China, job seekers from Siyi (one of the two major areas of emigration from Guangdong) had a better chance of obtaining loans through the credit-ticket system than did men from other parts of Guangdong. The importance of clan and regional ties in expediting emigration from certain areas should not be underestimated.[18]

Family ties have also played a major part in recent immigration from Asia, with family members of U.S. citizens and permanent residents constituting by far the predominant portion.[19]

An important economic by-product of kinship ties is the economic consequence of remittances. Although only a few would argue that remittances have contributed significantly to the economic development of the countries of origin, these remittances have been quite significant in volume and may have important consequences at the level of the local community, both in increasing the wealth of the community as a whole and in the redistribution of wealth in favor of emigrants' families.[20] They may also have long-term effects, I might add, both economically and culturally, as communities come to depend on outside sources for their income.

Finally, social ties between immigrant Asian communities and the countries of origin were not entirely haphazard, although the level of organization and its nature differed from one Asian group to another. In the case of Japanese Americans, social ties took the form almost of administrative control, as Japanese consuls became closely involved in the regulation of Japanese-American communities, in cooperation with local associations that were formed in the United States. The "Six Companies" in Chinatowns, a federation of locally oriented associations imported from China, were informal and yet they played a central part both in the organization of Chinatowns and the regulation of relationships between American Chinese and China.[21] Religious organizations of one kind or another have played comparable organizational roles in Korean and Indian communities.

Ironically, discrimination and oppression may have played an important part in perpetuating social ties of Asian Americans to countries of origin in ano 'her sense. Due to prohibitions against the immigration of women, Asian-American communities initially were bachelor societies. The prohibition against marriage with white women, as I noted above, forced them to look "home" for mates. But there was another product of such discrimination: it stunted the growth of a native Asian-American population, with the result that at any one time newly arrived immigrants have made up a substantial portion of the Asian-American population— except during the years of exclusion. After nearly a century and a half of Asian-American history, the newly arrived immigrants in most cases still make up half or more of the Asian-American populations today—with the exception of Japanese-Americans, once the largest group among Asian Americans, but relatively ever smaller as there has been little immigration from Japan since 1965.[22] Given that newly arrived immigrants are more likely to have strong ties to their country of origin than native-born Asian Americans, it may not be surprising that social ties of the kind discussed above loom large as a characteristic of Asian Americans in the United States. They do contribute significantly, nevertheless, to the constitution of Asia-Pacific as a *social* entity.

In addition, ties across the Pacific are also visible in the movements and organizations of a political nature that over the years involved Asian Americans in the political of their society of origin. The involvement of Chinese Americans in Chinese politics around the turn of the century, according to Eve Armentrout Ma, "altered their social structure and social order in a way that was probably more profound than anything that has taken place in the Chinatowns of the Americas up until the late 1970s."[23] The relationship of Chinese Americans to the People's Republic of China versus the Republic of China in Taiwan was to emerge as another divisive issue in the 1960s. Chinese Americans have also been involved in recent developments in Chinese socialism.

Similar ties are to be found among other Asian-American groups. Japanese Americans of the first generation (the *issei*) rallied to the support of Japanese government policies during the Sino-Japanese War (1894–1895), the Russo-Japanese War (1904–1905), World War I, and Japan's invasion of China from July 1937 to the beginning of the war between Japan and the United States. Conversely, radical and labor movements among Japanese Americans around the turn of the century had a significant impact on radical movements in Japan.[24] Political ties were most obsessively evident in the case of Korean Americans, for whom emigration to the United States appeared also as a political diaspora with Korea's annexation to Japan as a colony after 1910. As with Chinese Americans, the division of Korea (into north and south) after World War II was to complicate political ties to the society of origin among Korean Americans.[25] Issues arising from colonialism and national division have similarly affected Filipino and Southeast Asian Americans.

The issue of political ties is impossible to encapsulate in a brief space not just because of its complexities but more important because of its sensitivities for the groups involved and the whole question of Asian Americans as a group. More than one observer has suggested, validly in my opinion, that the exclusion of Asian Americans from politics in the United States helped perpetuate political ties across the Pacific; although such observations need to be qualified in light of the continuation of such ties even after World War II, when it became possible for Asian Americans to participate in U.S. politics.[26]

Most important, however, the question is sensitive both because of its implications for the status of Asian Americans in United States society and for its implications for the relationships of Asian Americans to one another. In the eyes of the dominant white population in the United States, which conveniently overlooked its denial of political rights to Asian Americans, the perception of political ties between Asian Americans and their society of origin rendered the former suspect as Americans, of which the most tragic consequence was the internment of Japanese Americans in concentration camps during World War II. These political ties also divided Asian Americans internally. The internment of Japanese Americans was welcomed by Chinese, Korean, and Filipino Americans, whose homelands had been colonized or invaded by Japan. Political ties on occasion even led to divisions within the same group. Chinese and Korean Americans have been divided over the years by conflicting loyalties to opposing political groupings in their society of origin. Ichioka has suggested that the support of first-generation Americans for Japan's policies in Asia even created a serious rift between the *issei* and their American-born children.[27] Such divisions imply that the various conflicts among and within Asian societies (as well as between the United States and Asian countries) have been replicated among Asian Americans and call into question the description of these peoples as a single ethnic minority. Divisions continue to this day as contests for power continues in the Asia-Pacific region.

As the Asia-Pacific region flourishes economically, another kind of tie between Asian Americans and their society of origin emerges to the foreground: economic ties. Such ties are not new; Asian Americans have been involved all along in the exchange of commodities between the United States and the various countries of immigrant origin. These ties have acquired a new significance, however, with the economic emergence of Asian societies and a simultaneous economic decline in the United States, which has intensified global competition for East Asian markets and capital. This has led to a new perception of Asian Americans as economic bridges between the United States and Asian countries, offering an edge for the United States within an overall regional economy.[28] The exact nature of these ties is yet unclear, and their significance probably belongs to a future yet to come. Suffice it to say here that this development may be more responsible than the factors described above for bringing to the foreground the Asia-Pacific ties of Asian Americans.

The final set of ties, and in my view the most fundamental, are cultural ties. They are fundamental not because they have played an integrative role in a regional formation comparable to the factors above—on the contrary, the issue of culture brings out fundamental ambiguities in the regional formation—but because culture, however perceived at different times by different protagonists, has provided the medium through which more concrete ties have been endowed with meaning. I will, therefore, return to the issue of culture after a few words on the national history of the United States as it appears in Asian-American perspective.

## Asian Americans, Asia-Pacific, and the United States: National History in Regional Perspective

Given the locus of Asian-American history within the national history of the United States, the trans-Pacific ties of Asian Americans would suggest that there has been all along an Asia-Pacific element in the construction of the United States as a national entity. Historically, however, a reverse image has been dominant. A culturally constructed definition of the United States has excluded any suggestion that the United States might be something other than a transplantation of a European civilization on the North American continent. To the extent that the trans-Pacific ties of Asian Americans have been recognized within the dominant culture, therefore, this recognition has served primarily to deny their "American-ness"—and their history. From the perspective of this dominant culture, the Pacific contrasts sharply with an Atlantic region. Ties across the Atlantic have derived their perceived cohesiveness ultimately from assumptions about a metahistorical cultural affinity between the United States and Europe. On the other side of the continent, even as the United States declared the Pacific to be an extension of its "Manifest Destiny," this same cultural self-image rendered the Pacific an alien territory, peopled by alien cultures that must be overcome in the realization of that destiny; the Pacific, in other words, must be conquered by remaking it in the U.S. image. The place assigned to Asian Americans in the history of the United States has been bound up with a profound ambivalence toward the Asia-Pacific articulated within the national history.

From the eighteenth century on, the United States was involved economically in the construction of an Asia-Pacific region, which set in motion the forces that would bring Asians to U.S. shores. Asian Americans in turn, in their trans-Pacific ties, introduced an Asia-Pacific element into the construction of the United States as a national entity. The history of the relationship of the United States to the Pacific, however, has been written entirely in terms of a U.S. expansion into the Pacific, an extension beyond the western shores of the continent of the same Manifest Destiny that had carried Americans across the continent, ultimately making the Pacific into a U.S. lake. The Asia-Pacific contribution to the construction of the United States has remained unacknowledged, suppressed beneath the cultural myth of a Manifest Destiny. The recovery of this Asian-American contribution to the history of the United States exposes a national history written as westward expansion as a hegemonic cultural construct; it also points to a profound ambivalence toward Asia-Pacific on the part of this hegemonic culture.

Asian-American scholarship has demonstrated that beginning with the Chinese in the middle of the nineteenth century, and well into the twentieth century, Asian labor made a significant contribution to the economic development of the North American West, from mining to railroad building to agriculture and fisheries.[29] One contemporary wrote, referring to the Chinese: "Without them the railroads could not have been built, nor the agricultural—and perhaps not even the mining—industries developed as they are."[30] The contribution was symbolized most dramatically in the contribution of Chinese labor to the building of the Central Pacific railroad, which when conjoined to the Union Pacific at Promontory Point, Utah, in 1869, symbolized the final unification of the continent. And as Chinese, and following them, Japanese laborers moved eastward from California and Washington with the railroads and expanding mining industries, they brought with them their trans-Pacific ties and their everyday cultures. Sam Wong's *English-Chinese Phrase Book*, printed in 1875, Frank Chin tells us, was distributed through Wells Fargo offices through nearly four hundred large and small Chinatowns scattered across the country west of the Mississippi.[31]

And yet even where such contribution was recognized, the Asian remained an exotic outsider. The same author who acknowledged the Chinese contribution to the building of the railroads observed that Chinese immigration had given San Francisco "the aspect of a settlement in the Flowery Kingdom."[32] Another contemporary observer, equally sympathetic, wrote in 1880:

> While gratifying my curiosity, and experiencing the pleasure of studying the habits and customs of a strange people during the recent Chinese civil and religious festival of the new year, it occurred to me that a short article giving the result of these observations might be of interest to readers, many of whom never have had, and possibly never will have, the opportunity to examine for themselves any of the peculiarities of this alien Asiatic race at present sojourning on the shores of the Pacific, apparently unaffected by contact with our Anglo-Saxon civilization. . . . Within a circle whose radius is half a mile, in the heart of an intensely Western American city, itself the growth of little more than a quarter of a century, is found what we might call an Asiatic colony, and a colony bringing with it and retaining in its new home all the characteristics of its Chinese parentage. Traverse but a few

feet, and the dividing line between a Mongolian and a Caucasian civilization, usually measured by an ocean, is crossed.[33]

Not without charm in their fascination with the exotic Chinese, these observations are testaments nevertheless to a generally agreed upon perception of the strangeness of the Chinese "sojourning" on the U.S. shore of the Pacific, separated by an "ocean" from "our Anglo-Saxon" civilization within the confines of the same city—a city that is itself only a quarter of a century old, but in the construction of which the Chinese population appears not as an integral part but rather as an exotic "Asiatic colony." It is not the status they assign to the Chinese in the growing civilization of the United States, but rather their sympathy for the exotic "Mongolian civilization" that distinguishes these writers from others who in the very same years called for and successfully achieved the exclusion of Chinese from immigration to the United States (1882). Those who wrote these lines objected to the rampant "anti-oriental" agitation in California, but the agitators themselves used the very same descriptions, in their case a cause for hostility to the Chinese, as the reason for their agitation.

As early as 1852, recent immigrants from Europe joined native-born Americans in demonstrating against the Chinese in San Francisco and calling for a "California for Americans."[34] The Chinese and subsequently other "Asiatics" were (in Ronald Takaki's term) "strangers," unassimilable to the "Anglo-Saxon civilization" that was to define United States culture. By 1924, all Asians, "ineligible for citizenship," were to be excluded from immigration to the United States. With that, their contribution to the construction of the United States was also "forgotten." In the recent fictional recreation of this history is Frank Chin's *Donald Duk*,[35] the Chinese-American boy Donald wonders as he comes of age why there are no Chinese in the pictures from Promontory Point in 1869, although Chinese labor had been crucial to taking the Central Pacific to where it met the Union Pacific. As they were left out of the photographs, so were they taken out of history, not to be recalled into it until recently in Asian-American historiography.

In the exclusion of Asians from the United States, the struggle between labor and capital played a prominent part. White laborers, concerned with the use of "docile" Asian labor by capital to deepen the exploitation of labor, played a vanguard role in the calls for Asian exclusion. Although the concerns may have been legitimate, they were expressed in a racist language that led to the racist oppression of a minority and the suppression of the part that the latter had played (and continued to play) in the construction of the United States as a nation. Labor did not invent racism, of course, and in some ways to view the problem of Asian Americans merely as a problem of race is misleading. In the exclusion from the United States of East Indians, who technically speaking were of the same race as the "Anglo-Saxons," the legal decision specifically stated that it was color, not race, that was the issue.[36] From its founding, the United States was conceived as a "white" civilization, and nonwhites were to be excluded from it.[37]

In order to appreciate the U.S. Asia-Pacific "problem," however, neither race nor color are sufficient categories. What has distinguished the Asian-American experience from that of other minorities subjected to racist or color oppression is an additional element: the element of culture; or as stated in the quotation above, the confrontation between "Anglo-Saxon" and "Mongolian" civilizations, which rendered the situation into a metahistorical problem of a confrontation between Eastern and Western civilizations.

In a letter he wrote to the Secretary of State in 1920, arguing for the prohibition of landownership by Japanese Americans (in effect since 1913), then governor of California William D. Stephens wrote:

We stand today at this point of western contact with the Orient, just as the Greeks who settled in Asia Minor three thousand years ago stood at its eastern point. And while Mesopotamia and the country to the east thereof were the highways of the intercourse between the Orient of that era and the Occident of that era, and while historically, there was much of contact and conflict between the types representing the two standards of civilization, history does not show any material fusion of either blood or idea between the two peoples.[38]

To Governor Stephens history was irrelevant before a metahistorical confrontation between two civilizations, oriental and occidental. So was geography. Americans such as the governor, facing west on the shores of the Pacific, saw the East. Geography, no less than history, was culturally constructed. In this cultural construction U.S. history itself appeared not as a historical product, to the construction of which many diverse peoples had made significant contributions, but rather as a cultural construct that excluded from the history those who did not fit in with its culturalist premises. Essential to those premises was the Eurocentric premise of the United States as an Anglo-Saxon civilization, ever moving west. The Pacific, which seemed so inviting as a space in this westward march of European (or "occidental") civilization, became a threat when it appeared on western U.S. shores in the persons of an Asian population in a possible eastern expansion from the other side of the ocean.

A contributor to *Harper's Magazine* wrote in 1900 that it was California, with all its wealth, part of which at least came from its Pacific connections, that had made the United States possible:

Our real West dates from California. It is not enough to remember that Minnesota, Oregon, Kansas, Nevada, Nebraska, Colorado, the two Dakotas, Montana, Washington, Idado, Wyoming, Utah, have been admitted as States, and New Mexico, Arizona, Oklahoma, and Alaska organized as Territories, since California came into the Union. The pertinent question is how many of them we should have if there had been no California. . . . The United States was mostly content to remain a narrow huddle of provinces when California, suddenly and almost empirically, unrolled our trivial halfway map to another ocean and gave us a national span, and pulled along population enough to vindicate the map. To this day there are many excellent people who never reflect what Uncle Sam's stature would have been if he had slept on with Canada as his head, Mexico for a foot-board, and his back against a British wall somewhere about the Platte.[39]

Arguing that "even American progress has to have reasons," the author went on to suggest that not only was California responsible for the physical unification of the continent by the railroads (without California, he stated, "there was not, nor has been, any other reason for mileages over three thousand"), but also for the shaping of the "American character" which was "woven of more threads than the stout one of birth."[40] We may note here not only that the spaces between the eastern United States and California were filled thanks to California, as this author suggests, but also as Asian American writers have argued, that those spaces were filled out from the west as well as from the east, and Asian Americans played a significant part with their labors in filling out those spaces. Asian American historiography, in recalling Asian Americans into the history of the United States, has made a significant contribution to U.S. historiography by challenging its dominant paradigm of an expanding western frontier and showing that there was an eastern frontier as well, with a significant Asian presence on its outposts. This is not to deny the significance of a western frontier, but only to recall that that western frontier in addition to exterminating (physically or culturally) the Native Americans who stood in its way, also had to roll back an Asian-American presence that for a while promised to add a significant Asian aspect to the visage of the United States in the role it played in the U.S. West. As Victor and Brett deBary Nee have written:

The arrival of . . . Chinese pioneers to the shores of California signalled the beginning of the first large-scale migration of a free, non-white people to the North American continent and with it California became the final battleground for the borders of the European New World. The struggle that followed unleashed on members of the Chinese race the same fury and violence with which large regions of the continent had already been won from the American Indians. The struggle left on the North American continent an infinitesimal minority of a people whose settlements had once spanned the Far West from the Rocky Mountains and the Sierra Nevadas to the swamplands of California and the deserts of the Southwest . . . through the defeat of Chinese migration by the passage of the Chinese Exclusion Act and the forceful expulsion of thousands of Chinese from the Far Western states, the entire North American continent had been secured as an extension of Western Europe and a preserve for the migration and regeneration of the European race.[41]

In the perception of the hegemonic "Anglo-Saxon" culture in the United States, Asian Americans were irretrievably Asians. Their trans-Pacific ties, of the kind discussed above, served not to further recognition of an Asian presence in the national formation of the United States, but to deny its members' "Americanness." The Asia-Pacific element they had introduced into the historical development of the United States was suppressed by a cultural construction of the United States as a western extremity of "occidental" civilization that faced the east in the west, as Asian Americans were suppressed in actuality by rolling back the inroads they had made into U.S. society thus conceived. The Asia-Pacific region, then, rather than a constituent of U.S. history, appeared as the next frontier to be conquered by this Occidental civilization.

## Cultural Hegemony/Cultural Resistance: Region, Nation, and Locality in Asian-American Discourse on Culture

Denied their Americanness because of their Asian origins and ties, Asian Americans as they have claimed their place in the history of the United States have done so by also reasserting their identity as Asians. The constitution of an Asian American cultural identity, one that is at once Asian *and* American, has been problematic for two reasons. First, an Asian-American identity presupposes rejection of a U.S. history without Asians as well as of an Asian culture without history (implicit in the affirmation of the Asianness of American Asians), problematizing the notions both of Asianness and Americanness; the elements out of which such a new identity is to be constructed, in other words, must be reconstituted themselves in the very process of constituting an Asian-American identity. Fixed notions of identity, therefore, give way to ethnic cultural identity as a historical process with unpredictable outcomes. This renders the process itself, into a contest both among Asian Americans themselves and between Asian Americans and the hegemonic culture that provides the immediate context for the constitution of such an identity; especially over the question of whether such an identity in the process of its formation should seek assimilation into its cultural environment or assert itself as a culture of resistance that should seek in constituting itself also to reconstitute its cultural environment. The question of Asian Americans' relationship to the cultures of their society of origin has been inextricably tied in with the question of their relationship to U.S. society.

These problems were sharply articulated early on in Asian-Americans' self-assertion in a remarkable essay, "Racist Love," written by two Chinese-American authors, Frank Chin and Jeffery Paul Chan. As the authors bluntly put it,

> White racism enforces white supremacy. White supremacy is a system of order and a way of perceiving reality. Its purpose is to keep whites on top and set them free. Colored minorities in white reality are stereotypes. Each racial stereotype comes in two models, the acceptable model and the unacceptable model. . . . The unacceptable model is unacceptable because he cannot be controlled by whites. The acceptable model is acceptable because he is tractable. . . . If the system works, the stereotypes assigned to the various races are accepted by the races themselves as reality, as fact, and racist love reigns. . . . One measure of the success of white racism is the silence of that race and the amount of white energy necessary to maintain or increase that silence. . . . the people of Chinese and Japanese ancestry stand out as white racism's only success.[42]

Central to the white stereotyping of Asian men, according to Chin and Chan, was the feminization of Asians: "The white stereotype of the Asian is unique in that it is the only racial stereotype complete devoid of manhood. Our nobility is that of an efficient housewife."[43] The stereotype had been perpetuated by the objects themselves, who "euphemized" it "as being successful assimilation, adoption and acculturation."[44]

The authors rejected the "concept of dual personality" as a means of constructing an Asian-American identity because rather than identify Asian Americans as Asian *and* American, the concept posited a "disintegrated personality" that concealed the "self contempt" that the internalization of the stereotype implied:

> The so-called "blending of East and West" divides the Chinese-American into two incompatible segments: (1) the *foreigner* whose status is dependent on his ability to be accepted by the white natives; and (2) the *handicapped native* who is taught that identification with his foreignness is the only way to "justify" his difference in skin color.[45] (emphasis in the original)

Rather, the authors argued, negation of these abstract premises of the dual personality concept (East and West, Chinese and White American; abstract because they forced a self-definition in terms alien to immediate experience) and simultaneous affirmation of the historicity of Asian

Americans' experience were crucial to the construction of an Asian-American cultural identity:

> The concept of the dual personality successfully deprives the Chinese-American of all authority over language and thus a means of codifying, communicating, and legitimizing experience. Because he is a foreigner, English is not his native tongue. Chinese from China, "real Chinese," make the Chinese-American aware of his lack of authority over Chinese, and the white American doesn't recognize the Chinese Americans' brand of English as a language, even a minority language, but as faulty English, an "accent." The notion of an organic, whole identity, a personality not explicable in either the terms of China or white America (in the same way the black experience is not explicable in either the terms of Africa or white America), has been precluded by the concept of dual personality. And the development of Chinese-American English has been prevented, much less recognized. The denial of language is the denial of culture. . . . Language is a medium of culture and the people's sensibility, including the style of manhood. Language coheres the people into a community by organizing and codifying the symbols of their own common experience.[46]

Neither Chinese nor white American, the Chinese-American sensibility was a product of the Chinese experience within United States history; and it was that historicity, imbedded in the very language of Chinese-American communities, that must be the point of departure for constructing a Chinese-American identity.

Such an identity, moreover, may be constructed only in resistance to white culture. Two decades later in another context, Frank Chin would refer to "death by assimilation."[47] A Chinese-American culture, he and Chan insisted at this time, would remain "emotionally-stunted" and "dependent" if it did not assert its autonomy of white culture in a relationship of antagonism:

> It is well-known that the cloying overwhelming love of a protective coddling mother produces an emotionally-stunted, dependent child. This is the Christian love, the bigoted love that has imprisoned the Chinese-American sensibility; whereas overt and prolonged expressions of hatred had the effect of liberating black, red, chicano and, to some degree, Japanese-American sensibilities.
>
> The hatred of whites freed them to return hate with hate and develop their own brigand languages, cultures, and sensibilities, all of which have at their roots an assumed arrogance in the face of white standards, and defiant mockery of white institutions, including white religion.[48]

In recent years, Frank Chin has engaged other major Chinese-American writers in acrimonious controversies, charging that in their urge to be assimilated to the hegemonic white culture, these writers have themselves assimilated, and perpetuated, white stereotypes of Chinese Americans. As he wrote recently,

> Kingston, Hwang and Tan are the first writers of any race, and certainly the first writers of Asian ancestry, to so boldly fake the best-known works from the most universally known body of Asian literature and lore in history. And to legitimize their faking, they have to fake all of Asian American history and literature, and argue that the immigrants who settled and established Chinese America lost touch with Chinese culture, and that a faulty memory combined with new experience produced new versions of these traditional stories. This version of history is their contribution to the stereotype.[49]

Chin's insistence on the need for "purity" in the Chinese-American relationship to a Chinese legacy, like his fear of "death by assimilation," yields the impression that he wishes to have nothing to do with U.S. culture, and seeks to isolate Asian-American culture from U.S. culture in general in order to construct an autonomous Asian-American culture from "purely" Asian ingredients. Although it is true, I think, that he insists uncompromisingly on the autonomy of Asian-American literature, it does not follow that this implies isolation from U.S. culture in general or a recovery of Asian purity.

What is at issue, I would like to suggest here, is an alternative vision of "Americanness" to that defined by the hegemonic white culture, one that resists assimilation into the received culture in order to create conditions for the reconstruction of U.S. culture in general. Chin has repeatedly pointed to the distance that divides Chinese Americans from Chinese in China; a distance that is at once the distance of history and language.[50] His own writing, arguably, is the most "American" of Asian-American writing in his incorporation of Western American lore into the Chinese-American experience; what he seeks to do, however, is to dissolve this lore into the Chinese lore that shaped the everyday culture of Chinese Americans.[51] Rather than repudiate "Americanness," his goal would seem to be to reject a hegemonic notion of Americanness that privileges white culture and to bring in an ethnic cultural formation as an equal partner in a redefinition of what it means to be American. He and Chan wrote in "Racist Love,"

> The concept of the dual personality deprives the Chinese-American of the means to develop his own terms of self-definition. It subjugates him by forcing him to define in terms he knows are not his. The tyranny of language has been used by white culture to suppress Chinese-American and Japanese-American culture and exclude the Asian-American sensibility from operating in the mainstream of American consciousness.[52]

Before an "Asian-American sensibility" can enter the "mainstream of American consciousness," the argument in "Racist Love" suggests, it must have its own space of cultural production; in other words, it must first develop fully as what we might call a "local" culture.

In a recent study of literary traditions in Hawaii, Stephen Sumida has explained that the term "local" may be understood in two senses. First is local in the sense of a parochial marginality, which is the sense in which it appears in hegemonic white conceptions of Asian-American literature. The other, the sense in which Sumida conceptualizes Hawaiian literature, is local in the sense of the articulation of a community's culture, which is central to the community itself:

> "Local" is today's shorthand by which people in Hawai'i—whether local or not, whether in pride or in derision—label a culture, a sensibility, an iden-tity, and, often forgotten despite how strongly it is valued, a personal, fam-ily, and community history.[53]

Local in this sense, rather than a resignation to the existing structure of hegemony, is an assertion of the community's identity in resistance to hegemony; that in its self-assertion challenges the claims of white culture to centrality by localizing it as the culture of one ethnic group among others:

> Hawaii's locals know very well that they are members of American society, because Hawai'i is a state of the Union. By itself, the term "local" does not imply a desire for separatism from America; it is indeed quintessentially American to assert one's individualism within a representative group, to enjoy, for instance, eating noisily with one's family in a local chop suey house without feeling that one is partaking in something alien. The term is thus inherently pluralistic in concept—it abhors assimilation even though there is plenty of evidence of assimilation too in Hawai'i, where many still think that the "melting pot" preserves racial and cultural diversity, which it expressly does not. Assimilation is opposite to the concept of pluralism. With its inherent value on history and the processes by which a community comes to be, pluralism implies that the kaleidoscopic (not melted) local sen-sibility continually changes.[54]

And so must U.S. society, and what it means to be American, change continually, as new ethnic groups enter into it and rather than melt into one big white pot, assert their own identities in an ongoing redefinition of the United States. Carlos Bulosan may have been the first Asian Ameri-can to make this point of the United States being an ongoing project rather than finished product when he wrote in *America Is in the Heart*:

America is not a land of one race or one class of men. We are all Americans that have toiled and suffered and known oppression and defeat, from the first Indian that offered peace in Manhattan to the last Filipino pea pickers. America is not bound by geographical latitudes. America is not merely a land or an institution. American is in the hearts of men that died for freedom; it is also in the eyes of men that are building a new world. America is a prophecy of a new society. . . .[55]

## Conclusion

As an Asia-Pacific regional perspective, personified here by Asian Americans, offers novel perspectives on U.S. national history, the cultural struggles of Asian Americans within U.S. history also offer insights into the structure of Asia-Pacific as a potential region. The struggle of Asian Americans against homogenization into a hegemonic culture is paradigmatic of Asia-Pacific as a space for cultural production. There, too, it is possible to detect an ongoing struggle of local culture against regional homogenization, whatever the source may be, of which Hawaii may be a prime example.

I started with the argument that the motions of people over the Pacific point to a constitution of an Asia-Pacific region as a social formation. In light of the discussion, I would like to qualify this observation. Although Asia-Pacific peoples have carried their cultural legacies across the Pacific, they also have been transformed by their host society without being absorbed into it beyond recognition. Rather, the histories of these peoples in their host society have produced a variety of local cultures. This has been the case with Chinese, who have moved across the length and breadth of the Asia-Pacific region in greater numbers than any other people, not just in the United States but in other societies as well.[56] The social constitution of the Pacific, in other words, ironically also points to a social dispersal when viewed from the perspective of these local cultural formations.

The Asia-Pacific idea has a significant social basis, which is evident in the motions of Asian and Pacific peoples as well as in their impact on the national histories of the societies that surround the Pacific or are located within it. As with the economic, political, and other relationships that endow the Asia-Pacific idea with some measure of material reality, however, socially, too, the region is as much a realm of contradiction and division as it is of mutuality of interest and unity. Cultural distance and dispersal articulate the contradictions that are built into the social dynamics of the regional formation. From this perspective, the Asia-Pacific idea appears simultaneously as an integrative discourse, one that suppresses its own contradictions in order to contain, hegemonically, the cultural formations that articulate community aspirations against the forces of cultural homogenization that emanate from the cores of the capitalist system that have shaped, and continue to shape, the region.

## Notes

1. Evelyn Hu-DeHart, "Chinese Coolie Labor in Cuba and Peru in the Nineteenth Century: Free Labor or Neo-Slavery?" (Unpublished paper presented at the annual meeting of the Association for Asian-American Studies, May 18–20, 1990, Santa Barbara, CA), p. 1. The number was 225,000. For comparable years (1847–1874), the number of Chinese immigrants to the United States was 171,171. See Fred Arnold, Urmil Minocha, and James T. Fawcett, "The Changing Face of Asian Immigration to the United States," in *Pacific Bridges: The New Immigration from Asia and the Pacific Islands,* ed. James T. Fawcett and Benjamin V. Carino (New York: Center for Migration Studies, 1990), p. 122.

2. Roger Daniels, *Asian America: Chinese and Japanese in the United States since 1850* (Seattle: University of Washington Press, 1988), pp. 4–6.

3. See *Amerasia Journal,* Vol. 15, No. 1 (1989) (Commemorative Issue: Salute to the 60s and 70s), for these themes.

4. Ignacio Lemuel, *Asian-Americans and Pacific Islanders: Is there Such an Ethnic Group?* (San Jose, CA: Pilipino Development Associates, 1976).

5. Stephen H. Sumida, *And the View from the Shore: Literary Traditions of Hawai'i* (Seattle: University of Washington Press, 1991), Preface.

6. Lucie Cheng and Edna Bonacich, eds., *Labor Immigration under Capitalism: Asian Workers in the United States before World War II* (Berkeley: University of California Press, 1984), Introduction, p. 2.

7. Fawcett and Carino, eds., *Pacific Bridges,* fn. 1.

8. Alejandro Portes, "One Field, Many Views: Competing Theories of International Migration," in Fawcett and Carino, eds., *Pacific Bridges,* pp. 53–70.

9. Fawcett and Carino, "International Migration and Pacific Basin Development," in Fawcett and Carino, eds., *Pacific Bridges,* pp. 8–12.

10. Edna Bonacich, "United States Capitalist Development: A Background to Asian Immigration," in Cheng and Bonacich, eds., *Labor Immigration,* pp. 79–129. For comparable arguments concerning other parts of the Pacific, see Charles A. Price, "The Asian and Pacific Island Peoples of Australia"; Andrew D. Trlin, "New Zealand's Admission of Asians and Pacific Islanders"; and Daniel Kubat, "Asian Immigrants to Canada," all in Fawcett and Carino, eds., *Pacific Bridges,* pp. 175–245.

11. William B. Johnston, "Global Work Force 2000: The New World Labor Market," *Harvard Business Review* (March-April 1991), pp. 115–127.

12. For an elaboration of this point, see Arif Dirlik, "The Asia-Pacific Idea: Reality and Representation in the Invention of a Regional Structure," *Journal of World History,* Vol. 3, No. 1 (Spring 1992).

13. For the application to Asian Americans of the concept of "strangers,"

originally from Georg Simmel, see Ronald Takaki, *Strangers from a Different Shore: A History of Asian Americans* (Boston: Little, Brown, 1989), pp. 11–12.

14. Portes, "One Field, Many Views," p. 57.

15. Victor G. Nee and Brett deBary Nee, *Longtime Californ': A Documentary Study of an American Chinatown* (New York: Pantheon Books, 1973), p. 19.

16. Ibid., pp. 17–19.

17. Ibid. For the case of another group, Japanese Americans, see Yuji Ichioka, *Issei: The World of the First Generation Japanese Immigrants, 1885–1924* (New York: Free Press, 1988), pp. 164–173.

18. June Mei, "Socioeconomic Origins of Emigration: Guangdong to California, 1850–1882," in Cheng and Bonacich, eds., *Labor Immigration,* pp. 219–247. Quotation on p. 237.

19. Peter S. Xenos, Robert W. Gardner, Herbert R. Barringer, and Michael J. Levin, "Asian Americans: Growth and Change in the 1970's," in Fawcett and Carino, eds., *Pacific Bridges,* pp. 249–284.

20. Carino, "Impacts of Emigration on Sending Countries," in Fawcett and Carino, eds., *Pacific Bridges,* pp. 407–426.

21. For discussions of associations for the different groups, see Ichioka, *Issei,* pp. 156-164; Nee and Nee, *Longtime Californ',* pp. 60–69; Takaki, *Strangers from a Different Shore,* pp. 270–314.

22. Xenos et al., "Asian Americans."

23. L. Eve Armentrout Ma, *Revolutionaries, Monarchists and Chinatowns: Chinese Politics in the Americas and the 1911 Revolution* (Honolulu: University of Hawaii Press, 1990), p. 1. See also Nee and Nee, *Longtime Californ',* pp. 72–72, 355–360.

24. Yuji Ichioka, "Japanese Immigrant Nationalism: The Issei and the Sino-Japanese War, 1937–1945," *California History,* Vol. 49, No. 3 (Fall 1990), pp. 260–274. See also Ichioka, *Issei,* Chapter 4, for the relationship between radical and labor movements in Japan and the United States.

25. Takaki, *Strangers from a Different Shore,* Chapter 7.

26. Ichioka, "Immigrant Nationalism," p. 274; Ma, *Revolutionaries, Monarchists and Chinatowns,* pp. 2–3.

27. Ichioka, "Immigrant Nationalism," pp. 273–274.

28. See for an example, Joel Kotkin, "The New Yankee Traders," *INC.* (March 1986), pp. 25–27. A recent conference on the Asian-American experience, sponsored by the Asia Society, included a panel on the role of Asian Americans in U.S.-Asian relations entitled, "Asian-Americans and U.S.-Asia Relations" (*The Asian-American Experience: Looking Ahead,* October 24–26, 1991, Los Angeles).

29. Ichioka, *Issei,* passim; Takaki, *Strangers from a Different Shore,* passim; Su Cheng-Chan, *The Chinese in California Agriculture* (Berkeley: University of California Press, 1986).

30. William Henry Bishop, "San Francisco," *Harper's Magazine,* Vol. 66, No. 396 (May 1883), pp. 813–832, reprinted in *The West: A Collection from Harper's Magazine* (New York: Gallery Books, 1990), pp. 75–92. Quotation on p. 92.

31. Frank Chin, "Come All Ye Asian American Writers of the Real and the Fake," in Jeffery Paul Chan, Frank Chin, Lawson Fuaso Inada, and Shawn Won, eds., *The Big Aiiieeeee! An Anthology of Chinese American and Japanese American Writing* (New York: Penguin Books, 1991), pp. 1–92, 44. For the phrase book itself, see pp. 93–110. For the Japanese presence in the West, see, Tsurutani Hisashi, *America-Bound: The Japanese and the Opening of the American West,* tr. into English by Betsey Scheiner with the assistance of Yamamura Mariko (Tokyo: Japan Times, 1989).

32. Bishop, "San Francisco," p. 83.

33. Catherine Baldwin, "The Chinese in San Francisco—the 6th Year of Qwong See [Guangxu]," *Harper's Magazine*, Vol. 62, No. 297 (December 1880), pp. 70–77, reprinted in *The West*, pp. 188–195. Quotation on p. 188.

34. Robert J. Schwendinger, *Ocean of Bitter Dreams: Maritime Relations between China and the United States, 1850–1915* (Tucson: Westernlore Press, 1988), p. 92. For the role of labor in anti-Chinese agitation, see Alexander Saxton, *The Indispensable Enemy: Labor and the Anti-Chinese Movement in California* (Berkeley: University of California Press, 1975).

35. Frank Chin, *Donald Duk* (Minneapolis, MN: Coffee House Press, 1991).

36. *U.S. v. Bhagat Singh Thind* (1923). See Takaki, *Strangers from a Different Shore, p. 299.*

37. *Ibid., pp. 15–16.*

38. *California Board of Control, California and the Oriental* (Sacramento: State Printing Office, 1922), p. 10.

39. Charles F. Lummis, "The Right Hand of the Continent," *Harper's Magazine*, Vol. 100, No. 596 (January 1900), pp. 171–185, reprinted in *The West*, pp. 416–430. Quotation on p. 420.

40. Ibid., p. 421.

41. Nee and Nee, *Longtime Californ',* p. 30. Roger Daniels expressed this point concisely: "To examine the Asian American experience involves, among other things, looking at American history the 'wrong way'; that is, from west to east rather than from east to west." *Asian America,* p. 3.

42. Frank Chin and Jeffrey Paul Chan, "Racist Love," in Richard Kostelanetz, ed., *Seeing through Shuck* (New York: Ballantine Books, 1972), pp. 65–79. Quotation on pp. 65–66. I am grateful to Ken Berger of the Perkins Library, Duke University, for helping me locate this article.

43. Ibid., p. 68.

44. Ibid., p. 67.

45. Ibid., p. 72.

46. Ibid., p. 76–77.

47. Edward Iwata, "Word Warriors," *Los Angeles Times*, June 24, 1990, Section E, pp. 1, 9. Statement on p. 9.

48. Chin and Chan, "Racist Love," p. 69.

49. Chin, "Come All Ye Asian American Writers of the Real and the Fake," p. 3. The references are to Maxine Hong Kingston, David Hwang, and Amy Tan. In approaching the problem here through Chin's writings I do not necessarily endorse Chin's views over that of these authors'. Indeed, Chin's approach is

rather one dimensional and ignores the fact that cultural experience differs not only by ethnic group but also by gender, class, and generational differences. Denial of such differences has led Chin to contradict his own injunction to be mindful of the historicity of the Asian-American experience. Moreover, in stressing myth over history in his recent writing (and his insistence that he alone has direct and "pure" access to Chinese myths), he disguises his own historically conditioned reading of those myths (as a Chinese American rather than Chinese) and confounds what would seem to be the more fundamental question, which is the relationship of Chinese-American writing to the hegemonic culture; in other words, what readings of Chinese myths lend themselves least to appropriation by white culture and therefore to a cultural assimilation that undercuts Chinese-American cultural autonomy? It is because Chin has raised *this* question most insistently, from "Racist Love" to the present, that I have chosen here to emphasize his writings.

50. Chin and Chan, "Racist Love," p. 76; Nee and Nee, *Longtime Californ'*, p. 383.

51. Chin and Chan, "Racist Love," p. 77.

52. Sumida, *And the View from the Shore*, p. xvi.

54. Ibid., p. xvii.

55. Carlos Bulosan, *America Is in the Heart* (Seattle: University of Washington Press, 1990), p. 189.

56. For brief discussions of the cultural transformation of the Chinese in different parts of the Asia-Pacific region, see *Free China Review* (July 1988).

# 13

# Pacific Island Responses to U.S. and French Hegemony

## GLENN ALCALAY

More than any other place on the globe, Oceania has been portrayed and popularized as an earthly paradise. Captain Cook's logs, Gauguin's canvases, Mead's anthropological tracts, Michener's tomes, and Hollywood films all contributed to the South Seas stereotype of "happy campers" living harmoniously in a sensuous nirvana. Yet, the highly militarized Oceania of the 1990s is one of the most nuclearized and colonized geopolitical regions in the world. In this chapter, I propose to lift the "coconut curtain" that has romanticized and distorted the Pacific for most people by challenging the Western popular images of these island people.

The anthropologist Bengt Danielsson—a Norwegian member of the 1947 Kon-Tiki expedition—has been residing in Tahiti for more than four decades and has been active (along with his wife, Marie-Therese) in the Pacific antinuclear and independence movement. According to Danielsson, the naming of the Pacific islands occurred this way:

> The term Polynesia was coined by Charles de Brosses in 1756 and applied to all the Pacific islands. The present restricted use was proposed by Dumont d'Urville during a famous lecture at the Geographical Society in Paris in 1831. At the same time he also proposed the terms Melanesia and Micronesia for the regions which still bear those names. The terms are not particularly good, considering that all three regions have "many islands" (polynesia) and "small islands" (micronesia); in Melanesia, it is not the islands, but the people who are black. (personal communication, 1991)

As for colorful names, the ambassador to the United Nations from Papua New Guinea, Renagi Lohia, has popularized the term "aquatic continent" to represent all of the Pacific islands (Lohia, 1989).

The more than 10,000 islands of the Pacific are home to roughly 6 million indigenous peoples in twenty-three microstates. Scattered over one-third of the earth's surface—but comprising a mere 0.5 million square kilometers of land—the Pacific islands were first encountered by European explorers 400 years ago (Walker and Sutherland, 1988, p. 6). Although the United States and France were late entrants into the Pacific region—preceded by the Spanish, the Dutch, and the British—their presence (along with Japanese investment) dominates the "Ocean of Peace" in the late twentieth century.

It will be my aim in this chapter to search beyond the tempting—but static—Western representation by analyzing the realpolitik interests of the United States and France in the Pacific region. An examination of how military and intelligence operations by these two Western nations have tampered with the postwar decolonization process will be featured. Additionally, I will explore the historic responses by the indigenous islanders to these metropolitan incursions in this vast (and underpublicized) oceanic expanse.

## Pax Americana in the Pacific

Early U.S. expansion into the Pacific was limited to Hawaii and the islands of Micronesia north of the equator: annexed in 1900, American Samoa (which became independent in 1962) was the sole island entity seized by the United States in the South Pacific. Congress annexed Hawaii in 1898, following the 1894 military coup by U.S. soldiers from the USS *Boston* overthrowing Queen Liliuokalani.

As booty in the Spanish-American War, the United States acquired Puerto Rico, the Philippines, and Guam in the Mariana Islands, an island outpost that has well served U.S. strategic interests for nearly a century. Nearby Tinian Island acted as the stationary aircraft carrier for the *Enola Gay* en route to Hiroshima.

The 2,100 islands of Micronesia were awarded to Japan at the Paris Peace Conference of 1919 as a class C mandate under the League of Nations (Heine, 1974, p. 14). Instrumental in its island outpost campaign, the Japanese mandated islands proved to be strategically useful for Japan's World War II military planners: the attack on Pearl Harbor was launched from aircraft carriers based in Micronesia.

In the Cairo Declaration, December 1, 1943, Churchill and Roosevelt announced that after the war, Japan would be relieved of the Pacific islands (north of the equator) granted in 1920. Of the 50,000 Micronesians living at the time, about 10 percent were killed in the bitter crossfire between foreign belligerents on island soil (Stanley, 1989a, p. 33).

At war's end, the United States engaged in an internal debate about the future administration of its newly won Micronesian isles. The War Department under Stimson advocated outright annexation of these useful isles, stretching past Hawaii and nearly to the Philippines; the State Department under Hull won out, getting them declared an unprecedented "strategic" trust territory under the newly spawned United Nations (McHenry, 1975, p. 56). Of the eleven newly created trust territories at the war's end, only Micronesia was designated a "strategic" trust and thus placed under the supervision of the Security Council.

The Pentagon had fixed its attention of the furtherance of its nuclear monopoly. A year before the United States formally signed the 1947 UN Trust Agreement, the 167 Marshall Island people of Bikini were forcibly evacuated from their ancestral atoll by the U.S. navy in preparation for the first series of postwar nuclear tests, "Operation Crossroads." The Bikinians today remain an exiled community awaiting return to their revered Eden.

From 1948 to 1958, at least sixty-six atomic and hydrogen bombs were exploded at Bikini and Eniwetok, another atoll similarly relieved of its original inhabitants in 1947. A monstrous series of hydrogen bombs designed by Edward Teller was exploded at Bikini and Eniwetok in spring 1954. The first H-bomb of the Castle series, code-named "Bravo," had a yield of fifteen megatons (over 1,000 Hiroshimas); this largest and dirtiest of U.S. hydrogen bombs blanketed countless inhabited atolls in the Marshalls with radioactive fallout. Aside from the Marshallese evacuees who were exposed on Rongelap and Utirik, U.S. service personnel on an adjacent atoll were likewise irradiated from the Bravo behemoth (Alcalay, 1987a, p. 237). Twenty-three Japanese fishermen were also caught in the lethal radioactive fallout.

The United States was eager to collect scientific data on how humans are affected by hydrogen bomb fallout and was quick to establish long-term health studies of the irradiated Marshallese: the Atomic Bomb Casualty Commission (now called the Radiation Effects Research Foundation) provided *only* data on the direct effects of radiation exposure. In his 1958 follow-up report, the chief scientist from Brookhaven National laboratory (under contract with the Atomic Energy Commission [AEC], now the Department of Energy) said:

> Greater knowledge of [radiation] effects on human beings is badly needed. Considerable research is being carried out on animals, but there are obvious limitations in extrapolating such data to the human species. The habitation of these people on the island will afford most valuable ecological radiation data on human beings. (Conrad, Zarsky, and Belloe, 1958, p. 22)

More recently, another document on Bravo from previously classified minutes of an AEC meeting revealed in the most bare-knuckled manner the actual rationale for conducting the follow-up Marshallese radiation studies. In January 1956, two years after Bravo, Merril Eisenbud, the AEC director of Health and Safety, addressed the radiation problems in the Marshalls:

> Now that island [Utirik] is safe to live on but is by far the most contaminated place in the world, and it will be very interesting to go back and get good environmental data. Now data of this type has never been available. While it is true that these people do not live, I would say, the way Westerners do, civilized people, it is nevertheless also true that these people are more like us than the mice. (Eisenbud, 1956, p. 232)

With several island communities remaining sociologically disrupted as "nuclear nomads" (Bikini, Eniwetok, and Rongelap), a key question today concerns the full extent of radiological contamination. A congressionally mandated Nuclear Claims Tribunal is currently attempting to sort out the radiation legacy in the Marshall Islands (Nuclear Claims Tribunal, 1992, p. 3).

The Marshall Islands continue to serve U.S. strategic interests. Kwajalein Atoll, 4,200 miles west of California's Vandenberg Air Force Base, is well sited for a U.S. $2 billion secret Pentagon laboratory. Used for development, missile testing, and perfecting ICBM warhead accuracy, the facility is key to "Star Wars" and the new emphasis on "smart" weaponry (Johnson, 1984, p. 23).

Now that the United States has been forced to vacate Clark Air Base and Subic Naval Base in the Philippines, the importance of Guam's strategic location just off the Asian mainland will increase dramatically. The largest island in Micronesia, Guam was originally claimed by the explorer Magellan in 1521 after Spanish troops waged a war of extermination against the indigenous Chamorro people. With the help of introduced diseases like smallpox and syphilis, the Chamorros were reduced from an original population of 80,000 in 1668 to fewer than 5,000 in 1741. By 1783 their numbers had been further decimated to a mere 1,500 (Stanley, 1986, p. 180).

The Pentagon stations 21,000 U.S. military personnel, spends U.S. $750 million a year, and controls one-third of Guam's 216 square miles. The current population of 130,000—composed of mixed blood Chamorros, Japanese, Filipinos, Chinese, and Koreans—has been Westernized and disrupted by this overbearing presence.

The indigenous Chamorros have been protesting to the United Nations and the U.S. Congress for years about environmental contamination from the military bases and along with the other people of Guam have intensified their campaign to retake land seized by the United States for military purposes. With growing Chamorro nationalism pitted against a huge influx of military hardware and personnel expected over the next few years (principally from the Philippines), and as the Pentagon pushes to militarize the adjacent islands of Saipan, Tinian, and Rota in the Northern Marianas, increased social and political unrest is practically guaranteed in this distant colony of the United States.

When the New Zealand Labour government under David Lange declared its ports and airfields off-limits to nuclear-laden ships and aircraft in 1984, the United States perceived its interests threatened in its "American Lake." Three years later, a military coup in Fiji—the first in the region—crushed another Labour government's threat to likewise adopt an antinuclear policy. The antinuclear thrust originated within the more progressive and newly independent Pacific microstates of Vanuatu (formerly New Hebrides), Papua New Guinea, and the Solomon Islands, known within the region as the Melanesian Spearhead Group.

While in New Zealand in 1987, I spoke with Graham Kelly, a New Zealand member of Parliament, about outside interference in the Pacific region. Because of the insights Kelly offered, I shall quote at some length from my interview with him:

> I worked for 25 years in the trade union movement, and it doesn't take you very long when you see events taking place to politicize you very quickly about the very subtle—and sometimes not so subtle—activities of people and organizations from outside your own country that want to determine your future and the way you should operate. There was a scandal that broke in Australia in 1975 where the CIA was known to be involved in the trade union movement there. The labor attache working out of the U.S. Embassy in Canberra was CIA-trained, as they are in New Zealand and elsewhere.
>
> These labor attaches work to influence the course of elections and to influence the policy of unions at the national level on their political and economic international issues. We found in New Zealand in 1977 a spin-off of that. In my own case with my own union we were challenging the then-Tory government over some national legislation on shop trading hours, and in the course of that we shut New Zealand down for two days; it was unprecedented. It was a golden opportunity for those who would like to see some dissent within the union to capitalize on that, and they did. We later learned that the dissenters were being orchestrated with the help of the U.S. labor attache from the embassy, and we resented the heavy-handed nature of U.S. involvement in our internal affairs.
>
> Various U.S. agencies have poured money into third world countries, whether it is Turkey or South American nations, or Asia and the Pacific. The American Federation of Labor–Congress of Industrial Organizations in fact financed an office in Fiji for the trade union movement—the Asian-American Free Labor Institute (AAFLI). It was an offer that was too good to be missed by the Fijians who haven't got much money, and in fact, they're

doing this in other Pacific island countries as well. AAFLI, as it is called, is one of three foreign affairs arms of the AFL-CIO; there is AAFLI in the Asia-Pacific region. These have been known to have CIA involvement from its formation during the Cold War.

Also, we now know about the National Endowment for Democracy, which has been used around the world to intervene in the electoral affairs of many nations. Now we know that all of these things are going on, so, for example, when the Fiji coup occurred [in May 1987], it didn't happen in isolation. (Kelly, 1987)

Further evidence of U.S. clandestine activities in the Pacific may be gleaned from the following passages contained in documents released under the Freedom of Information Act. For example, funding submissions from the AFL-CIO's Free Trade Union Institute, AAFLI's parent, to the National Endowment for Democracy, state:

> The trade unions located in the island nations of the South Pacific are fragile institutions. . . . Their ability to draw distinctions between the Soviet bloc and the democratic nations of the world is sometimes clouded, especially when emotional issues such as colonialism, nuclear testing and economic protection zones are introduced. (Wypijewski, 1987, p. 684)

Another document recounts the proceedings of a 1985 Pacific conference of the International Confederation of Free Trade Unions:

> The Australian and New Zealand representatives attempted to gain approval for a political resolution endorsing a Pacific "nuclear freeze" [sic] zone and supporting New Zealand in its dispute with the U.S. However, only one South Pacific delegate spoke up in favor of their approach, and the conference rejected it. This was in no small measure due to close collaboration and friendship nurtured between AAFLI and the South Pacific trade union leaders. (Wypijewski, 1987, p. 684).

U.S. concerns about Soviet and Libyan influence gained currency during the Reagan administration. One of the clearest statements came in the Hawaii Declaration issued in December 1987 at a major conference organized by the Moonie-funded International Security Council in New York City. In the Hawaii Declaration, the thirty-six scholars who signed the final document had these ominous and chilling things to say:

> The results of this comparative description and analysis provided a compelling picture of a Soviet strategic design to dominate the entire basin. That drive for preeminence employs a variety of means including intimidation, manipulation, regime transformation, subversion, the support of anti-American nationalism, and the promotion of chaos. The evidence of the Soviet

commitment to hegemony includes its own policy statements, naval deployments, covert activities, basing patterns, support of insurgencies and activities of its clients. (Hawaii Declaration, 1988, p. 218)

In 1984 the State Department commissioned the University of Hawaii anthropologist Robert Kiste and the New Zealand political scientist R. A. Herr (1984) to research Soviet penetration in the South Pacific. Their study, "The Potential for Soviet Penetration of the South Pacific Islands: An Assessment," concluded that Soviet influence in the Pacific was rather limited, and the authors pointed to the nearly universal perception by Pacific peoples that the United States and France posed a much greater threat to stability in the region. In their conclusion, Kiste and Herr noted:

By the usual objective criteria, the South Pacific ranks as one of the most vulnerable regions in the world and yet it has perhaps the least Soviet influence of any area of the globe. Further, as evidenced by Namaliu's [i.e., the former Prime Minister of Papua New Guinea] assessment of threat, the prospect of a physical or political danger from the Soviet Union was not regarded as high. (pp. 66–67)

This sentiment was shared by none other than Admiral William Crowe, the former chairman of the Joint Chiefs of Staff. In the July 26, 1986, issue of *U.S. News and World Report*, Crowe stated:

The Soviets are in real trouble in the Pacific. They haven't been able to make much headway ideologically or politically. They have acquired some shabby allies [e.g., Vanuatu and Kiribati, with whom the Soviets entered into fishing agreements] . . . whose economies are either stagnant or declining. The whole Far East—not just Japan—is becoming the most active, most prosperous market in the world, and the Soviets can't even penetrate it. (p. 23)

As the cold war quickly fades into memory, the U.S. military continues to show itself out of touch. According to the vice chairman of the Joint Chiefs of Staff, Admiral David Jeremiah, the United States has "absolutely no intention of ending its military presence in Asia and the Pacific." Addressing the Australian Royal United Services Institute in Canberra in September 1991, Jeremiah explained that despite troop reductions in Japan and Korea, the United States expects to "remain fully engaged in Asia through a program of frequent exercises, short term deployments and visits by units based in the U.S." (*Wellington Pacific Report*, 1991, p. 2). For an excellent analysis of the U.S. defense posture in the Asia-Pacific region, see *American Lake: Nuclear Peril in the Pacific* by Hayes (1986).

## La Bombe and La Force de Frappe

France's encroachment into the Pacific isles commenced in 1843 when Tahiti-Poynesia (known as "French Polynesia") was wrestled from the British and declared a French protectorate. This wide area, comprising the Society islands (including Tahiti), the Australs, the Tuamotus, the Gambiers, and the Marquesas, consisted of over five million square kilometers of French territory in the South Pacific (Stanley, 1989b, p. 15).

Additionally, with the idea of creating a penal colony similar to that in New South Wales in Australia, Emperor Napolean III ordered the annexation of New Caledonia in 1853. When nickel was discovered there in 1864—the world's largest nickel deposit—France saw economic advantage along with another far-flung strategic outpost.

The success of the Algerian independence struggle in 1962 meant that France had to move its nuclear weapons program from the Sahara Desert in that former colony. Beginning in 1966, France shifted its atmospheric nuclear experiments to its convenient Polynesian colony, and until 1974 exploded more than forty neutron and hydrogen bombs above the balmy lagoons at Moruroa and Fangataufa atolls near Tahiti. Following much regional protest—including litigation by New Zealand and Australia (which were hit with radioactive fallout from the French N-tests) before the International Court of Justice in the Hague—France drove its nuclear testing underground. Since 1966, France has exploded over 150 nuclear weapons in this Pacific colony more than 8,000 miles from Paris as part of its *force de frappe,* the French policy of nuclear deterrence.

In 1963, when all local political parties in Tahiti protested the invasion of Polynesia by thousands of French troops and technicians sent to create a nuclear test center, President Charles de Gaulle simply outlawed political parties. Since then the territorial assembly of Tahiti-Polynesia has adopted numerous resolutions asking the French government to halt the testing, without response (Stanley, 1989b, p. 33).

Indigenous protest in Tahiti was led by Pouvanaa a Oopa, an outspoken World War I hero. In 1949 Oopa became the first Polynesian to occupy a seat in the French Chamber of Deputies. In 1957 he was elected vice-president of the Government Council. A dedicated proponent of independence, Oopa was arrested in 1958 on trumped-up charges of arson and was sentenced to an eight-year prison term. Eventually freed in 1968, Oopa won the "French" Polynesia seat in the French Senate, a post he held until his death in 1977. Tahitians refer to Oopa as *metua* ("father") and his statue stands in front of Papeete's Territorial Assembly (Stanley, 1989b, p. 33). Other Tahitian independence leaders have since filled the vacuum, including Oscar Temaru, the mayor of Tahiti's second largest city, Faaa, and Charlie Ching, who has been repeatedly jailed and beaten for leading antinuclear and independence protests. As part of its international antinuclear campaign, Greenpeace planned a 1985 protest of France's nuclear weapons program in the Pacific (the United States ended its Marshall Islands nuclear tests in 1958, but tested H-bombs at Johnston Atoll [near Hawaii] until 1962). To draw attention to past as well as present nuclear testing in the Pacific, the Greenpeace flagship *Rainbow Warrior* helped to evacuate the Rongelap islanders in the Marshalls to another island in May 1985. As a member of the *Rainbow Warrior* evacuation team, I conducted interviews with the Rongelap people. A representative view about the Rongelap evacuation was expressed to me by Laim Anjain:

> The United States came and poisoned our islands and the people living here, and have thereby contaminated our once-untouched environment. We have had many problems over the years with our health and the health of our children.
>
> You have to understand that this is the island of my greatgrandparents, grandparents, and parents. Our decision to move was based on our concern for our children and the persistent fears we have about diseases that will affect the children in the future. We feel that the radiation from the Bravo bomb is still too dangerous for us to continue living here without fears and anxieties. (Liam Anjain, 1985, p. 27)

After the Rongelap evacuation in the Marshalls, the *Rainbow Warrior* headed south to New Zealand en route to completing the Greenpeace campaign of protest at the French nuclear test sites near Tahiti. While docked in Auckland, French military intelligence commandoes sabotaged the ship, killing one crew member in the bombing. French fears of drawing international attention to its clandestine N-testing in the Pacific were revealed when it became known that France's intelligence agency—the General Directorate for Foreign Security (DGSE)—carried out this terrorist act against Greenpeace (Robie, 1986, p. 105). Ironically, the world's attention was drawn to the French N-tests in the Pacific by its bungled act of violence against the environmental organization. In 1987 the UN Secretary General Javier Perez de Cuellar brokered a settlement between New Zealand and France, whereby the latter paid US$3 million in damages for the sunken ship and the death of a crew member.

New Caledonia, France's other Pacific colony, is a simmering cauldron waiting to explode. Located about 800 miles east of Australia, New Caledonia's tensions revolve around demography and land disputes. The indigenous Kanaks, like the Melanesian Fijians, have become a minority in their own land. They make up about 42 percent of the total population of 150,000, but reside on only 15 percent of the habitable land, in reservations not unlike South Africa's bantustans.

French settlers, known as Caldoches, have been migrating to the colony for more than a century. Included in this group are hundreds of right-wing militarists who fled Indochina in 1954, Algeria in 1962, and most recently Vanuatu (a former French-British colony) in 1980 and now view New Caledonia as their last stand. Today there are some 55,000 Caldoches. Centered around the "Paris of the Pacific" capital of Noumea, the heavily armed Caldoches control the lion's share of the economy.

The remainder of the population consists of 30,000 Pacific islanders and Asians who were lured to the Melanesian nation by lucrative employment opportunities in the now-depressed nickel industry. Included in the ethnic brew are some 10,000 French soldiers stationed in the island outposts to "maintain order."

Following a series of violent skirmishes between the Kanaks and the Caldoches, the majority of Kanak factions merged into the Kanak Socialist National Liberation Front (FLNKS) in 1984. In December of that year, the FLNKS swore in a provisional government as the first step in creating the independent state of Kanaky and installed independence leader (and Catholic priest) Jean-Marie Tjibaou as president. The organization demanded an immediate referendum on independence in which only Kanaks could vote, realizing that they would be outflanked by a coalition of the more numerous Caldoches, Polynesians, and Asians, who are economically linked by the nickel industry. Clashes between anti-independence Caldoche factions and the FLNKS erupted in late 1984, and by January of the following year violence brought the death toll of twenty, including two of Tjibaou's brothers (Robie, 1989, pp. 92–104).

Violence continued in France's Pacific outpost of New Caledonia with scores of new fatalities, and in May 1988—following repeated setbacks for the independence struggle—hooded Kanak militants seized a heavily armed French gendarme post on the island of Ouvea in New Caledonia. Armed with machetes, axes, and a handful of sporting guns, the Kanak militants killed four gendarmes who resisted, injured five others, and captured twenty-seven as hostages.

The Kanak militants hid their hostages underground in a cave on Ouvea Island. Flying in additional gendarmes from Tahiti, France launched an attack on the cave, and in the ensuing violence killed nineteen Kanaks. After the dust settled from the "Ouvea massacre," French President Mitterand offered a ten-year plan of development for New Caledonia, known as the Matignon Accord. Under the accord, a referendum on independence would be offered at the end of the ten-year period in 1998. A controversial provision called for the stepped-up acculturation of the Kanaks into the Caldoche (French) culture, a proposal detested by many indigenous Melanesians. For many within the FLNKS coalition there was a feeling that Jean-Marie Tjibaou had compromised too much with the French government, especially by postponing a referendum on independence for ten long years. In 1989, one year after the Ouvea massacre, hard-line FLNKS radicals assassinated Jean-Marie Tjibaou—known affectionately as the "Gandhi of the Pacific"—and his deputy Yeiwene Yeiwene at point-blank range (Robie, 1989, pp. 275–80).

Today, New Caledonia simmers in ethnic and economic turmoil. And the volatile Melanesian nation is known throughout the region as the Pacific's tinderbox. Likewise, the mineral-rich island of Bougainville is embroiled in a violent struggle to secede from Papua New Guinea. And the island of East Timor (astride the lucrative oil-rich Timor Gap) is the continuing site of ongoing genocidal policies conducted by the Indonesian army. It has been reported that about one-third of East Timor's population of 700,000 has been killed since 1975. Portugal, which retains internationally recognized sovereignty over the island, is currently involved in an attempted negotiated settlement with the Jakarta government.

Interestingly, the former director of French intelligence provided a candid picture of French attempts to destabilize the region. In a revealing 1988 interview with the conservative *New Zealand International Review*, Count Alexandre de Marenches, who departed from the DGSE in 1981 (well before the *Rainbow Warrior* bombing), boasted that "During my eleven years (1970–1981) we carried out about fifty successful operations in the region. Now to me an intelligence operation is only successful if you never hear about it" (*Wellington Pacific Report*, 1988, p. 5).

## The Islanders' Response

Having suffered the most in the nuclear age—from Hiroshima and Nagasaki to Bikini, Eniwetok, and Christmas Island (where the British conducted nuclear tests in the 1950s), Pacific islanders are intimately aware of the destruction wrought by the atom. When the push for independence gained momentum in the 1970s (with Fiji becoming independent in 1970, Papua New Guinea in 1975, the Solomon Islands in 1978, and Vanuatu in 1980), the movements contained an admixture of national pride and opposition to French nuclear testing. This political thrust led ultimately to a dynamic grass roots drive for a nuclear-free Pacific.

This movement took organizational form in 1970 with the founding of the ATOM (Against Tests on Moruroa) committee in Fiji. The group was made up of activists from the University of the South Pacific in the Fijian capital of Suva, the Pacific Conference of Churches, and the Pacific trade union movement.

The ATOM committee organized the first nuclear-free Pacific conference in Fiji in 1975. The meeting drafted a People's Charter calling for the creation of a nuclear-free zone in the Pacific on the model of the 1959 Antarctic Treaty and the 1967 Treaty of Tlatelolco for a Latin American nuclear-free zone. A second conference on the Micronesian island of Pohnpei in 1978 officially endorses the People's Charter. In addition to demanding a ban on all nuclear tests and other nuclear-related activities, the charter asked that the dumping of nuclear waste into the Pacific be prohibited. At the time, Japan and the United States were actively seeking such dumping rights.

A third nuclear-free Pacific conference in 1980 drew fifty-five delegates from twenty Pacific Rim countries.

The 1983 regional conference expanded its scope to include ongoing Pacific independence struggles. Fittingly, delegates met in newly independent Vanuatu, considered the region's most progressive nation (and denounced by the U.S. State Department as the "Cuba of the Pacific"). There the more than 100 delegates renamed their campaign the Nuclear-Free and Independent Pacific (NFIP) movement, to stress their concern over the liberation struggles under way in New Caledonia, French Polynesia, East Timor, and West Papua.

Regional representatives came together in 1987 in Manila to hammer out a concrete twenty-four-point program. This program focused on economic justice and independence as integral features of the campaign for a nuclear-free Pacific.

The 1987 Manila conference examined three Pacific "hot spots"—Belau in Micronesia, postcoup Fiji, and New Caledonia—and condemned the United States and France for blocking the indigenous struggles for nuclear sovereignty and independence.

The most recent NFIP meeting was held in New Zealand in 1991, where the concerns centered around indigenous peoples from the Pacific, including the plight of the Maoris, the Australian Aboriginals, and Native Hawaiians. Native Americans—who refer to North America as "Turtle Island"—have merged their quest for sovereignty within the NFIP movement.

Following the UN Law of the Sea Treaty, the Pacific microstates in 1979 declared 200-mile exclusive economic zones (EEZs) around their archipelagoes in order to protect their valuable marine and mineral resources. Seabed minerals—especially manganese and cobalt—are abundant near many Pacific archipelagoes, and it is expected that at the turn of the century the potato-like nodules that contain them will be mined from the ocean's depths, with unknown environmental consequences. These EEZs greatly enlarge the territorial size of the tiny Pacific states, and help to explain why France and the United States are loath to relinquish their Pacific holdings.

The South Pacific Commission based in New Caledonia, the region's first governmental organization, was founded in 1947 by six metropolitan powers (Australia, France, the Netherlands, New Zealand, Great Britain, and the United States) to promote regional economic (i.e., fisheries and agriculture and social development of the Pacific island nations.

The South Pacific Forum, founded in 1971, grew out of dissatisfaction with the South Pacific Commission, which was perceived as being dominated by Great Britain and France. The forum is currently composed of fifteen member nations and meets annually to discuss pressing issues in the region. Agencies of the forum meet more frequently.

In 1973 the forum created the South Pacific Bureau for Economic Cooperation (SPEC, now called the Forum Secretariat and based in Suva, Fiji), which focuses on economic problems of the region.

The forum established a regional shipping line in 1976 (the Pacific Forum Line), a fisheries bureau (the Forum Fisheries Agency based in the Solomon Islands), and the South Pacific Trade Commission in 1979. The forum negotiated the South Pacific Regional Trade and Economic Agreement (SPARTECA) in 1980 to provide preferential nonreciprocal access to Australian and New Zealand markets. Also, the Forum Secretariat participates in the South Pacific Regional Environment Programme (SPREP), a cooperative effort of the forum, the South Pacific Commission and the United Nations started in 1986.

The South Pacific Forum has consistently called for an end to French nuclear testing. Crafted by the forum nations—and inspired by the grass roots NFIP movement—the South Pacific Nuclear Free Zone Treaty was finally endorsed by the Pacific nations on August 6, 1985 (exactly forty years after Horoshima), in Rarotonga, the capital of the Cook Islands. The accord, known as the Treaty of Rarotonga, has been signed by Beijing and Moscow; France, Great Britain and the United States remain the noteworthy recalcitrants, and are thus perceived as pariahs in the Pacific.

What is especially troubling about the U.S. refusal to sign the treaty is that the treaty would not restrict U.S. military activities insofar as it only applies to the South Pacific and therefore does not encroach upon U.S. missile testing at Kwajalein, militarization of Guam, and so on, which are occurring north of the equator and are not covered by the treaty. It has become apparent that the U.S. refusal to sign the Treaty of Rarotonga in part stems from its stand of nuclear solidarity with France.

Quite unexpectedly, France announced on April 9, 1992, that it was suspending its program of nuclear weapons testing at Moruroa until the end of the year and suggested that it would extend the moratorium in 1993 if other nuclear powers followed suit (Riding, 1992, p. A-5).

## Conclusion

In the late twentieth century, some interesting political developments are taking place in the Pacific. The five smallest members of the South Pacific Forum—the Cooks, Niue, Kiribati (formerly the Gilbert Islands), Nauru, and Tuvalu (formerly the Ellice Islands)—recently held their first summit at Rarotonga in January 1992 to form a new organization to increase their visibility in the region as they try to address concerns common to them (*Washington Pacific Report,* 1992, p. 1). Calling themselves the Small Islands States (SIS) the group initially will involve itself in negotiating fishing rights in EEZs, looking at the global warming issue, and surveying the potential of renting air space to aircraft overflying their countries. Also mentioned was the possibility of initiating an SIS development bank. The five nations have a combined population of only 100,000 people living on less than 1,300 square kilometers of land. However, their territories encompass more than seven million square kilometers of ocean, about two-thirds the size of the continental United States.

Another interesting development is the newly created Alliance of Small Island States (AOSIS, including the Seychelles in the Indian Ocean and others), formed by Vanuatu's UN representative. Based in New York, AOSIS is an ad hoc group of diplomats from island states all over the world who wish to maximize their impact at the UN-sponsored environmental summit to be held in Brazil in June 1992.

In the wake of the cold war, and with major trading blocks forming (Japan and the so-called Asian tigers; the European Community; the North American block of Canada, the United States, and Mexico), the island nations of the Pacific will increasingly expand their role as markets and sources of raw materials in a still-unraveling post–cold war world. Moreover, the potential for tourism has been accelerating in the Pacific microstates, as infrastructure development (including ultramodern airports and hotels) and hefty Japanese investment continue. But even tourism will bring severe social, economic, and psychological disruptions to the Pacific region, as described in Cynthia Biddlecomb's excellent 1981 monograph *Pacific Tourism: Contrasts in Values and Expectations.*

Because this chapter focused on the Pacific incursions by the French and U.S. governments, very little was mentioned about the influence of Western capital in the region. For an astute analysis of the role of transnational corporations in the Pacific Islands, the reader is directed to James Winkler's 1982 *Losing Control: Towards an Understanding of Transnational Corporations in the Pacific Island Context.* It is to be hoped that with the diminishing militarization of the Asia-Pacific region—as recently evidenced by France's cessation of nuclear testing and the drawing down of U.S. forces in Korea and the Philippines—the island peoples of Oceania will finally begin to achieve a measure of true sovereignty in the postcolonial Pacific. If the next century fulfills the prediction that it will be known as the "Pacific Century," the indigenous island people of the region should fare better than they have under the brutal ravages visited upon them by the militaristic and marauding metropolitan powers of centuries past.

# References

Alcalay, Glenn. (1987a). "Nuclear Hegemony: America in Micronesia," *Third World Affairs* 1987, pp. 236–50.

———. (1987b). "South Pacific Regionalism: Connecting the Dots on the Map." *Nation,* August 1–8, 1987, pp. 84–86.

———. (1988). "The Ethnography of Destabilization: Pacific Islanders in the Nuclear Age," *Dialectical Anthropology,* vol. 13, pp. 243–51.

Anjain, Liam. (1985). Interview conducted by Glenn Alcalay aboard the *Rainbow Warrior* in the Marshall Islands.

Biddlecomb, Cynthia. (1981). *Pacific Tourism: Contrasts in Values and Expectations.* Suva, Fiji: Pacific Conference of Churches.

Conrad, R. A., Lyuba Zarsky, and Walden Belloe. (1958, June). "March 1957 Medical Survey of Rongelap and Utirik People Three Years After Exposure to Radioactive Fallout." Brookhaven National Laboratory, BNL 501 (T-119).

Crowe, William. (1986, July 26). "Interview with Admiral William Crowe," *U.S. News and World Report,* p. 23.

Eisenbud, Merril. (1956, January 13–14). "Minutes of Advisory Committee on Biology and Medicine." U.S. Atomic Energy Commission.

Hawaii Declaration. (1988). *Global Affairs,* Spring 1988, pp. 217–20.

Hayes, Peter. (1986). *American Lake: Nuclear Peril in the Pacific.* New York: Penguin Books.

Heine, Carl. (1974). *Micronesia at the Crossroads: A Reappraisal of the Micronesian Political Dilemma.* Honolulu: University of Hawaii Press.

Johnson, Giff. (1984). *Collision Course at Kwajalein: Marshall Islanders in the Shadow of the Bomb.* Honolulu: Pacific Concerns Resource Center.

Kelly, Graham. (1987, October). Interview conducted by Glenn Alcalay in Auckland, New Zealand.

Kiste, Robert, and R. A. Herr. (1984). "The Potential for Soviet Penetration of the South Pacific Islands: An Assessment." Report commissioned by the U.S. State Department.

Lohia, Renagi. (1989, September 6–9). "Search for Genuine Security in the Aquatic Continent." Keynote address at the Global Security Studies conference, Seattle.

McHenry, Donald. (1975). *Micronesia: Trust Betrayed.* Washington, DC: Carnegie Endowment for International Peace.

Nuclear Claims Tribunal. (1992, January). *Executive Summary.* Majuro, Marshall Islands.

Riding, Alan. (1992). "France Suspends Its Testing of Nuclear Weapons," *New York Times,* April 9, 1992, p. A-5.

Robie, David. (1986). *Eyes of Fire: The Last Voyage of the Rainbow Warrior.* Auckland: Linden.

———. (1989a). *Micronesia Handbook: Guide to the Caroline, Gilbert, Mariana, and Marshall Islands.* Chico, CA: Moon Publications.

———. (1989b). *Tahiti-Polynesia Handbook.* Chico, CA: Moon Publications.

Walker, Ranginui, and William Sutherland. (1988). *The Pacific: Peace, Security and the Nuclear Issue.* London: United Nations University and Zed Books.

*Washington Pacific Report.* (1984–1992). Published biweekly in Washington, DC.

*Wellington Pacific Report.* (1987-1992). Published monthly in Wellington, New Zealand.

Winkler, James. (1982). *Losing Control: Towards an Understanding of Transnational Corporations in the Pacific Islands Context.* Suva, Fiji: Pacific Conference of Churches.

Wypijewski, JoAnn. (1987). "What's It All About AFFLI?" (Letter to the Editor), *Nation,* December 5, 1987, p. 684.

# 14

# Blue Hawaii: *Bamboo Ridge* as "Critical Regionalism"

## ROB WILSON

### Place and Displacement

When I look around the island space of Oahu where I have lived and worked at the University of Hawaii since 1976, toward lush green Manoa Valley in Honolulu or the expanding commercial area of Ala Moana and the military complex that is Pearl Harbor, I can no longer think "east" and "west" as primary geographical orientations. I have learned to posit *mauka* (Hawaiian for "toward the mountain") and *makai* ("toward the sea") as bioregional directions, though the interactions of East and West, Pacific and Atlantic, local and international, in cultural and economic senses, are so commingled that ocean-front Waikiki looks like a fusion of the Ginza malls of Tokyo and the sun-lotioned streets of Miami Beach. As Wing Tek Lum, a Chinese-American poet of *Bamboo Ridge* affiliation who lives in his native Honolulu, has phrased this problem of geopolitical *dislocation* and historical *displacement* while trying to figure his own tiny place, as a child growing up in multiethnic Hawaii, upon the map of world history and postcolonial torment:

> O
> East is East
> and
> West is West.
>
> but
> I never did
> understand
> why
> in Geography class
> the East was west
> and

the West was east
and that no
one ever
cared
about the difference.[1]

Using a micropolitics of careful perception and slow-moving syntax, Lum's poem defamiliarizes for readers of this "East/West Issue" of *Hawaii Review* that Kipling's late imperial project of Anglo-Saxon global redemption has in certain respects been discredited: where are "East" and "West" in a Pacific region wherein such Eurocentric orientations and EuroAmerican formations of "the Orient" and "the Far East" into commercial unity dissolve into social contradiction and fade into the horizon of the surrounding ocean?[2] In terms of world systems, how can anyone map or totalize the unstable relationship of core (center) and margin (periphery) when Tokyo, New York City, Hong Kong, Los Angeles, and Vancouver all override Lum's Honolulu with claims to be the financial and metropolitan "center" of this Asian/Pacific region? In a postmodern context, with universalizing tactics of "Orientalism" undermined and postcolonial politics of ethnic and racial identity emerging as strategies of resistance, a stance of local implication and global import has managed to worry and "care about" theorizing/imagining this very fate of regional *difference* as the Pacific Rim serves as testing ground and crossover site for currencies and standardized products (not the least simulacrous of which are the atomic bombs still tested by France in the oceans of Micronesia) from Asia, the Atlantic, and the Pacific. Lum's questioning of who he is as a Chinese American in Honolulu requires a concrete sense of where he and his community are classed in the "Asian and Pacific Rim" as a blissful/tormented space of cultural production/difference/resistance not only to the much dreaded/admired "Mainland" of Los Angeles and New York City but also in relation to those main-capital and high finance (yen) interactions of Tokyo, Hong Kong, Toronto, Sydney, and Kuwait.

This matter of geopolitical *dislocation* remains a plight of identity, audience, and commitment for writers in Hawaii as they try to imagine and figure forth, in literature as in ordinary language, their (un-represented or under-represented) place, literally, on or off the global map, as well as their exclusion/token inclusion within multicultural canons of national representation such as the *Heath Anthology of American Literature* (1990).[3] Some 2,397 miles west of San Francisco and Los Angeles, "place" (as well as particularities of language, history, and value) remains an enchanted ground and enigma of the imagination for such local authors. For Hawaii is a state whose special, noncontiguous location off the continental mainland cannot gainsay the fact that it abides within the U.S. historical project of Manifest Destiny as a site substantiating some outpost of imperial outreach in the Asian/Pacific region. Hawaii was annexed in 1898, five years after Queen Liliuokalani was deposed by white U.S. business/military interests, and this place remains the site, unavoidably, of the ongoing battle for modern supremacy that was initiated at Pearl Harbor by rival powers (Western/Asian) for Pacific regional hegemony.[4]

Though this threat of "haolification" through the white culture of English and its attendant dilemmas of self-division registers a theme of much of the literature of Hawaii, this enigma of Hawaii's relationship to "the Mainland" U.S.A. is diagnosed in a poem by Joe Balaz from the recent *Aloha 'Aina Concert* film, "Da Mainland to Me." Balaz uses a stubbornly pidgin English that embodies the very linguistic marginality (dialogue) of being identified as outside, minor, other, different, exotic, distant, unreal to a distant place of cultural domination (in this context, Northern California):

> *Eh, howzit brah,*
> *I heard you goin mainland, eh?*
>   No, I goin to the continent.
> *Wat? I taught you goin San Jose*
> *for visit your bradda?*
>   Dats right.
> *Den you goin mainland brah!*
>   No, I goin to da continent.
> *What you mean continent brah?!*
> *Dah mainland is dah mainland,*
> *dats where you goin, eh?!*
>   Eh, like I told you,
>   dats da continent—
>   Hawai'i
>   is da mainland to me.[5]

So reconfigured, which one is the *mainland* of power, work, community, and family, as providing a sense where one's language and culture fits in: Hawai'i or California, "the mainland" or "the island" of a (globalized, international, intertextual) workaday existence? Balaz's punning retort to his unquestioning friend is staunch, terse, and admirably *local* in a committed sense that speaks as grounded in the body and place of regional identidy: "Hawai'i is the mainland to me" becomes a slogan of regional resistance. Written in a minority diction, though, Balaz's pidgin poem of place was not published in the *New Yorker* or *Zyzzyva* (with workshop poets Garrett Hongo and Cathy Song, for example, who are used by Norton and Heath to represent—in token and palatable form of ethnic formality—the literature of Hawaii). Instead he was published in one of the staunchly local journals that has helped to promote and circulate such a "local" aesthetic. After the "Talk Story" conference of 1978 and 1979, this literature emerged and flourished, belatedly, in keeping with decolonizing trends in the "American Pacific."[6]

At least since the mixed blessings of U.S. statehood accelerated the impact of technocratic culture and imposed a tourist-driven economy of high rises, urban sprawl, and cash nexus upon the islands in 1959, "Hawaii" has remained a place/sign up for grabs within the literary and filmic capitals: something Hollywood or Joan Didion could inject as a backdrop for a detective series to work, use as an exotic landscape parading a Royal Hawaiian Hotel trope of pink-lady paradise and vacation bliss that airline companies refuse to let die, or disseminate around the globe as an ad-poem to sell punch and condominiums with. In short, Hawaii became a region that Westerners could reimagine as a place of surfer girl lyrics and guru initiation movies such as *North Shore* and *Joe and the Volcano* and so on. Against native opposition, Diamond Head, in fact, is slated to become the site of Hawaii's first state film studio, to fund and stimulate such commercial representations as Hawaii shifts from an agricultural to an all-out tourist mode.

So imagined within U.S. discourse, "Hawaii" gets dominantly projected as a region of fantasy and vacation and deployed as an ahistorical Eden of sexual excess that can situate longings for some precapitalist paradise of bodily fulfillment, tribal community, or release from the traumas of overwork in Tokyo or underemployment in Boston. Whatever its troubled history of colonization and plantation settlement, Hawaii flips into the stereotypical moviescape of "Blue Hawaii": a garden of the South Pacific as filmed in these islands, but scripted and made (conceptualized, narrated, and banked upon) for Elvis to play crooning tour guide "local," with lots of strings from the metropolis gleefully attached. Thus this Pacific region has been exoticized, reclaimed, and circulated from these troubled and racially conflicted islands, but made in Hollywood, Tokyo, and New York City. This reduction of history and cultural difference to lush backdrop or seascape of sublimity set apart from the migratory patterns and contradictions of social reality needs to be interrogated, challenged, if not undone by postmodern writers and subjects for whom "Hawaii" is more than a postcard from afar or a chunk of exoticism/orientalism full of lazy Kimos and sexy Suzy Wongs. Drive in along Pearl Harbor and the Nimitz Freeway from Honolulu International Airport, with its neon "Aloha," and your senses will soon confide an alternative message: Oahu and the Outer Islands are far from the simple pastoral "paradise" you had been promised from the snowy streets or toxic sunsets of afar. Neither is Maui just a suburb of California or site of Sierra

Club rejuvenation sessions in what Lawrence once labeled "the void Pacific."[7]

## The Local Meets the Global

The fears and desires that accompany this politics of regional identity formation as positing some act of local resistance to metropolitan centers of hegemonic culture have accelerated, by capitalist hook and cybernetic crook in these decades of postmodernism, into an even more decentered geopolitics of *dislocation* and *displacement.* "All that was local becomes increasingly globalized, all that is global becomes increasingly localized" as Edward Soja claims of urban transformations now taking place to restructure the Pacific Rim.[8] This push-and-pull aspect of postmodernity—argued in diverse cultural studies such as the formulation of the creolized recuperation of the anglophonic novel undertaken in "English" margins of the dismantled British commonwealth in *The Empire Writes Back,* Kenzaburo Oe's postwar commitment to the regional periphery of a residually imperial and centrist Japan, the literature of "the Pacific Way" as making up some region of postcolonial solidarity and resistance, as well as Kenneth Frampton's architectural advocacy of "a place-conscious poetic" of rearguard resistance to technocratic culture[9]—assumes that peripheral cultures are threatened, on several fronts, from pressures of global commodification and the push toward shopping mall unity. Even as these variously grounded "local" cultures try "to qualify the received consumerist civilization through a consciously cultivated 'culture of place,' " neighborhoods turn placeless and dissolve without trace of nostalgia, outside languages flow into and inhabit the inside, deregulated industry turns multiplex and liquid as flights of world capital flow into and out of any homegrown region with the speed of cyberpunk cowboys.[10]

If "the local" encounters "the global" under pressures from these international reconfigurations of region, language, identity, and place, it needs to be recognized that this dynamic of fluid capital still *molests* the local with effects of cultural and economic uprooting that entail bewilderment; mimicry of the metropolitan or imperial center; creolized pastiche; tactical resistance; and an unequal distribution of information, profit, and pain. Drinking a glass of Meadow Gold milk or eating one of the Dole pineapples in Hawaii, for example, you consume the synthetic byproduct of a Green Revolution with untoward local consequences. As Darrell Lum's anecdote of EDB trenchantly suggests, this version of "the local" may not be all that wholesome or natural and may, in fact, be toxic to your survival:

Of course, there are the nature themes which, according to some visiting writers, appear too much and too often in local literature. But why shouldn't we [Hawaiian authors] write about nature when locals know that the EDB (ethylene dimethylbromide, more simply, ant poison) sprayed on the pineapples shows up in the drinking water years after they stop using the insecticide. This isn't standing-in-awe-of or ain't-it-beautiful nature writing that we're talking about.[11]

These Dole pineapples, too, have gone the way of global postmodernism, become a simulacrum of the dying agricultural market in Hawaii that is forcefully phasing out the entire island of Lanai as I speak into a totally planned and manipulated space of golf courses and tourist resorts, again to the chagrin (and impotence) of local workers who have labored for three or four generations in such fields and now are asked to service these new hotels. Remember, as Wing Tek Lum urges in "Local Sensibilities," this pineapple is another object that is invested with local labor and memory: "When I see a pineapple, / I do not think of exotic fruit sliced in rings / to be served with ham, / more the summer jobs at the cannery / driving a forklift or packing wedges on the line."[12]

The end result of such a drive to economic homogenization may be a reconfiguring of the native Hawaiian landscape of Oahu, into an advanced tourist mode of shopping mall redemption. This will generate a space in "the American Pacific" fit for the well-off of the First World such as Japan, the United States, and the EU to vacation in, stylize, pacify, simulate, parody, desacralize, and consume. Any version of the *local* or *regional,* as I am urging, will have to be spread upon the cognitive map of *global postmodernity* that Fredric Jameson, David Harvey, Stuart Hall, Edward Soja, and other "post-Fordist" geographers and critical theorists have conceptualized as that "world space of multinational capital" in which the material/tropological production of Asian/Pacific culture, in Los Angeles or Vancouver as in Honolulu, now takes place. Describing the by-now-lost U.S.$15 billion that circulated in the seventy countries from Panama to Luxembourg, Hong Kong, and the Cayman Islands where the Bank of Credit and Commerce International (BCCI) was, as it were, located, a U.S. investigator puts the matter of this postmodern dislocation succinctly: "It [BCCI capital] was located everywhere but regulated nowhere," which recalls the medieval sense (still invoked by Emerson and William James) of an omnipotent Godhead whose "center [of power] was everywhere and whose circumference was located nowhere."[13]

Since places and languages no longer match or fit prior configurations of imperial domination, the spatial and temporal coordinates of such a condition of global/local interaction have to be imagined and brought to public consciousness, and culture as such "demands a priority of attention" as one site where such cognitive mapping, adjustment, and counterhegemonic resistance can take place.[14] Given these transformations of regional infrastructure, questions of where to locate emerging modes of postcolonial cultural production and strategies of "local literatures" within this globalizing economy of telematic instantaneity and environmental molestation can no longer be phrased as questions of "Who Am I?" or "Where Is My Origin?" but something like, "Where Are We?" or "Where Are We Going?" as a community with a disintegrating ethos of the tactile, natural, vernacular, and near. This dilemma of postmodern locality has been phrased contextually, as a rather Gramscian bumper sticker from the 1960s—"Think globally, act locally." Because local culture as such occurs within a boundary-bashing world system that goes on dismantling places and nation-states into transnational fusions, and more specifically, confuses and misrepresents whole regions of cultural and political-economic difference (such as that area that Japan and the United States have managed as "the Asia and Pacific Rim"), contemporary questions of "the local" or "regional" will have to be articulated in conjunction with thinking through these configurations of "the global" if any community of regional resistance is to have staying power.

Rejecting illusions of cultural purity or racial priority, those who promote cultural production in "the Pacific Way" aim to invent a syncretic culture of resistance grounded in place, language, and the will to collective decolonization. Albert Wendt argues from this Pan-Pacific perspective, using English as a language capable of regional linkage and historical solidarity between the Oceanic cultures of 1,200 indigenous languages, English, French, Hindi, and Spanish as well as various forms of pidgin: "Our quest should not be for a revival of our past cultures, but for the creation of new cultures, which are free of the taint of colonialism and based firmly on our own past." Since 1976, Wendt has called upon this collective process and named his work one of inventing the emerging postcolonial culture of "a new Oceania."[15]

As a cultural region, this formation of the Pacific (either in its hegemonic or counterhegemonic mode) remains a complex, contradictory, and multicentered space of production. As the Fijian critic Subramani has argued of these staggeringly complex cultures of the Pacific, "Each of the regions is oriented towards the power that colonized it: Papua New Guinea, after independence, is still linked to Australia; the French territories are connected to France; the American territories gravitate towards the United States; Easter Island is totally dependent on Chile"; whereas the Polynesian and Melenesian regions such as Fiji and Tonga that were grouped together during the British colonial era still look to London.[16] As one "American Pacific" case in point, I would elaborate

"Hawaii" as exactly such a region of cultural imagining and site of critical resistance that must be situated, in the territories of the so-called Asian/Pacific Rim, within a global context of hegemonic domination that we can denominate, after the dismantling of the Berlin Wall, the ratification of START, and the technoeuphoric war in the Persian Gulf, "the New World Order." Drawing upon my involvement as a writer and critic of the local-literature scene for fifteen years, I will focus upon the "authentically local" culture of Hawaii as positing one such discourse of "critical regionalism." My goal is to articulate the regionally and ethnically inflected literature that has materialized in Hawaii since 1975 as a protopolitical ground, however illusory or fragile, for cultural resistance, projected community, and the recovery of a labor-troubled history and multivoiced critique of imperial domination.

In positing Hawaii as the space of counterhegemonic discourse and a "critical regionalism" capable of resisting, by means of community imagination, threats of external domination and internal sublimation, I will foreground certain qualities, attitudes, and aspirations that would make up this culture of the "authentically local." I will go on to focus upon two institutions in contemporary Hawaii that have been crucial to the formation of a distinctly Hawaiian literature hallmarked by these voices and tones of regional resistance: (a) *Bamboo Ridge,* the largely Asian-American journal formed in 1978 (in conjunction with the Talk Story conference in Honolulu) that has been the main outlet for the publishing and support of literary regionalism in the islands; (b) I will also touch upon the work of the Hawaii Literary Arts Council (HLAC), a statewide and town-grown coalition based in Honolulu that was formed in 1974 and has challenged, stimulated, and at times opposed this local regionalism with outside influxes of national and international pluralism.

## "Authentically Local"

One of the buzzwords in American education and literature today is "multicultural." But Bamboo Ridge has been multi-cultural from the beginning [1978]. We didn't follow any Mainland trends. In this case, they chased after us.[17]

One of the distinguishing marks of "local" cultural production that has emerged in Hawaii since the Talk Story conference of 1978 and 1979 started shaking up the by-products and forms of local literature and history, especially as this literary scene has centered around *Bamboo Ridge, Ramrod, Seaweeds and Constructions,* as well as other cultural journals of local commitment, has been the claim that "local literature" can *some-*

*how* be recognized, by language, style, and cultural attitude, as "authentically local." All well and good—as strategic assertion of *difference.* but what exactly is this complex of qualities that can be validated as "authentically local"?

In a polemic for cultural authenticity called "Local Literature and Lunch" (1986), Darrell Lum brought some clarity to this unstable situation of defining the "authentically local" when he contended that "a number of Hawaiian writers choose to describe themselves as local writers of 'local literature' (as opposed to 'Asian American' literature, largely a mainland term, or 'Hawaiian' literature, which the locals know means native Hawaiian literature."[18] By theory as well as expressive practice in pidgin-based works of striking originality such as *Sun* and *Oranges Are Lucky,* the novelist and playwright Lum (along with poets of diverse cultural and political commitment such as Eric Chock, Joseph Balaz, Dana Naone Hall, Richard Hamasaki, Juliet Kono Lee and others) has gone on to align himself with this distinct and mainland-resistant category we would now differentiate and commend as "authentically local." Of course any invocation of liberal pluralism can be an easy, fake cure to soothing the tensions and contradictions that drive and animate the "authentically local." It can be a way, finally, of absorbing and containing the drive to Hawaiian sovereignty, land rights, native religion, and cultural recovery now taking place by those who identify themselves not as hyphenated Americans but as indigenous "Hawaiians."[19] But Lum's troubled three-category separation of "the local" from both "Asian-American" and "Hawaiian" literatures suggests some of the difficulties and dangers any exclusionary definition of "the local" would confront when articulating the racial, linguistic, and historical dynamics of the overdetermined multicultural literature scene now emerging in contemporary Hawaii.

Furthermore, if we could identify such a complex of styles and attitudes, rooted in a sensibility for place or an enduring taste for pidgin English, for example, what would "local" mean anymore in an era of international finance and global molestation when a colorful and funky surf shop calling itself "Local Motion" can be bought out lock, stock, and stylistic barrel by a corporate conglomerate from Japan? In other words, what kind of purchase would "the authentically local" imply toward articulating and *resisting* the larger hegemonic forces of a shopping mall world? (Ironically, Lum had used this very same Local Motion shop in 1986 to stand for one aspect of the local-culture movement in "Local Literature and Lunch.")[20]

In "Waiting for the Big Fish: Research in the Asian American Literature of Hawaii," an early foray into historicizing local literature in *The Best of Bamboo Ridge Anthology* (1986), Stephen H. Sumida had first begun to challenge the tired colonial commonplace that Hawaii had produced no distinctive literature of its own with a crucial counterargument contending that an "authentically local, Hawaii literature began unmistakably to sound its voice in the postwar years."[21] As one of the organizational participants in the Talk Story scene, circa 1978–1981, Sumida at least knew the impetus driving this local culture of Hawaii as it emerged and sought to counter the fake paradise and erotic primitivism images circulating in the mass media and mainland literature of "Blue Hawaii" as seen, say, from a whiskey-hazed 747 window or the hegemonic view from a Hollywood Porsche. Sumida, Lum, Chock, and others wanted to seize the narrative apparatus, as it were, to recall, represent, and begin to circulate images and "talk story" of a Hawaii they could recognize as cultural home. Journals, presses, and coalitions soon emerged in the 1980s to fill in the literary gap when such outlets, prior to this time, did not broadly exist. Theory and cultural criticism lagged along rather than led the way in trying to articulate what needed to be done.

As a student of English and American Studies at the University of Hawaii in the 1970s, Sumida had been stung and wounded by a remark made by James Michener while putting *A Hawaii Reader* anthology to market during the first year of statehood (1959), the same year that Michener's *Hawaii* propagated his pseudo-history novel of "Hawaii." Michener had stupidly—and repressively—urged that those Hawaiian citizens "Oriental in ancestry" "having arrived in the islands as laboring peasants . . . did not produce a literature of their own."[22] The blithe orientalism of such a remark helped to create a false canon and contributed to a dominant set of misrepresentations and cliches of Hawaii as propagated by mainland writers such as Twain, Longon, Taggard, and May Sarton, and Europeans like Stevenson and Maugham "shanghaied in Honolulu," as it were, or poets such as Rupert Brooke who amazingly wrote of "Waikiki" in 1913 that "Somewhere an ukelele thrills and cries / And stabs with pain the night's brown savagery" [sic].[23]

In *And the View from the Shore: Literary Traditions of Hawai'i* (1991), arguing a more fully grounded *countermemory* to Michener, Magnum, and crew who work in the tourist industry of pastoral-paradise schmaltz so as to recall how "night's brown savagery" still threatens the Royal Hawaiian Hotel with racial and cultural otherness, Sumida has gone on to flesh out some of the genres, themes, tones, language tactics, authors, and works that have counted as and would make up a multicultural literature of what I am calling the "authentically local."[24] Drawing sweepingly upon extraliterary genres such as newspaper writing, songs, hula chants, histories, and the work of stand-up comics as well as critically reading important narrative examples of the "local-literature" tradition such as Milton Murayama's *All I Asking For Is My Body* (1975),

John Dominis Holt's *Waimea Summer* (1976), and O. A. Bushnell's *The Return of Lono* (1956), Sumida has begun to articulate the specific textual/ideological and multicultural ingredients of what it means for the literature of Hawaii to become and remain "authentically local." For Sumida, "local" is not a racial nor even a geographical criterion so much as a sustained commitment to articulating a shared *ground* (Hawaii as place) and sense of *history* (one that recalls plantation history as well as forces of colonial appropriation) as well as embodiment in an authentic *language* (local style). As Sumida confessed to fellow local writer and critic, Tino Ramirez, while recalling his pastoral roots in his family's Aiea watercress farm, local means a commitment to cultivate the agricultural/cultural ground of Hawaii in both material and cultural senses: "You have to take care of the land because it supports you. If you don't the island turns into a dump for imported resources and there's no life. Culture is the same: The word implies planting, tending and nurturing."[25]

*And the View from the Shore* is in the author's own words, "intended as a catalyst" to the cultivating, preserving, and transmitting of this local culture of the "Asian Pacific," and it is certainly—if unevenly—that. As the first scholarly narrative to attempt to describe, in sweeping summary for local and mainland consumption, the "literary traditions of Hawaii" as a distinct set of genres (primarily the so-called complex idyll and heroic), language styles (vernacular values rooted in pidgin English, though not exclusively so), and cultural attitudes (largely an ethos of family, community, and commitment to local ecology as well as *aloha aina,* for example), Sumida's pioneering book is bound to evoke and provoke hard-hitting critiques, counternarratives, and critical perspectives that would challenge many aspects of his ground-breaking summation. Whatever reservations emerge, many writers and scholars immersed in the local-literary scene, myself included, have much to be grateful for in this generous-hearted, brave, and category-defining study.

Admitting my overall respect for this important study, I nevertheless find much to contend with in Sumida's analysis, not the least of which is its sublation of the indigenously Hawaiian perspective into that of a dominantly Asian-American one, its liberal-American pastoralism of child, laboring swain, and place, as well as its very recognizably EuroAmerican urge to categorize if not to compel literature from the "pastoral" to the "heroic" as dominant modes of local-cultural production. Virgil and Milton may have moved from youthful pastoral to the more heroic epic modes of representation in the *Aeniad* and *Paradise Lost,* establishing the canonical pattern of the Western imagination, but why should Hawaii's writers follow this very Eurocentric pattern so rooted in imperial ambition and the will to historical domination? Oddly enough, Sumida seems to second the Asian-American and mainlandish claim of Frank

Chin that in Sumida's words, Hawaii's writers should go "beyond the established limits to take pidgin [English] from the pastoral [as in Lum's short stories] into the heroic" [as in Bushnell's novels] (103). Resisting such a teleological use of generic categories, however, why should Hawaii's writers aspire to achieve works of "the heroic," that most Eurocentric, male-based, and even imperialist of forms as these literary prototypes come down "from da mainland" through Homer, Milton, and Whitman to these Polynesian shores?

In ironic respects, Sumida's study started out as a "view from the shore" of Hawaii to the mainland and thereby posited a perspective of marginalization, difference, and critique. But *And the View from the Shore* has ended up, by disciplinary reversal and the type-assimilating perspective and all-engulfing pluralism of American Studies, a "view from the shore" of the mainland to Hawaii as making up a rather recognizable literary territory after all. This scholarly pastoralism needs to be distanced and critiqued, however, because ("simple" or "complex," "hard" or "soft") such pastoralism remains, I would claim, the dominant ideology of liberal Americanists such as Sumida's mentor at Amherst, Leo Marx, who hovers over the central terms and literary mythology of this study.[26]

Emerging in the back-to-nature movement of the 1960s, American pastoralism would recycle a set of utopic conventions that allow "nature" to coexist as retreat from hegemonic forces of technology and industry, a green space of transcendence wherein (European) art and (American) nature could come into harmony and cultivation as an "earthly garden" that constitutes a recuperated Eden (at Walden Pond, for example). Such was and still is the dominant myth—or "myth at first sight"—of an American Studies beholden to the nineteenth-century romanticism of Thoreau and Muir. It is surprising and cumbersome to see Sumida read the literature of Hawaii through these very deeply *EuroAmerican* categories of pastoral/heroic and even posit the oddly aboriginal notion that pastoral seemingly sprang forth from Hawaiian volcanoes and indigenous chants, that is, that there was a primordial "Polynesian pastoral." "These concepts [of pastoral and heroic] were ready-made well before the arrival of James Cook's expedition in 1778" (4), Sumida claims, so that non-Western native mythologies and Eurocentric *haole* forms coconspired to produce the (pastoral) illusion and (heroic) adventure first conjuring "Hawaii as paradise." A more critical genealogy of Pacific/American pastoral is called for, one situated within colonial dynamics of translation and exchange.

Not until Sumida gets to critiquing Mark Twain's abandoned novel of Victorian Hawaii, by way of the Western primitivist and "noble savage" fantasies of Melville, Cooper, and James Jackson Jarves, does he brilliantly begin to acknowledge and more fully confront the troubled colonialist dynamics of such uneven cultural exchanges. Sumida argues that though Twain promoted a soft-pastoral and tourist-like image of Hawaii as "the loveliest fleet of islands that lies anchored in any ocean," he had thought more darkly and historically in this contradictory novel of the antipastoral impact of disease, greed, legalized theft, racism, and industrial capitalism upon the "island kingdom sitting in the path of America's Manifest Destiny" (39). As Twain intuited, this place of Diamond Head and Pearl Harbor still has much to teach any American Adam innocent how deeply and how early the United States was already grounded in the history of colonial appropriation and the policing of the South Pacific.

I would concede, nevertheless, that Sumida's last chapter, "Hawaii's Local Literary Tradition," provides a splendid summary and survey of the themes and tactics that first emerged in the context of Talk Story and Bamboo Ridge. Trying to acknowledge as well as come to terms with the very distinct and distinctive *Hawaiian* traditions running through and energizing the local, Sumida urges that "the Hawaiian culture was rich in chants, dance, poetry, history, legend, and countless other arts" (272), and goes on to draw this future-oriented moral from such authentically local cultural production: "It seems to me that in this [cultural production by Hawaiians] is a recognition—from a people's actual hard experience of living on islands—that the arts, too, are absolutely necessary for survival." The local, so stated, is not a residual regionality (as often seems the U.S. South) but an emergent one capable of claims upon the national center.

## Blue Hawaii and "Bamboo Ridge"

This issue of "Hawaii" as indigenous territory is one that Hawaiians, in a biological as well as a geopolitical sense, refuse to see as just another forgotten metaphor or semiotic dance by white men on English-speaking Bibles. Rather, they see the issue as a life-and-death imposition on their very language and ecology, their culture as a way of life. Confronting this historical displacement, it should come as no surprise that contemporary Hawaiian writers, both indigenous and "local," remain spiritually *blue*: blue as that tour guide pseudo-Hawaiian Elvis in *Blue Hawaii*, blue as a plantation worker before the war, blue as an oblivion-inducing tourist drink, blue despite being in a so-called biological paradise of flowing mai-tais and see-through clothes, blue as the Delta blues of Robert Johnson despite the lure of surf, the call of body-bliss, the way of the ocean and sky.

Given the heteroglossic diversity ranging from work-ethic Japanese to land-grabbing developers to the slower paced, generous, live-and-let-live Samoans, say, or the Koreans who seem (even displaced in the United States) to run on ginseng, Confucius, and moral methedrine, "Hawaii" needs to be taken into U.S. consideration as a region with a distinct history and multicultural diversity worthy of wider recognition. *Bamboo Ridge* has managed successfully, within a decade, to serve these diverse audiences, styles, and tastes since its Talk Story conference beginnings in creating a narrative/poetic outlet. Cultivating "local writing" in the islands, *Bamboo Ridge* has given ground and place to help materialize, in distinct language, the spirit of "local writing" since its inception after the Talk Story conference. The magazine and press has functioned like the fishing place near the waters off Koko Head on Oahu and the particular style of slide-bait fishing it is named after: at once as a place of nourishment and as a place of manna, diverse voices (poles) who go "searching for his/her god [poem] off Bamboo Ridge" as Tony Lee writes in his flashback story on the ways of old, "Nowadays Not Like Before."[27] "Bamboo Ridge": it remains a place and metaphor of spirit power and ecological poetics, *local* only in some William Carlos Williams sense of loving the ground and body of place in full particularity. A place of daily love and fish-filled survival, hardly at all like the Hanauma Bay (not so far from Bamboo Ridge, actually) that served as the silly backdrop for that local tour guide, Elvis Presley, to croon his moonstruck love songs to while courting a moonstruck tourist wahine in *Blue Hawaii*.

This journal of Hawaii writers called *Bamboo Ridge* depends upon an ethos and center, which remains a hardworking, voluntary, and plural-spirited group of locals based around Eric Chock, Mari Hara, Wing Tek Lum, and Darrell Lum whose goal remains much the same since its founding—to promote the literary arts in the island, both by nurturing an intricate array of local talents, old and young, and by juxtaposing their work with better known talents from the outside world like William Stafford or Garrett Hongo to challenge the writing that goes on here to make larger claims upon "America" as a cultural artifact.

It should now be recognized, too, given the plight of pidgin English to be expressed for imaginative uses as well as the reign of commodity forms within the literary marketplace where poetry, say, seems self-enclosed if not publicly irrelevant, that this nurturing of "literary pluralism"—in some full sense allowing for radically mingled subjects, plural cultures resisting any master narrative of racial or technocratic unity—is no small feat in so-called melting-pot and hodgepodge-quilt Hawaii. This need to enlist a "literary pluralism" remains necessary in Hawaii given the sway of mainstream (and mainland) marketings and genre categories over such minority languages and (merely) regional literatures. Such literature is for the most part ignored or reprocessed, given the territorializing reach of U.S. empire, as it were, that can encode the ordinary lyric subject with liberal arguments and terms, reifications of capital, its own brand of add-one-more-ethnic-and-stir pluralism turning the nation into a gigantic shopping mall of which Oahu's Ala Moana or Newport Beach's Fashion Island are U.S.-sublime instances.

Despite these forces of U.S. marketing and liberal crisis management, these outlets for Hawaiian writing have cultivated in the 1970s and 1980s a literary "heteroglossia" of mixed voices and tongues that might otherwise starve out or have gone unrecognized in this state so far as it is (in a way, *luckily*) from the bright-lights-and-big-city voices of New York and Hollywood. Thus, *Bamboo Ridge,* as the main literary outlet of such localism and Asian-American heteroglossia since 1978, has nur- tured not a "fantasy island" literature of the islands, written by clever (I could even say unwittingly imperialist) outsiders. An historically acute literature of Hawaii, *"local"* in this cutting sense means in touch with the traditions, forms, terms, the body and ground of this much-imaged and much-contested place. "Local," in this contestational sense, means the polyvocal enactment of critical regionalism, a strategy of resistance from postmodern architecture to which my argument will return.

Without committed journals such as Joe Balaz's pidgin-oriented *Ram- rod* or Richard Hamasaki's Pan-Pacific *Seaweeds and Constructions,* which has aligned local literary production with the decolonizing litera- ture of "the Pacific Way," many local writers would have been silenced or simply died off without writing. Not everybody can make the super- woman-like leap from teaching English at Midpac and UH to the Dick Cavett show through the worldwide distribution exposure of Random House like Maxine Hong Kingston. Not everybody, that is, has Max's amazingly graceful if not spiderlike patience and endurance, her touch of narrative genius and canny sense of market self-positioning—a "woman warrior" indeed who could even subvert the petunia elegies of the *New Yorker* with her tripmaster monkey rapping out urban trauma like a Chinese-American Whitman on acid. The eccentric fate of Milton Mura- yama, self-published and belatedly recognized, however, seems much more likely for any willfully local writer, committed to the terms and values of one place and off voices. Such a writer is committed, that is, to the narrating and lyric documenting of a particularly troubled history of Japanese-American plantation workers in wartime Hawaii, many of whom confronted cold war exclusion on into the 1950s and statehood, as Steve Sumida has exposed and as I have written about in my own analysis of Milton's multilanguaged novel of Japanese plantation life as a working-class pastoral.[28]

As for *Bamboo Ridge,* well, Bamboo Ridge is Bamboo Ridge. Spunky, vital, ongoing, recurring, broad hearted, ecological, political, spiritual, micropolitical, cosmic, poor, yet *blue: blue* in some sense early Elvis of Sun Records could figure out as heart tone; blue as the poetry of lyric Memphis and his gigantic-hearted mother; blue as the azure depths off Hanauma; blue as the uncapturable gratitude toward place; blue and refreshing in the glut and glamour of literary magazines like blue shave-ice or ice-shave. *The Best of Bamboo Ridge* anthology that came out in 1986 and is widely used in courses in Hawaii and on the mainland (for example, at UC Santa Cruz, where Sarah Wilson is studying "Asian-American Literature" and reading about her father's gratitude to Italian-American blue in "Anita Sky") is just one installment of an ongoing project in critical resistance and regional self-invention.[29] "Hawaii," as counterlanguage, is threatened by the antipluralist forces of homogenization. As Juliet Kono Lee portrays through her mishmash son in "Yonsei," U.S. pop culture threatens to abolish memory, override ethnic traditions, and render place unrecognizable to those who once inhabited it. The mother chides this fourth-generation son oblivious to Japanese-American traditions on the Big Island as he heads out to surf, "shouldering a radio, / smouldering the speaker / into your ear,"

> You live so far
> from what connects you.
> You have no recollection
> of old plantation towns,
> of rains that plummeted
> like the sheaves of cane,
> the song of flumes,
> the stink of rotting feet,
> the indignities of hard labor.
> Your blood runs free
> from the redness of soil.[30]

But just putting koa wood counters at McDonalds in Waikiki or Peggy Hopper sailboats on the McDonalds in the Hawaii Kai Shopping Mall does not constitute a "local style" of critical-regional resistance; nor does putting Suzy Wong dresses and white bucks on Hotel Street characters result in a distinctly "Hawaiian" literature, even if that convention-coded writer is/was "Hawaiian" and readers on the mainland, especially New York City, cannot tell or care to know the historically necessary *difference* as an act of critical/stylistic resistance. This strategy of a "critical regionalism" in postmodern culture would resist, through local styles and tones, the threat of technocratic modernization and Western "reason" to folk cultures and indigenous traditions or regional locales. As Kenneth Frampton outlines, such an aesthetic of "rear-guard" [*sic*] architecture is enunciated as a counterhegemonic discourse to Western modernity. As such, U.S. regionalism need not be the code term for a neoromantic retreat from history into boyhood sentiment or those hazy charms of pastoral submission. Frampton argues for deploying such tactics of "local culture" to resist the threat of global homogenization and Western modernism, assuming that counterlanguages and counterforms to the "logic" of high-tech capital can be consciously voiced and inflected as regional style without succumbing to decoration or decadence.[31]

Two works I would commend as exactly acts of such "critical regionalism" are the pidgin-rooted short stories of Darrell Lum in *Sun* (1980) and the politicized lyrics of place and voice in Eric Chock's *Last Days Here* (1990). Both of these authors have served, by necessity and vision, as founding editors of *Bamboo Ridge*. As Eric Chock depicts the sway of local culture as a ground of commitment and critique to international capital in a recent poem called "Home Free," for example, the sense of threat is imminent (as his book title, *Last Days Here*, suggests):

> I am like my father
> who never left Hawaii,
> working the dry docks at Pearl,
> sending the ships back
> to some foreign port
> or out at sea.
> He would rather go home after work
> to the quiet place beside the stream. [. . .]
> But now I stand beside
> what used to be our stream:
> the smell of grease or garbage reeks.
> The influx of certain birds
> limits the number of mangoes I can eat.
> Even the tv, where he used to say,
> "Come quick Mommy, we can go to Paris,
> for free!"
> is no longer clear enough
> without a cable hook-up
> so fenced in are we
> with condominiums walking up from town,
> into our valley.

Chock then turns from this register of local molestation to utter a future-oriented plea of entrenchment, the will to be "home free":

> Now that I've grown up, and gone away,
> I want to develop my own sense of green.
> I want to be able
> to cup my hands in a clear stream.
> All I want
> is to be home free.[32]

As ethnic writers such as Frank Chin, Richard Hamasaki, or Lawson Inada have done in different terms, I would reiterate that Americans of ethnic origin need *not* ride this hyphen of self-conflicted identity to mainstream marketings, self-positionings of "voice" still centered in New York. The stylistic result could be the authenticity of voice that the career of Milton Murayama embodies or the locally inflected poetry of Eric Chock, who registers this stance so far from the workshop spotlights of Wesleyan, Iowa, and Yale. The end result could as well be oblivion or regional marginalization, which means another form of national silence.

## The Labors of HLAC

Founded in 1974 with the institutional goal "to serve the literary arts in Hawaii," the Hawaii Literary Arts Council (HLAC), with funding from the State Foundation on Culture and the Arts and usually with supplemental funding from the National Endowment for the Arts, in addition to arranging an incredibly diverse program of readings for Oahu and the outer islands, has maintained such formative programs as the Poets in the Schools (again, under Eric Chock's leadership) and the useful Hawaii Children's Literature Conference and puts out a pluralistic magazine *Literary Arts Hawaii* (now called *Kaimana*) under the care of editors such as Jill Widner and Pat Matsueda in the past and Tony Quagliano, Anthony Friedson, and Joseph Stanton in the present.

The writers brought to read in Hawaii every month are strong in diversity and range: Margaret Atwood, Gary Snyder, Cathy Song, Albert Wendt, Arthur Sze, Ron Silliman, Victor Cruz, Milton Murayama, John Ashbery—just to name a few that remain vivid in my memory. Granted, most of these writers came from the mainland and this provoked some local controversy and resistance, as Steve Sumida has documented. Yet with such a cantankerous inside grounding in tradition (*Bamboo Ridge* et al.) and an outside influx of techniques and agonistic challenges (HLAC et al.), is it any wonder that a new literature has emerged so fully in the 1980s? Audiences for such HLAC-sponsored literary readings over the years have ranged in size from full houses of around 150 at Korean Studies Center and 1,200 at Church of the Crossroads (Gary Snyder), to those attended by three or four friends of the author and a flickering candle (Edith Shiffert of Kona, now of haiku-laden Japan). The glut of these myriad readings goes on until the would-be local poet might flee back to the oceans of the North Shore to get his/her head together; or to the sanctuary of actual fishing off Bamboo Ridge; or to drink alone with the radio; or (like myself) to play Robo-cop basketball on Roy Sakuma

Productions' court on Sunday instead of going to mass or staying home to become an NBA couch potato.

Beyond such sponsored events, HLAC encourages and honors resident writers in the state through awards such as the Hawaii Award for Literature (which was given at the State Capitol to Reuel Denney for 1988, for example) and the Elliot Cades awards (given to Juliet Kono Lee and Darrell H. Y. Lum in October 1991)—two substantial awards to recognize "promising" and "middle-level" local writers at points in their careers when such honors can do their writerly souls and pockets maximal good. I call attention to this HLAC history to suggest, in local terms, that there is a link between literacy and literature. The cultivation of reading and writing skills not only by *Bamboo Ridge* and HLAC but by ordinary citizens needs to be encouraged "at both ends of the spectrum," as Frank Stewart of the UH writing program has noted. Young people can encounter not only the basics of language but the most challenging and imaginative use of their language. The end result for Hawaiian-grown children will be that inward creativity, synthetic thinking, and metaphoric leaps across boundaries can come about in whatever field the student chooses to apply his/her talents.

I would like to narrate this collective work on the spirit-body of local literature and minority languages with one anecdote. In September 1987, I participated in a reading to celebrate the appearance of *Bamboo Ridge* 33. Such potluck-like readings to celebrate the appearance of *Bamboo Ridge, Hawaii Review, Ramrod,* or *Chaminade Literary Review* are sponsored by HLAC, often giving small funds for writers to come from the outer islands. These community-building readings of local imagination and regional commitment, like those of Language Poets in Berkeley, say, have become vital, necessary events for local writers to hear living tones, themes, terms, moves, images, challenges from the Outside— "voices"!

After I had read a few of my own poems on love and death in South Korea, I sat down next to Jonathan Penner (then a visiting novelist at UH Manoa from the U of Arizona) to hear other readers. I was struck by the usual diversity of voices and forms at any *Bamboo Ridge* event—the generational portraits of Mavis Hara, Diane Kahanu, and Wing Tek Lum; the growing-up-local narrative of Rodney Morales; the wry family images of Barbara Guerin; the highly aestheticized nature poems of Reuben Tam—but I was impressed, in particular, by a short story by Gary Pak—"The Valley of the Dead Air"—about a stench on a plantation that not even the old kahunas can remove. Pak's story uses a range of pidgin voices to capture folk culture, as well as a more sophisticated narrative voice with political insights that recalled the materialist perspectives into social community of Latin American novelists.

As place was given voice, I was really taken by this energetic Korean-American writer. I thought to my all-too-pedagogical soul, "Wow, here are new writers who are building on the narrative traditions of people like Milton Murayama and Maxine Kingston, but taking it further, in a new direction, writing about the state and its history in a way that still needs to be done. Hollywood watch out—Hawaii is so much more than the backdrop for a cops-and-robbers show with glitzy cars, Polynesian dolls, beach-bingo Republicans with Tiger caps whose ideal of U.S. womanhood is, well, Nancy Reagan."

As I mused upon this "local" story, Jonathan Penner turned to me, amazed, and asked, "Are your writers *all* this good here?" I wanted to say "Yes, of course," because my *local pride* had stemmed from a kind of maternal-parental delight in *generativity,* the sense that I myself (through teaching, through supporting such vital outlets such as *Bamboo Ridge* or Joe Balaz's even more pidgin-based *Ramrod,* through participating in events such as magazine reading cosponsored by HLAC) had helped to hand on literary traditions and tools that could serve to shape the future, in specific ways that I or any jaded literary "old-timer" could not foresee.

Though it may sound like something you add to pluralize U.S. milk, "HLAC" is something you can add to literacy/literature in Hawaii as a mysterious catalyst with benign effects. For, whatever contentious people are involved, this remains the kind of work that HLAC does: it is a kind of work upon and within the human spirit. The bottom line is, so to speak, these benefits are as real and as lasting as hotels or high-tech bombs, as the work of writers as diverse as Gary Pak, Richard Hamasaki, or Milton Murayama can attest.

## Conclusion: Thinking Locally

In conclusion, I would invoke that bumper sticker refrain of regional pride/identity that registers in tough-minded senses not yet coopted into a marketing strategy of local penetration by the *Harvard Business Review* and that more embittered writers of decadence or adaptation cannot grasp—"Lucky you live Hawaii [that is, *lucky you don't live in East Lansing!*]." Why remain *"local"*? Well, to my critical ally in San Francisco, Frank Chin, local is one rallying cry to get beyond some apolitical and white-left-brain generated "blue Hawaii" invented and marketed in Hollywood and New York for global distribution. Local in this dynamic and nomadic political sense means *thinking globally but acting locally,* as Darrell Lum's comment on the EDB sublime "nature" recognizes as the ground of Hawaii's commitment to preserve the land.

"Hawaii" is not just a trope of the South Pacific. It is not just a primitive myth of eros or native essence, nor a backdrop for Tom Selleck or Jack Lord to sport around in with some mixed-race locals. Hawaii is not just real estate; not just the site of "gee-ain't-it-beautiful" postcards and plumeria-laden love-lyrics.[33] "Hawaii" remains capable of adhering to and broadening the support for a "place-specific poetic," and thereby expressing in multivoiced styles of history the lived-in spirit of a place and region worth preserving and passing on through literature as through other spiritual-material means of struggle.

## Notes

1. Wing Tek Lum, "East/West Poem," *Hawaii Review* Number 10 (Spring/Fall 1980): 140. Lum's commitment to forging a Chinese-American identity particularized in a language of regional location occurs more fully in his first collection of poems, *Expounding the Doubtful Points* (Honolulu: Bamboo Ridge Press, 1987). For related concerns, see *Pake: Writings by Chinese in Hawaii,* ed. Eric Chock and Darrell H. Y. Lum (Honolulu: Bamboo Ridge Press, 1989).

2. On the EuroAmerican production of "the Pacific" as a commercial and geographical region, "Basin," and "Rim," as well as the way this largely occidental invention obfuscated the Asian and Pacific content and motions of this same region, see Arif Dirlik, "The Asia-Pacific Idea: Reality and Representation in the Invention of a Regional Structure," *Journal of World History* 3 (Spring 1992): 55–79. Japan's hegemonic impact upon this region since the 1970s, culturally and economically, cannot be gainsaid.

3. *Heath's* canonization of Hawaiian writers occurs in the Asian-American guise of a Los Angeles/UC Irvine poet, Garrett Hongo, as well as through the work of Cathy Song, a poet from rural Oahu who has after a decade returned from Wellesley and Denver to teach in the state. Ethnically inflected in theme and imagery, both of these much-anthologized writers have much to admire in their work. Although both have appeared in *Bamboo Ridge,* however, their poetry is not tied to any "local-literature" discourse as such but to forms, rhetorical protocols, tones, and terms of logocentric imagery that can be better identified with "workshop" poetry. Responding to a symposium question on "For Whom Does the Poet Write?" Song reveals the nature of this (hegemonic) commitment: "Let's face it—you write for that cold girl in graduate school, the one in the Advanced Writing Workshop, you know the one who could rattle off Yeats and Hopkins at the drop of a hat, who smoldered poems with allegorical themes on Desire, Love, Jealousy, and Hate, who dismissed every poem you ever brought to class. . . . You write with the hope that she'll read your gorgeous poems in *APR* and the *New Yorker,*" *Manoa: A Pacific Journal of International Writing* 3 (1991): 108.

4. For counterhistory of the state from a distinctly Hawaiian point of view and ecology, see Haunani Kay-Trask, "Hawaii: Colonization and Decolonization," in *Class and Culture in the South Pacific,* ed. Anthony Hooper, Steve Britton, Ron Crocombe, Judith Hunstman, and Cluny Macpherson (Suva, Fiji: University of the South Pacific and University of Auckland, 1987), pp. 154–175.

5. Joseph P. Balaz, "Da Mainland to Me," *Chaminade Literary Review* 2 (1989): 109.

6. For one of the first collective manifestations of the "local-culture" movement in Hawaii, see *Talk Story: An Anthology of Hawaii's Local Writers,* ed. Eric Chock, Darrell Lum, Gail Miyasaki, Dave Robb, Frank Stewart, and Kathy Uchida (Honolulu: Petronium Press/Talk Story Inc., 1978). The opposition between Maxine Hong Kingston and Frank Chin, her most forceful antagonist, accusing her (unlike Milton Murayama or Chin himself) of mainstream marketings that entail ideological mystifications of Asian-American dilemmas, was first staged at the Talk Story conference in Honolulu: see Edward Iwata's analysis of this ongoing confrontation of Kingston and Chin in "Word Warriors," *Los Angeles Times,* June 24, 1990, pp. E1–9.

7. In *West of the West: Imagining California,* ed. Leonard Michaels, David Reid, and Raquel Scherr (Berkeley, CA: North Point Press, 1989), D. H. Lawrence provides the Eurocentric orientation for such a *westward* march of culture across the continental frontier: "California is a queer place—in a way, it has turned its back on the world, and looks into the void Pacific." *West of the West* offers a feast of ideological imagining, starting with Theodore Roosevelt's closed-frontier lament for "the true west," "When I am in California, I am not in the west. I am west of the west" and ending with Christopher Isherwood's posthistorical glimpse of Edenic banishment into shopping mall sprawl, cinematic simulation, and freeway norm, "California is a tragic land—like Palestine, like every promised land." Needless to say, it never occurs to born-again Californians that there might be a U.S. geography west of their own Edenic dreaming, except to appropriate as a suburb or a mimic footnote, like Maui out glimmering in "the void Pacific." As Shiva Naipaul puts this hegemonic assumption, "What California is doing today, the rest of the United States will be doing tomorrow" (277). The local is posited exactly against such regional arrogance and vanguard domination of the periphery.

8. Edward Soja, "It All Comes Together in Los Angeles," *Postmodern Geographies: The Reassertion of Space in Critical Social Theory* (London and New York: Verso, 1989), p. 217. In a claim I will pluralize and dispute, Soja argues that this postmodernized Los Angeles has become "the financial hub of the Western USA and (with Tokyo) the 'capital of capital' in the Pacific Rim" (192) and later that "securing the Pacific rim has been the manifest destiny of Los Angeles" (225) from the U.S. financial and military perspective. (On such attitudes, see footnote 7 above.)

9. That " 'standard' British English" gets infiltrated with creolized pidgin "English" and "concerns with place and displacement" fill the postcolonial novel is outlined in Bill Ashcroft, Gareth Griffiths, and Helen Tiffin, *The Empire Writes Back: Theory and Practice in Post-Colonial Literatures* (London and New York: Routledge, 1989), pp. 8–77; Oe's poetic of Japanese regionality is articulated in Kenzaburo Oe, "The Centre and the Periphery," in *Writers in East-West Encounter: New Cultural Bearings,* ed. Guy Amirthanayagam (London: Macmillan, 1982), pp. 46–50, and Masao Miyoshi, *Off Center: Power and Culture Relations between Japan and the United States* (Cambridge, MA: Harvard University Press,

1991), pp. 238–241; the "Pacific Way" is articulated in Ron Crocombe, *The Pacific Way: An Emerging Identity* (Suva, Fiji: Lotu Pasifika Productions, 1976), and Subramani, *South Pacific Literature: From Myth to Fabulation* (Suva, Fiji: University of the South Pacific, 1985); and Frampton's position within postmodernity is outlined in "Towards a Critical Regionalism: Six Points for an Architecture of Resistance," in *The Anti-Aesthetic,* ed. Hal Foster (Port Townsend, WA: Bay Press, 1983), pp. 16–30.

10. See Kenneth Frampton, "Place-Form and Cultural Identity," in *Design After Modernism: Beyond the Object,* ed. John Thackara (London: Thames and Hudson, 1988), pp. 51–66. On restructurations of the "local" via tactics of flexible accumulation that have accelerated since the global recession of 1973, see David Harvey, *The Condition of Postmodernity* (Cambridge, UK: Basil Blackwell, 1989).

11. On this place-and-language ethos of "local writing" in Hawaii, see Darrell H. Y. Lum, "Hawaii's Literature and Lunch," *East Wind* (Spring/Summer 1986): 32–33.

12. Lum, *Expounding the Doubtful Points,* p. 67.

13. On the global preconditions of such postmodernity, see Fredric Jameson, *Postmodernism, or, The Cultural Logic of Late Capitalism* (Durham, NC: Duke University Press, 1990). On BCCI, I quote from Robert Jackson, "BCCI's Shadowy Web Aided Noreiga in 'Shell Game,'" *Honolulu Advertiser,* August 12, 1991, p. D2.

14. Arif Dirlik, "Culturalism as Hegemonic Ideology and Liberating Practice," *Cultural Critique* 6 (1987): 13–19.

15. See Albert Wendt, "Towards a New Oceania," in *Writers in East-West Encounter,* pp. 202–215; and Albert Wendt, "Novelists and Historians and the Art of Remembering," in *Class and Culture in the South Pacific,* pp. 78–91.

16. Subramani, *South Pacific Literature,* p. x.

17. Darrell Lum, quoted in Ronn Ronck, "Write On," *Honolulu Advertiser,* October 24, 1991, p. B2, on the occasion of Lum's winning the 1991 Elliot Cades Award for Hawaiian Literature with Juliet Kono Lee.

18. Darrell Lum, "Local Literature and Lunch," in *The Best of Bamboo Ridge,* ed. Eric Chock and Darrell H. Y. Lum (Honolulu: Bamboo Ridge Press, 1986), p. 3.

19. See Richard Hamasaki's master's thesis in the Ethnic Studies Department of the University of Hawaii, *Singing in Their Genealogical Trees* (1990), for a distinctly "Hawaiian" take on this literature as emerging from a Pan-Pacific territory of ecological, linguistic, and political sovereignty as well as the important anthologies of Hawaiian literature and history edited by Rodney Morales (*Ho'i Ho'i Hou [1984]*) and Dana Naone Hall (*Malama* [1982]), both published by Bamboo Ridge Press in Honolulu.

20. As Lum proudly claimed in "Local Literature and Lunch," p. 3, "There's an island surf shop called Local Motion where you can buy T-shirts that say 'Locals Only.' Anyone can shop there, even tourists. And locals and tourists alike buy 'Locals Only' shirts because they're brightly colored, full of geometric New Wave designs, and they say 'Hawaii' right there in front."

21. Stephen H. Sumida, "Waiting for the Big Fish: Recent Research in the Asian American Literature of Hawaii," in *The Best of Bamboo Ridge,* p. 312.

22. Michener's infamous comment from 1959 is quoted in Stephen H. Sumida, "Waiting for the Big Fish," p. 304.

23. See Rupert Brooke, "Waikiki," in *A Hawaiian Reader,* ed. A. Grove Day and Carl Stroven (Honolulu: Mutual, 1984), p. 217.

24. See Stephen H. Sumida, *And the View from the Shore: Literary Traditions of Hawaii* (Seattle: University of Washington Press, 1991). Subsequent references to this study will occur parenthically.

25. Tino Ramirez, *Honolulu Star-Bulletin,* April 13, 1991.

26. I argue a broadly counterpastoral way of looking at the U.S. landscape—and technoscape—in *American Sublime: The Genealogy of a Poetic Genre* (Madison: Wisconsin University Press, 1991), especially Chapter 9, "Towards the Nuclear Sublime." Simple or complex, *pastoral* can become a literary way of ignoring and containing the historical fact of how fully nuclearized, ecologically threatened, and commodified Hawaii and "the American Pacific" already are: we expect this from *New Yorker* poets writing landscape poems set in Hawaii, or racially obtuse movies like *North Shore,* but not from "authentically local" poets and critics of *Bamboo Ridge.* A study of "pastoral" that more trenchantly sets this literary mode (appropriated and transformed by Americans from Great Britain) within the class dynamics of labor, social community, and injustices of global capitalism remains Raymond Williams, *The Country and the City* (New York: Oxford University Press, 1973); but also see Lawrence Buell, "American Pastoral Ideology Reappraised," *American Literary History* 1 (1989): 1–29, for a more critical perspective on "pastoralism" as an American-liberal ideology. Neither of these works figure in Sumida's analysis of American/Hawaiian pastoral, however.

27. Tony Lee, "Nowadays Not Like Before," in *The Best of Bamboo Ridge,* pp. 167–174.

28. For a history of plantation communities and the ethnic determinations that marked the complex class warfare that dominated Hawaiian daily life from 1840 to 1960, see Ronald Takaki, *Pau Hana: Plantation Life and Labor in Hawaii* (Honolulu: University of Hawaii Press, 1983). On Murayama's plantation novel, in addition to the Sumida scholarship cited above, also see the heteroglossic analysis of dominant and minority "voices" in Rob Wilson, "The Language of Confinement and Liberation in Milton Murayama's *All I Asking For Is My Body"* in Eric Chock and Jody Manabe, eds., *Writers of Hawaii: A Focus on Our Literary Heritage* (Honolulu: Bamboo Ridge Press, 1981), pp. 62–65; and Rob Wilson, "Review: *All I Asking For Is My Body,"* *Bamboo Ridge* Number 5 (1979–1980): 2–5.

29. Rob Wilson, "Anita Sky," in *The Best of Bamboo Ridge,* p. 111.

30. Juliet S. Kono [Lee], "Yonsei," in *Hilo Rains* (Honolulu: Bamboo Ridge Press, 1988), pp. 102–103.

31. See Kenneth Frampton, "Towards a Critical Regionalism: Six Points for an Architecture of Resistance," in *The Anti-Aesthetic,* pp. 20–29.

32. Eric Chock, "Home Free," in *Last Days Here* (Honolulu: Bamboo Ridge Press, 1990), pp. 74–75.

33. Concerning this trope of Pacific domination—projected in EuroAmerican artists such as Paul Gauguin, Robert Louis Stevenson, Mark Twain, Wallace Stevens, and Marlin Brando—that "makes explicit the equation tropics / ecstasy / amorousness / native," see Abigail Solomon-Godeau's analysis of Gauguin's French-colonial primitivism in "Going Native," *Art in America* 77 (July 1989): 119–128. As a "Pacific paradise" extending the nineteenth-century myths of U.S. Manifest Destiny, "Hawaii" still functions as this displaced incarnation of a U.S. Edenic eros. So runs the ad-myth for "the friendly skies" of United Airlines.

# 15

# There Is More in the Rim Than Meets the Eye: Thoughts on the "Pacific Idea"

## ARIF DIRLIK

A few years back, a discussion of the current economic status of Pacific islands in *The Economist*, began with the line, referring to the Pacific, that "it is not just a piece of geography, it is an idea."[1] Ideas depend on who thinks them, in what context and to what purpose. I reflect below on two different ways of thinking the Pacific, one from within and the other from without, that in their contradictoriness have much to tell us about the historical formation of the Pacific. They are also relevant, I will suggest, to thinking the global future both within and without the Pacific, because their very contradictoriness raises questions concerning the ways in which we think about the past and the present.

### The Pacific Rim: EuroAmerican and Asian

The Pacific occupies the prominent place that it does in our consciousness today not because of what is happening within the Pacific, but because of developments on what has come to be called the Pacific Rim. The Rim, especially on the Asian side, has come to serve not only as a frontier of development, but provides a new paradigm for global economic organization and change. But the Rim is ultimately external to the Pacific; at various locations along it are arraigned economic, political, and military forces that gaze across an empty Pacific at imagined antagonists somewhere else on the Rim. The Rim in effect erases the spaces within it from which it derives its name. The *Economist* article cited above recognizes this curious situation when it remarks that:

> It is clear that this Pacific does not include Japan or Hong Kong or the west coast of America. These are the rich places in what has come to be called the Pacific Rim, which are convinced they are going to become even richer

**351**

in the coming "Pacific Century." Neither are Australia and New Zealand part of this Pacific. They are Pacific powers, as are America and the Soviet Union, no-nonsense places concerned with areas of influence and such-like.

The real Pacific, the proper Pacific, the one in the world's dream-mind, is made up of the small Pacific islands, mostly in the South Seas. . . . [Their] reality is that they are poor.[2]

Geography tells us little about these spaces; on the contrary, the spaces of wealth and power inscribe the boundaries of the Pacific. But the "poor" empty space within the Rim, in its very emptiness, has a part to play as the source of utopian longings that belies its insignificance in terms of wealth and power:

The Pacific Idea is important for the mental well-being of the world. There is another possibility, it insists. The globe has not become the same all over. The Pacific idea stands for a belief in the survival of innocence; the Pacific is not really innocent, but something primal lingers there, deeply attractive to the inhabitants of an increasingly uniform industrial society that has come to seem, somehow, rather disappointing.[3]

Herein are the two contradictory ideas generated by the Pacific, that have been integral to the history and, therefore, the formation of the region: the Pacific as a frontier of capitalist development, and the Pacific as an escape from the ravages of capitalism. Contradictory as they are, the two ideas are constituent of a single Pacific discourse; in either case, the Pacific is internalized as a problem in EuroAmerican well-being.[4]

What is absent from this discourse are the people of the Pacific. What happens to the discourse when we bring their voices in? Those voices, I would like to suggest below, are essential to any construction of a Pacific discourse that seeks to break with the hegemony of the past—actual EuroAmerican hegemony over the people of the Pacific, and an ideological hegemony of the past over the present in the consciousness of EuroAmericans themselves. In spite of conscious well-intentioned efforts on the part of many to break with past hegemonies, the latter persists in Pacific Rim discourse, which is the most recent expression of EuroAmerican hegemony over the Pacific (now joined, however, by Pacific-Asian discourses which are integral to the discourse of the Rim). Before they may aspire to liberating the Pacific from hegemony, I will argue, those on the Rim need as a first step to liberate themselves from the hegemony of a past consciousness—for which they may well need the help of the Pacific peoples, and their conceptions of themselves and of the world. Before I turn to that question, a few words first about the Pacific discourse which continues to dominate contemporary consciousness of the Pacific.

## The Pacific and EuroAmerican Vision

I reverse the terms in the title of Bernard Smith's seminal work with a purpose; to draw attention to the ways in which the Pacific altered EuroAmerican ways of seeing the world, which that work documents.[5] Put bluntly, the encounter with the Pacific was to culminate in an expansion of the EuroAmerican vision of the world both spatially and temporally. Shortly after the conclusion of Captain James Cook's third (and to him, fatal) voyage that was to delineate the boundaries of the Pacific as we know it, the Reverent Thomas Haweis, a founder of the London Missionary Society, observed in a sermon:

A new world hath lately opened to our view, call it Island or Continent, that exceeds Europe in size: New Holland; and now become the receptacles of our outcasts of society—New Zealand, and the innumerable islands, which spot the bosom of the Pacific Ocean, on each side of the Line, from Endeavor Straits to the Coasts of America, many of them full of inhabitants—occupying lands, which seem to generalize the fabled Gardens of the Hesperides,—where the fragrant groves, which cover them from the sultry beams of day, afford them food and clothing; whilst the sea offers continual plenty of its inexhaustible stores; and the day passes in ease and affluence, and the night in music and dancing.[6]

The "second new world" revealed by Cook's voyages to a Europe in the midst of a "Pacific Craze" not only expanded the known world by half, but brought into the European consciousness wonders hitherto unknown in the form of new flora and fauna, and new men, to "enlarge the sphere of contemplation"—as John Locke had said with reference to the "first new world."

A contemporary French scholar wrote that for the "philosophical traveller," scrutinizing the peoples of the Pacific showed the way "to the first periods of our own history . . . sailing to the ends of the earth, is in fact travelling in time; he is exploring the past; every step he makes is the passage of an age. Those unknown islands that he reaches are for him the passage of human society."[7] The illusion of panoptical vision engendered by the Pacific was to foster an even more illusory temporal vision that claimed comprehensive historical hindsight. In the guise of noble savage or brutal cannibal both, the Pacific Islanders exemplified even more thoroughly than the indigenous peoples of the Americas the primitivism that Europeans had long left behind. The construction of the primitive was part of the very process of constructing civilized Europe. Writing of European responses to the Americas, J. H. Elliott observes that, "if progress now became a conceivable possibility, this was partly on account of the discoveries themselves . . . the discovery of the New

World . . . strengthened the Christian providentialist interpretation of history as a progressive movement which would culminate in the evangelization of all mankind, it equally strengthened the more purely secular interpretation of history as a progressive movement which would culminate in the civilization of all mankind."[8]

Civilization was not necessarily an unqualified blessing and, in the middle of the eighteenth century, the "noble savage" of the Pacific served as the object of nostalgia for those who would escape its ravages. As the faith in European civilization took root, demonstrated by the very global conquest of Europeans, what came to the fore was the image of the uncouth savage, in need of Europeans' civilizing mission, chiefly through the agency of Christianity. Reverend Haweis, having described the enchanted "state of nature" in which the Islanders lived, proceeded immediately to disenchant it by concluding that "amidst these enchanting scenes, savage nature still feasts on the flesh of its prisoners—appeases its Gods with human sacrifices—whole societies of men and women live promiscuously, and murder every infant born amongst them." And as in the Americas earlier, it was unclear whether these savages were genuinely human; civilizing them also implied, therefore, their humanization—even if it meant depriving them of their idyllic existence. Charles de Brosses, the author of the first important and influential work on Pacific voyages in the middle of the eighteenth century, justified the colonization of the Pacific for, while colonization might deprive them of their innocence, it would bring them much benefit, and not just materially: "We must also remember how much they would profit, by adopting our ideas of a regular and well-ordered society; their minds would be opened, and formed, their savage manners softened: In short, those nations would become men, who have just now nothing human but their figure."[9]

The competing notions of the Pacific as idyllic Eden and empty savage land waiting for civilization emerged simultaneously. By the end of the eighteenth century, the latter had won over the former. The image of a Pacific Paradise would survive the progressive physical and cultural destruction of the Pacific over the next century in the nostalgic memories of EuroAmericans; ironically, for part of the destruction entailed the assimilation by the islanders of the EuroAmerican image of them as uncouth primitives.

As Bernard Smith and others have documented, the Pacific was to have a lasting impact on European thinking—from new orientations in the arts to the emergence of the Pacific as a great "laboratory of nature." Perhaps the most significant product of the latter would be the theories of natural and social evolution. If the evidence of the Pacific played a major part in Charles Darwin's formulation of the theory of evolution, the Pacific peoples would be among the first victims of the colonialism which the theory came to justify. The expansion of EuroAmerican spatial and temporal consciousness by the Pacific was in the end an integral part of the EuroAmerican colonization of the world, of which it was at once a product and an agent.[10]

While colonialism has not disappeared entirely, especially where indigenous peoples are concerned, it is only rarely in our day that we might find a defense of colonialism as a beneficent idea. Rather, since World War II, the diffusion of civilization from EuroAmerica has been transmuted to the idea of modernization. As with earlier notions of civilization, it is still a social order empowered by capitalism that defines modernity, although it is now a capitalism far in advance of its origins in early modern Europe, and no longer confined to Europe or the Americas. Indeed, it is their success with capitalist development that has brought societies of the Pacific Rim to the forefront of our consciousness. Similarly, the inability to assimilate the capitalist order serves as a marker of "backwardness" within the Rim. That capitalist modernity does not serve merely as a measure of welfare, but also of civilization, is implicit in the perverse judgment that *The Economist* passes on the Pacific Islanders, which differs from the judgments of early modern Europeans on the islands only in its vocabulary:

> If the Pacific Rim countries do prosper as they expect, investment, large or small, should not be a problem. The main problem may be the islanders themselves. The following paragraphs may offend them. . . . The Pacific islanders have to change their ways. They suffer from, to use a polite word, inertia. The basic needs of life are available with minimum effort. Nobody need go hungry. There are fish in the lagoon and almost anything grows in the climate of perpetual summer. The biggest effort may be deciding what to do with the day. Those who believe that life must offer more find their ambitions stifled by the confines of a small island. . . . in a place with a population the size of a small European town, there is not much scope for a clever man.[11]

It is a tribute to the power of the ideology of capitalist modernity that what might appear otherwise as an occasion for celebration appears here as a lack on the part of the islanders. After two centuries of ecological, social and cultural destruction, it may be miraculous that the Pacific islands may still provide the good life. But it is neither human welfare, nor the good life, that is the measure of development; rather, it is the "scope for the ambitious." The Paradise may still be a paradise, but only for those suffering from "inertia." They may have full bellies, but they are not civilized. The premises that shape this way of thinking the Pacific still belong in the discourse that was produced by the earlier contact with the Pacific. One solution *The Economist* offers to the dilemma of the Pacific

Islanders is tourism; to sell paradise, which will bring to the islands many jobs as restaurant waiters and hotel chambermaids. The other is to import "Indians and Chinese, those bustling, adaptable journeymen of the Pacific, who will bring vitality to the islands." It does not occur to the writer that there may be still another way: to restore a way of life that places human welfare and happiness ahead of development.

With this in mind, let me turn to what some Pacific Islanders may have to say about their own aspirations.

## Glimpses from the Inside

If for EuroAmericans the Pacific provided the materials for an expansion and enrichment of their world views, the consequences of the interaction for the Islanders was an impoverishment and contraction (if not the extinction) of the world they had known before European arrival. There, too, cultural restriction and impoverishment was intimately related to material circumstances or existence; the disenchantment of nature went hand-in-hand with the expropriation of material resources in land and sea, which in their case had shaped not only spatial location but the very notions of temporality.

In his comparative examination of native-white relations in Australia, New Guinea and North America, Wilbur Jacobs wrote:

> In a sense, the real test of survival was possession of the land. Next to outright extermination the best technique for destroying natives was dispossessing them of their land. Land for the aborigines was all important because it was a spiritual ingredient of their culture; it determined their social groupings and status; and, finally, it was the source of their livelihood. Thus, if there is a real test for the survival of a native people it is found in the answer to the question: how much of their land have they retained after the alien invasion?[12]

Not much, is the evident answer, and when natives retained land, it was totally reconfigured in settlements that broke with the past spatially, also reconfiguring social relations and cultural orientations. Ward Churchill writes that for the American Indian, even "engineering was and is permissible, but only insofar as it does not permanently alter the earth itself."[13] The white attitude toward the land was the opposite: if land was not "permanently altered" by human activity, it was empty land. Thus, white settlers in New Zealand viewed Maori use of the land to be "undirected and, at worst, wasteful to the point of disallowing indigenous claims to ownership." One English official, himself relatively sympathetic to the Maori, nevertheless could not refrain from carrying "the imagination to another century—when this now desert country will no doubt be peopled—when the plains will be grazed by numerous flocks of sheep, and the streams, now flowing idly through remote valleys, will be compelled to perform their share of labour in manufacturing of wool."[14] Maori notions of ownership, based on a complex interplay of kinship, residence and utilization, were perceived by the British to lie at the root of this wastefulness, which also accounted for their "backwardness." Dispossessing them of their land, by substituting private property relations for native notions of ownership, was a benign act of civilization which would launch the Maori on the way to progress. A report on land division in 1862 stated that:

> Communism in land is admitted to be the great obstacle to the social and material advancement of the Maori people. It is very certain that, under the present system of land tenure, the Natives will never be induced to give up their low Maori habits and adapt themselves to the requirements of a superior civilization. . . . nothing would tend to do more to call forth their industrial energies and to promote a desire for worldly improvement than the possession, in severity, of an exclusive title to a piece of land, *however small in extent.*[15]

The dispossession of the natives of their land, in remapping their world, would transform radically their social world, as well as the spatial and temporal configuration of their spirituality, which was bound up with the land and, for the Pacific peoples, the sea as well. From two ends of the Pacific, we have examples of the contraction of native worlds, which eloquently express the tragic disenchantment of nature that accompanied their forced entry into the world of progress.

The Australian aborigines believed that at the origins of creation in the Dreamtime, the world had been sung into existence by ancient ancestors, "who had wandered over the continent . . . singing out the name of everything that crossed their path—birds, animals, plants, rocks, waterholes—and so singing the world into existence."[16] The songs then became the legacies of the clans that claimed descent from the various ancestors. The Songlines served as maps as well as direction-finders: "providing you knew the song, you could always find your way across country."[17] It was the song that also served as the basis for property:

> Before the whites came . . . no one in Australia was landless, since everyone inherited, as his or her private property, a stretch of the Ancestor's song and the stretch of country over which the song passed. A man's verses were his title deeds to territory. He could lend them to others. He could borrow other verses in return. The one thing he couldn't do was sell or get rid of them.[18]

The songs did not just map out space, but also contained time. "Aboriginals could not believe the country existed until they could see and sing it." The world must be called into existence again and again through the song. And each time the song was sung, the Dreamtime of the Ancestors was recalled as well.[19] The past and the present were part of the same song, as creation was immanent within it.

At another end of the Pacific, the native peoples sang their way through the seas. In her account, *The Daughters of Copper Woman*, Anne Cameron recalls the words of her grandmother:

> Everythin' we ever knew about the movement of the sea was preserved in the verses of a song. For thousands of years we went where we wanted and came home safe, because of the song. On clear nights we had the stars to guide us, and in the fog we had the streams and creeks of the sea, the streams and creeks that flow into and become Klin Otto . . .
>
> There was a song for goin' to China and a song for goin' to Japan, a song for the big island and a song for the smaller one. All she had to know was the song and she knew where she was. To get back, she just sang the song in reverse. . . .[20]

Here, too, the songs were the legacies of the families who inherited them from their lineages.

"The sickness killed off the songs," Cameron's grandmother tells her, recounting the fate of the tribe with the arrival of the white people, "so many people died. So many songs and stories and sea routes and histories."[21] As the lineages died out, so did the songs, and with them were gone the spaces that the songs had marked—and the temporalities contained within the songs.

The Songlines, and the consequences of their extinction or transformation (as with railroads in Australia), stand as poetic metaphors for the ways in which Pacific spatialities and temporalities were transformed in the course of the invasion of the Pacific by the technologies, property relations, and moral assumptions of a new civilization of progress. In Hawai'i, where the great land redistribution of 1848 created private property relations, and led to a large scale transfer of land from native Hawai'ians to the white settlers, the result of the Hawai'ians was "cultural debasement, economic destitution, and a third-rate status in their own homeland."[22] In this case, Christian missionaries played a central role both in the institution of new property relations, and the direct "deculturation" of the native population. In the words of Haunani-Kay Trask,

> Hymns that told of a suffering Jesus and a sinful humanity replaced chants of the origins of the universe, the evolution of life forms, and the genealogy

of an entire people. No longer was an ancient history recited, no longer were new chants composed. A repressive sexual morality reduced the fecund, sensual imagery of the Hawaiians to concepts of evil and filth. For example, where Hawaiians once eroticized their environment with sexual names, they were, under Christian influence, to rename their natural world, as their children, with safe English language referents. . . . Native history and native culture were all but lost along the way.[23]

The respatialization that is implicit in the names, not to speak of the new property relations, served also to distance the Hawai'ian present from the Hawai'ian past which, when not "forgotten" actively, lived on as a cause for embarrassment. The British sociologist Peter Worsley, writing of the conceptions of time of hunting and gathering peoples, has observed that they were not "dedicated to the accumulation of material wealth. Hence their conception of time was not linear. If we deny them any importance in history, they denied history as a category of the understanding."[24] The peoples of the Pacific, as they were compelled into history, were also historicized as primitives. As their spaces were renamed to render them into foreigners in their land, so was their temporality transformed from mythic to linear time; in many cases beginning with their entry into "civilization" with their Christianization. The distinguished Samoan writer Albert Wendt observes:

> I said earlier that a society is what it remembers, we are what we remember.
>
> If we look at written Pacific history, we find that most of it is the work of papalagi/outsiders, and that most of it is based on records kept by papalagi explorers/missionairies/clerks/etc. so we can say that that history is a papalagi history of themselves and their activities in our region; it is an embodiment of their memories/perceptions/and interpretations of the Pacific. And when we teach that history in our schools we are transmitting their memories to our children, and consequently reordering our children's memories.[25]

Adds Malama Meleisea, "The division of time into Before Christ (BC) and the Year of Our Lord (AD) began for us in 1830 with the arrival of the Gospel. We divide our history into the *pouliuli,* the time of darkness, and the *malamalama,* the time of enlightenment."[26]

Given the colonial erasure of indigenous memory, "re-learning" (in Trask's terminology) or "singing into existence" native spatiality and temporality is an utmost concern for Pacific peoples in search of liberation from colonialism and its legacy—which may account for the prominence of literature and poetry in Pacific writing, or to put it more accurately perhaps, for the denial by prominent Pacific writers such as

Epeli Hau'ofa, Haunani-Kay Trask, or Albert Wendt of conventional distinctions between history, poetry, or politics. This is not to suggest that struggles in the Pacific are merely literary struggles; "the struggle for the land" is of crucial significance where colonial rule persists, as in Hawai'i. But at bottom the struggle in a broader sense is a struggle against ideological hegemony, to rescue from colonial erasure concepts of space and time that may enable the formulation of alternatives to modes of development which from indigenous perspectives are little more than modes of subjugation—of native lands, as well as of native sensibilities.

I would like to look briefly here at a recent essay by Epeli Hau'ofa which is exemplary of these themes, especially the theme of the recapturing of space as a prelude to recapturing an indigenous identity in development. What makes this piece doubly interesting is that Hau'ofa, an anthropologist by training, is a distinguished writer of fiction, and head of the School of Social and Economic Development at the University of the South Pacific in Fiji. The combination is an unlikely one, and the very poetry of Hau'ofa's writing, aside from its content, offers an indigenous paradigm of Pacific development that contrasts sharply with the prosaic greed that empowers the Pacific Rim discourse of global capital.

Hau'ofa's essay, entitled "Our Sea of Islands," sets out to refute the notion of the "smallness" of the Pacific islands, which implies that "even if we improved our approaches to production . . . the absolute size of our islands would still impose such severe limitations that we would be defeated in the end."[27] It was his concern as a teacher, Hau'ofa tells the reader, that first led him to question this idea: "What kind of teaching is it to stand in front of young people from your region, people you claim as your own, who have come to the university with high hopes for the future, and to tell them that their countries are hopeless? Is this not what neocolonialism is all about? To make people believe that they have no choice but to depend?"[28] Colonial hegemony is very much on Hau'ofa's mind when he states that "such views, which are often derogatory and belittling, are integral to most relationships of dominance and subordination, wherein superiors behave in ways or say things that are accepted by their inferiors who, in turn, behave in ways that serve to perpetuate the relationship."[29]

This head of a school of development acknowledges without apology that the inspiration for the essay came to him during a trip to Hawai'i, where he witnessed that "under the aegis of Pele, and before my very eyes, the Big Island was growing, rising from the depths of a mighty sea." "The world of Oceania is not small," he concluded, "it is huge and growing bigger every day."[30] The idea of smallness was created by Europeans and Americans "who drew imaginary lines across the sea, making the colonial boundaries that, for the first time, confined ocean peoples to tiny spaces." But, Hau'ofa states,

> if we look at the myths, legends and oral traditions, and the cosmologies of the people of Oceania, it will become evident that they did not conceive of their world in such microscopic proportions. Their universe comprised not only land surfaces, but the surrounding ocean as far as they could traverse and exploit it, the underworld with its fire-controlling and earth-shaking denizens, and the heavens above with their hierarchies of powerful gods and named stars and constellations that people could count on to guide their ways across the seas. They thought big and recounted their deeds in epic proportions. . . . Islanders today still relish exaggerating things out of all proportions. Smallness is a state of mind.[31]

"There is a gulf of difference," Hau'ofa continues, "between viewing the Pacific as 'islands in a far sea' and as 'a sea of islands.'" The difference, we might add, is the difference between living with the hegemony of a colonial past, and a reassertion of Pacific identity in search of new alternatives for the present and the future. He concludes:

> Oceania is vast, Oceania is expanding, Oceania is hospitable and generous, Oceania is humanity rising from the depths of brine and regions of fire deeper still, Oceania is us. We are the sea, we are the ocean, we must wake up to this ancient truth and together use it to overturn all hegemonic views that aim ultimately to confine us again, physically and psychologically, in the tiny spaces which we have resisted accepting as our sole appointed place, and from which we have recently liberated ourselves. We must not allow anyone to belittle us again, and take away our freedom.[32]

## Indigenous Visions/Pacific Rim Discourse

The hegemony that Hau'ofa seeks "to overturn" is the hegemony of Pacific Rim discourse. This discourse is heir to two centuries of domination of the Pacific by powers from the Rim, or outside of it, that has been accompanied ideologically by the erasure of the subjectivities of Pacific peoples, and the denial to them of a place in modernity. In our day, Pacific Rim discourse articulates the location on the Rim of new frontiers of capital that dynamize capitalism globally, and revitalize a teleology of capitalist modernity. This teleology continues to marginalize those who do not live up to its expectations; among those so marginalized, as *The Economist* article above exemplifies, are the people of the Pacific.

To recognize the voices of Pacific peoples, conversely, has a significance that is greater than rescuing them from historical oblivion, or recognizing that they have experienced modernity not as progress but as domination and cultural extinction. It is to recognize also the challenge to capitalist modernity that is imbedded in their historical experience and, even more importantly, in their efforts to recapture a way of life that presupposes alternative organization of social relationships, and an alternative relationship to nature. It is, in other words, to reconceive modernity so as to allow for alternatives to capitalist modernity, of which indigenous visions are integral premises. "The Pacific Way," which appears in Pacific Rim discourse as an alternative within capitalism, appears in this other perspective as a means to overcome capitalist modernity to serve as a guide in a global search for alternatives to capitalism.[33]

I have suggested in a recent essay that, with the passing of the idea of the Third World as a critique of capitalism, indigenous visions now remain as a source of critique, as well as new conceptualizations of alternative modernities.[34] Indigenous visions are significant in this regard for a variety of reasons. Chief among them is the challenge in the indigenous vision to a fetishism of development as a goal in itself, without consideration of what development may imply in terms of human welfare, social relations and relations to the natural environment. In this sense, the indigenous vision stands in criticism both of capitalist and socialist approaches to the question of modernity. But the indigenous vision is significant in another sense: in its challenge to our ways of thinking about the world. Hegemonic discourses, in both capitalist and socialist approaches to development, are universalizing discourses, that prescribe identical futures for people around the world universally. Indigeneous discourses are of necessity local in orientation, and resist hegemonic universalisms that rest epistemologically on the objectification of the world.[35]

Pacific peoples' visions occupy a particularly important place in the contemporary critique of capitalist teleology because Pacific Rim discourse has emerged as the most recent location for a fetishized developmentalism (recall *The Economist* article, and the priority it gives to the ambitious over human welfare). As is the case with all indigeneous visions, however, the use of Pacific indigenous visions in the critique of capitalism presents problems of a profoundly political nature. These problems pertain to the relationship between the aspirations of Pacific peoples, and a critique of capitalist modernity in general; or, more concretely, the relationship between Pacific peoples speaking for themselves, and those outside such as the present author, who find in Pacific visions sources for the critique of problems of a global nature, which may or may not be of relevance to the former.

In a recent article, the Pacific historian Klaus Neumann, has offered a cogent and sensitive account of such problems where they relate to "first contact" between Pacific Islanders and EuroAmericans. Neumann focuses on the "politics of historical representation"; in other words, who represents whom, and how. Neumann points out correctly that even those nonindigenous historians writing sympathetically about indigenous peoples' experiences may be complicitous in perpetuating a hegemonic relationship because of the "political economics of academic knowledge production." The very location of nonindigenous academic historians in First World institutions implies that they are speaking about the powerless from their own positions of power, assuming the prerogative of representing the powerless, which means that their discourses are shaped by First World concerns, rather than concerns of the indigenous peoples themselves. For the most part, moreover, nonindigenous historians, by the very requirements of their location, are subject to "the myths of a historiographical practice that pretends that history is merely an account of the past and that past and present do not and must not intrude upon each other."[36] This latter is obviously worlds apart from the historiographical practices of indigenous peoples, which are immediately political to the extent that they challenge hegemonic conceptions of their pasts, and profoundly political in asserting different possibilities of conceptualizing the past against the objectivist historiography of which Neumann speaks. But they, too, face a dilemma. Indigenous intellectuals, like other colonial or postcolonial intellectuals, themselves must abide by the assumptions of a hegemonic historiographical practice—or face marginalization, since they have few spaces of their own from which to voice alternative epistemologies. To be acceptable as respectable historians or academics, they must continue to represent themselves in epistemologies presupposed by the hegemonic culture surrounding them. In Hau'ofa's satire, "The Glorious Pacific Way," a successful player in cultural politics advises a would-be rebel that "in dealing with foreigners," who control the funds for cultural work, one should "never appear too smart; it's better that you look humble and half-primitive, especially while you are learning the ropes. And try to take off six stone. It's necessary that we're seen to be starved and needy. The reason why Tiko gets very little aid money is that our people are too fat and jolly."[37] Hau'ofa, as head of a school of development, may get away with his utopian visions of a Pacific because of his reputation as writer, which foregrounds the poetry of his utopia rather than its developmental relevance. It may be for the same reason that indigenous writers have on the whole chosen "fiction" over "history" in their self-representations.[38]

In addition to the question of "who," the problem of representation also involves the problem of "how." Again, to cite Neumann: "These days, Papua New Guineans . . . do not appear overtly interested in being told about the horrors of colonialism, as such accounts potentially belittle today's descendants of yesterday's victims."[39] Such accounts may be of greater relevance to self-flagellating nonindigenous historians than to indigenous peoples, seeking to make a life for themselves in the contemporary world. But I think there is here a deeper issue; the issue of a modern history for the indigenous peoples. The preoccupation with the past, either in terms of colonial horrors, or a revival of precolonial social and cultural formations, may fall into the same ideological trap of an earlier hegemonic history by ignoring the historicity of the indigenous peoples themselves and, therefore, their contemporaneity. A preoccupation with the past in terms of the horrors of colonial extinction may not be all that different epistemologically than the images of timeless paradise imposed on the Pacific by generations of EuroAmericans. For better or for worse, the indigenous peoples of the present are not the indigenous peoples of a bygone day; which is a different way of saying that they are products of a modern historical experience who are internally differentiated, partake of the social, ideological, and cultural diversities of the present, and, consequently, hold diverse views of the present, the past, and the future.[40] Epeli Hau'ofa's vision of a "New Oceania" is by no means shared by others in the islands. And the Pacific Islanders are themselves quite aware of the problems involved in the reassertion of native identities.[41] Trask, who is an eloquent spokesperson for the revival of native Hawai'ian conceptions of nature and society, conceded readily nevertheless that the struggle for Hawai'ian sovereignty is a very contemporary struggle, inspired by and similar to the struggles of African-Americans, Africans, and other colonial and indigenous peoples.[42] The point in every case is not to recover a past that is gone, but reasserting its values as the source of new visions for the future against hegemonic conceptions of history that deny all value to native traditions. Unlike the EuroAmerican utopian blueprints that were inspired by a faceless Pacific, the utopian longings expressed in the works of Hau'ofa, Trask, and others, are filled with the concreteness and warmth of immediate social and natural relationships.[43] The past in which they find inspiration is a past that has been worked over by a historical experience of modernity, that is animated by the social and political concerns of the present, and points to a future that is not a mere reproduction of itself, but of which it is an integral ingredient.

For a nonindigenous person speaking about the Pacific as a source of a critique of capitalist modernity, or of alternative paradigms of development, therefore, there is the ever-present danger of appropriating Pacific peoples' struggles for liberation and existence for ends that are not theirs. As we have come to recognize in recent decades, this is a danger implicit in all "politics of representation." It seems that, having recognized the problem of hegemony presented by a single discourse in the representation of the world, our generation faces a genuine epistemological dilemma: risk a renewed hegemony by reinventing a common discourse, or resign ourselves to discourses fragmented along ethnicities (that is implicit in the resolution of the problem by so-called "multiculturalism").

It is possible, and perhaps necessary, that ethnicization and indigenization of epistemology is a necessary first step before we can achieve a genuine interdiscursivity, which would seem to be ruled out so long as the structures of hegemony persist that were put in place by centuries of EuroAmerican domination of the world.[44] Only after the formerly colonized and oppressed have recovered their autonomous voices, will it be possible once again to negotiate a common discourse—negotiate not under conditions of an illusory market equality, but under conditions of social and political equality that remain to be achieved. In the meantime, however, there is room for struggle for such equality on many fronts. Where the Pacific is concerned, one such front is that presented by a hegemonic Pacific Rim discourse that subjects us all to the teleology of a Global Capitalism, as it seeks to erase native subjectivities within the Rim. The oppressors are not all on the Rim, just as the oppressed are not only within it. The Pacific itself is one location for oppressions that are global in scope, and in its reification in a contemporary fetishism of development serves in turn to legitimize oppression globally. The ability of Pacific Islanders to chart out autonomous visions for themselves may be contingent on the eradication of the hegemonic discourse of the Rim.

The question for the critical nonindigenous historian is: can we call on these visions in the creation of alternative modernities, without appropriating them, or turning them into contemporary versions of island paradise, in a common struggle to overturn a hegemonic modernity? Maybe, and maybe not. But definitely not, unless we are able to abolish our distinction of what is in the Rim from what is on or without it, for the distinction is increasingly part of an overall mystification of a world in which the motions of capital recognize no boundaries except those that serve it—mainly to divide people from one another by confining them in their little spaces, which rules out all possibility of resistance to those motions, and all possibility of imagining alternative futures except in the most localized ways. The problem of alternative paradigms presently is a problem of how to reconceive the local and the global simultaneously. That calls for new alliances, and new ways of thinking about the world, that is, new languages. The people of the Pacific have long had to learn to speak in languages that were initially not theirs, but are by now indispensable to their existence. The least we can do on the Rim is to recognize the existence of those new languages in the Rim, and in the process modify our ways of speaking about the Pacific. That may be the best we can do for the present, but it seems to me that it alone would represent an enormous step toward a common ground; a common ground constructed not on the basis of uniformity but on the basis of diverse localisms that do not deny but take as their point of departure the common concerns of a globalized world.

## Notes

This chapter was presented originally as a keynote address at the conference, "Reimagining the Pacific," University of British Columbia, 24–26 April 1995. I would like to thank the organizers (especially John Willinsky) for the opportunity, and the participants for the reception. Thanks also to Professor Johann Galtung for his comments and support.

1. "The Pacific Idea: There Is a Better World," *The Economist* (16 March 1991): 15–18, p. 15.

2. Ibid.

3. Ibid.

4. I am using "Pacific discourse" here in a slightly different sense than the "Pacific Rim discourse" suggested by Chris Connery; what is in the Rim is included here to disturb the latter. For "Pacific Rim discourse," see, Chris Connery, "Pacific Rim Discourse: The U.S. Global Imaginary in the Late Cold War Years," in Rob Wilson and Arif Dirlik (eds), *Asia/Pacific as Space of Cultural Production*, special issue of *boundary 2*, vol. 21, no. 1 (Spring 1994): 30–56.

5. Bernard Smith, *European Vision and the South Pacific*, second edition (New Haven and London: Yale University Press, 1985). See, also, O. H. K. Spate, *Paradise Found and Lost*, vol. III of his *The Pacific since Magellan* (Minneapolis: The University of Minnesota Press, 1988). Spate's volume deals mainly with the eighteenth century, Smith's with the nineteenth.

6. Quoted in Smith, p. 144.

7. Joseph-Marie Degerando, quoted in P. J. Marshall and Glyndwr Williams, *The Great Map of Mankind: British Perceptions of the World in the Age of Enlightenment* (London, Melborne and Toronto: J.M. Dent and Sons Ltd., 1982), p. 294.

8. J. H. Elliott, *The Old World and the New, 1492–1650* (Cambridge: Cambridge University Press, 1970), p. 52.

9. Quoted in Marshall and Williams, p. 262.

10. Bernard Smith argues this at length for the arts and sciences. See, also, the essays in Roy MacLeod and Philip F. Renbock, *Nature in Its Greatest Extent: Western Science in the Pacific* (Honolulu, HI: University of Hawai'i Press, 1988)

11. "The Pacific Idea," p. 18

12. Wilbur R. Jacobs, "The Fatal Confrontation: Early Native-White Relations on the Frontiers of Australia, New Guinea, and America—A Comparative Study," *Pacific Historical Review*, 40.3 (August 1971):283–309, pp. 284–285. The most thorough account of the devastation of nature and people in the Pacific is to be found in Alan Moorehead, *The Fatal Impact: The Invasion of the South Pacific, 1767–1840* (New York: Harper and Row Publishers, 1987) (first published, 1966).

13. Ward Churchill, *Struggle for the Land* (Monroe, ME: Common Courage Press, 1993), p. 17.

14. Deborah Montgomery, "Coming to Terms: Ngai Tahu, Robeson County Indians and the Garden River Band of Ojibwa, 1840–1940: Three Studies of Colonialism in Action," Ph.D. Dissertation, Department of History, Duke University (1993), p. 69.

15. Quoted in Ibid., p. 128.

16. Bruce Chatwin, *The Songlines* (New York: Penguin Books, 1987), p. 2.

17. Ibid., p. 13

18. Ibid., p. 57

19. W. E. H. Stanner, "The Dreaming," in T. A. G. Hungerford (ed), *Australian Signposts* (Melbourne: F.W. Cheshire Publishing Pty. Ltd., 1956), pp. 51–65.

20. Anne Cameron, *Daughters of Copper Woman* (Vancouver, B.C.: Press Gang Publishers, 1985), pp. 96–97.

21. Ibid., p. 98

22. Noel J. Kent, *Hawaii: Islands Under the Influence* (New York: Monthly Review Press, 1983), 32.

23. Haunani-Kay Trask, "Hawaii: Colonization and Decolonization," in Antony Hooper, et. al. (eds.), *Class and Culture in the South Pacific* (Auckland, N.Z. and Suva, Fiji: Centre for Pacific Studies, University of Auckland and Institute of Pacific Studies, University of the South Pacific, 1987): 154–174, p. 160.

24. Peter Worsley, *The Three Worlds: Culture and Development* (Chicago: The University of Chicago Press, 1984), p. 62.

25. Albert Wendt, "Novelists and Historians and the Art of Remembering," in *Class and Culture in the South Pacific*, pp. 78–91, pp. 86–87.

26. "Ideology in Pacific Studies: A Personal View," in Ibid., pp. 140–152, p. 144. *Pouliuli*, incidentally, is the title of Wendt's important fiction/history.

27. "Our Sea of Islands," in Eric Waddell, Vijay Naidu, and Epeli Hau'ofa, (eds.), *A New Oceania: Rediscovering Our Sea of Islands* (Suva, Fiji: School of Social and Economic Development, The University of the South Pacific in association with Beake House, 1993):2–16, p. 5. The essay is reprinted in Rob Wilson and Arif Dirlik (eds), *Asia/Pacific as Space of Cultural Production* (Durham, N.C.: Duke University Press, 1995).

28. Ibid.

29. Ibid., p. 3.

30. Ibid., pp. 5–6.

31. Ibid., p. 7.

32. Ibid., p. 16.

33. This other "Pacific Way" has been satirized by Epeli Hau'ofa in his short story, "The Glorious Pacific Way," in Epeli Hau'ofa, *Tales of the Tikongs* (Suva, Fiji: Beake House, University of the South Pacific, 1993), pp. 84–94.

34. Arif Dirlik, "Three Worlds, One or Many: The Reconfiguration of Global Relations under Contemporary Capitalism," *Nature, Society and Thought* (Spring 1995).

35. For a comprehensive collection on indigenous visions of the world, see, Roger Moody (ed), *The Indigeneous Voice: Visions and Realities* (Utrecht: Inter-

national Books, 1993), second edition. Indigenous critiques of the fetishism of development, in either bourgeois or Marxist version, are to be found in Ward Churchill (ed), *Marxism and Native Americans* (Boston: South End Press, n.d.). While Pacific writers such as Haunani-Kay Trask use Marxist analysis of the problems of the Pacific, they are wary of socialist solutions to those problems. For critique of Marxism for ignoring the particularity of Pacific peoples' problems, see the essays by Trask and Meleisea in *Class and Culture in the South Pacific* cited above.

36. Klaus Neumann, " 'In Order to Win Their Friendship': Renegotiating First Contact," *The Contemporary Pacific,* vol. 6, no. 1 (Spring 1994):111–145, p. 134.

37. Hau'ofa, op. cit., pp. 88–89.

38. See the discussion by Albert Wendt, cited above, in *Class and Culture in the South Pacific.* Wendt, needless to say, refuses to recognize to history greater truth value over fiction, which he describes as "an analog of the real world."

39. Neumann, p. 122.

40. Neumann's article cites many works, indigenous and otherwise, that address the question of history in the Pacific. Two systematic investigations are noteworthy here: Robert Borofsky, *Making History: Pukapukan and Anthropological Constructions of Knowledge* (Cambridge: Cambridge University Press, 1987), and, Geoffrey M. White, *Identity through History: Living Stories in a Solomon Islands Society* (Cambridge: Cambridge University Press, 1991). Meleisa's "Ideology in Pacific Studies," cited above, offers an incisive critique, as well an account of the ironies, of stereotyping the aspirations of Pacific peoples.

41. The essays collected in, *A New Oceania: Rediscovering Our Sea of Islands,* offer a wide range of responses to Hau'ofa's ideas. Hau'ofa himself has a complex vision that is anything but escapist. He, in fact, takes as his premise that contemporary capitalism in the Pacific, which has enabled Pacific Islanders once again to range over the ocean as in earlier days. Hau'ofa's literary work is distingusihed by a skillful use of Island pidgin as its language (which he distinguishes, as the living language of the people, from "World Bank English" that they need to teach their students in the University of the South Pacific in order that they may succeed in the world). For the perspective of literature on this complex problem, see, Mudrooroo Narogin, *Writing from the Fringe: A Study of Modern Aboriginal Literature* (Melbourne: Hyland House, 1990), and Albert Wendt, "Towards a New Oceania," in Guy Amirthanayagam (ed), *Writers in the East-West Encounter: New Cultural Bearings* (London: Macmillan, 1982), pp. 202–215.

42. See her essay, "Hawaii: Colonization and Decolonization," cited above, and the collection of her essays, *From a Native Daughter: Colonialism and Sovereignty in Hawai'i* (Monroe, ME: Common Courage Press, 1993). It is noteworthy that Trask's first book was a study of feminism, *Eros and Power: The Promise of Feminist Theory* (Philadelphia: University of Pennsylvania Press, 1986), and that her sister Milinani, another distinguished leader in the Hawai'ian sovereignty movement, is a lawyer.

43. Trask's passionate poetry that at once mourns and promises is testimonial

to her complexity. See the collection, *Light in the Crevice Never Seen* (Corvallis, OR: Calyx Books, 1994).

44. Let me note here a complex problem imbedded in my use of "indigenization" and "ethnicization." I do not mean to equate these terms, nor do I view the processes they describe as processes transitional to a new universalism. This is particularly the case with indigenization, which I use both literally (as with indigenous peoples) and metaphorically (in the sense of localization). It is the latter sense that to me is the most intriguing: indigenization as localization cuts across ethnic or indigenous groups (or, stated differently, localizes them in concrete circumstances), pointing to the creation of local languages, that contrast with the universal. This corresponds to what I mean below by the local and the global, interactive, and yet different. It is also in this sense that it is possible to refer to indigenous movements as paradigms for local political movements, which I have suggested in the essay to which I referred above, "Three Worlds, or One or Many."

# Index

# About the Book and the Editor

In this multidisciplinary volume, leading scholars question the current euphoria over the rapid growth of the "Pacific Rim"—as an economic region and as a political concept. "Pacific Rim" (or its correlate, "Asia-Pacific") has become one of the most important components of geopolitical vocabulary worldwide. In the United States, it has come to define a crucial arena of political and economic activity. Academic institutions are organized around it, and constant references to "the Pacific Rim" in newspapers, journals, and the titles of numerous books have rendered it a part of everyday language. Yet there has been little effort to explore what this ubiquitous term signifies.

The essays in this volume undertake two related tasks. First, they explore critically the meaning of "Asia-Pacific" as concept, in order to bring to the surface the relationships of power that dynamize but are disguised by ideological constructions of "Asia-Pacific." They suggest that much of the discourse on the region is highly ideological, focusing on its potential for capitalist development while ignoring the limitations of such development. Second, against celebrations of "Asia-Pacific" they seek to uncover fundamental contradictions in the region, including its human costs and consequences. In evaluating the idea of "Asia-Pacific," the book shifts attention from abstract relationships between capital and commodities to the human interactions that have played a formative part in the region's constitution.

Arif Dirlik is professor of history at Duke University. His most recent publications include *After the Revolution: Working to Global Capitalism* (1994), *The Postcolonial Aura: Third World Criticism in the Age of Global Capitalism* (1997), and an edited volume with Paul Healy and Nick Knight, *Critical Perspectives on Mao Zedung's Thought* (1997).

# About the Contributors

**Glenn Alcalay** is assistant professor of anthropology at the City College of New York. Alcalay has been conducting research in Micronesia for the past twenty-two years, and he recently did a study of the impact of nuclear weapons testing on women and reproduction in the Marshall Islands. He has written extensively and has appeared on numerous occasions before the United Nations, the U.S. Congress, and the British House of Commons as an advocate for the rights of the indigenous peoples of the Pacific.

**Xiangming Chen** is assistant professor of sociology at the University of Illinois at Chicago and a faculty associate with the Center for East Asian Studies at the University of Chicago. His research has focused on the interface between urban and economic development from a comparative perspective with a central focus on China. He recently coauthored "Urban Economic Reform and Public Housing Investment in China" in *Urban Affairs Quarterly* 29 (1), 1993.

**Bruce Cumings** is professor of international history and East Asian political economy at the University of Chicago. He is the author of a two-volume study, *The Origins of the Korean War* (1981, 1990), and *War and Television* (1993). His most recent book is *Korea's Place in the Sun: A Modern History.*

**Gary Gereffi** has been a member of the Department of Sociology at Duke University since 1980. His published works include *The Pharmaceutical Industry and Dependency in the Third World* (1983); *Manufacturing Miracles: Paths of Industrialization in Latin America and East Asia,* coedited with the late Donald Wyman (1990); and *Commodity Chains and Global Capitalism,* coedited with Miguel Korzeniewicz (1993).

**Evelyn Hu-DeHart** is professor of history and ethnic studies, chair of the Department of Ethnic Studies, and director of the Center for Studies of Ethnicity and Race in America (CSERA) at the University of Colorado at Boulder. Her current research concerns the Asian diaspora in Latin America and the Caribbean.

**Donald M. Nonini** is associate professor of anthropology at the University of North Carolina at Chapel Hill. He is author of *British Colonial Rule and Malay Peasant Resistance 1900–1957* (1993) and of numerous articles on social theory and the cultural politics of Southeast Asian societies. Most recently he has been coeditor (with Aihwa Ong) of *Undergrounded Empires: The Cultural Politics of Modern Chinese Transnationalism.*

**Neferti Xina M. Tadiar** teaches in the Board of Studies in the History of Consciousness at the University of California at Santa Cruz and in the Department of English and Comparative Literature at the University of the Philippines. Her recent work is on the feminization of labor in the Philippines, particularly of overseas Filipino domestic helpers.

**Rob Wilson** is a professor of English at the University of Hawaii in Honolulu. A member of the *boundary* 2 and *Bamboo Ridge* collectives and frequent contributor to *Korean Culture,* he is the author of two books: *Waking in Seoul,* a collection of poetry and prose anecdotes about the American presence in South Korea (1988); *American Sublime: The Genealogy of a Poetic Genre,* a study of the American poetics of national power (1991); and *Reimagining the American Pacific: From "South Pacific" to Bamboo Ridge and Beyond* (1998).

**Meredith Woo-Cumings** teaches in the Department of Political Science at Northwestern University. Her publications include *Race to the Swift: State and Finance in Korean Industrialization* (1991), and *Past as Prelude: History in the Making of a New World Order,* coedited with Michael Loriaux (Westview, 1993).

**Alexander Woodside** teaches Chinese and Southeast Asian history at the University of British Columbia in Vancouver. He is the author of *Vietnam and the Chinese Model* and *Community and Revolution in Modern Vietnam* and a coauthor of the forthcoming *Education and Society in Late Imperial China.*